VIDEO GAMES AND THE GLOBAL SOUTH

Video Games and the Global South

Phillip Penix-Tadsen

Carnegie Mellon University: ETC Press

Pittsburgh, PA

ISBN 978-0-359-64139-0 (Print)

ISBN 978-0-359-64141-3 (Online)

CONTENTS

FOREWORD

SEND IT TO URUGUAY!

GONZALO FRASCA

Ever heard the expression, "If you want something out of your way, you'd better send it to Uruguay"? No? Never? I'm not surprised, because it doesn't exist. I just made it up. And even in spite of this expression never having existed, a lot of things did end up in Uruguay, my home country.

Two blocks from my childhood home, there lived a guy who was rumored to be a smuggler. Nobody in the neighborhood really cared if it was true or not, as long as he kept selling electrical appliances at very affordable prices—this was the 1970s in Uruguay, where a simple electric toaster was considered to be high-tech and could cost almost one month's salary.

It was also rumored that he was connected to the New Jersey mob, and that this was how he managed to get thousands of Coleco Adam computers for next to nothing. These were computers that, again according to rumors, needed to disappear quickly from the States on account of some shady insurance deal. It's highly likely that this tale was made up either by my overactive teenage brain or by his envious neighbors, but in any case, I hope you'll agree it makes for a pretty good story.

I was hired by my neighbor to perform a very particular task. These computers featured dozens of games that my boss wanted to sell. The problem is that they lacked any instruction manuals and my boss, an adult, assumed that kids needed to read booklets to be able to play a video game. My job consisted of playing these games and then writing a two-page manual where I described the goals, controls, backstory and lore of each game. Most of this I deduced from what I could infer from playing the games, and the rest I just made up.

I'd like to add, for the record, that my so-called smuggler neighbor was an amazing boss. It was the first time in my life that somebody took my advice seriously: he always listened carefully to what I had to say and valued my knowledge in computers and video games so much that he paid me handsomely for it. Being treated with such respect by an adult at that early age meant the world to me, and I'll be always grateful to him.

Ten years later, when I was finishing college, I decided to write a dissertation about computer games. To my dismay, there was nothing filed under that category at the Uruguayan National Library…except for some booklets that I had written when I was twelve. They were filed under "Anonymous" because although I may have been twelve, I'd like to think I was old enough to know better than to leave my name written on any document.

Since I had no game-related bibliography, I had no choice but to frame my early research with any theories that could help me better understand games. Thankfully, the Uruguayan National Library had plenty of books on French Narratalogy, which I devoured to make the point that games could be connected to interactive narrative. All because some American computers from Jersey, created by a toy company from Connecticut—Coleco stands for "Connecticut Leather Company, a shoe manufacturer that later switched to toys and doll manufacturing and then to electronic games and computers—made their way to Uruguay.

Funny things happen when you move things around. Something actually transpired with all those video games when they literally went south. Most players probably never noticed it—I doubt many read the manuals I wrote—but I do believe those games mutated a little bit in their journey. This book is about some of those mutations.

On the first day of class I usually play a game with my students. Actually, let me rephrase that: I play a game on my students. I ask them what is the best beer in the world. After ten minutes, the discussions usually become heated and, as you might expect, involve terms such as "lupulus," "barley," "microbrewery," "hops," "priming" and "hipster."

By the end of the session, most student groups will have chosen the parameters to define their beer of choice and, almost invariably, some student asks me what is "my" best beer in the world. Because it was a trick question, I've already got my trick answer prepared. I tell them that, in my opinion, the best beer in the world is any of the beers they have chosen, on a beach, with friends. In other words, what makes it the best beer in the world is not just what lies inside the bottle but also what's outside it.

Rest assured that my goal is not show off my teaching skills: I never felt I was particularly good at that job and I am pretty sure many of my former students are still puzzled about the relationship between beer and video games. Hopefully writing it down here will help me make a better case next month when my semester's teaching begins.

Funny things happen when you move things around. One of the common meanings of the term "game" is its physicality: when we say that we buy a game we are talking about the set—the box that contains the board game or the disk that holds its data. For too long, we have fetishized what we consider solid and immutable—what lies inside the box. That which we generally discuss, review and rate with little stars or numbers from one to ten. Similarly—even though it happens far less frequently—, it can be tempting to pay too much attention to what lies outside the box and fool ourselves into thinking that it can all but erase its contents of any meaning.

Just like that ideal beer, the game is not simply what is inside its rules and physicality: it is the negotiation that happens between two worlds.

If video games are, as Espen Aarseth claimed, "allegories of space," I could perhaps claim—following my beer bottle analogy—that the space inside the screen negotiates its meaning with the space that surrounds it. This can extend not just to the act of play but also to a game's conception, design, sale, analysis, mutation and disappearance.

So far, I have never met anybody else in the world whose job was to reverse-engineer video game instructions and recreate fictional worlds. However, I am certain I was not the only one. Because—as this book is here to remind us—no matter what those spooky robots in Disneyland might sing, it's not such a small world after all.

INTRODUCTION

VIDEO GAMES AND THE GLOBAL SOUTH

PHILLIP PENIX-TADSEN

VIDEO GAMES AND THE GLOBAL SOUTH: FIVE SNAPSHOTS

Las Palmitas II, Dominican Republic, July 1995. As evening falls, the pastel-painted houses lining the earthen roads of Las Palmitas go dark and activities begin to wind down (see Image 0.1).[1] Electricity and running water have yet to reach this rural hillside community, and most people rise with the sun, early in the morning, and go to sleep shortly after dusk. But this evening, in addition to the faint lights of candles and oil lamps shining in the occasional alcove, kitchen or bedroom, a glow emanates from under the metal roof of one house, just inside the main entryway. There, in a small living room with a dirt floor, several children, their parents and grandparents are gathered around a television that has been modified to run on power provided by a car battery. Alongside the TV set there sits a small black box that is also connected to the battery: a video game console manufactured in Hong Kong and obtained by a relative in Santo Domingo, pre-loaded with dozens of classic games originally published for the Nintendo Entertainment System and Sega Genesis.[2] Several generations of family as well as neighbors and friends laugh and compete with one another as the evening wears on. Even (or especially) in locales with little-to-no technological access, sites that may seem situated beyond the boundaries mapping computer technologies, electronic games can represent a powerful force in the lives of their players.

Mumbai, India, May 2016. Eight-year-old game developer Medansh Mehta has just presented his game *Let There Be Light* to Microsoft CEO Satya Nadella—himself a product of the country's public schools in his birthplace of Hyderabad—, who now oversees his company's US$9 billion game operations (see Image 0.2). The game attracted Nadella's attention due to the way it requires the player to balance industrial growth and agriculture, controlling variables such as pollution and growth rate in order to create an industry that is both economically and environmentally sustainable. When the young Mehta proclaims that he aims to become Microsoft's CEO himself one day, Nadella suggests the boy is setting his sights too low, and that his ambition and sensitivity will bring him to unforeseen heights greater than he has yet imagined.[3] Just a few weeks later, Anvitha Vijay, a nine-year-old Australian of Indian origin with several iOS applications to her credit, becomes the youngest developer ever to receive an invite to participate in Apple's Worldwide Developers Conference in San Francisco (see Image 0.2).[4] Vijay had an idea for a mobile application, so she spent a year studying free YouTube tutorials on coding in order to produce *Smartkins Animals* (Jovoya 2016), an educational game for

1. Author's photograph, Las Palmitas II, Dominican Republic, July 1995.
2. This description is based on the author's personal experience in Las Palmitas II, Dominican Republic, July 1995.
3. Anjali Bisaria, "8-Year-Old Genius Impresses Satya Nadella With His Game, Aims to Be Microsoft CEO One Day!," *India Times*, 1 June 2016, http://www.indiatimes.com/news/india/8-year-old-genius-impresses-satya-nadella-with-his-game-aims-to-be-microsoft-ceo-one-day-256004.html.
4. Priyanka Sangami, "Rise of Young Supercoders: How Indian Kids are Making a Mark in the Coding World," *Economic Times*, 16 June 2016, https://economictimes.indiatimes.com/magazines/panache/rise-of-young-supercoders-how-indian-kids-are-making-a-mark-in-the-coding-world/articleshow/52771287.cms; Bisaria, "8-Year-Old Genius Impresses Satya Nadella," *India Times*, 1 June 2016, https://www.indiatimes.com/news/india/8-year-old-genius-impresses-satya-nadella-with-his-game-aims-to-be-microsoft-ceo-one-day-256004.html; Rutu Ladage, "Anvitha Vijay, 9 yr Kid is the Youngest Apple Developer!," *India.com*, 14 June 2016, https://www.india.com/buzz/anvitha-vijay-9-year-old-indian-origin-kid-is-the-youngest-apple-app-developer-at-wwdc16-1258554/.

Image 0.1. The author (rear left) with host family and friends in Las Palmitas II, Dominican Republic, 1995.

young players. As more young people learn coding and software programming skills from an earlier age and new game design tools are made available to a broader segment of the world's population, the landscape of game development is being radically transformed.

Image 0.2. Indian game developers Medansh Mehta (left) and Anvitha Vijay (right).

Jenin, Palestine, September 2003. During a field interview for an analysis of players' habits in the Middle East, a twelve-year-old girl excitedly pulls researcher Helga Tawil-Souri aside in order to share what she describes as "the best game ever," the first-person shooter *Special Force* (Hezbollah 2003; see Image 0.3).[5] This player is highly familiar with games in this genre, having played games that position the player as part of a U.S. military force intervening in Iraq, Iran, Lybia and Syria. The difference is that *Special Force* is a pro-Arab video game, indeed the very first (though not the only) game of this type that this Palestinian adolescent has encountered. In fact, she has never played a game set in the Arab world that would permit the player *not* to shoot at Arabs. As she explains to Tawil-Souri, prior to playing *Special Force,* "I always had to shoot at my own people."[6] As game development emerges among locales outside the major world centers of technological production, concerns particular to specific cultural contexts push game developers to break with design conventions established in the global north, so that other stories can be told, different audiences can be reached and new experiences can be created.

Image 0.3. A screenshot from Hezbollah-sponsored first-person shooter Special Force (2003).

Manila, Philippines, June 2017. Local 18-year-old eSports champ Andreij "Doujin" Albar has just defeated the world's "undisputed champion" of *Tekken 7* (Bandai Namco 2015), South Korean Jin-woo "Saint" Choi, in a major upset at the Rage Art Championship (see Image 0.4).[7] The phenomenon

5. *Digital Islam*, "Special Force (Al-Quwwat al-Khasa)," http://www.digitalislam.eu/videoAndGames.do?articleId=1314.
6. Helga Tawil-Souri, "The Political Battlefield of Pro-Arab Video Games on Palestinian Screens," *Comparative Studies of South Asia, Africa and the Middle East* 27.3 (2007): 545.

of eSports—professional competitive gaming—has risen rapidly to worldwide prominence as both a career possibility and a spectacle: in addition to the hundreds of spectators and players in attendance, thousands of fans around the world streamed the final match in which Doujin dethroned Saint. One reason for Saint's loss was his choice to play as the character Eddy Gordo, a Brazilian *capoeira* champion who is not usually used in competition, thinking this would give him an advantage. However, Saint failed to realize that Eddy Gordo is an avatar of longstanding popularity in the Philippines, meaning Doujin was readily familiar with his repertoire of moves and maneuvers. And one reason Filipino players tend to be so familiar with *Tekken* and its characters is that the game was made popular on the original PlayStation console, whose shift from cartridge to CD-ROM facilitated piracy, thus expanding access to players from lower income brackets or those who lived in regions outside the official market of major multinational game corporations. This combination of factors reflects the complex cultural dynamics at play in the circulation of a cultural product like *Tekken*, which was developed in Japan, uses representations of characters from countries such as Brazil and India, was both officially and unofficially copied in China and Hong Kong for worldwide distribution, and decades later came to be mastered by a professional gamer in South Korea who was in turn dethroned by an unlikely challenger from Manila, one who had grown up playing unofficial copies of games from the series like so many players in the Philippines and elsewhere in the global south.[8]

Image 0.4. Playbook eSports team members Alexandre "AK" Laverez (left) and Andrei "Doujin" Albar (right).

Al-Salam, Sudan, January 2014. A group of refugees from South Sudan, fleeing the deadly conflict that consumes the area, are huddled together in an improvised earthen structure with a corrugated tin door and a metal kitchen shelving unit that has been converted into a makeshift entertainment center

7. Ian Walker, "Local Player Defeats Tekken 7 World Champion at Philippines Event," *Kotaku Compete*, 9 June 2017, https://compete.kotaku.com/local-player-defeats-tekken-7-world-champion-at-philipp-1795967096; Gab Lazaro, "PH Players Impress at Rage Art," Mineski.net, 6 June 2017, https://www.mineski.net/news/ph-players-impress-at-rage-art.
8. The meaning and usage of the term "global south" is discussed in detail in the following section.

(see Image 0.5).[9] About half of them look intensely concentrated, lips pursed, eyes focused—their gazes are fixed on two television screens on atop the shelving unit, as they ably manipulating the controllers in their hands, playing an electronic game. The rest of those present are beaming with bright smiles, happy to find a moment of respite and enjoying some much-deserved entertainment and togetherness with others in their same situation. And that situation is dire indeed—the refugees' home of South Sudan is engulfed in a civil war, and the Sudanese government and South Sudanese rebels have mutually accused one another of violence that has fractured a cease-fire, which itself followed a series of Sudanese bombing raids over the impoverished communities in the region.[10] These are not the only factors that make it so unlikely for these children to have gotten their hands on computer gaming hardware and software—technological access is severely limited by sanctions on free access to information and communication technologies (ICTs) levied by the United States on Sudan along with North Korea, Iran, Syria and Cuba.[11] And in spite of it all, even in the most unlikely and precarious of situations, this moment of shared gameplay offers a reminder that people everywhere in the world place a great deal of personal value on their entertainment, including specific entertainment technologies such as video games.

Image 0.5. Locals and South Sudanese refugees play video games in a market near a refugee camp, 2014.

9. Reuters, "Locals and South Sudanese Refugees Play Video Games in a Market Near a Camp 10 km (6 miles) from al-Salam Locality at the Border of Sudan's White Nile State," 27 January 2014, http://cms.trust.org/item/20140127212510-9x8ha?view=print.

10. Olivia Warham, "A Deadly Sleight of Hand," *HuffPost Blog* (United Kingdom), 28 January 2014, http://www.huffingtonpost.co.uk/olivia-warham/south-sudan-africa_b_4678826.html.

11. Aala Abdelgadir, "The Push to Lift U.S. Communication Technology Sanctions on Sudan," *Council on Foreign Relations*, 28 January 2014, https://www.cfr.org/blog/push-lift-us-communication-technology-sanctions-sudan..

APPROACHES TO VIDEO GAMES AND THE GLOBAL SOUTH

The five snapshots that open this introductory essay offer a glimpse of video games and game cultures in the Caribbean, Indian subcontinent, Middle East, Asia-Pacific region and Africa, showing some of the ways games impact the daily lives of individuals across the globe, including and especially those that have long been considered "peripheral" to the global centers of technological production and consumption. As Adrienne Shaw has argued, to understand video games, we must look at them *in* culture, not just *as* culture: "games permeate education, mobile technologies, museum displays, social functions, family interactions, and workplaces" and they "are played by many if not all ages, genders, sexualities, races, religions, and nationalities,"[12] as reflected in the anecdotes above. Moreover, as Thomas Apperley explains, "the digital game ecology is shaped through myriad and plural local situations that collectively enact the global,"[13] and these snapshots demonstrate how local economic, political and cultural concerns affect the experience of gameplay, as well as the multiple ways in which site-specificity impacts the player's experience. Elsewhere, I have referred to academic research related to these factors as "cultural ludology," which "focuses on the analysis of video games as such, attending to the myriad ways culture is incorporated into game mechanics, but at the same time recognizes the signifying potential of the cultural environment in which games are created, designed, manufactured, purchased, played and otherwise put to use."[14] The examples above also evidence the popularity of gaming across cultures, socioeconomic classes and a variety of other demographics—gaming is a commonplace practice "embedded and situated in the material and mundane everyday,"[15] and software, video games and social networks are gaining increasing prominence vis-à-vis more conventional U.S. cultural exports like Hollywood movies and hip-hop and rock music.[16] This is true even in locales with strict cultural or political controls on gaming technologies—for example, gaming is highly popular among Iranians and Venezuelans, even among marginalized and impoverished groups.[17] Hence these five snapshots are also a reminder of the increasing impact of video game culture on the global south, and vice-versa. They show just how much of the "big picture" of gaming is lost when we neglect experiences outside of the presumed norm, and just how much perspective can be gained by understanding games as complex technological and cultural products whose creation, circulation, consumption and meaning are shaped by concerns and practices that are fundamentally local and situated in nature.

Video Games and the Global South aims to reimagine the place of gaming in the world, redefining game culture from south to north. While video games are a quintessentially global technology—with game consumption, production and related practices taking place in virtually every country in the world today—they have been received, created and even played differently in different regions, because cultural and national context impact the circulation and meaning of games in myriad ways. Many geographical locales once considered part of the high-tech "periphery" are in fact home to longstanding and widespread technocultures with their own unique characteristics, and with their own geometries of power.[18] This is readily evident in the contributions to this anthology, which examine the cultural impact of video games in regions including Africa, the Middle East, Central and South America, the Indian subcontinent and parts of Oceania and Asia. An analysis of the games and game cultures of the vast region referred to as the global south sheds light on the cultural impact of gaming in less-frequently-examined geographical areas, offering evidence of video games' impact

12. Adrienne Shaw, "What is Video Game Culture? Cultural Studies and Game Studies," *Games and Culture* 5.4 (2010): 416.
13. Thomas Apperley, *Gaming Rhythms: Play and Counterplay from the Situated to the Global* (Institute of Network Cultures, 2009), 18.
14. Phillip Penix-Tadsen, *Cultural Code: Video Games and Latin America* (MIT Press, 2016).
15. Apperley, *Gaming Rhythms*, 8.
16. Brian T. Edwards, *After the American Century: The Ends of U.S. Culture in the Middle East* (Columbia University Press, 2016), 49.
17. Thomas H. Apperley, "Venezuela," in Mark J. P. Wolf, ed., *Video Games Around the World* (MIT Press, 2015), 615.
18. Bjarke Liboriussen and Paul Martin, "Regional Game Studies," *Game Studies* 16.1 (October 2016).

on economics, creative production, education, popular culture and political discourse, as well as showing how cultural context impacts games on the levels of development, design, reception and play practices.

Analysis of video games and game cultures from the viewpoint of the global south invariably intersects with other perspectives in game studies and related disciplines, and the contributors to this volume are participating in several broader dialogues. Therefore it is important to confront several key issues from the outset, including: 1) the meaning and usage of the term "global south"; 2) the critical and theoretical contributions of decolonial and postcolonial perspectives on video games; 3) the problems with conventional perspectives on the "global" game industry and "global" game studies; and 4) the role of local and regional approaches vis-à-vis the discipline of game studies at large.

First, it is essential to describe the history, advantages and disadvantages of the concept of the "global south," a term which stems from anthropology and more specifically from postcolonial and decolonial trajectories within anthropological research. In the essay "The Global South and the World Dis/Order," Walter Mignolo explains that the global south "is not a geographic location; rather it is a metaphor that indicates regions of the world at the receiving end of globalization and suffering the consequences" and comprises "the places on the planet that endured the experience of coloniality—that suffered, and still suffer, the consequences of the colonial wound (e.g., humiliation, racism, genderism, in brief, the indignity of being considered lesser humans)."[19] Likewise, in the introduction to the first issue of the journal *The Global South*, Arif Dirlik explains that "there are certain affinities between these societies in terms of mutual recognition of historical experiences with colonialism and neocolonialism, a history not yet ended of economic, political and social (racial) marginalization, and, in some cases, memories of cooperation or common cause in struggles for global justice in past liberation movements."[20] Thus the global south is a movable and situational term referring to many areas with internal political and socioeconomic divisions as well as previously colonized societies that still endure the effects of colonialism.

But for these critics and others, the term "global south" has its limitations. Mehita Iqani explains that although the term is "prickly in its trendiness and complexity," it is useful in the way that it "'speaks back' by bringing together into one analytical project some of the cross-cutting flows and tensions relevant to contexts in Asia, Africa and Latin America without homogenizing their disparate and unique characteristics," rather than reaffirming the "position of deficiency" implied in outdated terminology such as the "underdeveloped," "developing," "post-colonial," "third" and "non-western" world.[21] Like Iqani, this anthology uses the term "global south" to describe "continents, countries and cultures that were historically interlinked with western power by imperialism yet whose populations did not profit as uniformly from colonial exploitation and its legacies, and where poverty, social ills and inequality are acutely visible in counterpoint with pockets of wealth, privilege and 'development,'" but understands the term "neither as an eliminating concept nor as one that homogenizes massive diversities and complexities into one all-consuming narrative," but rather a concept whose contradictions and fragmentations can provide the ground for productive dialogue. Thus, this anthology uses a focus on the global south to examine game culture throughout societies that differ in many regards but share other characteristics nonetheless, revealing unexpected

19. Walter Mignolo, "Introduction: The Global South and World Dis/Order," *Journal of Anthropological Research* 67.2 (2011): 185.
20. Arif Dirlik, "Global South: Predicament and Promise," *The Global South* 1.1 (2007): 16.
21. Mehita Iqani, "Introduction: The Mediation of Global South Consumption," *Consumption, Media and the Global South: Aspiration Contested* (Palgrave Macmillan, 2016), 2-4.

connections that bring together the diverse cultures of Pakistan and Peru, Chile and China, Colombia and Cameroon.

Video games can be decolonial, too. Mignolo explains that *decoloniality* is distinct from the *decolonization* of nations, in that it involves "the decolonization of knowledge and of being and assumes that the way out is to unlink from the colonial matrix of power."[22] A decolonial approach to cultural production poses crucial questions such as "what kind of knowledge, by whom, what for?"[23] Likewise, a decolonial approach to game design would ask what kinds of games can be produced, who can produce these games and what purposes they can fulfill. There is a long history of the development of political, ideological, pedagogical and otherwise "serious" or "persuasive" games in the global south. More than a decade and a half ago, Uruguayan theorist and game developer Gonzalo Frasca spoke of the possibility of creating "video games of the oppressed," using the medium as a tool for education, socio-political awareness and consciousness-raising.[24] In short, Frasca advocated for the appropriation of the means of (game) production by actors in the global south, and the repurposing of these technologies in ways that would benefit the region's inhabitants. Fifteen years later, we can see that many gamers and game developers from across the global south have taken up this challenge, contributing to game cultures and creating games that respond to the obstacles and affordances of their particular geographical, socioeconomic, political and cultural contexts.

In game studies scholarship, a decolonial trajectory has also been developing over the past several years, and various scholars have begun to revisit key questions from postcolonial studies by asking in their own ways, "Can the subaltern play?," or perhaps even, "Can the subaltern code?" While Souvik Mukherjee questions whether games protesting hegemony can truly be considered "subaltern," he nevertheless deems games "platforms of ideological protest" with the capacity to represent "voices from below."[25] Mukherjee and other postcolonial scholars whose work "critique[s] capitalist norms and the resultant hegemonies"[26] have brought much-needed perspective on game development, circulation and consumption outside of the global north. To date, Mukherjee's groundbreaking 2017 study *Videogames and Postcolonialism: Empire Plays Back* is the only book-length study specifically related to postcolonialism and video games, and in it the author explains, "it is high time that the concerns of the millions of gamers in the so-named postcolonial geographies are represented. With the growing attention to issues of diversity in video games, currently involving questions of gender, race, and religion, the intrinsically connected questions of the representations of empire and the post-colony need a separate and yet related consideration."[27] For the purposes of many of the scholars in the present anthology, this intersectional approach is key to understanding the complexities of the relationship between games and culture. This is indeed a late-breaking critical trajectory, and as recently as 2010 Shaw rightly pointed out that, by and large, "although game studies has come to draw on the concepts and subjects of cultural studies, it has not taken on the conflicts"[28] and dilemmas that could productively advance discussions of the impact of factors such as race, gender, nationality, sexual identity and socioeconomic class on games' meaning and the experience of gameplay. In their 2007 anthology *Latin American Cyberculture and Cyberliterature*, Claire Taylor and Thea Pitman point out that "[f]uture work on Latin American cyberculture needs to address more

22. Mignolo, "Introduction: The Global South and World Dis/Order," 183.
23. Walter Mignolo, *The Darker Side of Western Modernity: Global Futures, Decolonial Options* (Duke University Press, 2011), xvi.
24. Gonzalo Frasca, *Videogames of the Oppressed: Videogames as a Means for Critical Thinking and Debate*, Ph.D. Dissertation, Georgia Institute of Technology, 2001.
25. Souvik Mukherjee, "Playing Subaltern: Video Games and Postcolonialism," *Games and Culture* 13.5 (2016): 8.
26. Siddharta Chakraborti, Kwabena Opoku-Agyemang, and Dibyadyuti Roy, "Gaming, Culture, Hegemony: Introductory Remarks," *Journal of Gaming & Virtual Worlds* 7.2 (2015): 139.
27. Souvik Mukherjee, *Videogames and Postcolonialism: Empire Plays Back* (Palgrave Macmillan, 2017), 9.
28. Shaw, "What is Video Game Culture?," 411.

fully these intersections between cyberculture, postcolonial theory, and Latin American identities of the term 'postcolonial' to the region," while they see in digital media the potential for digital forms of "expression of postcolonial consciousness" and "new and resistant forms of identity online."[29]

A decade later, these predictions are clearly confirmed in the vast array of perspectives that have come into play in particular with the advent of "casual" game production and consumption, which focuses on games played on mobile devices and social media platforms, meaning they have a lower level of entry for players and developers alike, bringing new audiences and voices to the world of video games. Likewise, scholars have begun to answer the calls a greater focus on the diversity of gaming and related practices throughout the world that have been sounded over the past decade or so. In their article "Regional Game Studies," Bjarke Liboriussen and Paul Martin attempt to offer "a form of game scholarship more attuned to the challenges of globalization, internationalization and postcolonialism,"[30] authors like Pamela Wilson and Michelle Stewart have advanced the study of "indigenous media," or "forms of media expression conceptualized, produced, and/or created by Indigenous peoples across the globe,"[31] and Dale Hudson and Patricia R. Zimmerman have examined "forms of knowledge production that complicate and contradict the assumptions and expectations of mainstream media, whether European or East Asian, whether Kollywood, Nollywood, Bollywood, Hollywood, or Tollywood."[32] The centers for game production are diversifying as well, and today every country is not only working on its own Hollywood, but also its own Silicon Valley, through processes that are complicated and often skewed against developers in the global south. As Apperley explains in *Gaming Rhythms*, the structures and practices of the international game industry—as well as the industry's inflexible operations and unequal access to its tools and benefits—are key to understanding digital games globally.[33] An example of these structural imbalances is "platform imperialism," Dal Yong Jin's term for the "asymmetrical relationship of interdependence in platform technologies and political culture between the West, primarily the U.S., and many developing countries" which "is not only about the forms of technological disparities but also the forms of intellectual property, symbolic hegemony, and user commodity because these issues concentrate capital into the hands of a few U.S.-based platform owners, resulting in the expansion of the global divide."[34] These perspectives help highlight the uneven reach and impact of the "global" games industry among different geographical regions.

Too often, game scholarship is blind to its own cultural biases, making universal claims about gaming based on a limited number of conventional examples. When tracing the history of video games, scholars have at times abandoned decades' worth of insight on inclusiveness in analyzing historical and cultural developments in other disciplines, leading to "global" histories that entirely or mostly omit the global south from consideration. This view of the international game industry "suggests a particular smoothness in the description of the manifestations and praxis of that industry,"[35] an illusion which at its worst can mask "a decidedly Anglo-American bias, where gaming practices from specific parts of the world—especially United States and United Kingdom—have been understood to be representative of global gaming cultures."[36] The evidence of this is everywhere, even in some

29. Claire Taylor and Thea Pitman, "Conclusion: Latin American Identity and Cyberspace," in *Latin American Cyberculture and Cyberliterature*, eds. Claire Taylor and Thea Pitman (Liverpool University Press, 2007), 267.
30. Liboriussen and Martin, "Regional Game Studies."
31. Pamela Wilson and Michelle Stewart, "Introduction: Indigeneity and Indigenous Media on the Global Stage," in *Global Indigenous Media: Cultures, Poetics, and Politics*, eds. Pamela Wilson and Michelle Stewart (Duke University Press, 2008), 2.
32. Dale Hudson and Patricia R. Zimmermann, *Thinking Through Digital Media: Transnational Environments and Locative Places* (Palgrave Macmillan, 2015), 146.
33. Apperley, *Gaming Rhythms*, 17.
34. Dal Yong Jin, *Digital Platforms, Imperialism and Political Culture* (Taylor & Francis, 2015).
35. Apperley, *Gaming Rhythms*, 16.
36. Chakraborti, Kwabena and Dibyadyuti, 136.

of the best scholarship on game history and game culture. Whether in popular histories such as Steven L. Kent's *The Ultimate History of Video Games*[37] or scholarly critiques like Tristan Donovan's *Replay: The History of Video Games*, game historians frequently suggest that the history of video games started and ended in the United States, Western Europe, South Korea and Japan. And while Donovan takes on the subject directly, noting that "the attempts at writing the history of video games to date have been US rather than global histories" and arguing that there is a need "to redress the balance," his work still concentrates largely on a relatively limited gamut of nations, most of which are (or were) wealthy countries and conventional centers for the production and consumption of game technologies: the United States, the United Kingdom, France, the Soviet Union, Japan and South Korea. Other omissions seem to be less self-conscious, making for purportedly universal studies that omit the global south entirely from the scope of consideration, due to the apparently peripheral or economically "non-existent" nature of this broad and varied region. Peter Zackariasson and Timothy L. Wilson's 2012 work *The Video Game Industry: Formation, Present State, and Future* focuses almost entirely on video game production in the United States, Europe and Japan, and notes in its introduction that while the most successful game publishers are headquartered in North America, Japan and Europe, producers from "outside of these areas are close to non-existent on the international market."[38] Overall, works such as *The Video Game Industry* or *The Ultimate History of Video Games* are helpful for those focused on the regions in question and groundbreaking in their treatment of video games as a global industry of historical significance, but they are symptomatic of the discipline's general tendency to ignore the global south in discussions of games, game cultures and game studies as a worldwide phenomenon.

There are good reasons to make game studies more inclusive, and recent scholarship has carved out a path for more culturally comprehensive and geographically situated assessments of games' history and global reach. Research on regional or area-specific game studies, and in particular those studies focusing on "regions and localities that have traditionally been underserved by dominant industrial players and under-examined by both journalists and scholars"[39] and/or "areas outside of Western Europe and North America"[40] have made valuable contributions to the way we think about games as a global phenomenon.[41] As Mukherjee has argued, the inclusion of diverse perspectives is advantageous to the game industry and academia alike in simultaneously expanding the international games market and the spectrum of player cultures examined—and interpretations of games and game culture from the perspectives of the global south are important, "not least because they challenge the centrality and fixity of readings and offer a multiplicity of perspectives."[42] One of the primary objectives of this volume is to expand and diversify our methodology for studying games in the global south, building on this pioneering trajectory in recent area-specific games research.

Scholars working on digital culture in the global south have laid essential groundwork for understanding the role of place in games and other electronic media. First and foremost, it is important to recognize that, as Taylor explains, early visions of the internet as a "limitless, free-floating realm, divorced from offline place" quickly gave way to more nuanced interpretations recognizing that "whilst certain conventional understandings of geography and place may be

37. Steven L. Kent, *The Ultimate History of Video Games* (Three Rivers Press, 2001).

38. Peter Zackariasson and Timothy L. Wilson, *The Video Game Industry: Formation, Present State, and Future* (Routledge, 2012: 3-4).

39. Ben Aslinger and Nina B. Huntemann, "Introduction," in *Gaming Globally: Production, Play and Place*, eds. Nina B. Huntemann and Ben Aslinger (Palgrave Macmillan, 2013), 2.

40. Liboriussen and Martin, "Regional Game Studies."

41. See, for example, Larissa Hjorth and Dean Chan, eds. *Gaming Cultures and Place in Asia-Pacific* (Routledge, 2009), Mark J. P. Wolf, ed., *Video Games Around the World* (MIT Press, 2015), Dal Yong Jin, ed., *Mobile Gaming in Asia: Politics, Culture and Emerging Technologies* (Springer, 2016), Mia Consalvo, *Atari to Zelda: Japan's Videogames in Global Contexts* (MIT Press, 2016) and Penix-Tadsen, *Cultural Code: Video Games and Latin America* (MIT Press, 2016).

42. Mukherjee, *Videogames and Postcolonialism*, 109-111.

challenged online, this does not mean that place is erased altogether," and indeed, "place is found not to be lacking on the internet, but rather is transformed, given different meanings, or re-affirmed in a variety of contexts."[43] When we envision the places where gameplay occurs, we may immediately think of the living room or the video arcade, the cybercafé or a seat on the train for mobile gaming. Each of these sites impacts the experience of gameplay in different ways, and this is that much more evident if we expand our examination of the places of gaming to include the types of sites Jack Lanchuan Qiu examines in his work on the "information have-less" in urban China, in which he observes that in "[a] factory, a school, a residential community, or prison cell: through the intermingling of people in place, the information have-less and working-class ICTs reconfigure each other in complex ways, giving rise to infinite variations and producing a kaleidoscope of communication patterns."[44] When we look at less-frequently-examined places for the consumption of technology (such as prison cells and factories), we gain a more expansive and realistic understanding of how these technologies fit into the lives of everyday people. The games people play connect into a sense of place: game cultures both reflect local cultures and enable links between transnational communities,[45] while the gameplay experience is impacted by parameters such as socio-economic class, cultural background and geographic location.[46] In their introduction to *Gaming Globally*, Nina B. Huntemann and Ben Aslinger outline how place impacts games, focusing on "how local, national, regional, transnational, and translocal perspectives can add new levels of complexity to how we assess and experience the formal, textual, and representational content of games; discourses and practices of game development, distribution, policy, ratings, and censorship; historical, geographic, spatial, linguistic, racial, ethnic, and domestic contexts that influence design, hardware and software production; and embodied and networked play practices."[47] Together, these myriad factors create what Apperley refers to as the "situated ecology" of gaming, in reference to the ways "[d]ifferent contexts of play create completely different experiences" through "the materiality of the embodied experience of gaming" as well as the ways the game experience is played out as a negotiation between the "global" virtual worlds the material conditions of the "local."[48] By drawing attention to the situated ecology of gaming in distinct locales from across the global south, the work in this anthology offers new evidence and novel case studies that help emphasize the importance of place for the experience of gaming, building upon the critical and theoretical perspectives from scholars of area-specific game studies in order to expand our understanding of how games work as global technologies.

Redefining video games from the viewpoint of the global south involves certain risks. First, we run the risk of reinforcing the same binary, center-periphery paradigm that much of our work aims to challenge. No doubt it is important for game scholarship to take the global south into account, but at the same time we must avoid treating the analysis of games in the global south as separate from game studies overall, or approaching the subject in a way that upholds its marginality vis-à-vis a presumed "center" of global gaming culture.[49] Liboriussen and Martin warn of "falling into a naïve essentialism" by labeling scholarship "regional," which could be taken as "dismissive or, worse, as the validation of a centre-periphery model that characterises research from Europe and North America as fundamental."[50] Shaw has argued that "game studies scholars who study the 'others' to this dominant

43. Claire Taylor, *Place and Politics in Latin American Digital Culture: Location and Latin American Net Art* (Routledge, 2014), 3-4.
44. Jack Linchuan Qiu, *Working-Class Network Society: Communication Technology and the Information Have-Less in Urban China* (MIT Press, 2009), 15.
45. Larissa Hjorth, "Guest Editor's Introduction: Games@Neo-Regionalism: Locating Gaming in the Asia-Pacific," *Games and Culture* 3.1 (January 2008): 3.
46. Chakraborti, Kwabena and Dibyadyuti, 137.
47. Aslinger and Huntemann, "Introduction," 2.
48. Apperley, *Gaming Rhythms*, 35.
49. As Bjarke Liboriussen and Paul Martin explain in their essay "Regional Game Studies" (*Game Studies* 16.1, October 2016), "Regional game studies is not simply exotic ornamentation for the "real" game studies of Western Europe and North America. We claim that in time regional game studies can make significant theoretical contributions to the field."
50. Liboriussen and Martin, "Regional Game Studies."

definition are forced to talk about their subject in relation to the perceived center," noting that in the research she has conducted for two studies, neither Arab gamers nor gay, bisexual and transgender gamers "place themselves outside what is often called video game culture," and therefore research that reinforces this separation "privileges the dominant gamer identity while marginalizing all others."[51] Thus, it is essential that we pursue research on the video games and game cultures of the global south in a way that recognizes the uniqueness of the regions involved, but that also looks to how reimaging video games from the viewpoint of the global south can impact game studies as a discipline worldwide.

While approaching games from the global south brings risks, it also bears many rewards, opportunities and affordances for scholars of game studies and related disciplines. Liboriussen and Martin call for a recognition that "[t]he world is not flat, and there are significant challenges to the development of game scholarship conducted in, for example, regions of the global South, that are not encountered elsewhere,"[52] and in spite of these challenges, scholars in these regions find ways to persevere in order to impact the way we think about video games, as many of the contributors to this anthology demonstrate. As early as 2008, Larissa Hjorth was calling attention to "heterogeneous models for gaming production and consumption" in different locales throughout the Asia-Pacific region, examining "the region's various gaming cultures to reflect on social, cultural, political, and economic factors that are informing the new 'Global South.'"[53] These calls for greater diversity of perspectives and attention to the particular contexts and circumstances for video games and game culture in the global south represent prescient and cutting-edge voices in contemporary game scholarship, and as this anthology shows, such a focus does indeed bring together a vast array of approaches and points of view. Ultimately, we could consider an examination of contemporary technoculture from the viewpoint of the global south as an opportunity for "border thinking," which Mignolo defines as "a machine for intellectual decolonization" that conceives of "the modern/colonial world system [...] in terms of internal and external borders rather than centers, semiperipheries and peripheries."[54] Using border thinking to approach technologies such as video games allows us to understand the multi-tiered obstacles and affordances to game development and consumption that exist beyond nationality alone, delving into the particular subcultures, differences in player practices and inequalities in access to game hardware and software that can exist within a single nation. With any luck, the bonds and fractures that emerge through this approach will continue to spread and expand until they reach the very foundations of game studies and the ways we conceive of video games' role in the world.

GAMES AND GAME CULTURES OF THE GLOBAL SOUTH: KEY CHARACTERISTICS

No generalization holds true in every case, and there are innumerable differences that make each particular example and circumstance unique. Indeed, such differences are key to many of the chapters ahead. Even still, it is useful to take note of the points of contact that bring together disparate settings and situations, and therefore it will be helpful to keep in mind some key characteristics common to the video games and game cultures of regions, countries and locales within the global south. These characteristics include: 1) a reputation as part of the technological "periphery" or "margin," in spite of a considerable history of game consumption, production, circulation and related practices; 2) a shared set of historical obstacles and affordances to the development of local game culture and game

51. Shaw, "What is Video Game Culture?," 408-409.
52. Liboriussen and Martin, "Regional Game Studies."
53. Hjorth "Guest Editor's Introduction," 4, 6.
54. Walter Mignolo, *Local Histories/Global Designs: Coloniality, Subaltern Knowledges, and Border Thinking* (Princeton University Press, 2012), 45, 33.

industries; 3) a history of in-game representations of local culture, created by developers in the global north; and 4) a dual government role with regard to video games, split between censorship and regulation on one hand, and a growing push to promote national game industries on the other. The remainder of this section will dedicate particular attention to these characteristics, using them as a point of departure for understanding the similarities and differences among the contexts explored in the chapters ahead.

Models that distinguish between supposed "centers" of global technological culture and its "margins" or "peripheries" are highly problematic, due to their unidirectional conceptualization of the relationship between media producers (in the global north) and media consumers (in the global south). In fact, the global south has a powerful impact on the ways media is created, circulated and used worldwide. If we fail to understand how "global" media circulate in countries and regions like those explored in this anthology, then we fail to understand them as truly global media. And yet, in game studies and media studies discussions of media production and consumption, as well as debates surrounding the relationship between games and culture at large, it is common to find sweeping generalizations based primarily or solely on examples from the global north. As Marcos Cueto has argued, however, "technology should be understood as an arena contested by a wide variety of individuals, institutions and actors and through complex local processes of reception, rejection, adaptation and hybridization."[55] Technology, in other words, is not simply transmitted from center to periphery in a unilateral manner, but rather it is shaped and transformed by a continual process of mutual exchange between multiple actors in a global network.

With regard to game studies scholarship in particular, the impact of the global south has only begun to receive attention relatively recently, due in part to the many obstacles that scholars of game culture in these regions face. As Mark J. P. Wolf explains in *Video Games Around the World*, many countries outside the so-called "centers" of game culture "have their own video game industries and their own national histories of video games, many of which are only now beginning to be recorded."[56] Although nearly every country now has a game history that is decades old, those histories have often remained confined within their own national borders and languages, if they have been recorded at all. In the Arab world, for example, Vit Šisler explains that game-related research "remains largely anecdotal and focuses on isolated, albeit important, threads within the fabric of videogame culture and development in the Middle East," and while he argues that "a 'mainstream' Arab, or Pakistani gaming culture does not yet exist," he nevertheless cites "a relatively coherent set of concerns that most of the producers in Iran and the Arab world share," including an emphasis on self-representation, personal motivation, engagement and respect for traditions, religion and culture.[57] Research like Šisler's helps to document the ways global cultural products are adapted, transformed and molded by the local environments in which they are produced and those where they are consumed.

The distinct timelines and trajectories of local game histories show why certain "universal narratives" of technological history fail to account for the complexity and diversity of global media practices. For example, while in some countries early video game culture developed in the same manner as in the United States, starting in the late 1970s and early 1980s with the release of arcade cabinet machines and home consoles such as the PONG and the Atari VCS, this is not universally the case. The

55. Marcos Cueto, "Foreword," in *Beyond Imported Magic: Essays on Science, Technology and Society in Latin America*, eds. Eden Medina and Ivan da Costa Marques (MIT Press, 2014), vii.
56. Wolf, *Video Games Around the World*, 1.
57. Vit Šisler defines "Arab world" as "as an umbrella term for countries belonging to the Arab League of Nations and whose official language is Arabic." See Vit Šisler, "Video Game Development in the Middle East: Iran, the Arab World, and Beyond," in *Gaming Globally*, eds. Huntemann and Aslinger, 252-253, 267.

differences between this "standard" model and the "divergent" models throughout the global south speak to the importance of diversifying our understanding of gaming. In the case of the Arab world, for example, Radwan Kasmiya explains that early game consoles reached middle eastern markets around the same time as in the U.S. and Japan, leading to "the demand for video game consoles with an Arabic-friendly interface," and eventually to the development of the first Arabic home computer, the Sakhr (meaning "Rock"), developed in Kuwait in 1981 (see Image 0.6).[58] In Argentina, game consoles also began to arrive in the late 1970s, and while the country's economic twists and turns caused occasional booms for systems such as the Atari 2600 and ColecoVision, it was the Family Game, a pirated version of the Japanese Famicom (known in English as the Nintendo Entertainment System) that revolutionized local gaming due to its inexpensive software and hardware.[59] In China, arcade games began to arrive in the early 1980s after the nation's "post-Mao opening and reform drive," establishing the roots of a national game culture that now generates the greatest game revenues of any country in the world. India's case is unique, as Shaw explains, "because game systems did not enter India until the 1990s, even avid gamers have had comparatively little time with them," meaning that "India did not experience the evolution of digital gaming" at the same time or in the same way as the U.S., western Europe, Japan or other areas.[60]

Image 0.6. A later-model Kuwaiti Sakhr Logo home computer, 1987.

58. Radwan Kasmiya, "Arab World," in Wolf, *Video Games Around the World*, 29-30; *Generation MSX*, "Sakhr Logo," https://www.generation-msx.nl/software/al-alamiah-lcsi/sakhr-logo/release/1955/.

59. Graciela Alicia Esnaola Horacek, Alejandro Iparraguirre, Guillermo Averbuj and María Luján Oulton, "Argentina," in Wolf, *Video Games Around the World*, 51.

60. Adrienne Shaw, "How Do You Say Gamer in Hindi?: Exploratory Reseearch on the Indian Digital Game Industry and Culture," in *Gaming Globally*, eds. Huntemann and Aslinger, 184.

Like game audiences, our ideas of software and hardware development are often shaped by dominant models such as the one famously established by the homebrew computing ethic of figures such as Bill Gates, Steve Jobs and Steve Wozniak. While it is true that in many places, game developers are primarily motivated to pursue their career path due to a deep personal interest in games, this is not universally the case. In India, for example, Shaw found that most in the game industry "did not enter the field because of a passion for gaming" and that "game development in India did not stem from a 'hacker culture' history prominent in the United States," due to historical differences to the development of local technological culture.[61] Unlike some of the more well-known technological pioneers, many in the global south have pursued technological development primarily as a way of overcoming obstacles, approaching software and hardware development from the standpoint of resolving problems for the end user, or for themselves. In areas with no formal higher education in game development, for example, modding communities have provided a crash course in computer programming for many individuals. In cases such as these, technological development aims less at state-of-the-art innovation, and more at overcoming the many obstacles that stand in the way of game development in the global south. These often include factors such as U.S. embargoes on technology that prohibit developers from purchasing game design engines, middleware and development software in the Arab world and elsewhere.[62] One result of such trade restrictions is that in many countries of the global south, the first locally-developed home gaming consoles were copied versions of other companies' hardware. This was the case of Kuwaiti Sakhr computer, which "was essentially based on the well-known Japanese MSX,"[63] as well as consoles such as the Argentine Telematch, a 1975 Magnavox Odyssey clone. Other early examples of local hardware development include the NESA-Pong, a 1973 PONG clone developed by Mexican entrepreneur Morris Behar;[64] the Brazilian TK90X, a Sinclair ZX Spectrum clone from the mid-1980s (see Image 0.7);[65] and the Xiaobawang ("Big Brother"), recognized as China's first game console, developed in the late 1980s.[66] While such hardware adaptations initially served to fill the void created by the game industry's absence from the formal market in much of the global south, they ultimately laid the groundwork for the emergence of the regional game industries that are developing rapidly today.

In many areas of the global south, piracy is another significant factor in the use and distribution of software (see Image 0.8).[67] However, some readers might be surprised by the unanticipated effects of piracy, since pirated games and software can nurture audiences' media literacy and can even ultimately add to global media publishers' bottom lines. In cases from Mexico to China, Thailand and Indonesia, it has been shown that "gray market" goods—those that are smuggled into the country by travelers returning from trips abroad—have been a boon to gamers as well as the game industry at large.[68] The gray market has benefitted players by offering access to hardware and software that were otherwise unavailable locally on the formal market, lowering consumer prices by circumventing import taxes and expanding access to players of different socio-economic classes. On the other hand, the game industry has benefitted from local publishers' development of important localization practices, improved gaming literacy among local populations and increased brand allegiance when consumers of black or gray market games transition to purchasing licensed hardware and software.

61. Shaw, "How Do You Say Gamer in Hindi?," 185.
62. Šisler, "Video Game Development in the Middle East," 255.
63. Kasmiya, "Arab World," 29.
64. Humberto Cervera and Jacinto Quesnel, "Mexico," in Wolf, *Video Games Around the World*, 345-357.
65. Gonzalo Frasca, "Uruguay," in Wolf, *Video Games Around the World*, 609-612; *Clube do TK90X*, http://www.tk90x.com.br/imagens/propagTK90X(Jul-85).jpg.
66. Anthony Y. H. Fung and Sara Xueting Liao, "China," in Wolf , *Video Games Around the World*, 121.
67. Sketcz, "Videogames of Egypt," *Hardcore Gaming 101 Blog*, 22 March 2010. http://blog.hardcoregaming101.net/2010/03/videogames-of-egypt.html.
68. Fung and Liao, "China," 129; Cervera and Quesnel, "Mexico," 346, 350; Songsri Soranastoporn, "Thailand," in Wolf, *Video Games Around the World*, 546; Inaya Rakhmani and Hikmat Darmawan, "Indonesia," in Wolf, *Video Games Around the World*, 250, 256.

Image 0.7. Advertisement for the Brazilian TK90X personal computer, mid-1980s.

While pirated media can be found the world over, they are the standard rather than the exception in much of the global south—for example, in the Middle East, where the level of piracy is among the highest worldwide—,[69] "the majority of video games, no matter their origin, are either purchased as pirated copies or played in public venues where one copy suffices for tens, if not hundreds, of gamers."[70] This democratizing effect, spreading access to players with less disposable income whose game consumption lies outside the margins of official market data, is key to understanding the impact of piracy. Studies from Brazil and China show that piracy comes into being largely to help overcome the significant obstacles between consumers and content, such as tremendously high tariffs on imported tech goods.[71] Likewise, Apperley's research on Venezuela suggests that piracy is crucial

69. Mohammed Ibahrine, "Video Games as Civilizational Configurations: US-Arab Encounters," in *Islamism and Cultural Expression in the Arab World*, eds. Abir Hamdar and Lindsey Moore (Routledge, 2015), 206-221.
70. Tawil-Souri, "The Political Battlefield of Pro-Arab Video Games," 538.

for the sustainability and profitability of businesses in the ICT sector of the economy, and argues that in "a global economy based on knowledge and networks, exclusion equals poverty, and in some cases, piracy enables inclusion in the economy."[72] Elsewhere, Apperley has pointed out that black market software use in the global south is a tactical response to global inequalities, one that is only logical given the structural unevenness of an industry with ever-growing demands for hardware and internet performance.[73] Moreover, in a global society where participation means not only consuming but producing, sharing and reproducing media, this is essential, as Lars Eckstein and Anja Schwarz explain in *Postcolonial Piracy*: "Cultures of piracy across the globe [...] have performed as crucial sites in which various ways of being modern have been negotiated and acted out."[74] Since global citizenship increasingly requires participation in media networks and a knowledge of computer hardware and software, one of piracy's greatest benefits for the global south is an expansion in overall access to those networks and technologies.

Image 0.8. Market stalls selling black market video game hardware and software, Cairo, Egypt, 2010.

Public gaming facilities such as cybercafés, LAN centers, PC Bangs and other game rental spaces are another significant factor in expanding access to gaming technology across the global south (see Image 0.9).[75] Anthony Y. H. Fung and Sara Xueting Liao note that in China's early game culture, cybercafés were both the primary sites in which games were played and also the locales in which piracy spread most rapidly, expanding access to players but cutting into profits for formal-market developers, at least temporarily.[76] Likewise, in many areas of Latin America, the cybercafé has served both "as a democratizing market force spreading game access far beyond the reach of official sales data" and also as "a shared space that has fostered the development of a community of gamers, game developers, and game industry professionals."[77] As Hjorth has noted, the PC bang, the variation of the

71. James Portnow, Arthur Protasio and Kate Donaldson, "Brazil: Tomorrow's Market," in *Gaming Globally*, ed. Huntemann and Aslinger, 76; Fung and Liao, "China," 122.
72. Apperley, "Venezuela," 619.
73. Apperley, *Gaming Rhythms*, 15.
74. Lars Eckstein and Anja Schwarz, *Postcolonial Piracy: Media Distribution and Cultural Production in the Global South* (Bloomsbury, 2014), 18.
75. Lina Andrea Plazas Lizcano, "Cuatro niños se encuentran en un local de videojuegos," 24 June 2005, Biblioteca Departamental Jorge Garces Borrero, http://hdl.handle.net/123456789/57283; Aura Cristina Alzate Vargas, "Jóvenes reunidos en la puerta de entrada a un local de videojuegos," 24 June 2005, Biblioteca Departamental Jorge Garces Borrero, http://hdl.handle.net/123456789/57299.
76. Fung and Liao, "China," 129.
77. Penix-Tadsen, *Cultural Code*, 53.

cybercafé prevalent in South Korea and other parts of Asia that is also the birthplace of competitive online gaming, has played a "pivotal role" in the development of games and game culture across the region.[78] Not only in Korea but in many areas worldwide, the first wave of cybercafés gave way to the development of LAN centers, which further helped to expand the reach of gaming and encourage multiplayer interactions through local area networks (LANs; see Image 0.10).[79] In Thailand, for example, LAN centers began to spring up in the late 1990s near schools and universities in the capital city of Bangkok, and eventually spread to all of the country's provinces.[80] Sites like cybercafés, PC bangs and LAN centers have served as the physical locales that have established the parameters for game culture in many countries, making them crucial for understanding the economic and social dimensions of gaming and game culture in the global south.

Image 0.9. Young patrons gather at two cybercafés in Cali, Colombia, 2005.

In addition to key factors that have helped to nurture regional game cultures such as hardware and software modification, software piracy and social gaming institutions like the cybercafé, many areas in the global south share a history of common obstacles to the development of local game culture and game industries. These obstacles include internal economic divisions between rich and poor, overall digital poverty, urban/rural divides in technological access, an absence of major game industry corporations and a lack of cultural and monetary localization to make games appealing to local audiences. In the Middle East, for example, common challenges to game development include not only those related to the state, such as a lack of intellectual property protection, regulation of cultural production and censorship, but also "social and cultural aspects" including "communication patterns, cultural identity, and religious values."[81] Likewise, the Indian game industry has faced obstacles including include infrastructure barriers such as low PC and Internet penetration, industry-related issues such as piracy and lack of development experience, and consumer-related impediments such as negative perceptions regarding games.[82] And in India as well as many parts of Africa and other areas of the global south, one of the most significant barriers to the establishment of a firm, legitimate local gaming market is the commonplace use of electronic microtransactions and autopayment mechanisms in games designed primarily for users with credit cards, which are extremely uncommon throughout the global south.[83]

78. Hjorth, "Guest Editor's Introduction," 7.
79. @Vainglory, "Had an awesome time meeting and engaging with 300 fans at the #HalcyonGathering LAN Party at Ho Chi Minh, Vietnam! Community OP!," Twitter, 14 January 2017, https://twitter.com/vainglory/status/820282926411776001.
80. Soranastoporn, "Thailand," 555.
81. Šisler, "Video Game Development in the Middle East," 252.
82. Shaw "How Do You Say Gamer in Hindi?," 193.

Image 0.10. LAN Party at the Halcyon Gathering, Ho Chi Minh City, Vietnam, 2017.

And nevertheless, the global south's gamers and game-makers have persisted. When we focus on the processes through which technologies that are frequently developed in the global north have been adapted and transformed to make them useful to consumers and creators in the global south, a new picture of worldwide technological evolution emerges. Rather than a globe that is simplistically divided between technological haves and have-nots on either side of a digital divide, we observe the way active agents around the globe are finding ways to work around the legal, economic, political and social obstacles to the development of regional games and game culture. This is why, in his research on technological adaptation among the Chinese working class, Jack Linchuan Qiu refers to the "information have-less," a "new social category" consisting of "low-end ICT users, service providers, and laborers who are manufacturing these electronics."[84] Though Qiu's work focuses on China specifically, his observation that "ICTs are becoming less expensive, more widespread, and more closely integrated with the life of working-class people" certainly holds true in many other areas across the global south, and it is an example of the steps that have been taken to allow people of different socioeconomic backgrounds to access technologies, as well as the obstacles they have faced.

The absence of major game industry corporations has been a catch-22 for the global south:

83. Wesley Kirinya, "Africa," in Wolf, *Video Games Around the World*, 28; Mukherjee, "Playing Subaltern," 242.

84. Qiu, *Working-Class Network Society*, 3-4.

multinational game companies are hesitant to invest in the global south because of the dominance of piracy and the difficulty of marketing their products to consumers; as a result, hardware and software piracy continue to expand, and the black market becomes the only source of many technological brands in countries across the global south. Historically, the "global" game industry has taken much longer to show an interest in the players and markets of the global south than those in the global north, though there have been some notable outreach efforts along the way. This generalized industry absence includes not only hardware companies such as Nintendo, Sony and Microsoft; but also software developers like Square Enix, Electronic Arts and Namco Bandai; and also online distribution networks like Steam, PlayStation Network and Xbox Live. Even as recently as 2008, multinational game corporations like Sony and Microsoft were practically absent from the Chinese market, which was dominated by producers from China, Taiwan and Korea.[85] In India, Microsoft marketed the Xbox but failed to provide development licenses for Indian developers—reflecting a general tendency of game corporations who *manufacture* but do not *develop* games in the global south—while Sony bucked the trend by engaging in the development of original titles from local developers.[86] In Latin America, major game industry players like Sony and Square Enix have begun incubator programs to help local developers create games for distribution on their platforms, but only after the 2009 economic downturn drove them to seek new customers in the region's untapped markets.[87] And in the Middle East and many other areas of the global south, services such as Xbox Live are not supported, and though Sony's game consoles are popular, Sony does not extend PlayStation Network access to many Middle Eastern countries, making it impossible for console gamers to play online.[88]

Cultural norms and expectations can also affect the development of games and game culture in different regions. The Arab world is a key case in point, as numerous games developed in the West contain elements that are at odds with an Islamic worldview, with the potential for sparking controversy or provoking censorship if they are not localized with care. Brian T. Edwards explains that many in the global south have associated "globalization" with "Americanization," but while in some more extreme cases "the disenfranchised could turn toward a resurgent fundamentalist version of Islam as an alternative globalism," their views of the West have also inevitably been impacted by the ways "the digital revolution made American movies, comics, fiction, music, video games, and websites easily accessible, opening a new way of life that set uneasily with a legend of US imperial designs."[89] Still, the relationship between video games and the audiences of the Arab world is complex, its history fraught with missteps by developers, even those from within the region itself. For example, the cool public reception of *Zoya: A Warrior from Palmyra* (2002), a *Tomb Raider*-inspired adventure game from Syrian developer Techniat3D, has been attributed to the "'improper attire' of the female warrior featured on the cover" of the game.[90] And cultural localization is not always as simple as adhering to local norms for characters' costumes. In his research on game development in the Middle East, Šisler argues that understanding key Arab cultural values such as modesty and honor are essential for addressing contemporary Arab video game production, and explains that regional game developers take a number of measures to "ensure the effective use of design concepts based on prevailing cultural values," including "(a) culturally sensitive design, in general, and (b) religious sensitivity, (c) identity construction, (d) educational appeal, and (e) self-censorship in particular."[91] Ahmad Ahmadi echoes this observation in his research on Iranian game culture, explaining that

85. Yong Cao and John D. H. Downing, "The Realities of Virtual Play: Video Games and their Industry in China," *Media, Culture & Society*, 30.4 (2008): 517-519.
86. Shaw "How Do You Say Gamer in Hindi?," 183-201.
87. Penix-Tadsen, *Cultural Code*, 120-122.
88. Kasmiya, "Arab World," 33.
89. Edwards, *After the American Century*, 21.
90. Kasmiya, "Arab World," 30.
91. Šisler, "Video Game Development in the Middle East," 254.

Iranian culture influences national game development on many levels, including the adaptation of cultural heritage and mythology; the depiction of cultural norms, traditions, customs and rituals; and the representation of modernity, "including free will, the rule of law and freedom of speech."[92] So while cultural differences can serve as obstacles to the development or reception of games throughout the Arab world, it is just as important to note that those same cultural differences produce new opportunities for developers who are able to capitalize on their familiarity with their region's cultural contexts and player profiles.

The representation of local, national and regional cultures of the global south in video games has a lengthy and at times controversial history. Most audiences in the global south grew accustomed to seeing their cultures depicted in games created by developers in the global north long before locally produced games began to appear, and many of these depictions from the outside were predictably reductive and stereotypical. Apperley cites public outcry over depictions of local environments from Seoul to Rio de Janeiro as demonstrations that national, regional and local identity can affect the way hegemonic depictions of "global" concerns are assimilated at the local level.[93] This is why it is so displeasing to see one's own culture depicted poorly, and conversely why it can be so surprisingly pleasant to see a more complex and nuanced depiction of one's culture in a game. Too often players in different parts of the global south are forced to play versions of their homelands sketched out through stereotypical generalizations and clichés, for example the countless Middle Eastern game environments across the medium's history that have used Orientalist imagery to depict the Middle East as either a quasi-historical fantasy landscape, or as a space for contemporary conflicts that situate Arabs and Muslims as enemies.[94] The same is true for other cases where cultures of the global south are represented: Siddhartha Chakraborti argues that in games produced in the global north such as *Tomb Raider III: Adventures of Lara Croft* (1998), *Prince of Persia: The Sands of Time* (2003) and *Call of Duty: Black Ops II* (2012), "India is never seen as a sovereign nation but rather as a location for the use of the western outsider," a framework that perceives India not as a nation but a destination, "a destination ripe for western intervention by denying the nation any sovereignty and agency of its own."[95] As these and many other cases show, the legacy of colonialism and orientalist depictions of cultures outside the global north—a legacy that responds to lengthy traditions in literature, the visual arts, film and other representational media—remains key to understanding the ways video games relate to the global south.

Just as interesting is how players from the global south have found ways to "play back" against colonialist tendencies in video games. Mukherjee has argued that "just as postcolonial historiography and narratives foster 'reading against the grain' of imperial chronicles," video games and play practices produced from a postcolonial or decolonial viewpoint "can be said to be 'playing against the grain'" or "playing back."[96] Mukherjee explains that in his view, playing back "is the playing of the plural; it disrupts linear chronologies and centers of truth; implicitly, it speaks for those voices that cannot be heard in the colonial archives; and it presents scenarios where both colonial stereotypes can be simulated and anticolonial alternative stories can be told." And indeed, there are many cases across the global south that show how game players and designers are developing practices that utilize the medium "against the grain" of its standard use for entertainment in order to represent the cultural and political concerns particular to the designated audience. For example, in his research

92. Ahmad Ahmadi, "Iran," in Wolf, *Video Games Around the World*, 284-285.
93. Apperley, *Gaming Rhythms*, 119.
94. Vit Šisler, "Palestine in Pixels: The Holy Land, Arab-Israeli Conflict, and Reality Construction in Video Games," *Middle East Journal of Culture and Communication* 2 (2009): 278-279; Vit Šisler, "Digital Arabs: Representation in Video Games," *European Journal of Cultural Studies* 11.2 (2008): 214.
95. Siddhartha Chakraborti, "From Destination to Nation and Back: The Hyperreal Journey of Incredible India," *Journal of Gaming & Virtual Worlds* 7.2 (2015): 183-202.
96. Mukherjee, *Videogames and Postcolonialism*, 103.

on game development in the Arab world, Mohammed Ibahrine distinguishes "Islamist" games—those developed by "groups that are radical and violent," a category that could include the Al-Qaeda sponsored *Quest for Bush* (Global Islamic Media Front, 2006), as well as the Hezbollah-backed games *Special Force* (2003) and *Special Force 2* (2007)—from "Islamic" games—those developed by groups that are moderate and non-violent—such as *Under Ash* (Dar al-Fikr 2001) and *Quraish* (Dar al-Fikr 2005), concluding that by representing perspectives that diverge from the common Western game narratives, video games offer developers "an extraordinary medium for non-state actors to culturally resist and confront hegemonic discourses and institutions, and these actors exercise considerable influence over Arab youth."[97] Ibahrine further argues that playing Islamic games can be "an act of emancipation from the American images that have previously dominated the world of video games,"[98] a thesis that would seem to be evidenced in the joy Palestinian player cited in a snapshot at the beginning of this introductory chapter, and others who have found profound self-affirmation in games offering a positive depiction of their own cultures. Still, other critics argue that these games frequently reproduce the militaristic worldview and violent standards typical of the medium, making games like *Special Force* fundamentally similar to western first-person shooters despite their attempts to transcend the limitations of the genre.[99] More recently, as Aslinger and Huntemann have argued, expansions in mobile technology and improvements in internet connectivity have spread access to gaming, game developers working on relatively small-scale smartphone applications and online games have encountered expanded opportunities for the creation of "more local and individualized experiences," while "industries and governments (among others) are jockeying for position in a fast growing market."[100] For example, although games developed in Latin America have not typically been marketed to the region's consumers, that tendency has begun to shift with the expansion of social networking and mobile internet access.[101] Indeed, at this very moment, we are experiencing an explosion in the development of local and regional games corresponding to the particular cultural environments in which they are created, and this boom in self-representation is likely just one of the early steps in the evolution of gaming as a global phenomenon.

In much of the global south, the state has played a split role with regard to video games: on one hand, games are seen as a dangerous concern to public health and morality, the focus of censorship, restriction and regulation in response to hegemonic representations and culturally controversial material; on the other hand, many governments seek to support of the game industry as a chance to partake more fully in the international knowledge economy through investment in national creative industries. This push-and-pull between governmental attacks on games and support for their development can be observed in cases from across the global south, in varying levels of extremity. China is a paradigmatic case of this dual state role. Dirlik sees China's visible contradictions as exemplary of the possibilities and the challenges facing the global south, with its high level of national economic development and integration in the international neoliberal economy balanced by its cultural autonomy and socialist-rooted ideas of equity and justice.[102] Certainly, these contradictions and fragmentations are as visible in China's video game culture as anywhere else. First, there is the heavy hand of state control: fueled by rising public controversies and alarms raised concerning childhood game addiction over the course of the 1990s, the Chinese Ministry of Culture demanded in 2000 that all companies and individuals to cease to produce, distribute and circulate video game

97. Ibahrine, "Video Games as Civilizational Configurations," 213-214.
98. Ibid., 216.
99. Šisler, "Video Game Development in the Middle East," 211.
100. Aslinger and Huntemann, "Introduction," 1.
101. Agustín Pérez-Fernández, "Video Game Development in Argentina," in *Gaming Globally*, eds. Huntemann and Aslinger: 80.
102. Dirlik, "Global South: Predicament and Promise," 17-18.

hardware domestically, a ruling which led to a longstanding ban on game consoles in China that also had the unforeseen effect of forcing all production, distribution and circulation of Chinese games to move online.[103] Fung and Liao argue that this ban was motivated by "economic and national protectionism," as a measure aimed at reducing the dominance of foreign game companies in China, where domestic companies had little experience other than importing and cloning foreign games.[104] Additionally, the Chinese "censorship mechanism" involves a combination of state and market procedures that range from official licensing and censorship of foreign games featuring violence, sex, superstition or seen as threatening to national sovereignty, to market functions such as self-censorship by game developers and publishers, who, for example, avoid all political content.[105]

But just as the state can frequently serve as an obstacle to the development of games and game culture, it can seek to advance national interests by investing in game development. In cases from across the global south from China to Colombia and from Thailand to Iran, governmental support has been cited as a key piece of the puzzle that leads to successful game development and a sustainable game development ecosystem.[106] Many of the most forward-thinking state agencies and political voices in the global south have begun to embrace gaming and game development as positive elements of national culture and areas of potential growth for the national economy, helping to strengthen the optimistic view that the balance in the state's dual role regarding video games will tip away from censorship and control, and toward nurturing and support.

Together, these four key factors—a reputation as part of the technological margins despite a longstanding game culture, a shared set of historical obstacles and affordances to game development, a legacy of cultural representation at the hands of game developers in the global north and a divided official perspective on video games—help understand the ways that games have been uniquely adapted and transformed by actors in the global south in order to ensure their compatibility with the parameters of local cultural expectations, technological capabilities and economic circumstances. While the situation of every region, country and locale is irreducibly unique, these factors illuminate some of the points of contact that can bring together otherwise disparate countries and regions, showing that an understanding of the games and game cultures of the global south is essential to an understanding of games and game culture in general.

REDEFINING VIDEO GAMES AND GAME CULTURE, FROM SOUTH TO NORTH

Today, video games are a major part of culture in the global south, and likewise, in order to understand contemporary game culture, it is essential to take into account how games are created, circulated and put to use in regions like Africa, the Middle East, the Caribbean, Central and South America, the Indian subcontinent and developing areas of Oceania and Asia. In order to better comprehend video games as a global phenomenon, it is essential to learn from the experiences of game players and developers from these regions, helping redefine games and game studies from south to north. Video games have never just "fallen into place" in the global south—instead, they have been situated and contextualized, made playable and accessible by the active efforts of countless groups and individuals whose endeavors are landmarks in the development of global game culture. Today a number of factors have paved the way for a boom in game access and game development alike across the global south, including an increase in mobile internet access and use; a concomitant increase in developers'

103. Fung and Liao, "China," 127.
104. Fung and Liao, "China," 132.
105. Cao and Downing, "The Realities of Virtual Play," 523-524.
106. Cao and Downing, "The Realities of Virtual Play," 524; Luis Parra and Global Game Designers Guild, "Colombia," in Wolf, *Video Games Around the World*, 142; Soranastoporn, "Thailand," 552; Šisler, "Video Game Development in the Middle East," 255.

access to the casual game market; public and private efforts to nurture a healthy game development ecosystem; and increased crossover, visibility and relevance to other facets of culture such as sports, music and art. These elements are making the global south's impact on game culture clear in new and undeniable ways, and they show why the development of games and game culture in the global south is likely to continue its exponential expansion for the foreseeable future.

Increased access to games in the global south means increased game literacy among today's players, who are tomorrow's game developers. Over the past decade, an explosion of cellular and mobile internet access have made video games and other interactive media accessible for the first time to many audiences in the global south. In India, for example, Shaw explains that "massive growth in mobile phone use" has increased the popularity of social networking games and motivated a shift in focus toward the development of mobile games, with mobile gaming being heralded as a major boon to the local game market due to "high consumer adoption, micropayment models, cheaper development costs, and lower piracy risk."[107] And indeed, similar factors are motivating a shift toward the mobile market in many other areas of the global south. In Africa, mobile phones outnumber PCs and game consoles combined,[108] while in Latin America mobile subscriptions now outpace land lines by a factor of more than 4 to 1.[109] Research on the use of ICTs in development projects highlights the role played by state-funded and NGO-supported programs focused on improving access to the internet and related technologies. Chile, for example, is considered a leader in ICT policy across Latin America and the global south due to its hybrid approach to expanding access, which focused on the creation of school programs (Enlaces) and access points in public libraries (BiblioRedes) as well as schools and stand-alone telecenters (Infocentros).[110] At the same time, the good intentions of development projects run up against the media uses and desires of actual users—for Chile's library-based BiblioRedes access points, for example, content-control policies grouped gaming along with other restricted or forbidden uses such as online chatting and pornography.[111] The Chilean case illustrates some of the obstacles that have lay upon the path to an expansion in access to gaming technologies across the global south in recent years, as well as some of the collective efforts and innovations that have helped resolve these issues.

An expansion in mobile technology use and the booming popularity of casual games have not only led to new and more diversified gaming audiences, they have opened up new opportunities for game development across the global south, as small independent game studios have brought their products to the international market thanks to the lower investment necessary to create games designed for mobile devices and social media platforms. Research across the global south, from India, Thailand and Indonesia to Latin America, demonstrates that there is a major game development boom has been building up over the first two decades of the 21st century.[112] In his research on Africa, Wesley Kirinya traces the history of regional game development to South Africa in the early 2000s, going on to discuss the establishment of new studios around the same time in Kenya and Ghana, as well as in the mid-2000s in Nigeria, Kenya, South Africa and Morocco.[113] As the first generations to grow up playing video games have come to maturity across the globe, games have become an integrated part of their cultural experiences, and the desire to contribute to game development has expanded. This has led to some creative integration of local culture into locally-developed video games, a practice

107. Shaw, "How Do You Say Gamer in Hindi?," 189-190.
108. Kirinya, "Africa," 28.
109. Penix-Tadsen, *Cultural Code*, 57.
110. Dorothea Kleine, *Technologies of Choice?: ICTs, Development, and the Capabilities Approach* (MIT Press, 2013), 10-13.
111. Kleine, *Technologies of Choice?*, 90
112. Mukherjee, "India," 138; Soranastoporn, "Thailand," 552; Rakhmani and Darmawan, "Indonesia," 263; Penix-Tadsen, *Cultural Code*, 136-138.
113. Kirinya, "Africa," 17-28.

which is itself fraught with controversy for developers in the global south, who may question the pros and cons of tying game development to the depiction of "local color." As Wolf explains, there is "tension between foreign imports and indigenous production" in every country that produces video games, with foreign games establishing design conventions and audience expectations alike.[114] While multinational corporations and government agencies seem to have an insatiable thirst for things like "local color" and "Latin flavor" in games developed in Latin America, for example, game developers may be hesitant to pigeonhole themselves professionally and creatively into what some see as tired tropes and cultural stereotypes.[115] The game cultures of the global south have come into being as part of the struggle and synchronicity between the local and the global within the contemporary media landscape.

A spectrum of official, private and hybrid efforts have also worked in concert to prepare the terrain for this recent increase in game development and game culture in the global south. In terms of financing for game development, the degree to which the balance tilts toward government support on the one hand, or industry support on the other, varies from case to case. In China, the game industry's success has been based less on ties to large, established state-owned media conglomerates, and more on private investment and the support of non-state entities.[116] Colombian game development, for its part, has been nurtured by grassroots associations of game developers such as SOMOS as well as those with ties with international organizations, such as the International Game Developers Association in Colombia and the Global Game Designers Guild.[117] In a number of African contexts, along with growth in the mobile game market, game development has been driven by a focus on the creation of digital development games (DDGs), a trajectory that is not without its problems—Jolene Fisher argues that DDGs are far from radical or revolutionary in their approach to development issues, and indeed that "the production of DDGs is directly tied to the worldwide growth of the digital games sector, a highly concentrated media system in which the Western loci of production, technology, and skills reinforces established North/South knowledge/power divides."[118] While there are many individuals and organizations willing to support game development in the global south, each one has its own agenda and its own objectives. Therefore, the types of development that are most heavily promoted often depend upon the interests being served, whether they are focused on creative production, community building or economic development. These are just some of the considerations and choices that game developers in the global south must make to get their games to players, showing how the interests and expectations of supporting entities can impact the types of games that can potentially be produced within a given set of circumstances.

Critical perspectives, theoretical frameworks and case studies of game culture from the global south are essential to make game studies more diverse, inclusive and complete in its analysis of games and game culture as worldwide phenomena. As this introduction has attempted to make clear, we can no longer think of video games and game culture as phenomena that originate in the global north, but rather the technocultures surrounding video games are developed simultaneously and divergently in different locales throughout the globe. Looking at games from the perspective of the global south means understanding the steps that must be taken in order to make global culture local, and the processes involved in bringing local culture to a global audience. The critical perspectives of scholars from the global south enrich the spectrum of viewpoints on the role of games in culture, and provide

114. Wolf, *Video Games Around the World*, 6.
115. Penix-Tadsen, *Cultural Code*, 101-104.
116. Cao and Downing, "The Realities of Virtual Play," 523.
117. Parra and Global Game Designers Guild, "Colombia," 143.
118. Jolene Fisher, "Toward a Political Economic Framework for Analyzing Digital Development Games: A Case Study of Three Games for Africa," *Communication, Culture & Critique* 9 (2016): 44.

a more nuanced background for understanding games as a truly global phenomenon. And universal attempts to theorize what video games are and how they function will inevitably fall short if they fail to take into account the limitations of the perspective being imposed, or if they are blind to the game-related practices and traditions of regions other than those in which their own theories originate. In other words, game studies as a whole has much perspective to gain from the global south, and it is no longer enough to study the games and game cultures of this vast and varied region as a marginal add-on or peripheral appendage to game culture as envisioned from the viewpoint of the global north. As the work of this anthology's contributors demonstrates, the time has come to redefine video games and game culture from the perspective of the global south.

STRUCTURE OF THE BOOK

Video Games and the Global South is divided into three sections, each thematically organized around a significant point of intersection between the chapters in the section.

Part One, "Serious Games and the Politics of Play" focuses on the relationship between video games, politics, economics and cultural identity, using a variety of approaches including the analysis of "serious" game design and procedural rhetoric, aesthetics of art games, modification practices of player communities and the representation of cultures of the global south by game developers in the global north. In "Replaying the Digital Divide: Video Games in India," Souvik Mukherjee responds to several currents in recent postcolonial critiques of gaming, using them to help reveal the mechanisms that influence views on India's video game industry by analyzing the rhetoric employed by both the state and actors in the country's game industry. Claire Taylor's chapter "Serious Gaming: Critiques of Neoliberalism in the Works of Ricardo Miranda Zúñiga" examines this Chilean artist's interactive works, which combine street interactions with digital/online games in order to maximize audience engagement and encourage players to question the rules of the system in which they are playing. This thread of art game analysis is continued in Jenna Ann Altomonte's chapter, "Playing *Killbox*: Didactic Gaming and Drone Warfare," which shows how DeLappe's multimedia art works as a critique of drone warfare's violent effects on perpetrators as well as victims, putting players in each position in order to force them into an ethical conundrum. In "Playing Beyond Precariousness: The Political Aspect of Brazilian Modding in *Pro Evolution Soccer*," Thaiane Oliveira, José Messias and Diego Amaral apply Walter Mignolo's concept of epistemic disobedience to an analysis of the practices of Brazilian software modifiers and hackers, showing how their work uses state-of-the-art design practices to foreground the interests of subaltern communities at a particular geographical and historical junctures. Rhett Loban and Thomas Apperley shed further light on the cultural role of software modification in their chapter "Eurocentric Values at Play: Modding the Colonial from the Indigenous Perspective," which examines how indigenous culture, history and issues have conventionally been depicted in video games, as well as how they are being reimagined by communities of strategy gamers and game modders. In the final chapter of Section One, "Digital Masks and *Lucha Libre*: Visual Subjectification and Allegory of Mexico in Video Games," Daniel Calleros Villareal explores the history of the lucha libre mask as a ludic symbol of Mexico, analyzing the ways video game luchadores impact Mexican gamers' self-images and notions of cultural identity. Together, these six chapters break new ground in research on the relationship between games and culture in the global south by applying a postcolonial or decolonial perspective to the analysis of regional game industries, serious game design, software modification and in-game cultural representation's impact on players, providing an in-depth examination of serious games and the politics of play in the global south today.

Part Two, "Gaming Communities and Subcultures," includes six chapters focusing on the unique practices, identities and interactions of player communities from across the global south. In the first chapter, "Not Waiting for Other Players Anymore: Gaming in the Middle East between Assignation, Resistance and Normalization," Pierre-Alain Clement provides a framework for the analysis of current video game practices in the Middle East by exploring games' development process, content, audience and user-produced content in light of recent regional data related to online gaming. Verónica Valdivia Medina's chapter "National Cultures and Digital Space: The Case of *World of Warcraft*" uses a comparative analysis of player interactions on North and South American *WoW* servers to identify significant elements of national culture that players bring to this platform, as well as the profound effects of cultural perspective on the meaning of games for players from different backgrounds. Jules Skotnes-Brown, in the chapter "Colonized Play: Racism, Sexism and Colonial Legacies in the *Dota 2* South Africa Gaming Community," analyzes interactions among South African players of *Dota 2* to explain why racism and sexism are allowed to thrive in an online community amidst widespread national attempts to rid the country of such prejudices. Also focusing on *Dota 2* player communities but in the context of Peru, Jerjes Loayza's chapter "Ludic Solidarity and Sociality: An Analysis of the Impact of *Dota 2* on Lima's Youth" argues that, though consumers of video games are sometimes stigmatized as isolated or even antisocial, *Dota 2* players in Peru's capital city not only prefer to share common spaces for the purpose of team interaction, but also because they form long-lasting friendships, bonds and interpersonal relationships in public gaming centers that extend beyond the games themselves. In "Arab Gamers: An Identity Inclusivity Study," Bushra Alfaraj offers a systematic analysis of interview data from Arab-identifying players to learn how audiences from this identity group make sense of the current state of lacking Arab representations in video games. Finally, in "eSports Gamers in China: Career, Lifestyle and Public Discourse among Professional *League of Legends* Competitors," Boris Pun, Yiyi Yin and Anthony Y. H. Fung explore eSports in China from the perspective of political economics, showing how this phenomenon is representative of game culture in a country where the economy is booming but political controls are strict, a situation typical to a number of other locales in the global south. The six chapters that make up Part Two serve to illustrate how the practices of player communities and subcultures throughout the global south correspond to the cultural, technological, social, political and economic conditions in which games are played, offering insights that can help enhance our overall understanding of the relationship between player practices and cultural context.

Part Three, "Circulation of Games and Game Culture," explores emergent practices related to gaming and the multimodal networks through which games are produced, circulated, consumed and otherwise put to use across the global south today. In "Digital Gaming's South-South Connection," Thomas Apperley compares ethnographic player data with participant observations from cybercafés in Melbourne, Australia and Caracas, Venezuela to explore how networked gaming uses globally scaled real-time cross-cultural and transnational communication to connect and reconnect regions in ways that realign local and regional geographic imaginaries. Also shedding light on an underexplored game culture within the global south, Rebecca Yvonne Bayeck's chapter "The Emerging African Video Game Industry: An Analysis of the Narratives of Games Developed in Cameroon and Nigeria" offers key insights into the burgeoning west African game industry, exploring the relationship between the narratives of regional games and the local cultures of the countries in which they were produced in order to offer insights that are relevant to game development on a global level. In "Video Game-Related Engagement on Social Media in the Middle East," Ahmed Al-Rawi and Mia Consalvo examine how Middle Eastern audiences engage with video games and game-related topics on social media, using data from Facebook and Twitter to show how these online platforms serve as extensions of the offline debates that occur around key cultural issues. María Luján Oulton examines how the Southern Cone is responding to global cultural shifts in "The Nuances of Video Game Curation: Lessons from Argentina," analyzing the interaction between art and video games over the last decade in Argentina to show how societies of the global south not only consume cultural products but remix and recreate their own content, shaped by their cultural identity and context. In the chapter "Mobility through Games: Gaming Cultures and Migration," Will Balmford, Larissa Hjorth, Ingrid Richardson and Joshua Wong use an ethnographic analysis of Asian international students in Melbourne, Australia to explore the role of migration in the circuits of game consumption, showing the complex ways in which distance and intimacy are interwoven within the practices of being home and away. Part Three concludes with the chapter "Whose 'Game Culture' is It, Anyway? Exploring Children's Gameplay across Cape Town," in which Nicola Pallitt, Muya Koloko and Anja Venter examine children's gameplay across settings in Cape Town including suburban schools, holiday clubs, township libraries and family households in order to show that the physical location in which a game is played can be as important as who plays, what they play and how they play. These six chapters offer a concerted view of emergent practices that can help expand our understanding of games and game culture by highlighting the unique transmedial relationships that connect previously divided regions, revive cultural traditions by merging them with media of increasing relevance to audiences, bring together the worlds of video games and other forms of art and establish new forms of player communities that may be intimately tied to a precise location, or may cross geographic expanses that were once unimaginable.

WORKS CITED

Abdelgadir, Aala. "The Push to Lift U.S. Communication Technology Sanctions on Sudan." *Council on Foreign Relations,* 28 January 2014, https://www.cfr.org/blog/push-lift-us-communication-technology-sanctions-sudan.

Ahmadi, Ahmad. "Iran." In *Video Games Around the World,* edited by Mark J. P. Wolf, 271-291. MIT Press, 2015.

Apperley, Thomas H. "Venezuela." In *Video Games Around the World,* edited by Mark J. P. Wolf, 613-628. MIT Press, 2015.

—. *Gaming Rhythms: Play and Counterplay from the Situated to the Global.* Institute of Network Cultures, 2009.

Aslinger, Ben and Nina B. Huntemann. "Introduction." In *Gaming Globally: Production, Play and Place,* edited by Nina B. Huntemann and Ben Aslinger, 1-15. Palgrave Macmillan, 2013.

Bisaria, Anjali. "8-Year-Old Genius Impresses Satya Nadella With His Game, Aims to Be Microsoft CEO One Day!" *India Times,* 1 June 2016, http://www.indiatimes.com/news/india/8-year-old-genius-impresses-satya-nadella-with-his-game-aims-to-be-microsoft-ceo-one-day-256004.html.

Cao, Yong and John D. H. Downing. "The Realities of Virtual Play: Video Games and their Industry in China." *Media, Culture & Society* 30.4 (2008): 515-529.

Cervera, Humberto and Jacinto Quesnel. "Mexico." In *Video Games Around the World,* edited by Mark J. P. Wolf, 345-357. MIT Press, 2015.

Chakraborti, Siddharta, Kwabena Opoku-Agyemang and Dibyadyuti Roy. "Gaming, Culture, Hegemony: Introductory Remarks." *Journal of Gaming & Virtual Worlds* 7.2 (2015): 137-140.

—. "From Destination to Nation and Back: The Hyperreal Journey of Incredible India." *Journal of Gaming & Virtual Worlds* 7.2 (2015): 183-202.

Consalvo, Mia. *Atari to Zelda: Japan's Videogames in Global Contexts*. MIT Press, 2016.

Dirlik, Arif. "Global South: Predicament and Promise." *The Global South* 1.1 (2007): 12-23.

Donovan, Tristan. *Replay: The History of Video Games*. Yellow Ant, 2010.

Eckstein, Lars and Anja Schwarz. *Postcolonial Piracy: Media Distribution and Cultural Production in the Global South*. Bloomsbury, 2014.

Edwards, Brian T. *After the American Century: The Ends of U.S. Culture in the Middle East*. Columbia University Press, 2016.

Esnaola Horacek, Graciela Alicia, Alejandro Iparraguirre, Guillermo Averbuj and María Luján Oulton. "Argentina." In *Video Games Around the World,* edited by Mark J. P. Wolf, 35-55. MIT Press, 2015.

Fisher, Jolene. "Toward a Political Economic Framework for Analyzing Digital Development Games: A Case Study of Three Games for Africa." *Communication, Culture & Critique* 9 (2016): 30-48.

Frasca, Gonzalo. "Uruguay." In *Video Games Around the World,* edited by Mark J. P. Wolf, 609-612. MIT Press, 2015.

—. "Videogames of the Oppressed: Videogames as a Means for Critical Thinking and Debate." Ph.D. Dissertation, Georgia Institute of Technology, 2001.

Fung, Anthony Y. H. and Sara Xueting Liao. "China." In *Video Games Around the World,* edited by Mark J. P. Wolf, 119-135. MIT Press, 2015.

Gama Alves, Lynn Rosalina. "Brazil." In *Video Games Around the World,* edited by Mark J. P. Wolf, 88-104. MIT Press, 2015.

Hjorth, Larissa and Dean Chan, eds. *Gaming Cultures and Place in Asia-Pacific*. Routledge, 2009.

Hjorth, Larissa and Dean Chan. "Locating the Game: Gaming Cultures in/and the Asia-Pacific." In *Gaming Cultures and Place in Asia-Pacific,* edited by Larissa Hjorth and Dean Chan. Routledge, 2009: 1-14.

Hjorth, Larissa. "Guest Editor's Introduction: Games@Neo-Regionalism: Locating Gaming in the Asia-Pacific." *Games and Culture* 3.1, January 2008: 3-12.

Hudson, Dale and Patricia R. Zimmermann. *Thinking Through Digital Media: Transnational Environments and Locative Places*. Palgrave Macmillan, 2015.

Ibahrine, Mohammed. "Video Games as Civilizational Configurations: US-Arab Encounters."

Islamism and Cultural Expression in the Arab World, edited by Abir Hamdar and Lindsey Moore, 206-221. Routledge, 2015.

Iqani, Mehita. *Consumption, Media and the Global South: Aspiration Contested.* Palgrave Macmillan 2016.

Jin, Dal Yong, ed. *Mobile Gaming in Asia: Politics, Culture and Emerging Technologies.* Springer, 2016.

Kasmiya, Radwan. "Arab World." In *Video Games Around the World,* edited by Mark J. P. Wolf, 29-34. MIT Press, 2015.

Kent, Steven L. *The Ultimate History of Video Games.* Three Rivers Press, 2001.

Kirinya, Wesley. "Africa." In *Video Games Around the World,* edited by Mark J. P. Wolf, 17-28. MIT Press, 2015.

Kleine, Dorothea. *Technologies of Choice?: ICTs, Development, and the Capabilities Approach.* MIT Press, 2013.

Ladage, Rutu. "Anvitha Vijay, 9 yr Kid is the Youngest Apple Developer!" *India.com,* 14 June 2016, https://www.india.com/buzz/anvitha-vijay-9-year-old-indian-origin-kid-is-the-youngest-apple-app-developer-at-wwdc16-1258554/.

Lazaro, Gab. "PH Players Impress at Rage Art." *Mineski.net,* 6 June 2017, https://www.mineski.net/news/ph-players-impress-at-rage-art.

Liboriussen, Bjarke and Paul Martin. "Regional Game Studies." *Game Studies* 16.1 (October 2016).

Medina, Eden and Ivan da Costa Marques, eds. *Beyond Imported Magic: Essays on Science, Technology and Society in Latin America.* MIT Press, 2014.

Mignolo, Walter. "Introduction: The Global South and World Dis/Order." *Journal of Anthropological Research,* 67.2 (2011): 165-188.

—. *Local Histories/Global Designs: Coloniality, Subaltern Knowledges, and Border Thinking.* Princeton University Press, 2012.

—. *The Darker Side of Western Modernity: Global Futures, Decolonial Options.* Duke University Press, 2011.

Mukherjee, Souvik. "India." In *Video Games Around the World,* edited by Mark J. P. Wolf, 137-144. MIT Press, 2015.

—. "Playing Subaltern: Video Games and Postcolonialism." *Games and Culture* 13.5 (2016): 1-17.

—. *Videogames and Postcolonialism: Empire Plays Back.* Palgrave Macmillan, 2017.

Nakasone, Arturo. "Peru." In *Video Games Around the World,* edited by Mark J. P. Wolf, 393-398. MIT Press, 2015.

Parra, Luis and Global Game Designers Guild. "Colombia." In *Video Games Around the World,* edited by Mark J. P. Wolf, 137-144. MIT Press, 2015.

Penix-Tadsen, Phillip. *Cultural Code: Video Games and Latin America*. MIT Press, 2016.

Portnow, James, Arthur Protasio and Kate Donaldson. "Brazil: Tomorrow's Market." In *Gaming Globally: Production, Play and Place*, edited by Nina B. Huntemann and Ben Aslinger, 75-78. Palgrave Macmillan, 2013.

Qiu, Jack Linchuan. *Working-Class Network Society: Communication Technology and the Information Have-Less in Urban China*. MIT Press, 2009.

Rakhmani, Inaya and Hikmat Darmawan. "Indonesia." In *Video Games Around the World*, edited by Mark J. P. Wolf, 249-270. MIT Press, 2015.

Reuters, "Locals and South Sudanese Refugees Play Video Games in a Market Near a Camp 10 km (6 miles) from al-Salam Locality at the Border of Sudan's White Nile State," 27 January 2014, http://cms.trust.org/item/20140127212510-9x8ha?view=print.

Sangami, Priyanka. "Rise of Young Supercoders: How Indian Kids are Making a Mark in the Coding World," *Economic Times*, 16 June 2016, http://tech.economictimes.indiatimes.com/news/internet/ibm-apple-microsoft-and-others-fuel-the-rise-of-young-supercoders/52772626.

Shaw, Adrienne. "How Do You Say Gamer in Hindi?: Exploratory Research on the Indian Digital Game Industry and Culture." In *Gaming Globally: Production, Play and Place*, edited by Nina B. Huntemann and Ben Aslinger, 183-201. Palgrave Macmillan, 2013.

—. "What is Video Game Culture? Cultural Studies and Game Studies." *Games and Culture* 5.4 (2010): 403-424.

Šisler, Vit. "Digital Arabs: Representation in Video Games." *European Journal of Cultural Studies* 11.2 (2008): 203-219.

—. "Palestine in Pixels: The Holy Land, Arab-Israeli Conflict, and Reality Construction in Video Games." *Middle East Journal of Culture and Communication* 2 (2009): 275-292.

—. "Video Game Development in the Middle East: Iran, the Arab World, and Beyond." *Gaming Globally: Production, Play and Place*, edited by Nina B. Huntemann and Ben Aslinger, 251-271. Palgrave Macmillan, 2013.

Soranastoporn, Songsri. "Thailand." In *Video Games Around the World*, edited by Mark J. P. Wolf, 545-564. MIT Press, 2015.

Tawil-Souri, Helga. "The Political Battlefield of Pro-Arab Video Games on Palestinian Screens." *Comparative Studies of South Asia, Africa and the Middle East* 27.3 (2007): 536-551.

Taylor, Claire and Thea Pitman. "Conclusion: Latin American Identity and Cyberspace." In *Latin American Cyberculture and Cyberliterature*, edited by Claire Taylor and Thea Pitman, 263-267. Liverpool University Press, 2007.

Taylor, Claire. *Place and Politics in Latin American Digital Culture: Location and Latin American Net Art*. Routledge, 2014.

Walker, Ian. "Local Player Defeats Tekken 7 World Champion at Philippines Event." *Kotaku Compete,* 9 June 2017, https://compete.kotaku.com/local-player-defeats-tekken-7-world-champion-at-philipp-1795967096.

Warham, Olivia. "A Deadly Sleight of Hand." *HuffPost Blog* (United Kingdom), 28 January 2014, http://www.huffingtonpost.co.uk/olivia-warham/south-sudan-africa_b_4678826.html.

Wilson, Pamela and Michelle Stewart. "Introduction: Indigeneity and Indigenous Media on the Global Stage." In *Global Indigenous Media: Cultures, Poetics, and Politics,* edited by Pamela Wilson and Michelle Stewart, 1-55. Duke University Press, 2008.

Wolf, Mark J. P. *Video Games Around the World.* MIT Press, 2015.

Zackariasson, Peter and Timothy L. Wilson. *The Video Game Industry: Formation, Present State, and Future.* Routledge, 2012.

PART ONE: SERIOUS GAMES AND THE POLITICS OF PLAY

REPLAYING THE DIGITAL DIVIDE

VIDEO GAMES IN INDIA

SOUVIK MUKHERJEE

THE NORTH-SOUTH AND THE SOUTH-SOUTH IN INDIAN VIDEO GAMES: OPENING QUESTIONS

As the armies of the wintry and impoverished north move towards the rich and powerful south in the episodes of *The Game of Thrones*, the north-south divide has currently "arrived" on television screens the world over. The reverse of the global north vs. south in academic discussions, *Game of Thrones* nevertheless perpetuates the north-south binary that academia has comparatively recently posited to describe the economically prosperous and developed countries in the global north vis-a-vis the poorer and less developed ones in the global south (earlier called the "developing countries" or the "third world: variously). While the geographical north-south binary does not fit as comfortably as in fictional worlds (for example, countries such as Singapore, Australia, New Zealand and China are major outliers), the term global south is used here as an accepted shorthand within which the digital gaming scenario in India is assessed in comparison to the gaming industry and culture worldwide as well as in connection with other countries that are considered part of the so-called global south. Phillip Penix-Tadsen,[1] in his introductory chapter, acknowledges the limitations and the prickly complexity of the term (following Mehita Iqani) and invokes Walter Mignolo's definition, whereby the term signifies those regions that faced and are still facing the consequences of being colonized, so as to provide a coherent framework to understanding the global south.

Clearly linked with Mignolo's position and often connected with the north-south divide is the "Digital Divide," or the division between those countries that have access to advanced knowledge-systems in the digital world and those that do not. As far as India is concerned, how the digital divide affects India and links to its positioning within the global south is a moot question. Then again, following Iqani's argument that the global south is more complex even in the way it understands itself, one should neither forget claims of an internal north-south cultural divide in India, nor ignore the uneven distribution of access to digital knowledge within the vastly discrepant socio-economic tiers in the country. Also intriguing is whether the purported south-south collaboration that is supposed to occur within the countries of the global south is relevant to video games in India. Earlier publications and industry reports have drawn attention to the promise and the challenges of India's video game industry; however, set against the backdrop of the global south and the recent focus on closing the digital divide, in the rhetoric employed by both the state and the industries, this appraisal aims to highlight deeper mechanisms that influence views on India's video game industry.

DIGITAL INDIA AND VIDEO GAMES

In what is a promising statistic for the proponents of the digital, the number of Internet users in India has grown phenomenally in recent years and this is likely a continuing trend—*The Economic Times* reports a

1. See Phillip Penix-Tadsen, "Introduction: Video Games and the Global South," in this volume.

jump of 15% between October 2015 and a year later;[2] the global statistics portal Statista sees the number of Internet users growing to 511.89 million in 2022 from 331.77 million at present.[3] Considering that India is a rather late entrant to public Internet—VSNL (Videsh Sanchar Nigam Limited) introduced the first public dial-up service in 1995—this is a significant statistic. India's large and growing mobile phone penetration is one of the factors considered responsible for this spike in numbers. The Indian government celebrates this as a closing of the north-south divide and uses the digital as its watchword in most of its recent policymaking. In fact, the Digital India initiative of the Ministry of Electronics and Information Technology makes it clear that the "vision of Digital India programme is to transform India into a digitally empowered society and knowledge economy," and this echoes the current Prime Minister's exhortation to "take the nation forward—economically and digitally."[4] The connection of the digital with the economy is well evident in such manifestos and there is a further link with both knowledge and empowerment. The previous government also saw the importance of stressing the rise of the global south and of south-south collaborations and the former UN under-secretary general and current parliamentarian, Shashi Tharoor states that one of the aims of the global vision for India was "the management of outer space and cyberspace in the common interests of humanity."[5] As India moves rapidly towards digital governance by bringing all its residents' biometric information, financial and welfare data under the panopticon of its digital databases, the awareness of the digital spreads to its remotest corners and the "closing" of the digital divide is being celebrated all the more. Speaking from a different political standpoint, the Nobel-laureate economist Amartya Sen also shares the promise of Information Technology (IT) as having "inspired Indian industrialists to face the world economy as a potentially big participant, not a tiny bit player."[6] Sen also sees in the IT industry benefits in education and gender-equality. As commentator Dinesh Sharma sees it, it is the digital that is perceived as having caused a sea-change in global perceptions of India: "from a meager $30 million of exports in 1981 to $100 billion in 2013, the Indian IT industry's remarkable success story has made the country one of the leading destinations for software and outsourced services. The success of this one industry has given rise to the notion of Brand India or India Inc. among potential investors and international financial institutions."[7]

As Arif Dirlik points out, "[w]ith the so-called globalization of the 1990s, the geographies of development have been reconfigured, calling into question not only the earlier Three Worlds idea, but the viability of the North/South distinction."[8] Thomas Friedman, proposing a "flattening of the globe" or the playing-field of global economy being levelled, claimed to find inspiration for his theory in the software hubs of Bangalore. Friedman was writing after the "outsourcing" boom in India. Speaking to Rajesh Rao, CEO of the digital games company Dhruva Interactive, Friedman saw huge potential in the then almost non-existent video games industry in India in harnessing the ambitions of globalization:

> Well I'll give you an example of a company—you've never heard of it—Dhruva. Dhruva is a little game company in Bangalore, founded by a guy named Rajesh Rao, a young man who is really into games. You know the gaming business today is bigger than Hollywood. The Xboxes, all those things—more of those games are sold and downloaded off the internet than movies! So this is big business. Well, Rajesh, he wanted to get into this business. And he thought India had a lot of unique skills because there are a lot of sons and daughters of Indian Hindu

2. Surabhi Agarwal, "Mobile Internet: Internet Users to Touch 420 Million by June 2017: IAMAI Report," *The Economic Times*, 5 February 2017, http://economictimes.indiatimes.com/tech/internet/420-million-to-access-internet-on-mobile-in-india-by-june-iamai/articleshow/58475622.cms.
3. "India: Number of Internet Users 2022 | Statistic," *Statista*, 2017, https://www.statista.com/statistics/255146/number-of-internet-users-in-india/.
4. Ministry of Electronics and Information Technology Government of India, "Vision and Vision Areas | Digital India Programme," *Digital India*, 8 November 2017, http://www.digitalindia.gov.in/content/vision-and-vision-areas.
5. Shashi Tharoor, "From Aid-Taker to Donor, India Is Now Global Rule-Maker: Tharoor," *The Quint*, 19 October 2016, https://www.thequint.com/opinion/2016/10/19/being-aid-donor-establishes-india-as-the-globes-fulcrum-tharoor-g-20-president-obama-africa-india-summit.
6. Amartya Sen, "What Can IT Industry Do For India?," *Outlook India*, 16 February 2017, https://www.outlookindia.com/website/story/what-can-it-industry-do-for-india/233893.
7. Dinesh C. Sharma, *The Outsourcer: The Story of India's IT Revolution*, Revised ed. (MIT Press, 2015), 2.
8. Arif Dirlik, "Global South: Predicament and Promise," *The Global South* 1.1 (2007): 12-23.

> temple artists, where drawing and painting have been elevated to a high art, who are very adept at transferring those skills to computer-assisted design to draw up characters. And he thought, "Whoa! If I could use all this technology to connect these Indian artists to the game industry, I could be part of this game! So what did he do? He started a company! They bought some PCs, got a fiber-optic Internet connection—the pipes and the PCs. And then they used the software that is now available to offer their services to draw characters for American or European game companies. So they downloaded from Google all this Wild West imagery. They used email, and all these new software for computer-aided design, and they developed a whole game which they marketed over the internet, which so attracted American companies that some of the biggest game companies in American now are outsourcing characters to little Dhruva on a backstreet in Bangalore. That's a world gone tiny.[9]

This is Friedman's classic example for Globalization 3.0, a concept for which he is popular the world over. Whereas other advocates of Digital India failed to notice them, video games figured importantly in Friedman's experience of the changing landscape of Indian technology. Rao himself is now President of the NASSCOM Gaming forum, which is affiliated to National Association of Software Services and Companies (NASSCOM), itself one of the primary influences on the IT policy-making in India. NASSCOM brings out annual reports about the gaming industry in India and in its recent report on mobile gaming in India it forecast "stellar growth" amounting to $1.1 billion in 2020.[10] Similar promises are to be seen in the reports created by KPMG and Price Waterhouse Cooper in recent years. The FICCI-KPMG Indian Media and Entertainment Industry Report 2014 predicts a growth of 22% in CAGR between 2013 to 2018 and amounting to around INR 6.9 billion in 2018 for the entire PC and TV gaming market.[11] The quantitative predictions of huge potential success are backed up qualitatively by leading game development figures such as Ernest Adams. Adams states that "India has the talent, the resources, and the attitudes required to become a major player in this industry. All [they are] lacking is experience, and that will come with training and time."[12] In a blog post written after visiting the country, he calls India a "sleeping giant" in the video game industry. Video games, just like other spheres of IT in India, seem to be poised towards equalizing the north-south imbalance and the digital divide.

INDIAN VIDEO GAMES: THE JOURNEY TOWARDS THE PROMISE

Any discussion of video games in India must also point out that although India made some progress in information technology immediately after independence, in the late 1970s with the expulsion of IBM (and Coca Cola, incidentally) by the government, the country was largely unfamiliar with personal computing until the late 1980s and even more so during the liberalization of the 1990s. The Nintendo boom passed India by and barring a few scattered arcade machines and smuggled or imported devices that were beyond the reach of even the middle classes, video games were not well known in the country. Consoles are still not as popular (and the reasons for this will be addressed in depth subsequently) but in the early days of gaming, Amiga, Nintendo Gameboy or even personal computers used for gaming such as Amstrad were almost unknown. There is little literature about Information and Computer Technology (ICT) teaching in the early 1990s and the author must, therefore, rely on memory—even in a comparatively elite English-medium school, computer classes were a novelty and many class-periods were spent in letting the children play *Dig Dug* (Atarisoft, 1983) on BBC Micro Computers or IBM PCs. In the late 1990s, computer magazines such as *Digit* (published by Jasubhai Media) would provide demo or shareware versions of PC games and the cybercafes and internet parlors that mushroomed across the cities would also let people play video games for a small hourly fee. In a survey aimed at

9. Thomas Friedman, "Globalization 3.0 Has Shrunk the World to Size Tiny," *YaleGlobal Online*, 4 July 2004, http://yaleglobal.yale.edu/content/globalization-30-has-shrunk-world-size-tiny.
10. NASSCOM, "Digitizing India: NASSCOM Annual Report 2016-17," *NASSCOM*, 2017, http://www.nasscom.in/sites/default/files/NASSCOM_Annual_Report_2016-17.pdf.
11. KPMG, "The Stage Is Set: FICCI-KPMG Indian Media and Entertainment Industry Report 2014," *KPMG*, 2014, http://ficci.in/spdocument/20372/FICCI-Frames-2014-KPMG-Report-Summary.pdf.
12. Ernest Adams, "The Promise of India," *The Designer's Notebook*, 7 November 2009, http://www.designersnotebook.com/Lectures/India/india.htm.

analyzing the experience of Indian game developers vis-à-vis players in India, conducted by Padmini Ray Murray and Souvik Mukherjee in 2014, a respondent comments: "Dad got home a 386 [Intel i386 32-bit], and I first laid eyes on *Prince of Persia* and *Dave*. In final year of school, made a game project. While I was studying engineering, I joined a games dev startup. Never looked back."[13] Another respondent reveals that his first console was a Nintendo but that it had been brought by his father from a trip to Thailand. This respondent would have been part of a select few as not many people would have been able to afford the "imported" tag electronics goods. As Penix-Tadsen says in the introduction, the gray market is another popular source of such technology in the global south; in India, however, despite the flood of video-cassette recorders and Walkman personal stereos, video game consoles did not make a significant appearance in Indian drawing rooms. Indeed many households were still using black-and-white television sets well into the mid-nineties. Not surprisingly, the entrance of Indians to game development also came comparatively late. As another respondent comments, "First exposure to video games was through the old coin-operated arcade machines in the 80s, True love though happened in 1995 when I chanced upon Doom, and I was hooked! Stumbled into video game design in 1997 (I was probably one of the [few?] game designers in India)."[14] The first PC game released in India is either *Bhagat Singh* (Mitashi, 1999), which is about an Indian freedom fighter who tries to assassinate the British viceroy, or *Yoddha*, which is about the Kargil war fought with Pakistan. Both of the games were released in 1999 and have heavily nationalistic content that is influenced by the trending movies in Bollywood. *Bhagat Singh* is also postcolonial in its protest against the colonial rule of India (one might risk calling it one of the first "postcolonial video games"). Neither game was popular among players although *Yoddha* was noted for its soundtrack. There haven't been any globally recognized Indian PC-game bestsellers so far and the industry is a far cry from Bollywood. Piggybacking on Bollywood films continued in games such *Dhoom* and *Ghajini*, both of which were released after the eponymous movies. Megastar Shahrukh Khan starred in a video game-themed movie, *Ra-One* and a game based on the film neither of which had any lasting impact.

Recent Indian games have moved beyond Bollywood and *Unrest* (Pyrodactyl Games, 2014), *Bird of Light* (Zen Labs, 2016) and *Switch—or die trying* (Threye Interactive 2017) are prominent among the few PC titles from India that can be found on the online distribution platform Steam (a handful more have been greenlit on that platform). Out of these, *Unrest* is set in a fictional town in ancient India and is about negotiating dialogue choices to solve some very complex moral conflicts. A GameSpot review has mixed feelings about the game but lauds its unconventional morality structure: "though flawed, Unrest's system of cause and effect is a refreshing change from traditional conversation mechanics and deserves appreciation. In a sea of clearly defined morality systems, Unrest proves that sometimes the best waters consist of infinite shades of gray."[15] Arvind Raja Yadav, the designer, says that he wanted the game to dispel the notion that India was all about Bollywood and Cricket and in that he has largely succeeded. Other notable recent titles from Indian developers are *Hanuman: Boy Warrior* (SCEE, 2009) and *Street Cricket* (SCEE, 2011) both of which were released for PlayStation consoles. *Hanuman: Boy Warrior* is based on the adventures of the monkey-god, Hanuman, from the popular Hindu epic *The Ramayana*. *Street Cricket*, as the name suggests, is the digital version of the mostly commonly played game for the man-in-the-street.

Despite their popular appeal, both *Hanuman* and *Street Cricket* struggled in the market mainly because console games are still not as popular in India due to the heavy import duties and costs. In fact, the

13. P. Ray Murray and S. Mukherjee, "From the Outside Looking In: Creating a Serious 'Art Game' in India—A Case Study," Paper presented at the 5th International Conference on Games and Virtual Worlds for Serious Applications (VS-GAMES), 2013, 1-3.
14. Ibid.
15. Cameron Woolsey, "Unrest Review," *GameSpot*, 22 July 2014, https://www.gamespot.com/reviews/unrest-review/1900-6415822/.

Nintendo Wii has not been released in India although the latest versions of PlayStation and Xbox are now available. The low-cost console Zeebo, which was intended for release in India, did not finally launch in the country despite doing so in other global south markets such as Brazil and Mexico. Mobile devices represent the most popular gaming platform by far, and developers all over the country have invested much in Android and, to a lesser extent, iOS titles. In 2011, Rolocule won the People's Choice Award at the 8th IMGA awards ceremony held in the Mobile World Congress 2012 in Barcelona with its *Flick Tennis* (Rolocule, 2012) and developers such as Shailesh Prabhu of Yellow Monkey Studio have won international acclaim with games such as *Huebrix* (Yellow Monkey Studios, 2013) and *Socioball* (Yellow Monkey Studios, 2015). NASSCOM's annual Game Development Conference is one of the biggest such events in the region and is the venue for launching new titles.

Much of India's recent game development is being done by smaller indie studios, and the availability of the Unity game design engine and other free development software has been a big advantage. While many developers are based in metropolises such as Bangalore, Mumbai and New Delhi, there are a few from remote locations. Indie games have seen a steady growth in recent times and Prabhu says that "they are small but very dynamic groups with very interesting developers from all aspects of game development."[16] Among other indie games of note are *Asura* (Ogre Head Studios, 2014) and the upcoming *Raji* (Nodding Heads, in development) , both of which contain elements from Indian mythology. India has also seen an entry to serious games with *Missing* (Flying Robot Studios, 2016), a game addressing the horrors of child-trafficking and prostitution. Satyajit Chakraborty and Leena Kejriwal visited red-light areas and conducted interviews in their research for the game. *Missing* is also available in Bengali and the developers aim to have it in other Indian languages too. Besides *Missing*, there is a growing number of games in serious games genre: Studio Oleomingus's *Somewhere* (Studio Oleomingus, in-development) is about subalternity and voicelessness, drawing from postcolonialism as well as other philosophical standpoints and the forthcoming *Antariksh Samachar* (Indian Sandbox Games Lab, in-development) is based on the life of the mathematician Sreenivasa Ramanujan and is also an adaptation of an eponymous opera by *Bharatnatyam* dancer, Jayalakshmi Eshwar. All of these titles have been acclaimed in both national and international exhibitions and festivals.

Nevertheless, the promise is only part of the scenario. As a respondent from survey conveys, it is not all such a smooth ride: "[d]esign is extremely weak. Indies are not focussed enough. People are not efficient, a project that should ideally take 6 months goes on forever. No real support from the government. The varies bodies are not really doing a lot. Indies and investors don't really look eye to eye. Too much idealism, it sounds like a good thing but trust me when you have a crazy number of things against you ….."[17] Although just a two-decade old industry, game development has still not picked up as much as one would expect given the larger Digital India initiatives and the country's recent IT boom. Asking the players, one gets a different picture. Until recently, the prices of games were prohibitively high and piracy was a big problem. Aniket Majumdar, a regular contributor to the *Haogamers* blog, laments the general lack of awareness among the populace and also the reasons behind piracy:

> If you are a gamer in India, you would be used to glares as well as giggles. Those are pretty much the only two reactions you are likely to receive when you tell someone that you love video games, because it is widely believed by the majority that gaming is either a massive waste of time preventing you from studying or focusing on your career, or that it is an acceptable way for children to pass time, and adults (or even teenagers) who waste their time with such nonsense must be emotionally and intellectually stunted. Add this to the fact that most people here do not see piracy as a crime, or hold ludicrous assumptions like "The internet provider must pay the game

16. Souvik Mukherjee, "India," in *Video Games Around the World*, ed. Mark J. P. Wolf (MIT Press, 2015), 239.
17. Ray Murray and Mukherjee, "From the Outside Looking In."

developer when I download a torrent!" (actual personal experience, not made up) and you will understand why, even in 2015, Steam is an unfamiliar name in India.[18]

Steam, nevertheless, has made a successful entry in India after introducing Indian pricing and Majumder is hopeful: "Being a gamer in a poor country, especially one so prejudiced against gaming (a topic for another day), is not easy. What Valve did in bringing the changes in currency and regional prices is nothing short of commendable, even if it isn't perfect. [...] If publishers take advantage of this change and treat India as the large untapped market it is, we might be looking at the beginning of the end of widespread piracy here, and also the beginning of a whole new era of gaming."[19] Going by the stats on Steamspy.com, the Indian market seems to be doing well with well over a million users. In a country of one billion, though, there's much untapped potential. As in the Oleomingus game, *Somewhere*, there are also many voices that go unheard and many challenges to overcome.

"DOES THE DIGITAL DELIVER?": GROUND REALITIES IN THE GLOBAL SOUTH

Despite the promise of south-south collaboration and that of the rise of the global south (to which the closing of the digital divide contributes signally), there are still many apprehensions. Shantanu Chakrabarti points out the conflicting scenarios in conceptualizing the global south in India: "The Global South is not a uniform entity in binary opposition to the developed North. This simple truth finds expression when it tries to define and characterise itself (multilaterally or singularly) as empowering itself within a restructured global order. India's projection as one of the leaders of the global south which has 'arrived' on the global stage continues to be dependent upon its role in ensuring regional stabilisation in South Asia and addressing internal inequalities."[20] Chakrabarti addresses the internal conflicts within India (there is a north-south divide based on linguistic, cultural and economic issues and there is widespread socio-economic inequality based on class and caste) and also among the partners in the south-south collaboration; he also indicates the possibility of a hegemonic order where India is considered to have "arrived" on the global scene of development. Speaking of the inequalities, Radhika Gajjala raises the question, "When is the subaltern brought online and for what purpose?,"[21] in which she adopts the term "subaltern" to describe those who are rendered voiceless in the contexts established by colonial, postcolonial and third-world systems of knowledge and communication as a result of which they lose their identities, embodiment and their social presence. Gajjala is quick to observe how the discourse of "India Shining" is instrumental in "breaks up these [she studies handloom weavers, in particular] communities through its need to individualize the labor force and draw it into (in)secure low-skilled IT jobs and call center work that will service the global economy and neo-colonial hierarchies therein."[22] Without access to the discourse and technical knowledge of the digital, these communities are rendered voiceless in the digital economy and the digital divide, instead of being closed as the state's rhetoric claims, is only reconfigured: "thus, in the case of the third-world subaltern (rural) "Other," there are more learning steps for access and more gatekeeping issues both culturally and technically, in addition to actual material access to the technological artifact itself."[23] As Pramod Nayar observes,[24] another area that remains virtually unaddressed in the digital narrative of India is that of caste—how the digital is either absent in the lives of the *dalit* community (the traditionally repressed castes and groups) or how digital tools are coopted to reveal further issues of discrimination and deprivation.

18. Aniket Majumdar, "Steam Is Supporting Indian Gamers with Its New Changes," *Haogamers*, 11 November 2015, https://haogamers.com/steam-is-supporting-indian-gamers-with-its-new-changes-4a0f482a354.
19. Ibid.
20. Shantanu Chakrabarti, "Global South Rhetoric in India's Policy Projection," *Third World Quarterly* 38.8 (August 3, 2017): 1909-1920.
21. Radhika Gajjala, ed., *Cyberculture and the Subaltern: Weavings of the Virtual and Real* (Lexington Books, 2012), 3.
22. Ibid.
23. Ibid., 4-5.
24. Pramod Nayar, "The Digital Dalit: Subalternity and Cyberspace," *Sri Lanka Journal of Humanities* 37.1-2 (26 July 2014).

Besides the reconfiguring of the digital divide, one also needs to consider the unique scenario of "making" in the Indian scenario: Padmini Ray Murray and Chris Hand refer to the practice of *jugaad* which they describe as "an indigenous form of hacking that differs from its western counterpart in its ubiquity, precipitated by economic constraints and lack of resources."[25] How far *jugaad* translates as hacking is a moot question but as Ray Murray and Hand clarify, the significant difference is that it arises out of a lack of resources and facilities. Therein, they also illustrate the difference with DIY practices in the global north, where such "making" is a hobby rather than an activity driven by basic need. In fact, even when compared to "modding" practices in other regions of the global south, as reflected in the chapters by Thaiane Oliveira, José Messias and Diego Amaral[26] and by Rhett Loban and Thomas Apperley,[27] *jugaad* is much more of a quick and temporary solution to quotidian problems. Unlike the skill base that is assumed in relation to mods, the *jugaad* is more of a making-do than a making—it is something that arises out of a socio-economic lack and is more of an quick innovation that is often unstable and unreliable. The need for *jugaad,* whether it is in villages of India or in the laptop repair shops in Nehru Place in the capital city, New Delhi, makes the north-south gap even more evident and also shows how and why the digital divide is difficult to wish away by simply promoting digital technology in the country's systems of governance and finance. This is very evident in the case of video games.

As Prabhu bluntly states it:

> Poverty problems aside, there are several cultural and technological barriers to games in India. Most of India's large population lives in over-crowded cities with poor infrastructure. Our traffic jams are so severe that more often than not, we lose mobile internet when stuck in one. Being one of the more popular use cases for mobile games, this is definitely a problem. At the same time, our local trains are so crowded that it is largely impossible to play a game while stuck in a crowded train, yet another popular use case for the mobile game. Hell, a HUGE majority of India uses squatting toilets, ever tried playing *Candy Crush* while you have to squat to "go" and use water to clean up after? [Sic] Yet another popular use case down the drain.[28]

Prabhu questions the rhetoric of the success of the breakdown of the digital divide and indeed also the narrative of promise for the Indian games industry that earlier accounts had addressed. Together with the rosier picture, the reality check that Prabhu calls for is also necessary. It is also important to note that despite the aforementioned problems, the industry continues to make progress. When Indian video games researcher Marcus Toftedahl was asked about his observations on the Indian gaming scene, he stated, "Sure, the business reports say that India will be a big player, but it is all up to the people involved,"[29] and in this, he includes both the developers and the players. Casey O'Donnell makes perhaps the most astute observation when he says, "video games [in India] are still viewed as a diversion from those educational tasks students ought to be preparing for. For this reason design is a difficult leap in the Indian industry."[30] No wonder, then, that despite commentators such as Friedman seeing the promise of globalization in the video game industry, video games do not figure anywhere in the grand narrative of digital India, whether it be the state-sponsored projects or the awareness of citizens. O'Donnell further notes how the channels of communication between designers, programmers, engineers and artists are unorganized and, therefore, lack documentation. Adrienne Shaw picks up on the fact that even Indian languages struggle to find a word for "Gamer" (the Hindi word *khiladi* meaning "player" is hardly ever

25. Padmini Ray Murray and Chris Hand, "Making Culture: Locating the Digital Humanities in India," *Visible Language* 49.3 (December 2015): 141-155.
26. Thaiane Oliveira, José Messias and Diego Amaral, "Playing Beyond Precariousness: The Political Aspect of Brazilian Modding in Pro Evolution Soccer," in this collection.
27. Rhett Loban and Thomas Apperley, "Eurocentric Values at Play: Modding the Colonial from the Indigenous Perspective," in this collection.
28. Shailesh Prabhu, "Breaking down the Billion," *GamesIndustry.Biz*, 11 February 2016, http://www.gamesindustry.biz/articles/2016-11-02-breaking-down-the-billion.
29. Team Haogamers, "'I See a Lot of Promise': Swedish Researcher Marcus Toftedahl on Indian Gaming Scene," *Haogamers*, 8 December 2016, https://haogamers.com/i-see-a-lot-of-promise-swedish-researcher-marcus-toftedahl-on-indian-gaming-scene-a3876948cc3d.
30. Casey O'Donnell, *Developer's Dilemma: The Secret World of Videogame Creators, Inside Technology* (MIT Press, 2014).

used) and this is perhaps because games are seen as historically external to Indian media culture.[31] By this, one assumes that Shaw means video games as opposed to games in general since the Indian T20 Cricket is by far one of the biggest cash sources for the media. As she observes, mainly the lack of resources and access makes video games more of a "foreign" concept in India. Sadly, however, the huge potential of video games as a medium of both entertainment and education has not been adequately tapped in the country.

PLAYING THE SUBALTERN: NARROWING THE DIGITAL GAPS

Recent articles on video games in India also point out how the Western discourses often elide or oversimplify key elements of Indian culture making the domination of the global north even more prominent. As I say elsewhere, *Age of Empires III: The Asian Dynasties* (Microsoft, 2005), has Brahmin healers riding elephants and Sepoys (which means "soldier" in many Indian languages) being described as a separate race—a portrayal that is inadequately researched and even orientalist in nature. This, too, makes up the digital divide that digital India is so desperately trying to close. Any discussion of India's gaming industry and culture vis-à-vis the global south needs, therefore, to first acknowledge the digital divide on its multiple planes such as access, awareness, resources and global perceptions, among other things. Video games should also enable the reopening of subaltern discourses and create platforms for subaltern voices to be heard, for example by placing players in positions they would never have faced before. A reviewer of *Missing* on the Google Play store remarks that the game makes the player experience the lives of victims of trafficking—"the characters are about people we hear of in the news."[32] *Somewhere* has as its very premise the condition of the subaltern, where certain groups are rendered powerless and voiceless.

Commentators on bridging the digital divide see the implausibility of a solely knowledge-based narrowing of the digital divide. According to some, although India "has created a strong ICT industrial base and capacity to compete in some areas such as IT software and ITES-BPO [Information Technology Enabled Services/Business Process Outsourcing] in the global market, it does not appear to have achieved same level of capacity in the area of utilizing ICT for socio-economic changes, that is, in terms of e-education, e-health, e-government, and so on."[33] Successive governments have stressed on ICT as a panacea but again most of the services do not permeate to cities and towns besides the major metropolises. Access, training and resources are any attempts to establish digital equality. Rural India is an even bigger challenge. Despite the efforts elsewhere, the quickly burgeoning field of video games has never figured in the policymaking and the potential of the medium as an opinion-shaping and experience-forming tool has been consistently missed. With additional support provided to the industry and the recognition of the so-far semi-neglected gaming culture, many more will be able to participate and the hitherto negative cultural attitudes can also be countered by creating awareness and providing quality education on video games and game development.

Discussions of video games in the global south also need to take into account indigenous practices of making such as *jugaad*, their drivers in resource-strapped locales, the many unrepresented voices in the official narratives of development and how these can be potentially better represented in a participatory and immersive medium such as video games. The video game industry and the gaming culture in India is certainly on an upswing in comparison to what it was three decades ago but instead of only focusing

31. Adrienne Shaw, "How Do You Say Gamer in Hindi?: Exploratory Research on the Indian Digital Game Industry and Culture," in *Gaming Globally*, eds. Nina B. Huntemann and Ben Aslinger (Palgrave Macmillan, 2013), 183-201.
32. Souvik Mukherjee, "Difficult Choices, Distressing Answers," *Times of India*, 12 October 2016.
33. Angathevar Baskaran and Mammo Muchie, *Bridging the Digital Divide: Innovation Systems for ICT in Brazil, China, India, Thailand, and Southern Africa* (Adonis & Abbey, 2007), 43.

on information, perhaps by focusing on the gaps in the digital discourses and by literally replaying the digital divide by promoting the making and cultural dissemination of crucial technologies of the future such as video games.

WORKS CITED

Agarwal, Surabhi. "Mobile Internet: Internet Users to Touch 420 Million by June 2017: IAMAI Report." *The Economic Times*, 5 February 2017, http://economictimes.indiatimes.com/tech/internet/420-million-to-access-internet-on-mobile-in-india-by-june-iamai/articleshow/58475622.cms.

Baskaran, Angathevar and Mammo Muchie. *Bridging the Digital Divide: Innovation Systems for ICT in Brazil, China, India, Thailand, and Southern Africa*. Adonis & Abbey, 2007.

Chakrabarti, Shantanu. "Global South Rhetoric in India's Policy Projection." *Third World Quarterly* 38.8 (3 August 2017): 1909-20.

Dirlik, Arif. "Global South: Predicament and Promise." *The Global South* 1.1 (2007): 12-23.

Friedman, Thomas. "Globalization 3.0 Has Shrunk the World to Size Tiny." *YaleGlobal Online*, 4 July 2004, http://yaleglobal.yale.edu/content/globalization-30-has-shrunk-world-size-tiny.

Gajjala, Radhika, ed. *Cyberculture and the Subaltern: Weavings of the Virtual and Real*. Lexington Books, 2012.

KPMG. "The Stage Is Set: FICCI-KPMG Indian Media and Entertainment Industry Report 2014." *KPMG*, 2014, http://ficci.in/spdocument/20372/FICCI-Frames-2014-KPMG-Report-Summary.pdf.

Majumdar, Aniket. "Steam Is Supporting Indian Gamers with Its New Changes." *Haogamers*, 11 November 2015, https://haogamers.com/steam-is-supporting-indian-gamers-with-its-new-changes-4a0f482a354.

Ministry of Electronics and Information Technology Government of India. "Vision and Vision Areas | Digital India Programme." *Digital India*, 8 November 2017, http://www.digitalindia.gov.in/content/vision-and-vision-areas.

Mukherjee, Souvik. "Difficult Choices, Distressing Answers." *Times of India*, 12 October 2016.

—. "India." In *Video Games Around the World*, edited by Mark J. P. Wolf. MIT Press, 2015.

Murray, Padmini Ray and S. Mukherjee. "From the Outside Looking In: Creating a Serious 'Art Game in India – A Case Study." Paper presented at the 5th International Conference on Games and Virtual Worlds for Serious Applications (VS-GAMES), 2013.

Murray, Padmini Ray and Chris Hand. "Making Culture: Locating the Digital Humanities in India." *Visible Language* 49.3 (December 2015): 141-155.

NASSCOM. "Digitizing India: NASSCOM Annual Report 2016-17." *NASSCOM*, 2017, http://www.nasscom.in/sites/default/files/NASSCOM_Annual_Report_2016-17.pdf.

Nayar, Pramod. "The Digital Dalit: Subalternity and Cyberspace." *Sri Lanka Journal of Humanities* 37.1-2 (26 July 2014).

O'Donnell, Casey. *Developer's Dilemma: The Secret World of Videogame Creators*. MIT Press, 2014.

Prabhu, Shailesh. "Breaking down the Billion." *GamesIndustry.Biz,* 11 February 2016, http://www.gamesindustry.biz/articles/2016-11-02-breaking-down-the-billion.

Sen, Amartya. "What Can IT Industry Do For India?" *Outlook India,* 16 February 2017, https://www.outlookindia.com/website/story/what-can-it-industry-do-for-india/233893.

Sharma, Dinesh C. *The Outsourcer: The Story of India's IT Revolution*. Revised ed. MIT Press, 2015.

Shaw, Adrienne. "How Do You Say Gamer in Hindi?: Exploratory Research on the Indian Digital Game Industry and Culture." In *Gaming Globally,* edited by Nina B. Huntemann and Ben Aslinger, 183-201. Palgrave Macmillan, 2013.

Statista. "India: Number of Internet Users 2022 | Statistic." *Statista,* 2017, https://www.statista.com/statistics/255146/number-of-internet-users-in-india/.

Team Haogamers. "'I See a Lot of Promise': Swedish Researcher Marcus Toftedahl on Indian Gaming Scene." *Haogamers,* 8 December 2016, https://haogamers.com/i-see-a-lot-of-promise-swedish-researcher-marcus-toftedahl-on-indian-gaming-scene-a3876948cc3d.

Tharoor, Shashi. "From Aid-Taker to Donor, India Is Now Global Rule-Maker: Tharoor." *The Quint,* 19 October 2016, https://www.thequint.com/opinion/2016/10/19/being-aid-donor-establishes-india-as-the-globes-fulcrum-tharoor-g-20-president-obama-africa-india-summit.

LUDOGRAPHY

Arvind Raja Yadav. *Unrest*. Pyrodactyl Games, 2014.

Aurona Technologies. *Hanuman: Boy Warrior*: SCEE, 2009.

Avichal Singh. *Raji: An Ancient Epic*. Nodding Heads (in development).

Avinash Kumar. *Antariksha Samachar*. Indian Sandbox Games Lab (in development).

Dhruv Jani. *Somewhere*. Studio Oleomingus (in development).

FX Labs and Geetha Arts. *Ghajini*. FXLabs, 2008.

FX Labs. *Dhoom 2*. FXLabs, 2007.

Ensemble Studios. *Age of Empires 3*. Microsoft Games, 2015.

Mitashi. *Bhagat Singh*. Mitashi Edutainment, 2002.

Roach Interactive. *Bird of Light*. Zen Labs, 2016.

Rolocule. *Flick Tennis*. Rolocule, 2012.

Satyajit Chakraborty. *Missing*. Flying Robot Studios, 2016.

Shailesh Prabhu. *Huebrix*. Yellow Monkey Studios, 2013.

—. *Socioball.* Yellow Monkey Studios, 2015.

Threye Interactive. *Switch—or Die Trying*. Threye Interactive, 2017.

Trine. *Move Street Cricket 2.* SCEE, 2011.

—. *Ra-One*. SCEE, 2011

Vishal Gondal. *Yoddha: The Warrior*. Indiagames, 2000.

Zainuddin Fahad. *Asura*. Ogre Head Studio, 2014.

SERIOUS GAMING

CRITIQUES OF NEOLIBERALISM IN THE WORKS OF RICARDO MIRANDA ZÚÑIGA

CLAIRE TAYLOR

This chapter considers the serious game/alternative game projects of the U.S.-Nicaraguan artist Ricardo Miranda Zúñiga, whose works often draw on his bi-cultural heritage and display a strong awareness of social inequality and discrimination. His projects combine digital technologies with physical objects, installations and audience interaction, creating artworks that involve both online interaction and public participation in the streets. The first of Miranda Zúñiga's works under consideration in this chapter is the collaborative project, *The Miracle of Chile* of 2010. Involving workshops, an interactive game, posters on public transport and street interaction with portable electronic devices, *The Miracle of Chile* explores the contradictions in Milton Freidman's model, and invites participants to submit their own responses to his famous slogan. The chapter analyzes how, through resistant gaming techniques, this work interrogates Milton Friedman's famous assertions regarding the "economic miracle" of Chile as representing the purported success of the neoliberal, free-market model and encourages participants to question this model.

The second work under consideration is Miranda Zúñiga's *A Geography of Being: una geografía de ser*, an interactive installation consisting of a video game along with sculptures that contain electronic circuits and react to the game. The chapter analyzes how this video game functions as a resistant game that, far from drawing the user into a purely ludic, pleasurable world, encourages him or her to reflect on social issues. As the player is positioned in the role of an undocumented youth, s/he needs to negotiate the game and learns about the hardships that these young people face.

Ricardo Miranda Zúñiga is one of the leading artists of Latin American origin living and working in the U.S. today. Born of immigrant parents, and growing up between Nicaragua and San Francisco, his artworks often draw on this bi-cultural heritage and display a strong awareness of social inequality and discrimination. His art combines digital technologies with physical objects, installations and audience interaction, creating artworks that involve both online interaction and public participation in the streets. Amongst his many artistic projects are early pieces such as *U.S. Authorities Say...* (1999), which combines a video camera with an audio recording of a montage of excerpts from news reports, or *Cargo Load* (also 1999), which is a performance piece based around a sculptural vehicle and a digital short-wave radio. More recent pieces include *Vagamundo: A Migrant's Tale* (2002), which was the first of his artworks that ventured into the video game format as an art form; *Dentimundo* (2005), comprising an interactive website with an avatar promising us a "cybernetic tour of the Mexican border"; *Carreta nagua, siglo XXI* (2007), combining physical installation, digital animation and citizen participation; and *Votemos.us ¡México decide!* (2008), which consists of a website that proposes that, due to the constant circulation of people, products and capital between the U.S., Mexicans should be invited to vote for the U.S. president.

In all of these works, Miranda Zúñiga combines digital technologies with face-to-face interaction. As Miranda Zúñiga himself stresses:

> With each project, I approach art as a social practice that seeks to establish dialogue in public spaces (both physical and virtual) to broaden the work of art. I view the street as an incredibly rich arena for interactive works that employ illustration, animation, sound and interactivity to draw an audience and ideally initiate a fruitful discussion.[1]

Miranda Zúñiga often makes use of gaming formats, such as computer games or puzzles, and it is two such works that are under analysis in this chapter. As the chapter argues, through the critical stance that we are encouraged to take in the game, and through the insertion of socio-political commentary into the game world, the conventional scope of the game is challenged. In this way, Miranda Zúñiga's artistic practice shares similarities with other of the projects examined in this volume, particularly in his attempts to critique the structural inequalities that underpin the gameworld; see, for example, Loban and Apperley, who talk about software modification in grand strategy games as ways of reimagining indigenous communities, and how, through process such as oral history and inserting cultural information into the game, those who are conventionally depicted in such games as subjects of European colonialism can be given agency. Miranda Zúñiga's practice can be understood in terms of recent trends in what has been variously termed alternative gaming, political game-art, or experimental game projects.[2] Often conceived of in opposition to, or as a critical development of, the commercial entertainment games industry, alternative gaming can be seen as a response to the forces of neoliberalism that commercial games are frequently seen to uphold.[3] In her overview of the growing alternative computer games scene, Tiffany Holmes proposes the term "art games" to describe "an interactive work, usually humorous, by a visual artist that does one or more of the following: challenges cultural stereotypes, offers meaningful social or historical critique, or tells a story in a novel manner."[4] I argue that Miranda Zúñiga's work can be understood within this trend of "art games," through his deliberate use of gaming techniques in order to critique the current socio-political conditions depicted in his game world.

The first of Miranda Zúñiga's works under consideration in this chapter is the collaborative project *The Miracle of Chile* (2010), on which Miranda Zúñiga worked in conjunction with Kurt Olmstead, and which was presented as part of the *Portables* exhibition curated by Ignacio Nieto. The work is a multimedia project, involving workshops, an interactive game, posters on public transport and street interaction involving portable electronic devices. In their blurb about the project, Miranda Zúñiga and Olmstead state that when they were invited to participate, they were "already deep into investigating the root causes of the current financial crisis," and that, as a result, it seemed "natural"

1. Ricardo Miranda Zúñiga, "Artist Statement," http://www.ambriente.com
2. Laetitia J. Wilson uses the term "political game-art" to describe games in which the political content works to "morph the play-space into a think-space"; see Wilson, "Encountering the Unexpected: Play Perversion in the Political Art-game and Game-art," in *Proceedings of the 2006 International Conference on Game Research and Development* (Perth, 2006), 269. Patrick Crogan uses the term "experimental game projects" to describe works which involve a "critical interrogation of gaming culture"—see Crogan, "Playing Through: the Future of Alternative and Critical Game Projects," in *Worlds in Play: International Perspectives on Computer Games Research*, eds. Suzanne de Castell and Jennifer Jenson (Peter Lang, 2007), 88. Andreas Jahn-Sudmann, meanwhile, lists the terms "Games with an Agenda," "Serious Games," "Persuasive Games" or "Social Change Games" to describe the types of games which "are explicitly arranged as a critical, interceding practice in order to call attention to social problems in the 'real world'"—see Jahn-Sudmann, "Innovation NOT Opposition the Logic of Distinction of Independent Games," *Eludamos: Journal for Computer Game Culture* 2 (2008): 9.
3. This is not to say, of course, that players of commercial gaming environments do not engage in resistance practice, and attempt to challenge the ideologies underpinning the game world; as Nick Dyer-Witherford and Grieg de Peuter have noted, gamers "sometimes resist the dominant messages" encoded within games and manage to produce "alternative expressions" from within; see Dyer-Witherford and de Peuter, *Games of Empire: Global Capitalism and Video Games* (University of Minnesota Press, 2009): 193. Rather, the point is that the implied player (to follow Wolfgang Iser's notion of the implied reader) of the commercial video game is meant to comply with the ideologies of the game world, whereas in alternative gaming, the player is encouraged to resist or trouble the ideologies; see Iser, *The Act of Reading: A Theory of Aesthetic Response* (Johns Hopkins University Press, 1980).
4. Tiffany Holmes, "Arcade Classics Spawn Art? Current Trends in the Art Game Genre," in *Proceedings of the 5th International Digital Arts and Culture Conference* (RMIT University, 2003): 46.

to think of a link to Chile.[5] They go on to say that they became very interested in "the use of Chile by the neoliberals as a rhetorical weapon in their ideological battle."[6] Here, their words make reference to the now infamous phrase attributed to Milton Friedman, that of Chile as an "economic miracle" as a result of the implementations of neoliberal policies by the so-called "Chicago boys."

The term "Chicago boys" refers to the group of Chilean economists who studied in the U.S. under Milton Friedman, and who became, as Silva terms it, his "unconditional disciples."[7] Convinced that the implementation of a free market economy was the solution to Chile's problems, the Chicago boys were leading figures in this implementation under the Pinochet military regime of 1973-1990, and they advocated privatization, deregulation, cuts to social security programs and new labor laws. Yet more than just neoliberal technocrats, the Chicago boys were very closely allied with, and played a strategic role in, Pinochet's regime;[8] they were, as Silva puts it, the "organic intellectuals of the military regime," because they "played a key role in the attempt to institutionalize the dictatorship," and "elaborated sophisticated discursive answer to the latent contradiction in the co-existence of economic liberalism and political authoritarianism."[9] Indeed, Orlando Letelier, shortly before his murder in 1976—widely believed to be due to his opposition to the Pinochet regime—described the role of the Chicago boys as lying in the fact that they were "prepared to supplement the brutality, which the military possessed, with the intellectual assets it lacked."[10]

Moreover, in addition to the fact that the Chicago Boys, in their implementation of the "Chilean miracle," propped up and provided the technocratic-intellectual justification for the Pinochet regime, the long-lasting effects of their policies also had serious social consequences. Their neoliberal model slashed the public sector, undertook mass privatizations, restricted workers' rights and labor laws and opened up Chile's economy to foreign markets. In the words of Winn, the neoliberalism imposed during the Pinochet regime was a "highly ideological version," and a "vehicle for an aggressive attack on Chile's workers and the labor rights they had acquired during decades of struggle," and he notes the loss of labor rights, the stagnation in real wages and the maldistribution of income as a legacy of the Pinochet dictatorship.[11]

The phrase "the miracle of Chile" is, thus, a highly contentious expression, which glosses over both the shocking human rights abuses, state-sponsored murder, torture and forced disappearances of the Pinochet regime *and* the longer-term effects on the Chilean people, including widening inequality, labor insecurity and a reduced public sector. It is, thus, highly significant that Miranda Zúñiga and Olmstead choose this term for the title of their work, and, even more so, that they note that their aim is to "interrogate it, disrupt it, wrest control of its meaning from its makers."[12] This project is, thus, about disrupting the phrase and questioning it, rather than endorsing it.

They go on to explain that they created three main elements to "trouble" this doctrine, these being: a labyrinth which was overlaid by photographs that were generated at workshops; bricks with computer boards, used on the streets; and the re-writing of public space on buses.

5. Ricardo Miranda Zúñiga and Kurt Olmstead, "About," *The Miracle of Chile*, 2010, http://miracleofchile.com/about.php.
6. Ibid.
7. Patricio Silva, "Technocrats and Politics in Chile: From the Chicago Boys to the CIEPLAN Monks," *Journal of Latin American Studies* 23.2 (1991): 390.
8. For more on their role, see Carlos Huneeus, "Technocrats and Politicians in an Authoritarian Regime," *Journal of Latin American Studies* 32 (2000): 461-501.
9. Silva, "Technocrats and Politics in Chile," 393, 395. Silva is here making reference to Gramsci's concept of the organic intellectual, this being the member of a hegemonic class whose role is to formulate and spread the ideologies of that class; see Antonio Gramsci, *Selections from the Prison Notebooks* (New York: International Publishers, 1971).
10. Orlando Letelier, "Economic 'Freedom's' Awful Toll: The 'Chicago Boys' in Chile," *Review of Radical Political Economics* 8.3 (1976): 46.
11. Peter Winn, ed., *Victims of the Chilean Miracle: Workers and Neoliberalism in the Pinochet Era*, 1972-2002, (Duke University Press, 2004), 3-4.
12. Miranda Zúñiga and Olmstead, "About."

Regarding the first of these, the interactive game takes the form of a labyrinth in which the spectator-player is invited to negotiate, and is based on a workshop undertaken with children, who were asked to document what the phrase "the miracle of Chile" meant to them. The images that they captured were then fed into this maze. Miranda Zúñiga and Olmstead explain that their aim during the workshop was to question the meaning of the phrase "miracle of Chile" which had widely been seen as embodying the triumph of neoliberalism. Participants in the workshop were given a brief talk about economics, followed by a discussion, and then asked to walk through the city and document their understanding of what the phrase "Miracle of Chile" meant. As Miranda Zúñiga says, "The goal was to capture a sense of how ideology inscribes itself into the public space."[13]

Their practice here can be understood through theorizations of Debord and other Situationists regarding urban space. Debord's proposed "psychogeographical" method aimed to expose "the precise laws and specific effects of the geographical environment,"[14] and was inspired by Marxist thought, aiming to resist established meanings of urban space, particularly as these were regulated by capitalism, or, in the words of Hancox, "combat[ting] the alienating effects of the city's compartmentalization into zones that facilitated capitalist productivity."[15] In this way, the actions of the participants of *Miracle of Chile*, in their dérive around the city, documenting its spaces, can be seen as a type of neo-situationist approach for late capitalism, as they attempt to uncover the ideology that has been inscribed into public space.

Following the walk, participants returned to upload their images to the project's Flickr account, which were then used to populate the virtual labyrinth. In this way, as players when we negotiate the labyrinth, we, too, are negotiating and uncovering the ideology of the city space, with Santiago as the embodiment of neoliberalism. What immediately becomes obvious from these images are the stark contrasts that emerge between the phrase "miracle of Chile" and the images that have been captured. For in these images, this is not the Santiago of the finance district—which would be emblematic of the "success" of the purported miracle—but in fact side-streets and run-down areas of the city, as we see dilapidated buildings, rusting equipment in children's play parks, dogs behind railings with the paint peeling off and so forth. Whilst there are too many images to mention each of them, it is worth noting, for instance, one of a disused shop front, daubed with graffiti, with the slogan "Para que nunca más" running across the top and photographs pinned up across the window (see Image 1.2.1). The phrase is immediately recognizable as a reference to the Pinochet dictatorship, with "nunca más" being a highly-charged slogan representative of the investigation into the human rights abuses of the Pinochet regime.[16] The photographic images, whilst we cannot see the full details at this resolution, must therefore be of the disappeared, and indeed, the format of the photographs—the classic head-and-shoulders ID shot—is emblematic of the human rights protests calling for the truth of what happened to the disappeared. This image, therefore, makes reference to the stark reality of the purported "miracle of Chile," namely: to the state-sponsored imprisonment, torture and murder of thousands of Chilean citizens during the Pinochet regime.[17]

If this image in the labyrinth makes us question the prior regime under which the "miracle" of Chile was implemented, other images encourage us to question the contemporary conditions of neoliberal

13. Ricardo Miranda Zúñiga and Kurt Olmstead, "Workshop," *The Miracle of Chile*, 2010,http://miracleofchile.com/workshop.php.
14. Guy Debord, "Introduction to a Critique of Urban Geography," in *Situationist International Anthology*, ed. Ken Knabb (Bureau of Public Secrets, 1995), 3.
15. Simone Hancox, "Contemporary Walking Practices and the Situationist International: The Politics of Perambulating the Boundaries Between Art and Life," *Contemporary Theatre Review* 22.2 (2012): 237.
16. See the use of the term "Nunca más" as the title of the 1999 summary version of the Rettig report (see Comisión Chilena de Derechos Humanos), and also its use by Ricardo Lagos in his prologue to the 2005 Valech report.
17. While, due to the clandestine nature of the arrests and the torture centers, exact figures are hard to gain, the Valech Commission documented over 27,000 victims (Comisión Nacional sobre Prisión Política y Tortura 2005).

Image 1.2.1. The Miracle of Chile, 2010 (detail).

Chile. This is the case, for instance, of a photographic image of a scrap material merchant, who pushes his handcart along the sidewalk, loaded with cardboard, bags of garbage and other refuse (see Image 1.2.2). The presence of the scrap merchant can be read as emblematic of the longer-term consequences of neoliberalism, and the growing inequalities of the city.

As we navigate through these images, we thus we uncover the underside of the city, or, to use Debord's term, we see what lies beneath the "spectacle" of the city.[18] Our navigation of these images enables to understand both how the "economic miracle" was undertaken during a brutally repressive dictatorship with complete disregard for human rights and, furthermore, how it created, and continues to create, the "uneven geography" of late capitalism.[19]

The second element of this work—the street interaction—involved the creation of an object consisting of electronic circuits mounted onto broken street tiles from the city of Santiago. The tiles with the circuits were placed onto the pavement with a set of instructions for interested pedestrians who were then encouraged to find another passer-by, ask them the question posed—what the Miracle of Chile is—and then pass the object on.

18. Guy Debord, *The Society of the Spectacle*, trans. Donald Nicholson-Smith (Zone Books, 1994), 29.
19. Manuel Castells, *End of Millennium* (Blackwell, 2010), 73.

Image 1.2.2. The Miracle of Chile, 2010 (detail).

In this part of the work, Miranda Zúñiga and Olmstead are playing with the notion of the brick or the "ladrillo," and its multiple meanings. On the one hand, their tactic of taking up a broken piece of the street paving is a deliberate attempt to engage with the fabric of the cityspace, and furthers their aim of interrogating the ideology of the city. On the other hand, as well as referring to the literal paving stone, the term "ladrillo" is immediately recognizable in a Chilean context as the term given to the 500-page document created by the Chicago Boys, which set out Friedman and his teaching as a "remedy" to Chile's economic problems.[20] Dubbed "el ladrillo" due to its huge size, the document prescribed privatization, deregulation, cuts to social programs, and was central to the implementation of neoliberalism under Pinochet. In this part of the project, then, the artists combine the multiple meanings of "ladrillo," and in so doing closely tie the cityspace to ideology.

20. The document has since been made available through the Centro de Estudios Públicos; see Centro de Estudios Públicos (1992).

The third element of the project involved a tactic of re-writing public space on buses. In this part of the project, the artists used the advertising spaces that are inserted into the straps that passengers hold on the buses to interrogate the "miracle of Chile." In so doing, they disrupt the uses of these spaces in two ways. Firstly, they take up a space conceived of for advertising—and so, promoting products and the ideology of capitalism—but do so in order to encourage the passengers to question capitalism, rather than comply with it by buying new products and being seduced by commodity fetishism. Secondly, the disruption also comes about in relation to the geographical spaces that are traversed by the bus. For, the bus line that was selected for this part of the project is that which leads from the wealthy business district of Santiago to one of the most impoverished neighborhoods of the city, La Victoria. This is a deliberate tactic to draw attention to the spaces of uneven development of late capitalism. As Castells and others have argued, the process of capitalist restructuring under neoliberalism has resulted in an "extremely uneven geography of social/territorial exclusion and inclusion," resulting in a "new geography of social exclusion" which is visible in every country, and every city, around the globe.[21] The structural inequalities of late capitalism thus create what Christian Fuchs has called "segmented spaces" (Fuchs 2008: 94), in which these inequalities are visible in the very spaces of the city itself. Travelling along this bus line, then, is a process of witnessing the "two Santiagos" and "two Chiles"[22] which subtend the "miracle of Chile," and of understanding the living conditions of the millions of Chilean workers whose long hours, poor pay and precarious living conditions have made the "miracle" possible.

One example of the type of intervention that was inserted into these advertising spaces is the following (see Image 1.2.3):

Image 1.2.3. The Miracle of Chile, 2010 (detail).

21. Castells, *End of Millennium*, 73.
22. Winn, *Victims of the Chilean Miracle*, 1-4.

Using bright, contrasting colors, this mock advertisement displays a grimacing, deliberately cartoon-esque Friedman in the bottom left corner; such a cartoon reworking of images is common to Miranda Zúñiga's aesthetic in many of his works. Here, we can see the way in which the work plays with the notion of "estar en tus manos" [to be in your hands]: the strap we hold as we ride the bus is indeed, literally in our hands, but we are also encouraged to reflect upon how the economy may be in our hands in a figurative way: how the purported economic miracle is due to the hard work of millions of working class laborers – known as "mano de obra" in Spanish. As a whole, then, *Miracle of Chile* interrogates Milton Friedman's famous assertions regarding the "economic miracle" of Chile as representing the purported success of the neoliberal, free-market model, and the work encourages participants to question this model.

If the above example is of a game art project that contests the uneven spaces of neoliberalism which, albeit influenced by global economic theories, was implemented largely within the same country, the next example under analysis in this chapter demonstrates how these uneven spaces transcend nation-state borders. This is the case with Miranda Zúñiga's *A Geography of Being: una geografía de ser* (2012), an interactive installation consisting of a video game along with sculptures that contain electronic circuits that react to the game, which was exhibited at the New York Hall of Science in 2012 as part of the *ReGeneration* exhibition.

In a similar fashion to *Miracle of Chile*, which encouraged us to resist rather than comply with the ideologies of the city space, *A Geography of Being* is a resistant game that, far from drawing the user into a purely ludic, pleasurable world, encourages him or her to reflect on social issues. The game narrates the experiences of undocumented young immigrants in the U.S., and is based on interviews that the artist undertook with two young men who immigrated to the U.S. as young children.

The experiences of these two interviewees—one from Latin America, the other from Asia—influence the narrative and the visuals of the game, and, significantly represent key points of U.S. domestic and foreign policy. As regards the Latin American context, the experience narrated in the game makes reference to the growing numbers of Mexican, Central American and other Latin American migrants attempting to enter the U.S. The rise in these numbers is due to a number of factors, including fleeing pervasive violence, persecution and extreme poverty, with some describing them as "de facto refugees, not illegal border crossers."[23]

One particular driver in the numbers of undocumented migrants attempting to cross the border has been the neoliberalization of the Mexican economy, with the 1994 implementation of NAFTA as a defining moment; Rosas, for instance, has described NAFTA and the accompanying structural transformations in Mexico as marking "the consolidation of neoliberalism in Mexico."[24] NAFTA ensured the U.S. access to an abundant supply of cheap labor south of the border, and has long been the subject of criticism by Mexican activists for its devastation of the traditional Mexican rural economy.[25]

One of the effects of NAFTA was the creation of a dispossessed underclass; as Valdes and others have argued, NAFTA resulted in the creation of "a newly dispossessed class of agricultural workers, many of whom were compelled to migrate to the United States."[26] In this way, the implementation of

23. Robert Warren and Donald Kerwin, "The 2,000 Mile Wall in Search of a Purpose: Since 2007 Visa Overstays have Outnumbered Undocumented Border Crossers by Half a Million," *Journal on Migration and Human Security* 5.1 (2017): 125.
24. Gilberto Rosas, *Barrio Libre: Criminalizing States and Delinquent Refusals of the New Frontier* (Duke University Press, 2012), 50.
25. See, for instance, Irma Lorena Acosta Reveles, "Fifteen Years of NAFTA: The Impact on Rural Mexico," in *Social Change, Resistance, and Social Practices*, eds. Richard A. Dello Buono and David Fasenfest (Brill, 2010.), 93-102.

neoliberal policies that devastated the Mexican rural economy was one of the contributing factors to the waves of migration from Mexico and Central American countries to the U.S.

The game positions the player in the role of one of these undocumented youths, and s/he needs to negotiate the game and learns about the hardships that these young people face. Visually, the game is very striking, with bold outlines, bright colors and collage-like images (see Image 1.2.4). The visual references within the game are taken from the experiences of these undocumented youth, and represent both their homeland they have come from, and their trials and tribulations in the U.S.

Image 1.2.4. Screen capture of A Geography of Being: una geografía de ser, 2012.

Our avatar is a young male, dressed in black, whom we need to move through the gameworld via a limited number of movements using the arrow keys and the space bar of our keyboard. No instructions are provided to us, and we have to navigate our way through, and work out how to navigate the gameworld as we go along—much as the undocumented migrants must learn to understand and navigate their new environments.

The backdrop to the game in the first level contains a number of cultural references to Latin America, including indigenous figures who fought against the colonizing Spanish, or the colonial cathedral in the city of Granada, Nicaragua. Subsequently, in the second level of the game we are located within a complex system of cogs, with each cog containing an image of a manual worker, such as a delivery man or cook. If we fail to jump successfully from one cog to another, we get crushed between the cogs; in this level, we are trapped within the system, and must frantically negotiate our way out. The

26. Dennis N. Valdes, "Legal Status and the Struggles of Farmworkers in West Texas and New Mexico, 1942-1993," *Latin American Perspectives* 22.1 (1995): 128.

third level of the game locates us in an underworld beneath the streets of New York, in which we must avoid certain hazards in order to progress upwards towards the surface.

The game narrative, running throughout these three levels, is, broadly speaking, one of assimilation, as we move from our cultural homeland to try to survive in New York. Yet a particular feature is the sound in the game, which encourages us to critique rather than comply with the notion of ludic/narrative progression that the gameworld implies. For the sound in the game, rather than being diegetic sounds of the gameworld, is an extended extra-diegetic sound, which runs over the game introduction and the game itself. These sounds comprise excerpts from the interviews, as well as comments from activist and community groups; these tell us about the difficulties faced by undocumented migrants. In this way, the sound disrupts the gameworld, and does not allow us to get caught up in the game world; instead, we are encouraged to critique it. Given that the game largely about progression (and its associated sense of assimilation) we are encouraged to critique, rather than comply with, this concept.

In addition to the gameplay itself, another highly important features of the installation is the presence of the wooden sculptures that accompany the video game, and take the form of three humanoid figures: a mother, a father and a child. Each sculpture, approximately half a meter in height, contains within it an animated display that is shown on a small screen installed in their midriff and connects to the video game (see Image 1.2.5). These robots react to the game as it is being played, and can provide the eagle-eyed player with shortcuts to help them through the game levels.

The provocative name given to these robots by Miranda Zúñiga is "Undocumented Drones"—a reference both to the status of these young men as undocumented, and to the increasing use of drones by U.S. forces in zones around the globe. Here, Miranda Zúñiga's use of the term makes reference to the geopolitical realities that underpin the waves of migration that his work represents. Re-semanticizing the term "drone," Miranda Zúñiga provides a critique of the use of drones in U.S. national and foreign policy, both in their use in policing the U.S.-Mexico border, and in policing the virtual borders of the U.S. elsewhere around the globe. Regarding firstly the U.S.-Mexico border, the drone has become a key component of the so-called "virtual wall"; the complex system in which drones are employed, along with sensors, cameras and other equipment to police the border, track migrants and arrest them.[27]

But the drone has not just been used to police this particular border space; its use in a variety of conflicts around the globe has meant that it has become emblematic of U.S. foreign policy, and, in particular of U.S. attempts to protect its (imagined, extended) borders. Here, I draw on Feldman's arguments regarding the U.S. homeland security state as creating "a cartography of open-ended counterinsurgency in West and Central Asia."[28] Viewing this as a "resuscitation of frontier violence," Feldman argues that the contemporary U.S. homeland security state engages in "practices of 'ubiquitous bordering' at a variety of local, regional and transnational scales," and that, following Kaplan, "the ideological function of the term 'homeland security' itself is meant to legitimate these practices by suturing the intra-national contraction of proper spaces and subjects of the political with the transnational expansion of U.S. imperial sovereignty." The notion of homeland security, thus attempts to "stabilize, make legible, and manage the ineluctable plurality of a population," and, at the same time, "the extension of bordering processes outside the geography of the nation-state creates

27. For analysis of other game art or "didactic game" projects that engage with and critique the drone as telepresent technology in modern warfare, see Jenna Ann Altomonte's chapter in this volume, "Didactic Gaming Online: Joseph DeLappe's Killbox."

28. Keith P. Feldman, "Empire's Verticality: The Af/Pak Frontier, Visual Culture, and Racialization from Above," *Comparative American Studies* 9.4 (2011): 326.

Image 1.2.5. A Geography of Being: una geografía de ser, 2012 (installation detail).

flexible biopolitical zones capable of traversing the globe, in which certain subjects [...] are invited to occupy categories of life and wield power over the lives of others, while others are banished from sociality to the point of death."[29]

I argue that the way in which the term "drone" is used in Miranda Zúñiga's work is an attempt to lay bare, and to critique, the structures underlying these technologies. If drones are symptomatic of the flexible borders of "homeland security," then the fact that Miranda Zúñiga turns them on their head, encourages us to critique this. This is done firstly through their nomenclature where, in place of the standard terminology, in which "drone" is taken to mean "un*manned* aircraft," these are now un*documented* drones (my emphasis), with the drones representing not the forces of law, but the experience of the undocumented migrant. In addition to this, the physical manifestation of the drones is a further way in which the trope of the drone is troubled.

Now, in this game, the drones are humanoid figures and indeed, according to Miranda Zúñiga, are intended to "represent the traditional nuclear families: father, mother, the sibling. If people

29. Ibid., 327-328.

cannot figure out the game they can talk with the figures—this is like talking with families who help them through their lives and tell them about reality."[30] The drones in Miranda Zúñiga's game, then, are no longer the external surveillance system enacting U.S. homeland security policy, but fellow undocumented migrants whose presence is essential for survival. In this way, the technologically-enhanced surveillance system offered by the conventional drone is now replaced with a technologically-enhanced helping hand—helping the migrant in his/her experience, and helping us as player by means of the shortcuts through the game. In summary, the drone is a reference to both to the increasing militarization of the border *and* a reference to U.S. foreign policy and intervention in other areas of the globe, yet Miranda Zúñiga's tactic is to question the semantics of the drone and the power structures that it represents.

In conclusion, this article has analyzed two different works by Miranda Zúñiga which employ gaming techniques as part of their strategy. Both combine online and digital space with offline, concrete place, in their different ways, and both involve questioning dominant ideologies. Through their combination of audience and street interaction with digital and online games, *Miracle of Chile* and *A Geography of Being* aim for maximum audience engagement, and encourage the player to question the rules of the system in which they are playing.

WORKS CITED

Acosta Reveles, Irma Lorena. "Fifteen Years of NAFTA: The Impact on Rural Mexico." In *Social Change, Resistance, and Social Practices*, edited by Richard A. Dello Buono and David Fasenfest, 93-102. Brill, 2010.

Centro de Estudios Públicos. *"El Ladrillo": bases de la política económica del gobierno militar chileno.* Prologue by Sergio de Castro. 2nd ed. Centro de Estudios Públicos, 1992.

Comisión Chilena de Derechos Humanos. *Nunca más en Chile: síntesis corregida y actualizada del informe Rettig*. LOM Ediciones, 1999.

Comisión Nacional sobre Prisión Política y Tortura. *Informe de la Comisión Nacional sobre Prisión Política y Tortura.* Ministro del Interior, 2005.

Debord, Guy. *The Society of the Spectacle*, translated by Donald Nicholson-Smith. Zone, 1994.

—. "Introduction to a Critique of Urban Geography." In *Situationist International Anthology*, edited by Ken Knabb, 5-8. Bureau of Public Secrets, 1995 (first published 1955).

Dyer-Witheford, Nick and Grieg de Peuter. *Games of Empire: Global Capitalism and Video Games.* University of Minnesota Press, 2009.

Fuchs, Christian. *Internet and Society: Social Theory in the Information Age*. Routledge, 2008.

Castells, Manuel. *End of Millennium*. 2nd edition. Blackwell, 2010.

Crogan, Patrick. "Playing Through: the Future of Alternative and Critical Game Projects." In *Worlds in Play: International Perspectives on Computer Games Research*, edited by Suzanne de Castell and Jennifer Jenson, 87-100. Peter Lang, 2007.

30. Cited in Claire Taylor, *Cities in Dialogue* (Liverpool University Press, 2016), 60.

Feldman, Keith P. "Empire's Verticality: the Af/Pak Frontier, Visual Culture, and Racialization from Above," *Comparative American Studies* 9.4 (2011): 325-341.

Gramsci, Antonio. *Selections from the Prison Notebooks.* International Publishers, 1971.

Hancox, Simone. "Contemporary Walking Practices and the Situationist International: The Politics of Perambulating the Boundaries Between Art and Life." *Contemporary Theatre Review* 22.2 (2012): 237-250.

Holmes, Tiffany. "Arcade Classics Spawn Art? Current Trends in the Art Game Genre." In *Proceedings of the 5th International Digital Arts and Culture Conference* (RMIT University, 2003), 46-52.

Huneeus, Carlos. "Technocrats and Politicians in an Authoritarian Regime." *Journal of Latin American Studies* 32 (2000): 461-501.

Iser, Wolfgang. *The Act of Reading: A Theory of Aesthetic Response.* Johns Hopkins University Press, 1980.

Jahn-Sudmann, Andreas. "Innovation NOT Opposition the Logic of Distinction of Independent Games." *Eludamos: Journal for Computer Game Culture* 2 (2008): 5-10.

Letelier, Orlando. "Economic 'Freedom's' Awful Toll: The 'Chicago Boys' in Chile." *Review of Radical Political Economics* 8.3 (1976): 44-52.

Miranda Zúñiga, Ricardo. *U.S. Authorities Say...*, 1999, http://www.ambriente.com/sculpture/mfaudio.htm.

—. *Cargo Load*, 1999, http://www.ambriente.com/sculpture/cargo.htm.

—. *Vagamundo: A Migrant's Tale*, 2002, http://www.ambriente.com/cart/index.html.

—. *Dentimundo*, 2005, http://www.dentimundo.com/.

—. *Carreta nagua, siglo XXI*, 2007, http://ambriente.com/carreta_nagua/.

—. *Votemos.us ¡México decide!*, 2007-2008, http://votemos.us/.

—. *A Geography of Being: una geografía de ser*, 2012, http://ambriente.com/gob/.

Miranda Zúñiga, Ricardo and Kurt Olmstead. *The Miracle of Chile*, 2010, http://miracleofchile.com/.

Rosas, Gilberto. *Barrio Libre: Criminalizing States and Delinquent Refusals of the New Frontier*. Duke University Press, 2012.

Silva, Patricio. "Technocrats and Politics in Chile: From the Chicago Boys to the CIEPLAN Monks." *Journal of Latin American Studies* 23.2 (1991): 385-410.

Taylor, Claire. *Cities in Dialogue*. Liverpool University Press, 2016.

Warren, Robert and Donald Kerwin. "The 2,000 Mile Wall in Search of a Purpose: Since 2007 Visa Overstays have Outnumbered Undocumented Border Crossers by Half a Million." *Journal on Migration and Human Security* 5.1 (2017): 124-136.

Winn, Peter, ed. *Victims of the Chilean Miracle: Workers and Neoliberalism in the Pinochet Era, 1972-2002.* Duke University Press, 2004.

Wilson, Laetitia J. "Encountering the Unexpected: Play Perversion in the Political Art-game and Game-art." In *Proceedings of the 2006 International Conference on Game Research and Development* (Perth, 2006), 269-274.

Valdes, Dennis N. "Legal Status and the Struggles of Farmworkers in West Texas and New Mexico, 1942-1993," *Latin American Perspectives* 22.1 (1995): 117-137.

PLAYING KILLBOX

DIDACTIC GAMING AND DRONE WARFARE

JENNA ANN ALTOMONTE

Who is remembered? Who is mourned? Who is responsible for remembering and mourning, and how can artists respond?

– Joseph DeLappe

In 2015, artist-activist Joseph DeLappe developed *Killbox,* a politically motivated online gaming experience. The premise for the game centered on the use of unmanned aerial vehicles (UAVs, also known as Drones) used in Northern Pakistan since the mid-2000s. Currently available for play, the game seeks to educate user-participants about *telepresent technology* used in both active and inactive warzones. Employed in the context of modern warfare, telepresent technology may be defined as a system used to connect actual users/operators to distant, geographical regions via telerobotic and/or telecommunication devices.[1] UAVs serve as an example of telepresent technology developed to reduce the presence of ground troops and decrease civilian casualties in war/conflict zones.

Recent projects by DeLappe and his collaborators investigate the execution and after-effects of UAV technology since the onset of the Iraq and Afghanistan Wars of the 2000s. Throughout this chapter, *Killbox* will serve as the primary example of his collaborative work, supported by several other projects that examine the tension between telepresent technology and modern warfare. *Killbox* may be defined as a *didactic game,* a type of *serious game* that serves the primary purpose of educating and informing users about cultural, social and/or political issues. Originating from Clark C. Abt's influential text, *Serious Games,* and expanded by Ian Bogost in *Serious Games: The Expressive Power of Videogames,* a *serious game* is defined as "a videogame created to support the existing and established interests of political, corporate, and social institutions."[2] However, Bogost also suggests that *serious games* are "not games in the service of governments, corporations, educational institutions, and their kindred but games that challenge such institutions, creating opportunities to question, change, or eliminate them.[3]

In *Killbox,* the game serves to educate the participant about UAV-initiated violence, challenging perceptions about telepresent technology. I apply the concept of didactic gaming as a tool for political activism centered on UAV criticism. This approach appears in other serious or politically-motived games like Miranda Zúñiga's *A Geography of Being,* a game that subverts that "purely ludic, pleasurable world" of virtual gaming space by exposing players to the fraught social climate occupied by undocumented immigrants in the United States.[4]

1. James Der Derian, "Global Swarming, Virtual Security, and Bosnia," *The Washington Quarterly* 19.3 (1996): 46
2. Ian Bogost, *Persuasive Games: The Expressive Power of Videogames* (MIT Press, 2007), 55.
3. Bogost, *Persuasive Games,* 58.
4. Claire Taylor, "Serious Gaming: Critiques of Neoliberalism in the Works of Ricardo Miranda Zúñiga," in this anthology.

The didactic approach to *Killbox* centers on the gaming format used to instruct participants about the technology used in both active and inactive warzones. The game exposes users to the function, execution, and after-effects of UAV-initiated attacks, using basic interface that focuses on the *actions,* rather than visual effects. Rather than use human avatars, DeLappe opted for colored spheres without vocal or gestural signifiers. Thus, the game removes the visual identifiers of both operator and ground civilian, a trait offered by Phillip Penix-Tadsen that emphasizes the politics of play, rather then the visuality of game design.[5]

To further understand the premise/function of the piece for my research, I downloaded a version of the game and played the role of both a UAV operator and civilian on the ground. Included throughout this chapter, personal commentary on the effects of playing both operator and civilian explicate the function of the game as a critical evaluation of UAV technology. By playing the game, the participant is made aware about the process of engagement, issues of visibility, and the unpredictability of UAV strikes in both active and inactive warzones.

EARLY INFLUENCES

DeLappe's exposure to experimental and technology-based art practices originates from his youth and post-secondary education. Born in San Francisco, California in 1963, DeLappe grew up in a fertile atmosphere of political and social activism. After graduating high school, he contemplated joining the military, however a chance meeting with a Vietnam veteran recruiter changed his perspective:

> actually contacted a recruiter who had come to our school. I had a recruiter in my living room and the next step was to take this test in the Presidio, in San Francisco. There they classify where they would have you go. This guy actually talked me out of it. The recruiter—he was a Vietnam vet—probably just saw something in me; he said "You know, you really need to be sure there's something very specific you want to get out of this because it's not always for everybody." You may want to think about not doing this. It changed my life. This one person saying it maybe was not the right thing. And it wasn't the right thing.[6]

Instead of enlisting, DeLappe enrolled in San Jose State University (SJSU). At the time, San Jose stood at the intersection of the booming 1980s tech scene and the radical Bay Area punk movement. The tech/punk combination influenced his early creative process, namely through the anti-establishment lyrics of the musical scene and the interactive, collaborative approaches used in the digital arts milieu. With regards to his punk influence, DeLappe states, "I was, at the time, immersed in the hardcore punk rock scene in San Francisco: the Dead Kennedys, Flipper, DOA, Black Flag, etc.—these groups influenced my political stance in a rather radical way and at the same time they inspired me with their DIY sensibility."[7] While at SJSU, DeLappe enrolled in courses that challenged the relationship between technology and the visual arts. One of the more progressive programs offered by the university was the Computers in Art, Design, Research and Education, or CADRE.[8] The CADRE program, formed in 1984, still serves as a source for utilizing the "tech-heavy" resources in Silicon Valley. Their current mission statement emphasizes the following:

5. See Phillip Penix-Tadsen, "Introduction: Video Games and the Global South," in this anthology.
6. Stephen Duncombe and Steve Lambert, "Joseph DeLappe," *Center for Artistic Activism*, 28 January 2012, http://artisticactivism.org/2012/01/joseph-DeLappe/.
7. In a 2016 interview with DeLappe, the artist cites a famous quote by Dead Kennedys lead singer Jello Biafra that perfectly encapsulates many of his digital intervention pieces: "Don't fight the media. Become the media." As evident in works like *dead-in-iraq* and *Twitter Torture/MGandhi in Jail*, DeLappe chooses not to "fight" against the power of the media, instead choosing to use digital and online space as a didactic tool for educating users about war and the plight of civilians caught in spaces of violence. See Scott Beauchamp, "A Critique of Conscience in Joseph DeLappe's Video Games," *Pacific Standard*, 4 May 2016, https://psmag.com/a-critique-of-conscience-in-joseph-DeLappes-video-games-7b21fad381dc#.yquxcrw5v.
8. Beauchamp, "A Critique of Conscience."

> [CADRE] is dedicated to research and experimentation in a multitude of areas. It has branched out from the Art Department to become a truly interdisciplinary program that has included courses from Engineering, Computer Science, Theatre Arts, and Library Science. Topics of study include surveillance, digital media aesthetics, artificial life, robotics, mobile computing, and databases as art.[9]

During his undergraduate career, the curriculum focused on pushing the limits and definitions of art through technological interventions. For example, in an early digital art work titled *Computerized Confessional,* DeLappe examined the relationship between machine and human. In the piece, participants engaged an Apple IIe computer by kneeling in front of the screen and confessing their sins. As in *Killbox,* the premise for the piece required direct exchange between the digital interface and participant, detailing the role of technology as the "higher power." This encounter between a human and computer device remains a constant in many of DeLappe's projects, representing human dependence on technology.

During his MFA residency at SJSU, DeLappe was exposed to the performances of Linda Montano and Laurie Anderson. He recalls the following about his contact with feminist performance art from the 1970s and 1980s:

> It has been primarily women performance artists whom I find most interesting—excluded from the galleries and museums they took to the streets and to life to make their creative statements. I first engaged in performing in game spaces upon the realization that these online environments could be considered a new type of public space. I definitely consider my work to have a direct lineage to street theater/interventions, etc.

The link to intervention-based art serves as the main thematic drive for many of DeLappe's works. Since the invasion of Iraq in 2003, many of his performances and installations challenge online presence through virtual occupation/intervention. The works selected for this chapter utilize the performance-based intervention methods influenced by Montano and Anderson and furthered by the rise of gaming and gaming-based art in the early 2000s.

OCCUPYING ONLINE SPACE: *DEAD-IN-IRAQ*

In an example from 2002, DeLappe occupied the online MMORPG (massively multiplayer online role-playing game) site *Quake III: Arena.* In a performance titled *Quake/Friends,* DeLappe and a group of students created avatars based on the popular television series *Friends.* They used the online message box to recite, verbatim, lines from one of the episodes. Other users continuously shot and killed the avatars, causing each student to "respawn" and continue reading the lines from the episode. After three hours, the performance concluded. In 2006, DeLappe would build upon this MMORPG experience with the creation of *dead-in-iraq,* one of his more critical contributions to intervention art and digital performance.

Unlike the collaborative effort in *Quake/Friends, dead-in-Iraq* involved a single avatar created by DeLappe. The location of the digital performance took place over the course of five years within the online MMORPG space of *America's Army,* a virtual location which proved pivotal to DeLappe's performance. Produced under the direction of Col. Casey Wardynski, the *America's Army* series dates to 1999. Influenced by his son's interest in video games, Wardynski sought to develop a gaming platform that would appeal to America's youth. Used to influence younger generations of potential

9. "History," *CADRE Media Lab,* http://cadre.sjsu.edu/?page_id=59.

military recruits, the game provided participants access to simulated military campaigns combined with rules and regulations enforced in actual warzones. Per *America's Army* objective, the game:

> ...provides civilians with an inside perspective and a virtual role in today's high-tech Army. The game reflects the bedrocks of Soldiering to include adherence to Army Values, the importance of training and individual development, as well as the necessity of teamwork and leadership for success in small unit actions and missions. In the *America's Army* game, players are bound by Rules of Engagement (ROE) as they take part in multiplayer force on force operations.[10]

Using commentary and testimony from actual soldiers and veterans, the game was advertised as an authentic experience within the online gaming environment. After several years of development and design, the game became active on July 4, 2002 and cost the U.S. Army $7.5 million to produce. Currently, over nine million online accounts are registered with 42.6 million downloads from 60 countries since the game's creation.

Users "play" numerous scenarios within the gaming space. As in actual military training, users must pass combat and rifle marksmanship courses before advancing to actual group gameplay.[11] After passing the courses, users may choose to lead a raid attack in Iraq or negotiate a domestic hostage exchange in the U.S.. In each case, users must work with other participants to problem solve the scenario and work together to successfully complete each task. To complement each scenario, users face a high-tech environment that mimics desert villages and urban city scenes. The sophisticated design of the game supersedes many top-game developing firms like Activision, Infinity Ward and Ubisoft. Seamless graphics add to the "realism" of the gaming environment, challenging users to traverse complex terrain and urban structures. Rules of engagement also apply and violating such rules can disqualify players from the game. If a player fails a mission or accidently shoots a fellow team member, consequences include imprisonment in the digital Ft. Leavenworth prison, arrest as a prisoner-of-war, or death of the user's avatar.

One of the key issues with the game centers on youth engagement. Although marketed as T for Teen, or available for children ages 13 and up, many critics view the game as inappropriate for young adolescents. Wardynski insists that the game "is definitely not" a recruiting device, but instead a "communication tool designed to show players that the army is a high tech, exciting organization with lots to do." James Paul Gee provides commentary on the function of *America's Army* and the methods of recruiting youth using the video game:

> I don't think they wanted it to be just a recruiting device, but to brand the Army. They wanted to say...a modern army is high-tech, collaborative. You have to be on a team, got to be a team player, and have to use pretty sophisticated technology. Games are very good to let the world know what your world looks like. If I want you to know- how does the world look to me? One way to do that is to put you in it. And the Army did it.

Gee and many critics of the game argue that *America's Army* lacks a certain level of "transparency." Many users are unaware that the U.S. Army tracks successful progress within the game, actively engaging participants that succeed within the MMO environment. This could be viewed as a type of youth recruiting device, using the video game platform to encourage children to "play" war games sanctioned by the U.S. government.

10. "America's Army PC Game Fact Sheet," *America's Army*, http://assets.americasarmy.com/americas_army_fact_sheet_sept_15_for_aapg_launch_final.doc.
11. Bogost, *Persuasive Games*, 75.

A consequence of playing *America's Army* centers on the disjuncture between the actual warzone in Iraq and the digital gaming space. Outlined in "Social Realism and Gaming," Alexander Galloway considers the method of play and the gaming environment in *America's Army*. He argues that the game fails his *congruence requirement*, a method of measuring the relationship between the virtual gaming environment to actual spaces:

> I suggest there must be some kind of congruence, some type of *fidelity of context* that transliterates itself from the social reality of the gamer, through one's thumbs, into the game environment and back again. This is what I call the "congruence requirement" and it is necessary for achieving realism in gaming. Without it there is no true realism.[12]

This disjuncture occurs due to the lack of realism produced by both the gaming environment and method of play. The game only presents one position, that of the American soldier. Thus, there is a fixed narrative that requires players to perform a single role without playing the "Other." In *Performance, Politics, and the War on Terror: 'Whatever it Takes,'* Sara Brady criticizes *America's Army* for forcing players to play the "good guys,"

> We, as US soldiers, as ourselves (and global players also playing US soldiers, playing "other"), fight an amorphous enemy. By doing so "we," the players, participate in cultural myths acquiescing to hegemonic US geopolitical force…the enemy of *America's Army* is unformed, "unreal," it was designed only to represent the *behavior* of the terrorist, void of ethnic or religious identity.[13]

In *dead-in-iraq*, DeLappe worked to fracture the single mode of play by making visible the actual consequences of war via textual intervention.

Many users play the game without understanding the after-effects of *actual* warfare. As a means of disrupting the space occupied by players, DeLappe created an account under the name *dead-in-iraq* with the intention of dismissing acts of violence in exchange for memorializing real American troops killed since the invasion of Iraq in 2003. The layout of the game permitted DeLappe the opportunity to chat with other users via a text box located in the upper left corner of the screen. On the lower portion, a health tab and ammunition gauge tracked the number of bullets left in the weapons cache. As DeLappe traversed the terrain, he sought to pacify the scene by dropping his weapon and typing the names of American soldiers killed in the Iraq war. The text included their date of death and branch of military service. The names of the deceased were copied from the online death count website, icasualties.org, a website that logs the number of Coalition Military deaths from both the Iraq and Afghanistan wars. By using the names of actual troops killed in the Iraq War, DeLappe fractured the simulated warzone in *America's Army*. The inclusion of actual names removed the façade of gameplay, making visible the consequential after-effects of war.

One major component of the piece centered on how other users engaged DeLappe. Some users messaged DeLappe or asked questions about the performance, while others forced him off the site by killing his avatar or complaining to the site administrator. A typical screen transcript reads as follows:

[US Army] –hk-burritoman#1 messaged: i think they are dates of deaths of soldiers

[US Army] dead-in-iraq messaged: CEDRIC LAMONT LENNON 32 ARMY JUN 24 2003

[US Army] BgRobSmith messaged: are those real people??

12. Alexander R. Galloway, "Social Realism and Gaming," *Game Studies* 4.1 (2004).
13. Sara Brady, *Performance, Politics, and the War on Terror: 'Whatever It Takes'* (Palgrave, 2012), 88-89.

[US Army] dead-in-iraq messaged: JOHN ELI BROWN 21 ARMY APR 14 2003

[OpFor] bin-lad-e-nG.W.B messaged: I am srry

[US Army] dead-in-iraq messaged: JOSEPH ACEVEDO 46 NAVY APR 13 2003

[OpFor] bin-lad-e-nG.W.B messaged: I am srry

KICK NOTIFICATION: dead-in-iraq has been kicked by an Administrator

[US Army] dead-in-iraq messaged: JIMMY J ARROYAVE 30 MARINE APR 15 2004

[Admin] [BM]LoftyDog ADMIN MESSAGE: cause i dont need to sit through a list of over 1000 deaths

[Enemy] stepdown messaged: RIP, THIS IS A GAME

[US Army] dead-in-iraq messaged: HESLEY BOX JR 24 ARMY MAY 6 2004

[US Army] dead-in-iraq: ERICK J HODGES 21 MARINE NOV 10 2004

[US Army] –os-zelptic messaged: dead stfu you dumb **** {FUBAR}rtftd was shot by {-Boomer-}

[US Army] turkeybird messaged: who cares

[US Army] dead-in-iraq messaged: GEORGE T ALEXANDER JR 34 ARMY OCT 22 2005

[US Army] Pvt_Styx messaged: jeeez shut up already we get it people died

[US Army} ={UMD}=HairyJohnson messaged: hmmm so whats your point?

XSTALKERX89 was shot by {UMD}=MORE_BEER.

As evident in the transcript, some users verbally assaulted him by cursing, condemning his actions or shooting his avatar. The administrator of the gaming simulation even forcibly removed DeLappe several times from active game play.

While part of the performance of *dead-in-iraq* includes social intervention within online space, the piece also serves as a memorial to the nearly 4,500 American soldiers killed in the Iraq War (2003-2018). The appearance of victims' names is a trait common to several post-Vietnam memorials like Maya Lin's Vietnam Veteran's Memorial, the Oklahoma City National Memorial and several of the 9/11 Memorials, where names appear etched onto the surfaces of granite tablets or slabs. Through his avatar *dead-in-iraq*, DeLappe typed the names of each fallen soldier as a memorial to the deceased. Many of the users from *America's Army* reacted by complaining to administrators that DeLappe made the game *too real* and took away the joy of escapism within the online gaming environment. However, since the game serves to recruit users to join the armed forces, should users be aware of the real casualties of war? DeLappe responded with the following criticism:

> One of the things that has intrigued people about this work is that it is in this online context. It is essentially military territory online. It's a kind of base if you will. People who have…complained to me about this, like "this is not the place to protest go do this on the federal building steps." And I'll respond to them…and I said look I'm taking this to the source. There's a reason why in the '60s blacks went to lunch counters. They created meaning by actually going into that context. It's the same thing I'm doing here. I mean I could go to

the federal building and stand there and read a list of these names but who's going to pay attention to that? This got your attention.

By finding an online location where young users convene, DeLappe used the site to memorialize, but to also expose players to the harmful possibilities of joining the U.S. military during an active war. By continuously performing the piece in *America's Army,* he served as a constant reminder to users about violent after-effects of warfare.

KILLBOX AND OTHER UAV-THEMED WORKS

Unlike the occupation of a pre-designed gaming site in *America's Army,* DeLappe and a group of collaborators created the online game *Killbox* as an independent digital intervention about UAV technology. *Killbox* serves as one of several other projects in a series by DeLappe that critically evaluates the use of UAVs in both active and inactive war zones. Other works in the series include *Project 929: Mapping the Solar* (2013), a 10-day performance in which DeLappe rode a bicycle around Nellis Air Force Base in Nevada, dragging a piece of chalk for 460 miles. The piece sought to highlight the amount of space needed to create a solar farm large enough to power the entire continental United States.[14] *Cowardly Drones* (2013) was an intervention piece where DeLappe added the word "Cowardly" to the body of General Atomic's MQ1-Predator and MQ9 Reaper Drones and uploaded the doctored images as searchable jpgs in Google and Bing. Created in 2014, *Me and My Predator* permitted participants to download schematics for a wearable art piece—still available at http://www.instructables.com/, users can create an exact 1/72 scale replica of a Predator Drone, fastened to a carbon-fiber rod measuring roughly three feet in length.[15] The rod attaches to a metal C-clamp head strap made of aluminum that rests on the posterior of the head. Once secured in place, the drone hovers above the participant's head. DeLappe states that "the Personal Drone System is designed for insecurity and comfort—to simulate using analog technologies and what it might be like to live under droned skies…." *Drone Strike Visualization* (2014-2015) mapped UAV-initiated bombing sites in Mir Ali, Pakistan, highlighting the number of deaths caused from aerial attacks. In each piece, the UAV objects serve to explicate locations of action and occupation, making visible places (and spaces) traversed by UAVs.

Killbox is the most recent piece in this series of UAV-inspired works. Building off the other pieces in the series, DeLappe teamed up with several artists and software engineers to create an interactive gaming site that focused on the implementation and after-effects of UAV strikes. Collaborators include: Malath Abbas, co-founder of Quartic Llama, Tom deMajo, head game designer and sound engineer, and Albert Elwin, a programmer and founder of Space Budgie.[16]

The title for the game originates from the military term: the U.S. Department of Defense (DOD) defines a *kill box* as "a three-dimensional area reference that enables timely, effective coordination and controls and facilitates rapid attacks."[17] Put simply, a kill box space serves as an open-range kill zone where targets may be neutralized based on threat levels. With the onset of urban warfare, a kill box requires efficient data analysis, cartographic expertise and technological prowess. In "The Moral Cost of the Kill Box," Scott Beauchamp discusses how modern kill boxes are used:

14. Joseph DeLappe, "On the Making of Killbox…," *Killbox*, 29 March 2016, https://www.killbox.info/killbox/.
15. Joseph DeLappe, "Me and My Predator," *Joseph DeLappe*, http://www.DeLappe.net/sculptureinstallation/me-and-my-predator/.
16. Jo-Ann Green, "Turbulence.org Commission: 'Killbox' by Joseph DeLappe, et al.," *Networked Performance*, http://archive.turbulence.org/blog/2015/09/22/turbulenceorg-commission-kill-box-by-joseph-DeLappe-et-al/.
17. Scott Beauchamp, "The Moral Cost of the Kill Box," *The Atlantic*, 26 February 2016, http://www.theatlantic.com/politics/archive/2016/02/the-cost-of-the-kill-box/470751/.

> First, kill boxes have materialized in places the local population might not expect. And second, kill boxes have been used in conjunction with disposition matrices, or "kill lists." The DOD uses these to target people whose "pattern of life" fits the parameters of an algorithm, rather than specific individuals. For example: Say someone who owns a cellphone has been calling numbers that trigger a response from a computer at the Pentagon. Analysts will triangulate the cellphone's whereabouts, and military leaders might initiate a 'kill box' at that location, authorizing soldiers to kill everyone within the 'box.' Mission accomplished.[18]

For example, if a suspected ISIS cell in Iraq makes a series of references to terrorist attacks using cellphones or computers, surveillance teams can pinpoint the location of the suspected cell and decide to survey the region for possible threats. If the threat is imminent and the region is properly surveyed according to the "pattern of life" parameter, then the target is neutralized.

In the past, warfare required the actual visualization of hostile enemies by ground units, supplemented by aerial surveillance devices. Beginning with the Persian Gulf War and the weaponization of UAVs, the need for ground troops decreased, relying on telepresent technology and aerial surveillance devices. Beauchamp continues his critique of the UAV-kill box marriage by stating:

> The military began using kill boxes in the so-called war on terror as a technique to exert force in "ungoverned spaces," territories that are not controlled by a state and are populated by people who might not share American cultural values... The innocent people living in Afghanistan or Yemen, however, are apparently judged by a different standard. And this is the moral cost of the kill box: When used widely and indiscriminately, the tactic devalues human life.[19]

This facet of military UAV warfare deserves attention, specifically in the aftermath of several bombings on civilian hospitals run by Doctors without Borders (DWB) in Syria. In fact, several reports claim that DWB-sponsored facilities have been hit over 50 times in the past several years in Iraq and Syria alone, killing civilians, doctors and staff.[20] DeLappe's game serves to educate the public about the loss of innocent life with regards to UAVs and how operators risk civilian casualties in combat zones.

Unlike *America's Army, Killbox* focuses primarily on the objective/task of the designated avatar. Rather than inundate the player with a sophisticated, three-dimensional environment, the game's landscape is reduced to rudimentary, geometric shapes and basic terrain indicators. Instead of sharp, high-contrast shadows and detailed color graphics, buildings appear as square blocks. Monochrome colored dots replace the realistic bodies found in *America's Army.* Although the game's designers have the necessary credentials to create a highly sophisticated game, their decision to create a rudimentary design serves a strategic purpose: their reasoning is based on "the setting of cultural signifiers that may trigger a player's prejudices, and to show how artificial the world may feel when viewed through a circling camera." Without the distraction of realistic set designs, the user can focus on the *process* of playing, rather than the graphics or plethora of action options provided to players in *America's Army.*

Unlike *dead-in-iraq,* the premise of *Killbox* requires users to download the game from http://turbulence.org/commissions/Killbox/ and play one of two roles available (see Image 1.3.1, Image 1.3.3).[21] To fully understand the premise and objective behind the game for my research, I downloaded a version of *Killbox* from the website and documented my experience. The following details my movement through the space:

18. Beauchamp, "The Moral Cost of the Kill Box."
19. Ibid.
20. Rudaw, "'Syria Is a Kill Box' Says Medical NGO," *Rudaw,* 18 February 2016, http://rudaw.net/english/middleeast/syria/180220161.
21. Credit for all images belongs to Joseph DeLappe and the Biome Collective.

As a first-time user, I follow the link to turbulence.org, an online digital arts project. The link to Killbox leads me to a separate site that provides the basic premise for the piece, supplemented by two links to download the game (one for PC, the other MAC). Once the game is downloaded, the Killbox logo appears on a black screen, followed by two icons. On the left side of the screen, a green icon appears and the right, a red icon. When I guide the mouse over the icons, the green dot turns into a humanoid figure wearing a headset with the text "PLAYER 1" above the head. When the mouse hovers over the red dot, the icon rapidly changes from a child icon to a woman to a man. Above the flickering figures, a text box reads "PLAYER 2." I first venture into the PLAYER 1 scenario.

Image 1.3.1. Player 1 option, Killbox, 2016.

First, I type a username and password to start. Users must then press "L" to continue. The text line moves up. The name "CREECH AIRBASE 4320" appears, followed by a series of GPS coordinates. More numbers appear, seemingly arbitrarily in their sequence. The next action indicates that the drone is located over Waziristan, Pakistan. I continue through the space:

Next, the screen indicates a system check for a MQ-1 Predator. More numbers and coordinates appear. Slowly, the left 2/3 of the screen opens into a digital landscape. Rudimentary, white buildings, green grass, a beige walkway, and rows of green triangles appear in the scene. The lower right section displays actual instruments used by UAVs and military aircrafts, including the elevation and GPS coordinates while the left and upper portion displays distance measurements, the height above target, range, and bearings. The silence is interrupted by voices speaking over a radio. The voice over the radio is unclear, providing little to no information. I hear alphanumerical sequences. A command option tasks the player with testing camera keys to move the UAV camera left (A key), right (D key), up (W key), down (S key), zoom-in (I key), and zoom-out (O key) (see Image 1.3.2). *Once the keys are pressed, the text box reads "All Systems Operational." Next, I confirm the target by pressing the T key. The ground target is then locked. After several seconds, I press the M key in order to launch the missile. Upon closer inspection, small dots move around the space, some in clusters, others alone. A red square appears around one of the dots. Once the missile makes contact, two black spheres appear on the target site as the buildings crumble and the surviving dots cluster away from the target zone. The user can then shoot another missile at the target. The screen fades to black.*

A small red dot appears on the black screen (see Image 1.3.3). *I am now in the role of Player 2. The occasional bird chirp breaks the silence of the gaming space. Waziristan, Pakistan is written on the side of a low building, coupled with the command keys: MOVE: W/A/S/D LOOK: MOUSE JUMP: SPACE. As I traverse the terrain,*

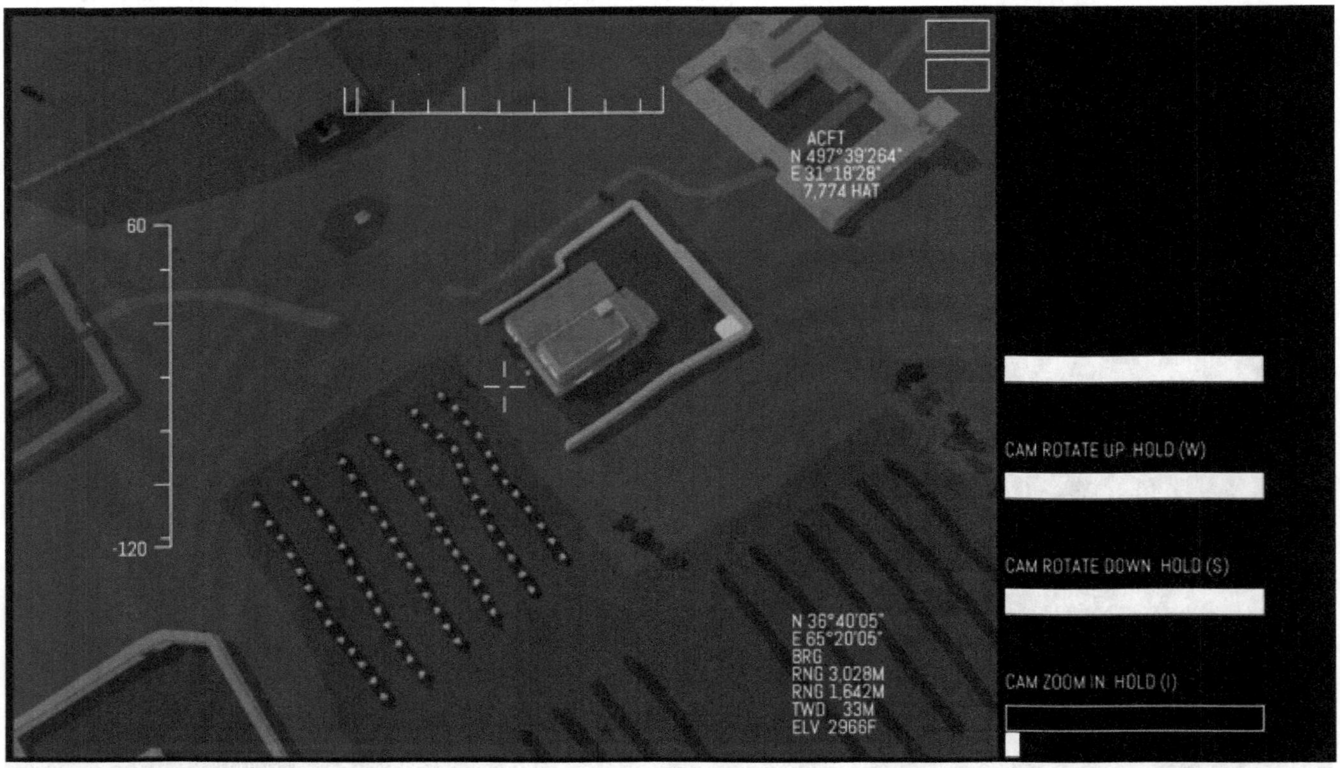

Image 1.3.2. Command key test, Killbox, 2016.

the dots disappear when the player 2 sphere runs over them. Gelatinous, multi-colored forms move through the space.

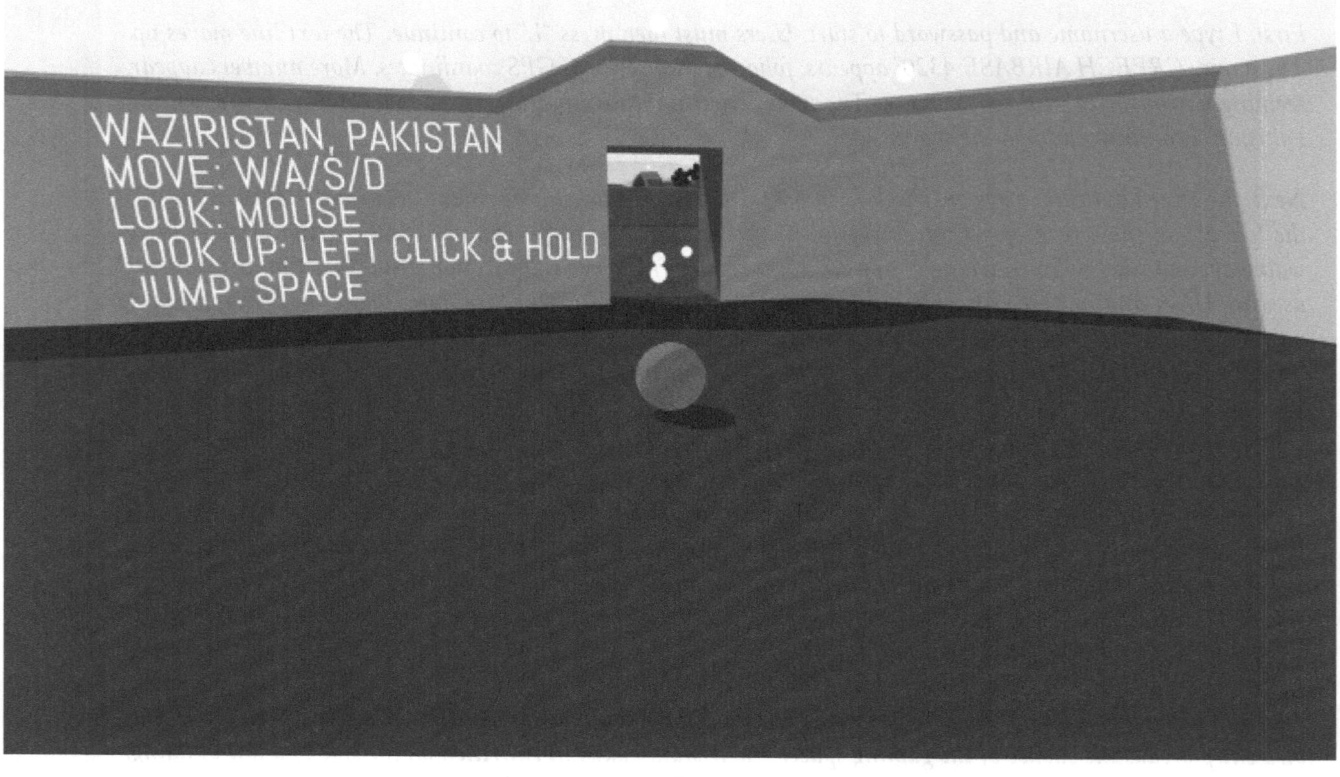

Image 1.3.3. Player 2 point-of-view, Killbox, 2016.

A loud explosion followed by a black scene interrupts my movement (see Image 1.3.4). *The scene turns to a grey overlay and then fades to black. The screen remains black for several seconds.*

Image 1.3.4. Aerial UAV hit, moment of impact, Killbox, 2016.

An information box appears (see Image 1.3.5).

The text reads:

In 2004 the first Unmanned Aerial Vehicle missile strike in an unofficial war zone was carried out in North Pakistan, killing four people including two children.

Since then over three thousand people have been killed by UAV-or Drone- strikes piloted from screens in cubicles thousands of miles away. Press any key to continue.

CONCLUSION: DIDACTIC GAMING

Killbox serves as a didactic tool for educating gamers about the accessibility of violent technology used in modern warfare. One issue with telepresent technology centers on the sanitized nature of UAV use. Building on cruise missile technology from the 1970s, the UAV was created to reduce both military and civilian casualties. Operators guiding UAVs could use the devices to reduce collateral damage, decrease ground troop presence and provide long-range support to remote regions. However, the main concern from UAV critics centers on the idea that "drones make killing too easy" and may blur geopolitical borders by major military powers. Reputable data on UAV collateral and civilian damage remains an issue, however, as cited in a report from 2012 by the Human Rights Clinic at Columbia Law School. Due to media bias and source tampering, there are issues gathering reliable information about civilian casualty rates associated with UAV-related strikes.[22] This issue is parlayed by Larry Lewis in *Rethinking the Drone War: National Security, Legitimacy, and Civilian Casualties in*

22. Chantal Grut, et. al. *Counting Drone Strike Deaths* (Human Rights Clinic, Columbia Law School, 2012), 5-6.

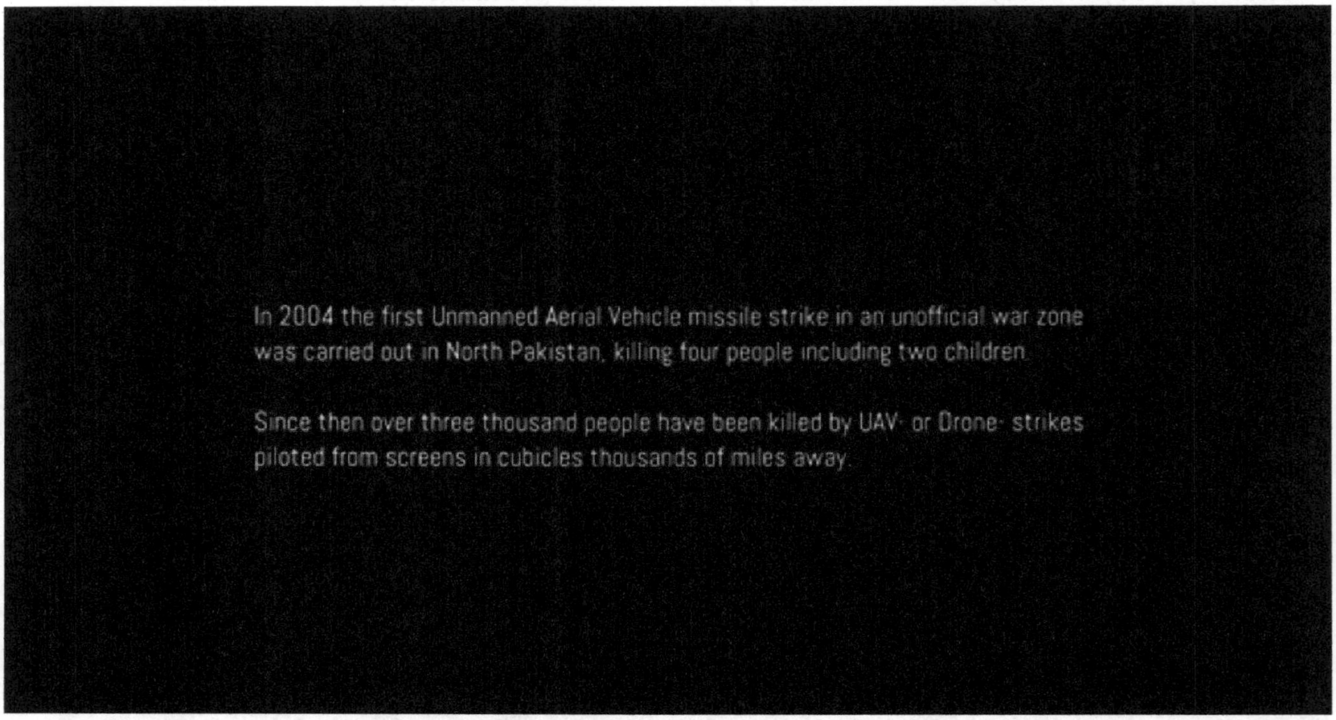

Image 1.3.5. Information screen, Killbox, 2016.

U.S. Counterterrorism Operations, where he extrapolates on how NGOs and government organizations gather data used to collect collateral and casualty statistics. Lewis estimates that UAV-related fatalities occur due to the "misidentification [of] civilians as enemy combatants [and] inaccurate assessments based on aerial surveillance." From this position, suspected terrorists often "co-locate" with civilians, obfuscating their identity.[23]

From a geopolitical standpoint, Tom deMajo, one of the collaborators on *Killbox*, explains that drones "bend legal boundaries, definitely territorial boundaries, but also psychological boundaries as well," asking "[h]ow do you reconcile yourself with killing on a screen, when you're used to doing it for fun?" In *Killbox*, the choice to use colored dots, rather than realistic bodies or avatars, serves a strategic purpose. For many UAV pilots and sensor operators, ground targets resemble small dots, making it very difficult to distinguish enemy combatants from civilians, especially in co-location scenarios. In the game, the user bombs these targets without consideration for what they may or may not represent. The same issue remains present for many UAV pilots when confronted with targets in regions where visibility may be low or targets undefined.

Killbox is not just a "video game" or form of entertainment, but a tool used to educate users about the power of violence produced by telepresent technology. The problem with the statement "killing made easy" derives from out-of-date research involving UAV crew and operator data. Cases of Post-Traumatic Stress Disorder (PTSD) for UAV pilots and sensor operators has increased exponentially, suggesting that "killing too easy" may be correct in terms of technological intervention, but not with regards to the humans operating the devices.

In 2014, 1,064 UAV pilots and operators were included in a United States Air Force study that

23. Larry Lewis and Diane Vavrichek, eds., *Rethinking the Drone War: National Security, Legitimacy, and Civilian Casualties in U.S. Counterterrorism Operations* (Marine Corps University Press, 2016), 12-13.

focused on the relationship between PTSD and indirect exposure to combat scenarios. Many UAV pilots and operators suffered from extreme exhaustion from working in isolation for 12 hours per day, up to six days a week. Others experienced depressive disorders after witnessing the deaths of civilians, combatants and fellow soldiers via the screen within their operator units. By using the monochrome figures in *Killbox,* DeLappe and his collaborators showed the difficulty of identifying figures as combatants or non-combatants from the position of the operator. Thus, *Killbox* provides users the opportunity to experience, albeit on a minimal scale, the issues many operators face when having to strike targets on the ground.

Currently, the deployment of UAV and other telepresent devices serves to prevent acts of terrorism and neutralize potential threats in both active and inactive warzones. Using the game to inform participants about the various complications involved in the deployment of UAV devices, *Killbox* continues to operate as a downloadable game for play. The game functions not only as a video game or form of entertainment, but a didactic tool used to educate participants about the visibility issues affecting operators, the violent after-effects of UAV strikes, and the rise of civilian casualties in both declared and undeclare warzones.

WORKS CITED

"America's Army PC Game Fact Sheet." *America's Army,* http://assets.americasarmy.com/americas_army_fact_sheet_sept_15_for_aapg_launch_final.doc.

Beauchamp, Scott. "A Critique of Conscience in Joseph DeLappe's Video Games." *Pacific Standard.* 4 May 2016. https://psmag.com/a-critique-of-conscience-in-joseph-DeLappes-video-games-7b21fad381dc#.yquxcrw5v.

—."The Moral Cost of the Kill Box." 26 February 2016. http://www.theatlantic.com/politics/archive/2016/02/the-cost-of-the-kill-box/470751/.

Bittanti, Matthew. "Interview: Joseph DeLappe, Pioneer of Online Game Performance Art." *Game Scenes: Art in the Age of Videogames,* 20 March 2010, http://artisticactivism.org/2012/01/joseph-DeLappe/.

Bogost, Ian. *Persuasive Games: The Expressive Power of Videogames.* MIT Press, 2007.

Brady, Sara. *Performance, Politics, and the War on Terror: "Whatever It Takes."* Palgrave, 2012.

Bumiller, Elisabeth. "Defense Chief Lifts Ban on Pictures of Coffins." *The New York Times,* 26 February 2009, http://www.nytimes.com/2009/02/27/washington/27coffins.html?_r=0.

Chappelle, Wayne, Tanya Goodman, Laura Reardon and William Thompson. "An Analysis of Post-Traumatic Stress Symptoms in United States Air Force Drone Operators." *Journal of Anxiety Disorders* 28 (2014): 480-487.

Coll, Steve. "The Unblinking Stare: The drone war in Pakistan." *The New Yorker,* 24 November 2014, http://www.newyorker.com/magazine/2014/11/24/unblinking-stare.

Der Derian, James. "Global Swarming, Virtual Security, and Bosnia." *The Washington Quarterly* 19.3 (1996): 45-56.

DeLappe, Joseph. "Drone Strike Visualization." *Joseph DeLappe*. http://www.DeLappe.net/installation/drone-strike-installation-prototype/.

—. "Me and My Predator." *Joseph DeLappe*, http://www.DeLappe.net/sculptureinstallation/me-and-my-predator/.

—. "On the Making of Killbox…." *Killbox*, 29 March 2016, http://www.killbox.info/killbox/

—. "Quake/Friends.1." *Joseph DeLappe*, http://www.DeLappe.net/game-art/quakefriends/.

—. "Virtual Commemoration: The Iraqi Memorial Project." Last modified 2011, http://www.iraqimemorial.org.

Duncombe, Stephen and Steve Lambert. "*Joseph DeLappe*." The Center for Artistic Activism, 28 January 2012, http://artisticactivism.org/2012/01/joseph-DeLappe/.

Galloway, Alexander R. "Social Realism and Gaming." *Games Studies* 4.1 (2004).

Grut, Chantal, et. al. *Counting Drone Strike Deaths*. Human Rights Clinic, Columbia Law School, 2012.

"History." *CADRE Media Lab*, http://cadre.sjsu.edu/?page_id=59.

Lewis, Larry and Diane Vavrichek, eds. *Rethinking the Drone War: National Security, Legitimacy, and Civilian Casualties in U.S. Counterterrorism Operations*. Marine Corps University Press, 2016.

"MQ-1B Predator." *U.S. Air Force*, 23 September 2015, http://www.af.mil/AboutUs/FactSheets/Display/tabid/224/Article/104469/mq-1b-predator.aspx.

"Playing America's Army." *PBS Frontline*. Last modified 2010, http://www.pbs.org/wgbh/pages/frontline/digitalnation/waging-war/a-new-generation/playing-americas-army.html.

Rudaw. "'Syria Is a Kill Box' Says Medical NGO," *Rudaw*, 28 February 2016, http://rudaw.net/english/middleeast/syria/180220161.

Stahl, Roger. *Militainment, Inc.: War, Media, and Popular Culture*. Routledge, 2010.

Wetzel, TSgt. Greg and MSgt. Ryan Wollenberg (Air Force In-flight Refuelers). Interview by Jenna Altomonte. 1 August 2016 and 15 July 2017.

PLAYING BEYOND PRECARIOUSNESS

THE POLITICAL DIMENSION OF BRAZILIAN MODDING IN PRO EVOLUTION SOCCER

JOSÉ MESSIAS, DIEGO AMARAL, AND THAIANE OLIVEIRA

INTRODUCTION: PRECARIOUSNESS AND PLAY IN BRAZIL

Video games and other forms of entertainment reproduce the power and knowledge relationships characteristic of what Walter Mignolo[1] refers to as the Modern/Colonial World-System.[2] This concept, as developed by Mignolo, asserts that an entanglement with coloniality is a fundamental pillar of modernity. Arguing that modernity and coloniality are two sides of the same coin, the author also suggests that our body of knowledge is determined by the ways in which the colonial power structure formulates paradigms of knowledge. Thus, following Mignolo, this chapter aims to promote epistemic disobedience, a transition to new ways of thinking and perceiving that has originated in the countries of the global south, former colonies whose knowledge and modes of being have been profoundly distorted by the so-called "canonical knowledge" institutionalized by the (former) colonizers.

In this chapter, we aim to highlight the normative potential of video games, products of an industry that is highly influenced by canonical standards. More importantly, as can be seen in the film industry in general and in Hollywood in particular, these norms are often dictated by market interests. By examining the friction between large-scale commercial games and individually or collectively customized versions of these same games, this article aims to cast a light on the power-knowledge relations among hegemonic powers, as seen in the ways Brazilian player communities respond to massive multinational game corporations and global industry standards with their locally-based initiatives. Looking at this side of the spectrum, we see how interactive digital culture has enabled a variety of anti-hegemonic initiatives, among which video game *mods*—modifications of commercial games that have been altered by individuals or communities of software modifiers or *modders*—are an important example.

In this context, we intend to look into the political and affective implications of the customization of video games and game related content. It is not just modding itself that is of interests, but also the relationship between modding and broader aspects of the production and appropriation of global technologies for the development of regional initiatives. As a result of these configurations, new possibilities for exploring the mainstream gaming experience have emerged that have allowed individuals living below the imaginary line of the equator to insert their own imaginaries into gameplay and game design.

With this in mind, this chapter specifically focuses on the creation of Bomba Patch mods for the game *Pro-Evolution Soccer* (*PES*, Konami, 2001-), which constitute an unintentional but still-relevant

1. Walter Mignolo, "Histórias locais/Projetos globais: Colonialidade, saberes subalternos e pensamento liminar," *GEOgraphia* 7.13 (2009).
2. The term refers to the world-system theory developed by Wallerstein (1974) among others. See also *The Modern World-System: Capitalist Agriculture and the Origins of the European World-Economy in the 16th Century* (Academic Press, 1974), v. 1.

decolonial exercise in inventing new ways for the communities of the global south to explore mainstream video games. Bomba Patch in this hybrid Portuguese-English form means a patch—a small mod—and *bomba* is the word for "bomb," but it can also be a slang term that translates to "hype" or "hyped." Its origins can be traced back to 2005, when a local video game store commissioned a customized edition of *PES* for a tournament between clients. At the time, the game did not feature Brazilian football teams, so one of the clients created a version of the national championship including not only first but also second and third tier teams. Given the low commercial appeal of the Brazilian market and these globally unknown squads, this kind of hacker intervention was the only way to play the game in a manner that reflected these players' taste, culture and subjectivity. Therefore, these mods encourage the emergence of affective communities and the subversion of popular, stereotypical representations by inserting local cultural elements such as slang, values and player personalities into blockbuster "global" games like *PES*.

We believe these customization-related practices enable an affective reconfiguration of the world by establishing new existential/affective territories that pertain to a particular intersection of space and time. In order to better understand these spaces and temporalities, this chapter builds upon the premises developed by Doreen Massey,[3] who defines space as a product of interactions, always under construction and marked by the coexistence of diversity.

In this sense, game mods developed by the communities of the global south gain a special relevance due to their capacity to merge world-class design tools with the interests of subaltern communities at particular intersections of space and time. Inspired by Mignolo's notion of epistemic disobedience, and focused on communities of gamers who challenge the spatial and temporal relations dictated by the global market, this chapter will show how hacking and software modification practices can contribute to the development of local—and decolonial—projects in precarious areas.

Precariousness can be defined in different ways within the current world system. It is not merely a matter of socioeconomic scarcity, or actual poverty. Taken more broadly, precariousness relates to what Hardt and Negri have called the "common condition of poverty of the Multitude."[4] It means precarious—or *conditioned*—access to infrastructure, education, culture, quality of life, mobility and so on: conditioned by market demands, geographical location, public perception and political interests. The richest person in Cuba cannot purchase a broadband connection as strong as the average South Korean's. Likewise, in many neoliberal capitalist societies like the U.S., access to knowledge is blocked by publishers' interests and the generalized privatization of higher education.

To discuss structural precariousness in the global south one must take in consideration the inner contradictions within each country. In this volume, Mukherjee underlines that an analysis of the digital divide in India must also regard the inequalities within the country such as the north/south division or class inequality consequent of the caste system. The Indian situation becomes relevant to illustrate the digital divide and, thereby, the precariousness in Brazil. Despite of not having multiple major languages or castes, Brazilian society is highly divided. The country's GDP is highly dependent on the southern regions, which tend to be home to the majority of technological and industrial development.

In order to better understand these issues' intertwined relationship with environmental scarcity and the socio-affective (ultimately political) appropriations of technical objects in zones of the global

3. Doreen Massey, *Por um sentido global do lugar* (Papirus, 2000).
4. Antonio Negri and Michael Hardt, *Multitude* (Penguin Books, 2004).

south, this chapter adopts an ethnographic approach to the analysis of Brazilian networks of player-editors who customize the *PES* franchise, also known as *Winning Eleven* in the Japanese market, by using the Bomba Patch to create their own versions of the game.

Three *mods* were selected for this study: Bomba Patch GeoMatrix, Bomba Patch União PI/Gospel K and Bomba Patch Jacaré.[5] We followed these mods' Facebook pages, tracing interactions between fans, and ultimately interviewed the modders behind them. Among our findings is that the PS2 console is experiencing a resurgence among Brazilian players, mainly due to the popularity of football/soccer simulations based on game series like *PES* and *FIFA* (EA Sports, 1993), along with other games like the *Guitar Hero* and *Grand Theft Auto* (GTA) franchises, which go beyond the scope of this analysis.

Modding football simulation games is a global trend, with players from around the world finding ways to circumvent licensing arrangements such as those between Konami, professional teams and national leagues, in order to create new names, kits (uniforms) and other copyrighted content. When game manufacturers fail to acquire some of those licenses, it falls to player communities to "fix" the game, hence the popularity of *patches* that contribute to this type of modding. In the cases analyzed in this chapter, a preference for the discontinued technology of the PS2 leads to particular strategies that harness social, improvisational and cognitive skills in order to shape modders' efforts and manifest their creativity. Moreover, these mods and communities are responsible for the creation of new spheres for socialization, and have developed a unique economy based on their own shared ethics, as we will see in the remainder of this chapter.

AFFECT, POWER AND EPISTEMIC DISOBEDIENCE

Hacking, modding and patching are part of the basic vocabulary for some within Brazil's gaming community. These groups of people participate in a network that involves the production (adaptation) of goods, their circulation and, as a consequence, the establishment of a micro-market that runs parallel to the official video game market. In so doing, these individuals create bonds that go beyond strictly commercial relationships and move toward the construction of spaces where affective, commercial and technological-aesthetic innovations arise.

Our usage of the term *space* here follows Massey, for whom space is "a product of interrelations" determined by interactions; heterogeneous, constituted by difference in relation; and always "under construction."[6] Using this provocative alternate concept of space as a point of departure, we can think of the culture of video game modification in Brazil as a way of enabling the constitution of micro-spaces, or rather, the modification of affective spaces to attain a desired composition.

At this point, it is important to point out that this affective network of players/producers/consumers, with the same person occupying multiple positions in many cases, takes place in precarious environments. In the 2006 book *Convergence Culture*, Henry Jenkins adopted the term "prosumer" to refer to these fans, especially the Japanese animation and comic book (manga) aficionados that translated and distributed this content online before it was licensed by publishers, but also writers of fan fiction and creators of Machinima and other remixes and parodies of movies and games. In response to the game industry's incapacity to provide ideal products, players overcome

5. As is further explained below, the names are a mix of Portuguese and English. GeoMatrix is the name of the local game store in the state of São Paulo that first "ordered" the mod. The second is a "joint venture" between two modding groups, one from the city of União (Union) in the state of Piauí, and the other Gospel K, a modder from Rio de Janeiro who added his evangelical beliefs and the first letter of his name to his group moniker. Finally, Bomba Patch Jacaré, which means alligator in Portuguese, is the modder's alias as a local DJ.

6. Massey, *Por um sentido global do lugar*, 8-9.

precariousness by using inventive solutions that allow them to insert their own feelings and desires into the game. "Game" here has a double meaning: it refers to the very objects modified, but also to a chain of production and distribution which marches towards the standardization of time and taste. In this sense, such locally produced game mods are an attempt to reorganize the system from within. Without the ambition of creating a worldwide impact, competing with or challenging the game industry, Brazilian gamers are creating new ways of relating to their preferred games without relying on the help of game companies.

By connecting people through affective links, these groups create networks with their own particular traits, such as: a specific temporality, since the editions of the mods frequently disregard and/or challenge the market calendar established by official games; a particular sense of "realism," given that the modders impact characters' overall ratings within the games in favor of "more credible ones"; and more importantly, the sense of community, which is a consequence of the direct relationship between producers and gamers. This final characteristic seems to be a major aspect of nearly all such mods. Indeed, all the nodes of this network are connected in a horizontal manner, as opposed to the top-down distribution and consumption of the official versions. As a result, the cultural misrepresentations and impositions produced by hegemonic industry powers in response to market interests are being fractured and distorted, and a community is emerging in the global south.

MODDING *PRO EVOLUTION SOCCER*

Group formation is a core element in the analysis of customization as a process. Individuals are known to gather around a cultural product, idea, feeling/sensation, etc., and in the case of *Pro Evolution Soccer/Winning Eleven*, a degree of dissatisfaction with the franchise has been a constant factor motivating software modders, who are equipped with the ability to effectively act on their frustration with the help of digital tools.

Open-source software and user-produced content bring about the possibility of direct intervention in the object of the user's affection, which is different from writing a review, creating fan fiction or undertaking other creative endeavors enabled by the convergence of media. Although it can be a controversial subject in the industry, some game publishers insert editing features in their games in order to make them more modifiable, which extends their shelf life and appeal to diverse audiences. Though its publishers were resistant at first, this took place with *The Elder Scrolls V: Skyrim* (Bethesda, 2011), while it is an approach Konami adheres to more wittingly. The editing feature in *PES* allows players to customize the unlicensed content filling the gaps the company contractually cannot. Thus, in subjective terms, the mod does become "another game," since the act of modifying and later playing it represents a certain rupture/break with mainstream market agenda, reliant upon both affective and commercial bonds, even if it is still the same product from a practical point of view. Modding is more akin to having the possibility to re-record the end of a movie or rewrite or (re)score a song to make it more to your liking.

In the case of the particular network of player-editors we are examining in this chapter, the group came together as a result of their attachment to the PS2 and to the Bomba Patch "brand," in a deliberate rejection of the new generation of consoles. This retro movement is driven less by nostalgia than by a serious dissatisfaction or displeasure with current football games. Their most common complaints are both the inaccuracy of players' attributes or overall ratings—a constant criticism among Brazilian players—and changes to the latest generation of games in and of itself. The examples below reflect this general discontent.

It is no coincidence that the PS2, though familiar to many players, also represents the most restrictive generation of consoles in terms of user handling and control. It is harder to manipulate or intervene in this platform even if one is willing to hack, damage or sacrifice some features in response to the demands of the console hardware or the game software. In pursuit of commercial and legal protections and marketing deals, console manufactures like Sony, Microsoft or Nintendo (and game and software companies in general) have decided to focus on user-friendly technology that is ready to play/use and difficult to share or modify/configure.

Game publishers have tried to restrict user manipulation of game software in a number of ways. For example, Microsoft's decision to link Xbox One games to the user's online account on their Xbox Live online service, for instance, made news and generated a great deal of backlash from fans. This decision was later revoked, but it still shows how online connectivity has gone from being an additional feature to a standard requirement.[7] There are innumerable other company policies intended to curb users' abilities to tinker or interfere with their intellectual property. Likewise, Lori Emerson has criticized Apple's platforms and business models for their strict controls on user-generated content:

> If the iPad signals the future of computing and of ubicomp-related computers, then perhaps it also simultaneously signals a future generation of hackers who will be driven to find a way out of this flat notion of creativity that amounts to little more than consumption and manipulation as users are turned into audience members watching their devices perform magic tricks before their very eyes.[8]

This critique also applies to a broader business model based on licensing, rather than purchasing, of media. Video game developers are frequently left with no other option than to "license" their games to consumers through publishers and distributors, which can leave them with reduced access and curtailed copyright protections, accompanied by an increase in licensed digital sales over transferable hard copies. Again, Emerson hits the nail on the head—even if she is not talking about video games specifically, her comments pertain the situation of digital technology in the last 10 to 20 years: "what concerns me is that the user-friendly now takes the shape of keeping users steadfastly unaware and uninformed about how their computers, their reading/writing interfaces, work, let alone how they shape and determine their access to knowledge and their ability to produce knowledge."[9] We consider this another form of market-imposed precariousness, this time one that is not restricted to communities of the global south.

Precariousness here takes on another meaning, one that has already been addressed by Mia Consalvo in her analysis of decoding chips, GameGenies, Code Breakers, Free Loaders and other popular tools for unlocking the content of consoles and cartridges in the U.S.[10] These popular hacking tools were popular among consumers for playing Japanese games, running homebrew games, or using the console as a Linux machines on early game hardware. However, we must consider the socioeconomic factors behind the rejection of the latest generation of consoles, at least in parts of Brazil: consoles and games are extremely expensive, costing upwards of US$600-700 (R$2000) at the time of release, and remaining close to US$350-400 (R$1000-1200) for years. These are 2019 prices for the PS3 and Xbox 360, each launched more than a decade ago. This price inflation takes place because of the country's high import taxes and other fees, even when the consoles are manufactured in Brazil. In the end,

7. Jon M. Chang, "Xbox 180: Microsoft Backpedals on 2 Controversial Xbox One Features," *ABC News*, 20 June 2013, http://abcnews.go.com/Technology/microsoft-backpedals-controversial-xbox-features/story?id=19449001.
8. Lori Emerson, *Reading Writing Interfaces: From the Digital to the Bookbound* (University of Minnesota Press, 2014).
9. Emerson, *Reading Writing Interfaces*, 49
10. Mia Consalvo, *Cheating: Gaining Advantage in Videogames* (MIT Press, 2007).

the final retail price of 7th generation consoles ends up being at least 50% higher than the national minimum wage of R$880/month (roughly US$ 210 to 230/month).[11]

THE BOMBA PATCH UPRISING

The Bomba Patch mod for the PS2 version of *PES* appeared in 2005, initially in connection to a single group on the social network Orkut. Later, as it became more and more popular, the name "Bomba Patch" turned into a synonym in Brazil for all PS2 football mods, and every group or individual interested in creating a *PES* mod for the console started using the term in their work.

Bomba Patch GeoMatrix was named after the video game store that "sponsored" its development. Its creators consider it the "official" Bomba Patch mod because it rose to fame in 2005, and they also claim to have created the name, as they were the first group to publish a Bomba Patch for *PES*.[12]

The GeoMatrix shop is located in the state of São Paulo, in the city of Mogi Mirim, considered small by Brazilian standards with its 90 thousand inhabitants. GeoMetrix's staff has explained that the person responsible for the mod was actually a client of the store, and that they first ordered the development of the mod for the local *PES* tournaments that they hosted there. According to GeoMatrix's spokesperson, editing was a requirement, because "the *PES* games came all wrong. There were no Brazilian teams and players overall ratings were all messed up."[13]

Since then, GeoMatrix has assumed the Bomba Patch "brand" and supports the creation of other mods for the PS2, which they sell in both their physical store and website. They also have their primary social media account as well as another for Bomba Patch releases—the latter's YouTube channel has more than six million views. When PS2 consoles and games for them were discontinued around 2012, the GeoMatrix team began specializing in launching versions of *GTA IV* (Rockstar 2008) and *GTA V* (Rockstar 2013) as well as recent *PES* games not available to the platform. Among other "store exclusives" are classic editions, with football legends from the past, Portuguese translations of in-game content and even commentary and broadcasting from different networks.

The "new" *GTA* releases are usually overhaul mods of *GTA San Andreas* (Rockstar, 2004), the last game in the series officially launched for the PS2 platform. The Portuguese subtitled or even dubbed versions of games like *GTA*, *PES* and more recently *God of War* (Sony, 2005) are available at GeoMatrix website along with the gameplay videos in their YouTube Channel.[14] Using editing software, it is possible to translate the text from the menus and dialog boxes and add audio and video files of non-player characters' speeches or whole dubbed cutscenes. The same is done with television broadcast narration and commentary, where the recorded audio is inserted in specific matching situations such as passing the ball, making a kick, committing a foul and, most importantly, scoring goals. In this case, synchronization is not always perfect (actually far from it), thus the names of players and teams are often mixed up, and the narrator often says the wrong score.

It is worth noting that football simulation franchises generally do not attempt to remediate the feel of an actual football match, but rather its television broadcast. For this reason, sportscasters have been a part of these games since the beginning. The companies hire actual TV personalities for this

11. Available at https://www.polygon.com/2013/10/21/4863954/ps4s-brazil-import-fees-taxes and https://www.polygon.com/2015/1/10/7524759/nintendo-brazil-wii-u-3ds-tariffs-taxes.
12. Unidentified spokesperson, GeoMatrix store, personal communication, 15 October 2015.
13. Ibid.
14. Available at http://geomatrixgames.com/loja/index.php?cPath=88_169 and https://www.youtube.com/watch?v=_KOPgAQgIIY&list=PLNybNY_6F-9g0sGx5b65ok1rEoE9dyEOS.

job and they record game commentary, player's names, their distinctive catch phrases and so on. However, with Bomba Patch, the modders add "alternative commentary" by extracting audio from TV broadcasts. The recent Bomba Patch 75 from GeoMatrix, which features the 2017 squads, has 11 commentary options drawn from four major Brazilian free-to-air and cable channels. This very flawed and artisanal process takes place because *PES 6* (Konami, 2006), the base for most Bomba Patch mods, does not have official commentary in Portuguese, which was only added with *PES 2011* (Konami, 2010).

GeoMatrix sells the hard copies of its mods in their store and website for R$10 to R$25 (US$3-8), a controversial practice that has been heavily criticized by other modders, as we will see. Geomatrix has explained:

> charge for early/advanced copies of the game, but 30 days later it is available for free. Those who buy help with the costs of production. They are basically other stores [likely street vendors too] that would like to sell the modded game before it becomes free. Whether you liked it or not, Bomba Patch is a source of income for the [street] stalls that increase their sales in each new version, which helps folks support themselves.[15]

The games can indeed be downloaded for free on their website, though not usually within the first 30 days after release but rather upon the release of the next new mod. To date, they claim Konami has never contacted them regarding copyright infringement.

It is vital to note that these mods are not made from scratch, nor do they require any elaborate programming skills—there is no actual adaptation or transfer of files from PS3 or PS4 versions to the PS2 "format." Most modders use *Winning Eleven 10* (*WE10*), also known as *PES 6* (Konami 2006), as a base from which they alter the content and in-game text using a highly intuitive and easy-to-use graphic user interface. No line of code or script is rewritten. And indeed, there are good reasons for game publishers to permit this type of unofficial local development. As Geomatrix explains, "We never had problems with Konami because we use their own in-game editing tools. We do everything there and later apply it to the game. You just have a save file with your achievements and progress and then you sell it to your friends. The editing is similar to the one that *Dota* gave us, and now *Dota 2* is sold separately as a game too."[16] The reference to known case of *Defense of the Ancients* (*DOTA*)—a mod of *World of Warcraft III* (Blizzard, 2002), that spawned a whole new genre called the Multiplayer Online Battle Arena (MOBA)—only strengthen the argument for a closer look at modding practices. Modding not only has educational and political significance, but can contribute to multibillion dollar industries with many examples of commercial success like the often-mentioned *Counter Strike* franchise (Valve, 2000) or the *Dota*-like game *League of Legends* (Riot Games, 2009).

The new groups that don the Bomba Patch name have a tense relationship with GeoMatrix, in part because of their pricing. A Facebook and blog post by the Bomba Patch União PI, dated November 2015, includes the following discouraging message: "A warning and announcement to GeoMatrix. Shame on you, create your own patch instead of stealing and redoing ours only changing the images in the j_text file. União PI and Gospel K appreciate the understanding."[17] The União PI group thus publicly denounced Geomatrix as frauds. In another blog post, now in the release of Bomba Patch Gospel K - Classics, from November 2015, the modder warns originally in all caps: "GeoMatrix, we do not accept [online] visits from mercenaries that sell defective patches full of bugs. Shame on you do not come back here."[18] It is worth noting that GeoMatrix has roughly 37,000 likes on their Facebook

15. Unidentified spokesperson, GeoMatrix store, personal communication, 15 October 2015.
16. Ibid.
17. Available in Portuguese at http://bombapatchgospel-k.blogspot.com/2015/10/bomba-patch-uniao-pi-2016.html.

page, while União PI and Gospel K have around 1,800 and 2,300 likes respectively. In these public denunciations of Geomatrix, clearly the issue is not only the money, but also the higher visibility of GeoMatrix's Bomba Patch.

COLLABORATION AND INNOVATION THROUGH MODDING

Rivalries are not the only relationships that have been sparked within the Bomb Patch modding community—it has brought forth collaboration as well. Bomba Patch Gospel K derives its name from the main contributor, Kelfany, who lives in city of São Gonçalo, in Rio de Janeiro state. Kelfany states in his social media profiles that his protestant Christian beliefs led to the name of the mod.[19] Kelfany is the main contributor, but not the only one, as there are several online nicknames listed in the group blog. There are also video tutorials dealing with the customization of each individual aspect of the game: shoes, balls, players' faces and hairstyles, commentary, stadiums, etc.

Bomba Patch Gospel K even includes a "map" of the game, a digital spreadsheet containing the main "customizable" elements like teams, leagues, stadiums and their "position" within the game file, indexed with an identification number. The pedagogical aspect of Bomba Patch Gospel K's social media is so evident that Kelfany once posted a 53-minute video class, recorded on Google Hangout, in which he commented on the kit (home team and away team jerseys) made by one of the page's followers, by that individual's request. In the video, he opens the files sent by this follower on Photoshop and shows the mistakes and how to correct them in order to improve customization. This kind of commitment to open-source software sharing and inter-generational mentorship definitely sheds some light on Kelfany's criticism of GeoMatrix's policies.

On the other hand, the Bomba Patch União PI comes from the homonymous city in state of Piauí, commonly abbreviated "PI." Three friends—Leonardo, 22, Wyllame, 24 and Diego, 26—are behind the patch, and the youngest jokingly boasts about their trajectory via Facebook Messenger:

> [...] we have always liked Bomba Patch and the football games for PS3, like PES and FIFA, never pleased us [...] we were going to create one just for ourselves, because we hated the [other Bomba Patches from street vendors] we bought, with messed up graphics. Everything was poorly done and lagged. Then, we started doing ours and we saw it was getting really good, so we decided to share it with the rest of country. And from that first one we already became a sensation.[20]

There are similar stories being told across the web and social media as a sort of Bomba Patch movement seems to be growing. Hubs like the YouTube channel, blog and Facebook profile for The Ruivo (meaning "redhead" in English), which has 4,000 likes and a little over one million views, promote retro gaming in general and PS2 mods specifically. Ruivo encourages these hacker-players to send their creations and later records gameplay videos critically evaluating them. The community converges around these spaces, playing and producing new patches and eventually collaborating, as was the case with União PI and Gospel K. Leonardo says: "Gospel [Kelfany] creates the jerseys. That is his specialty, he makes the best ones. We update the squads [current players and overall ratings]."[21] This type of collaboration is a key aspect of modding communities in the global south, as it offers mentorship and competence development opportunities that are often otherwise lacking. Inspired by the games they like, people from different parts of the country, and most importantly different

18. Available in Portuguese at http://bombapatchmineirao.blogspot.com/2015/11/bomba-patch-gospel-k-especial-classicos.html.

19. Kelfany, Blogspot personal profile, https://www.blogger.com/profile/14217809495392374004; for another perspective on this topic, see Rhett Loban and Thomas Apperley's chapter "Eurocentric Values at Play: Modding the Colonial from the Indigenous Perspective," in this volume.

20. Leonardo from Bomba Patch União PI, personal communication, 19 January 2016.

21. Ibid.

infrastructural challenges, are able work together, like the historically poorer Northeastern city of União, in inner Piaui, and São Gonçalo, in the metropolitan area of Rio de Janeiro.

Finally, beyond these structured groups, there are some individual tinkerers and hackers that take on modding as a pastime or hobby, since it can be as fun and challenging as actually playing. Game scholars like Ian Bogost,[22] Stuart Moulthrop,[23] Alexander R. Galloway[24] and others have analyzed the configurative or action-oriented nature of games. Eric Zimmerman take this one step further with the concept of gaming literacy, a skill set that promotes cognitive capabilities and influences behavior.[25] This helps us see configuring and tinkering with games as not just a nontrivial effort in media, but something that is applicable to other areas of life.[26] Zimmerman explains: "Gaming a system, means finding hidden shortcuts and cheats, and bending and modifying rules in order to move through the system more efficiently— perhaps to misbehave, but perhaps to change that system for the better."[27] By stating that a "tinkering logic" embedded in modding practices transcends the realm of video games and entertainment, this chapter focus on the immediate educational potential of technological appropriation and on a broader spectrum the political implications of self-definition and representation, access to information and culture and so on.

Straight out of the tiny town of São Miguel do Guaporé in the state of Rondônia, DJ Jacaré (meaning "alligator"), the moniker of Hemersom Rodrigo, started out modding very "casually." He was just 21 years old when we talked, and had begun modding four years earlier, as a high school freshman: "I just watched a bunch of videos on YouTube. And I had my PS2, however continuing to buy games was too expensive. Then, I had internet installed at home, watched the videos and acquired a taste for modding," Hemerson recollects.[28]

Again, the precariousness of infrastructure faced by many Brazilian modders deserves attention—it was only in 2013 that Hemerson gained internet access at home, and while it was far from an ideal connection, it still made significant difference in his life. There is a point to be made here about games as entry points to broader digital literacy, which is nourished by the cognitive skills and technological mediation provided through direct contact with video games as digital objects and the creation of spaces of affinity using the tools provided by this medium.[29]

Gaming and digital literacy often go hand in hand, relying on the non-written languages of the audio-visual spectrum. This can be seen by the extensive use and production of video classes and tutorials by the Brazilian player-hackers examined here. This visual performativity of the image combined with intervention and configuration skills are in high demand in these customizations. There is an aesthetic quality or mediation to learning methodologies employed in digital platforms that is manifested in a number of ways.

Given the procedural nature of these manifestations, games' algorithmic functions[30] converge with the computer to result, according to James Paul Gee and Elisabeth R. Haynes, in a greater degree of

22. Ian Bogost, *Unit Operations: An Approach to Videogame Criticism* (MIT Press, 2006).
23. Stuart Moulthrop, "From Work to Play: Molecular Culture in the Time of Deadly Games," in *First Person: New Media as Story, Performance and Game*, eds. Noah Wardrip-Fruin and Pat Harrigan (MIT Press, 2004).
24. Alexander R. Galloway, *Gaming: Essays on Algorithmic Culture* (University of Minnesota Press, 2006).
25. Eric Zimmerman, "Gaming Literacy: Game Design as a Model for Literacy in the Twenty-First Century," in *The Video Game Theory Reader 2*, eds. Bernard Perron and Mark J. P. Wolf (Routledge, 2009).
26. Espen J. Aarseth, *Cybertext: Perspectives on Ergodic Literature* (John Hopkins University Press, 1997).
27. Zimmerman, "Gaming Literacy," 25.
28. Hemerson Rodrigo, personal communication, 19 January 2016.
29. James Paul Gee, *Literacy And Education* (Routledge, 2015).
30. Lev Manovich, *The Language of New Media* (MIT Press, 2002).

problem-solving aptitude.[31] Needless to say, this is a skill that can be very useful when dealing with defective infrastructure. Having launched eight Bomba Patch releases so far and by now established his own network, Hemerson jests:

> Dude, people say I am a wizard [laughs] My PC has 2GB RAM. My internet connection is 512 kbps. If I run too much software it crashes, but it's never happened with games. The crashes are more frequent with these two programs, Game graphic studio [an editing application] and PCSX2 [a PS2 emulator]. They are a handful, I can't run anything else.[32]

The informality of online lingo aside, Hemerson shows a particularly poor written register in the conversations on Facebook Messenger—he exhibits deep deficiencies in his usage of Portuguese, in sharp contrast to his natural aptitude in other areas. In a conversation that took place in 2016, he praised his own skill, boasting, "I quickly learned the skills to mod games. I started doing my own versions after watching only three videos. I downloaded the necessary software and I am now on my third year making mods."[33] These learn-on-demand methods certainly do not replace formal training and education, but based on the principles of convergence of media and a booming contemporary visual culture, they need to be better understood. Self-tutoring by video has become an increasing trend especially among the youth and these practices can inform us, among other things, about the attention span of these audiences, their multitasking skills, information gathering and organization in audiovisual and text-based media.

The accessibility of digital interfaces makes learning easier by better "translating" or adapting content to an interactive, visual interface. This platform may not make a good fit every kind of discourse, such as a complex lecture with deep and abstract philosophical concepts, but an interactive format and aesthetic presentation are a logical fit with this mode of learning-on-demand. Nonetheless, as it is not our intention to romanticize poverty, it is important to recall that these initiatives are so deeply scarred by precariousness. Hemerson reports several problems due to his infrastructure situation, "4 GB RAM would solve most of my problems. Video and music editing software like sound forge and sony vegas give the hardest time. I already lost track of how many projects crashed when they were almost done."[34]

In this environment, users come up with other initiatives like the "personal patch," and less-experienced players ask veterans for custom-made mods, since most of them are willing to pay for them rather than having to go to the trouble of learning how to do it themselves. Even in his brief "career," Hemerson was approached by other players with such requests:

> I posted my first release in my blog, I didn't even know how a blog worked [...] it had only 200 downloads. After that I stopped doing it. I took a six-month break and only updated the mod for myself. Then I met this guy, a year or so ago. He owns a website with games and programs and stuff. He asked me for a personal patch with the page URL inside the mod. It got more than 1,000 downloads! I kept perfecting my skills. Fixed the blog. I started doing really cool image effects and then I was in this "market." I got to charge a guy R$40 (US$13) once and about four others bought my mods as well.[35]

Again, strategies for the circumvention of precariousness bring about novel initiatives and a degree of technological aptitude and methods in less-than-ideal socio-political and economic circumstances.

31. James Paul Gee and Elisabeth R. Hayes, *Women and Gaming: The Sims and 21st Century Learning* (Palgrave Macmillan, 2010).
32. Hemerson Rodrigo, personal communication, 19 January 2016.
33. Ibid.
34. Ibid.
35. Ibid.

When asked once more if people were really inclined to pay for a personal patch, since he uploads Bomba Patch Jacaré online for free, the DJ listed the several elements that can be modified and thus weigh on the decision to have an exclusive mod:

> I charge up to R$10 (US$3.20) for a personal patch if there's not much to be done. With more, the price goes up. You see, there's these opening images, cutscenes, they look like advertisements. So, I change that. The background image too. It's usually a famous player like CR7 [Cristiano Ronaldo], Neymar or Messi. I switch this for the picture of a place, a store [...] or just a name, like a LAN house [cybercafé] or the buyer's name. Picture this: a person calls his friends to play at his house, the game starts and the person's name is there on the screen. I only had one order from a website owner, it's usually for playing at home.[36]

Mods of football games were selected precisely for this factor of inclusivity and personalization. In Brazil, *PES* attracts a wide range of players, from police officers to delivery personnel, college graduates to high school dropouts. In the context of the global south, this personalization also indicates an inclusion of such "subaltern" voices to the larger discourse of mainstream video games. Similarly to the 12-year-old Palestinian girl playing *Special Force* (Hezbollah 2003) mentioned in the Introduction of this anthology, Brazilian players used the technology to feel closer to and better represented in globally distributed games.

Therefore, when examined closely, seemingly trivial entertainment practices evidence innovative intricacies as well as, we would argue, a strong political bias, even if at first glance they do not present themselves as intellectually or educationally significant.

CONCLUSION: THE POLITICAL DIMENSION OF PES MODDING IN BRAZIL

Through an analysis of this community of player-creators' bonds created around the *PES* franchise, we have aimed to portray the place of entertainment practices in the rearranging of space and power relations.

These stories of appropriation often go against industry mandates of standardization and quality that determine what is considered outdated or out of fashion, enjoyable or passé. Thus, the demands of the market and one's infrastructural background define what knowledge is and what being knowledgeable means, and therefore what can or cannot be done. Increasing digital literacy means increasing one's participation in contemporary culture and global networks of communication and commerce, in spite of the many challenges faced, for example, by software modders in the global south. This is how modding becomes epistemic disobedience.

In a precarious environment, where scarcity calls for innovation and the grassroots development of computational/media literacy, networks of collaboration and mentorship can emerge. These are less-than-optimal solutions to the deeply embedded social and economic problems of Brazil, and certainly, video games are not going to bring about the political and educational changes the country needs. However, tracing the untold history of this type of digital-savvy tinkering is key to unfolding video games' influence and potential in these areas. As an invitation to mobilization, the Bomba Patch mods and similar initiatives have, at the very least, allowed for the blossoming of a politically-oriented call for participation through affective technological innovation.

36. Ibid.

WORKS CITED

Aarseth, Espen J. *Cybertext: Perspectives on Ergodic Literature.* John Hopkins University Press, 1997.

Bogost, Ian. *Unit Operations: An Approach to Videogame Criticism.* MIT Press, 2006.

Chang, Jon M. "Xbox 180: Microsoft Backpedals on 2 Controversial Xbox One Features," *ABC News,* 20 June 2013, http://abcnews.go.com/Technology/microsoft-backpedals-controversial-xbox-features/story?id=19449001.

Consalvo, Mia. *Cheating: Gaining Advantage in Videogames.* MIT Press, 2007.

Emerson, Lori. *Reading Writing Interfaces: From the Digital to the Bookbound.* University of Minnesota Press, 2014.

Galloway, Alexander R. *Gaming: Essays on Algorithmic Culture.* University of Minnesota Press, 2006.

Gee, James Paul. *Literacy And Education.* Routledge, 2015.

Gee, James Pau and Elisabeth R. Hayes. *Women and Gaming: The Sims and 21st Century Learning.* Palgrave Macmillan, 2010

Jenkins, Henry. *Convergence Culture: Where Old and New Media Collide.* New York University Press, 2006.

Manovich, Lev. *Language of New Media.* MIT Press, 2002

Massey, Doreen. *Por um sentido global do lugar.* Papirus, 2000.

Mignolo, Walter. "Histórias locais/Projetos globais: Colonialidade, saberes subalternos e pensamento liminar." *GEOgraphia,* 7.13 (2009).

Moulthrop, Stuart. "From Work to Play: Molecular Culture in the Time of Deadly Games." In *First Person: New Media as Story, Performance and Game,* edited by Noah Wardrip-Fruin and Pat Harrigan. MIT Press, 2004.

Negri, Antonio and Michael Hardt. *Multitude.* Penguin Books, 2004.

Zimmerman, Eric. "Gaming Literacy: Game Design as a Model for Literacy in the Twenty-First Century." In *The Video Game Theory Reader 2,* edited by Bernard Perron and Mark J. P. Wolf. Routledge, 2009.

EUROCENTRIC VALUES AT PLAY

MODDING THE COLONIAL FROM THE INDIGENOUS PERSPECTIVE

RHETT LOBAN AND THOMAS APPERLEY

Indigenous people and cultures are rarely included in digital games, and if they are it is often in a rather thoughtless manner. The indigenous peoples and cultures of many parts of the world have been portrayed in digital games in several ways that show little respect or understanding of the important issues these populations face. For example, in the Australian-made *Ty the Tasmanian Tiger* (Electronic Arts, 2002), Australian Aboriginal people are completely absent, replaced by anthropomorphized indigenous animals some of whom wear traditional face paint, while the plot involves rescuing other animals from the "dreamtime." So while a secularized white settler version of Aboriginal culture is a core part of the game, the people are absent. The controversial mobile game *Survival Island 3: Australia Story* (NIL Entertainment, 2015), was removed from the Google Play and Apple stores in January 2016, largely because of an online petition that was concerned the game encouraged violence against indigenous Australians. The game portrayed Aboriginal people as "savages" who contributed to the difficulty of surviving in the Australian outback. Other games have appropriated indigenous iconography and culture, like *Mark of Kri* (Sony Computer Entertainment, 2002) which used traditional Māori (the indigenous people of Aotearoa/New Zealand) facial tattoo or Tā moko on characters in the game. These examples are disappointing, and seem to represent a common occurrence in commercial non-indigenous media.[1]

However, there have also recently been a number of critically acclaimed commercial gaming projects which deal with indigenous culture and issues from an indigenous perspective, for example the game *Never Alone/Kisima Iŋŋitchuŋa* (E-Line Media, 2014), made by Upper One Games in partnership with Alaska's Cook Inlet Tribal Council.[2] With an interest in exploring how an indigenous perspective can be brought to strategy and grand strategy digital games this chapter considers the practice of "modding" digital games. In strategy games, Indigenous people, like other non-Western peoples (see Souvik Muhkerjee's chapter in this volume) are often depicted in an ahistorical, generalized way, which ignores their unique cultures and histories as sovereign people. We are concerned with how these depictions could be fleshed out through modding original games, in order to create a more detailed and balanced experience for both indigenous and non-indigenous players. Strategy games are a high stakes area for indigenous representation as they simulate complex history processes, often—explicitly or implicitly—including the colonization of the world by European powers.

This chapter is a collaboration between two scholars, Rhett Loban and Thomas Apperley. Rhett is a Torres Strait Islander, one the indigenous people of the Torres Strait Islands, which are a chain of islands in the Torres Strait between Cape York, Australia and Papua New Guinea. Torres Strait Islanders are distinct from the Aboriginal people of the rest of Australia. This chapter details an

1. Non-commercial "serious" games that deal with indigenous content more respectfully and authentically have been developed; see Jakub Majewski, "Oldest Culture, Newest Medium: What Emerges from the Clash?," *Proceedings of DiGRAA 2016 National Conference: Tensions* (2016).
2. Elizabeth LaPensée, "Video Games Encourage Indigenous Cultural Expression," *The Conversation*, 22 March 2017.

element of his Ph.D. project, which examines the use of strategy games for history education in informal and formal contexts. Thomas is a Pakeha (settler) New Zealander, who has been studying and working in Australian tertiary institutions since 2004, and he is one of Rhett's three Ph.D. supervisors. This chapter brings together their mutual interest in grand strategy games and is primarily a collaboration, but the mod that is discussed was developed solely by Rhett through research with his family members and other Torres Strait Islanders. Therefore, this chapter has two voices: "we" which is Rhett and Tom, and Rhett speaking alone in the first person singular, which we will signal throughout.

The chapter proceeds in three parts. In the first part we reflect on how grand strategy games have represented indigenous people, with particular attention to both problematic issues and more recent efforts that have been made to be more inclusive. In the second, Rhett discusses his research and process of making his mod "Indigenous People of Oceania," which adds an indigenous perspective to *Europa Universalis IV* (*EUIV*) (Paradox Interactive, 2013). In the third section, we consider the limits of working with mods in these games, considering how Eurocentric models of nation and sovereignty are embedded in the game rules and mechanics. Through this journey we explore the question: can the Eurocentric version of history and culture that informs strategy games and places indigenous peoples and cultures on the outside of history be effectively given an indigenous perspective through practices like modding?

Before we go any further, the practice that we refer to as modding is an umbrella term that encompasses a large number of practices (see also the chapters by Mukherjee and Messias, Amaral and Oliveira in this volume). It can include modifying game software to such an extent that a new game is created.[3] But other practices of modding are less extensive, the software interventions make changes to existing games, or develop additional content for them. Some definitions of mods extend to game hardware.[4] But the key attribute of modding is that it involves customizing, tailoring or remixing the game or game content by players, in order to suit their desires and interests. In this chapter, "modding" refers to the process of altering the files of a game to create a new game content or a new version of the game; while a "mod" is the product of that alteration.

GRAND STRATEGY GAMES AND INDIGENOUS CULTURES

A key concern of many grand strategy games is European colonization, which makes the representation of Indigenous people a crucial issue as they are the key victims of the colonial process. While the United Nations has no strict definition for the word "indigenous," they do highlight key attributes including self-identification as indigenous, strong links to territories, distinct social, economic and political systems, unique languages, cultures and beliefs and, crucially, an existence as a pre-colonial society.[5] Indigenous people had autonomous histories prior to colonization,[6] and continue to struggle for preservation of their culture and way of life after colonization.[7] They are the "conquered descendants of earlier inhabitants of a region who live mainly in conformity with traditional social, economic and cultural customs that are sharply distinct from those of dominant

3. Baptiste Monterrat, Elise Lavoué and Sébastien George, "Learning Game 2.0: Support for Game Modding as a Learning Activity," *Proceedings of the 6th European Conference on Games Based Learning*, 2012, 340. See also Ibrahim Yucel, Joseph Zupko and Magy Seif El-Nasr, "It Education, Girls and Game Modding," *Interactive Technology and Smart Education* 3.2 (2006), 144.

4. Walt Scacchi, "Computer Game Mods, Modders, Modding, and the Mod Scene," *First Monday* 15.5 (2010), 2.

5. United Nations Permanent Forum on Indigenous Issues, "Fact Sheet: Who Are Indigenous Peoples?," *United Nations Permanent Forum on Indigenous Issues*, 2006, https://www.un.org/esa/socdev/unpfii/documents/5session_factsheet1.pdf.

6. Franke Wilmer, *The Indigenous Voice in World Politics: Since Time Immemorial* (Sage, 1993), 97. See also Ted Robert Gurr, *Peoples Versus States: Minorities at Risk in the New Century* (U.S. Institute of Peace Press, 2000), 17.

7. Wilmer, *The Indigenous Voice in World Politics*, 97.

groups."[8] Even though indigenous people often maintain many elements of their traditional way of life, they are still effectively defined by colonialism in settler versions of history.

Grand strategy games also tend to understand indigenous people in this way. They are presented not as sovereign people, but as potential subjects for European-style colonialism. The "actors" in these games are the nations and culture historically associated with colonization (e.g. the Netherlands, or Great Britain), and any conflict with indigenous peoples is uneven, both in terms of the relative resources available to each side in the game, and in the respect of the rich historical detail given to their culture and history. For example, there has been a tendency in strategy and grand strategy games to group indigenous people together in an ahistorical manner, and represent indigenous populations in a generic way, as is found in the *Sid Meier's Civilization* series, which used generic (and pejorative) term "barbarians," to describe nomadic populations.[9] In *Sid Meier's Civilization IV* (2K Games, 2005) indigenous nations such as the Aztec and Maya are individually represented, however the Native American tribes have been amalgamated into an ahistorical faction labeled "Native American." Similar issues have been noted in *The WarChiefs* expansion for the *Age of Empires III* (Microsoft Game Studios, 2006), which added greater detail to the playable Indigenous factions.[10] In *Sid Meier's Civilization V* the Polynesian faction is based on a muddled collection of Polynesian themes: the leader of the faction is Kamehameha, the first king of Hawai'i/Hawaii; their unique unit is the Māori warrior, referencing the indigenous people of Aotearoa/New Zealand; while their unique civilization improvement is the Moai (a giant stone head) from Rapanui/Easter Island.

Better depicting the world's indigenous people is not just the "right thing to do," it will also make games a more rewarding, vibrant and insightful experience for the community of players. Although some players will attempt to just "win" the game through following the colonial logic of world conquest, they may still be interested in the history in the game being "true" or "accurate."[11] Previous research has noted that some players also play strategy games to explore and roleplay alternative realities, also called counter-factual or "what if" histories.[12] Other players may try to "accurately" roleplay history attempting to recreate historical empires or nations, and sharing fictional accounts called after-action reports.[13] Many fans of history and strategic games enjoy playing them in part because of the histories, cultures and peoples depicted in them. Adding detail to indigenous peoples in the games would serve to enrich these players' experiences.

The Grand Strategy genre epitomized by *EUIV* has managed to depict Indigenous people with more detail than other strategy games. For example, in the *Europa Universalis IV: Conquest of Paradise* (Paradox Interactive, 2014) expansion and update, Native American tribes are developed as uniquely conceptualized cultures through game mechanics and pop-up decision and text boxes. All North American tribes (including Apache, Huron, Cherokee, Sioux, Comanche, Iroquois, etc.) have the Native American or tribe-specific benefits that are unique to each tribe or North American Indian group. They also introduced a specific government type "the Native Council," a unique religion called "Totemist," and a unique set of buildings that can only be constructed by Native American tribes. The

8. Jeff Corntassel, "Who Is Indigenous? 'Peoplehood' and Ethnonationalist Approaches to Rearticulating Indigenous Identity," *Nationalism and Ethnic Politics* 9.1 (2003), 78-80.

9. Emily Bembeneck, "Phantasms of Rome: Video Games and Cultural Identity," in *Playing with the Past: Videogames and the Simulation of History*, eds. M. Kapell and A. Elliot (Bloomsbury, 2013), 81-82.

10. Beth A. Dillon, "Signifying the West: Colonialist Design in Age of Empires III: The WarChiefs," *Eludamos. Journal for Computer Game Culture* 2.1 (2008): 129-144.

11. Apperley, "Modding the Historians' Code," 185-198.

12. Apperley, "Modding the historians' code," 8; Adam Chapman, *Digital Games as History: How Videogames Represent the Past and Offer Access to Historical Practice* (Routledge, 2016).

13. Thomas Apperley, "Counterfactual communities: Strategy games, paratexts and the player's experience of history," *Open Library of the Humanities* 4.1 (2018): 1-22.; Souvik Mukherjee, *Video Games and Storytelling: Reading Games and Playing Books* (Palgrave, 2015).

expansion also gives all Native American Tribes a special function called "Migration," which allows them to migrate from one province to another, reflecting the pre-colonial nomadic lifestyle of some of the tribes.[14] Federations between tribes may also be formed as a defensive alliance mechanism to ward off attackers and defend the tribe, an acknowledgement of the tribal organization use by the Iroquois from the fifteenth century.

In the *Europa Universalis IV: El Dorado* (Paradox Interactive, 2015) expansion and update, the Aztec, Maya and Inca nations are reflected in greater detail in terms of their religion which was fundamental to their society. For example, the Aztec religion is reflected by way of the Doom system, which simulates the millennial elements of Aztec religion and culture. Doom incrementally builds up from 0% to 100% over time and through events, and when it reaches 100% grave penalties are imposed on the Aztec faction. Doom can be decreased with sacrifices, which is reflected in the game by the option of declaring war on neighboring nations via the "Flower War" Casus Belli in order to capture sacrificial prisoners (a real historical reference), or by sacrificing the leaders of subject nations.[15] It should be noted that the elements of Aztec culture that are embedded in the software are based on an outsider perspective in the form of accounts by Spanish priests.

However, even with these expansion packs, in *EUIV* large parts of the Americas, Africa, Asia and Oceania are portrayed as "empty" lands ready for anyone to colonize. Each province does portray an indigenous population, but there are no ways to diplomatically interact with or playing these peoples like other nations (such as the Iroquois or Aztecs). Considering the overwhelming detail of the game, these areas stand out as peculiar. Inclusion of more indigenous specific nations, models, ideas and in-game content would provide players with a much more consistent and, to an extent, informative experience.

As games like *EUIV* have the potential to offer multiple perspectives on history,[16] adding an indigenous perspective through modding is consistent with an increasingly interactive and customizable player experience. As these games are often criticized for presenting "Western" version of history in a way that excludes other cultures,[17] developing a mod that augments the game with an Indigenous perspective is useful for establishing a version of history that embraces a version of multiplicity that includes Indigenous people. Other work on *Europa Universalis II* has underscored how the game may be used in ways that disrupt official versions of history.[18] For these reasons Rhett decided to develop a mod that added cultural details from the indigenous perspective to *EUIV*, in order to allow interested players to be exposed to the autonomous history and culture of indigenous people in a manner that may challenge and complicate the Eurocentric view of history that they have learned through schooling and exposure to popular culture, the same worldview portrayed and implicitly endorsed in *EUIV*.

A MODDING SOLUTION?

While playing a mod (just as you play a game) requires no initial training, some aspects of modding require quite specific skills. Games such as *EUIV* are designed to be modified and the Paradox Interactive online forums are explicitly mod-friendly, with community-developed wikis to guide the

14. History.com, "Native American Cultures," *A&E Networks*, 2009, https://www.history.com/topics/native-american-history/native-american-cultures.
15. Ross Hassig, *Aztec Warfare: Imperial Expansion and Political Control* (University of Oklahoma Press, 1995), 3, 10.
16. William Uricchio, "Simulation, History, and Computer Games," in *The Handbook of Computer Game Studies*, eds. J. Raessens and J. Goldstein (MIT Press 2005), 335-336.
17. Souvik Mukherjee, "Playing Subaltern: Video Games and Postcolonialism," *Games and Culture* 13.5 (2016), 3; Kacper Pobłocki, "Becoming-State," *Focaal - European Journal of Anthropology* 39 (2002), 166.
18. Apperley, "Modding the historians' code," 185-198; Chapman, *Digital Games as History*.

user through the mod making process. Modding is one of the elements of gaming cultures that is often pinpointed by educators as being a key area where unofficial but work-relevant literacies are developed.[19] There have been other initiatives to make game content more individual and relevant for indigenous communities through modding. This is in parallel to a widespread interest in modding from a cultural perspective by artists, activists and game designers as a way of remixing media from the point of view of local marginalized populations (see the chapters by Muhkerjee and Messias, Amaral and Oliveira in this volume).[20] Key indigenous initiatives include a recent project with Native American youths in Canada. Youths became involved in video game content creation to depict the histories of the Iroquois, as told by their families.[21] By persuading the Native American community in Montreal to become involved, Mohawk Youths were able to convey their stories in a creative and respectful manner while also allowing them to learn programming skills that are often confined to the non-indigenous population. In this respect making mods is a useful learning exercise. However, while it is often though modding served a mainly as IT, computer science and game development learning tool;[22] there is also potential for using modding as learning tool for other disciplines such as history and cultural studies.

Rhett chose to use *Europa Universalis IV* as a case study because the game aims to present a high degree of historical accuracy and also supports a large community of modders, who are able to circulate their mods through Paradox Interactive's official online forums. Mods in *EUIV* can vary from simple mods that change a few variables in order to add greater balance to the game, to complete overhauls of the game that replace the game scenario with a completely different setting, for example the "Song of Ice and Fire Mod"—a *Game of Thrones* for *Europa Universalis*. However, it is more common for modders to use mods to make adjustments to the game that they believe will further its historical realism and accuracy. *EUIV* modding usually takes the form of adding new data to existing game mechanics and data sets, as opposed to creating entirely new functions. Paradox Interactive, the developers of *EUIV*, encourage modding in the *EUIV* community and draw knowledge and information from them which they use in subsequent iterations of the game.[23]

Some modding tools are highly accessible and already built into game interfaces. Common examples are the *Age of Empires* (Microsoft, 1997) "Scenario Editor" and the *Warcraft III* (Blizzard, 2002) "World Editor," which are tools for making shareable and playable maps. Paradox Interactive grand strategy games are often accompanied by modding tools such as "Modder mode" in *Hearts of Iron IV* (Paradox Interactive, 2016), an in-game interface aimed at assisting with game modding and the "Clausewitz Maya Exporter," which allows the modder to export 3D models from Maya into Paradox Interactive games. The tools typically used to mod *EUIV* include:

- the *EUIV* software;
- a code editing program, or text editor such as notepad :
- specific tools like the "Clausewitz Maya Exporter" ; and
- access to the internet for historical research and modding guides

19. Thomas Apperley and Chris Walsh, "What Digital Games and Literacy Have in Common: A Heuristic for Understanding Pupils' Gaming Literacy," *Literacy* 46.3 (2012): 115-122.
20. Padmini Ray Murray and Chris Hand, "Making Culture: Locating the Digital Humanities in India," *Visible Language* 49.3 (2015): 141-155.
21. Beth Aileen Lameman, Jason E Lewis and Skawennati Fragnito, "Skins 1.0: A Curriculum for Designing Games with First Nations Youth," *Proceedings of the International Academic Conference on the Future of Game Design and Technology* (2010): 105, 111.
22. Magy Seif El-Nasr and Brian Smith, "Learning through Game Modding," *Computers in Entertainment* 4.1 (2006): 18-19; Yucel, Zupko and El-Nasr, "IT Education, Girls and Game Modding," 154.
23. Trin Tragula, "Eu4—Development Diary—2nd of May 2017," *Paradox Interactive*, 2 May 2017, https://forum.paradoxplaza.com/forum/index.php?threads/eu4-development-diary-2nd-of-may-2017.1018557/.

Typically, when modifying a file, modders will only change the more accessible script files in the game files, rather than the deeper level code that makes up the core functions of the game. Through the script files a potential modder can access and alter most of the graphical interfaces and models, most in-game variables/datasets and in-game texts.

What makes the process of creating a mod for *EUIV* different from other forms of modding is that it often requires additional history research. In a developer diary, Trin Tragula, a content designer at Paradox interactive describes how the development team divided historical research conducted during game development into two categories:

- Database/Setup Research which relates to game mechanics (like religious mechanics) and pop-up boxes about history; and
- Background/Content Research which entails the initial and historical staring condition of the game and the variables/characterizes of each game province.[24]

These are also the typical points where modders will mod the game, unless they are developing completely new in-game mechanics.

As mods are often implemented to "correct" perceived inaccuracies it is important that thorough research is conducted. Many information sources can be used, but most often the internet has the most readily available information, though it may be less reliable than other sources. Other common resources include books and documentaries (like those found on YouTube). For the *EUIV* mod Rhett developed, the "Indigenous People of Oceania," oral accounts from family and other members of the Torres Strait Islander community were important. Family and oral history can provide insight into indigenous history and culture that is not otherwise available in other sources. In some instances, these oral accounts can reconfirm what are in other sources, or they can provide an important variation that diverges from other sources.

The next step requires inserting the historical and cultural information into the game. This can be done in many ways, for example the simplest and most obvious way to do this in *EUIV* is through pop-up boxes or other text based aspects of the game such as national ideas. These are short pieces of text that convey an event, cultural practices, or other sorts of historical or cultural information. The pop-up box might outline a significant event in a history or culture, usually accompanied by an in-game positive or negative modifier. The approach Rhett took with the "Indigenous People of Oceania" mod was to create a playable nation where in the original game there is only a blank piece of land. Quite a lot of information is required to flesh this out, so that there is a comparable level of detail to existing playable nations. These details include national flags, graphic models, national ideas, provincial information, extra mechanics and so on.

For the "Indigenous People of Oceania," Rhett used modding techniques to create new technology groups that reflect the differing lifestyles (land-based or seafaring) of the oceanic peoples, and many new indigenous pacific nations (including Mabuiag, Fiji, Hawai'i, Ngāi Tahu, Asaro, Gubbi Gubbi) with their ideas in game bonuses and information about the nations people's history, as well as the addition of new religious faiths present at the time. A comparison between the original *EUIV* map and *EUIV* "Indigenous People of Oceania" mod map shows the inclusion of many cultural groups in the Pacific region in the IPO map (see Image 1.5.1 and Image 1.5.2). The mod is far from perfect, but it

24. Ibid.

gives the game an indigenous perspective on the region's history, mainly by providing specific detail about the different indigenous nations of the Pacific.

Image 1.5.1. EUIV original map showing Oceania.

Image 1.5.2. EUIV "Indigenous People of Oceania" map.

THE SOVEREIGN CODE

In spite of the strengths mentioned above, Rhett found that the modding tools that were easily available had some crucial limitations because of the Eurocentric frameworks in which issues such as sovereignty and even the concept of the nation are embedded in the game's rules and mechanics. While the "Indigenous People of Oceania" mod was able to successfully add details which portrayed many aspects of indigenous culture, the mod still had to work within European concepts of nationhood, territory and sovereignty. In this sense Rhett's process pinpointed the limitations of modding by demonstrating how the structure of *EUIV* limited the extent to which indigenous people could be represented. From a game design and technical standpoint, modding games such as *EUIV* to portray indigenous people from their own perspective is difficult, particularly because of centrality of very Eurocentric notions of the state, nation and sovereignty that are embedded in the game software.

Sovereignty is understood as having sole control or authority of a given geographic area. Liberal independent theorists might say sovereignty is state ability to control actors within its defined borders, while realists might say it is in the ability to make great decisions such as war.[25] For Weber, sovereignty is the "monopoly of the legitimate use of physical force" as a defining characteristic of the state.[26] Sovereignty appears to be a defining feature of a state, and it is noted that a state is not just a government, as a state rules over a defined area and continues to exist even if the government changes. In *EUIV*, historic states which exercised sovereignty over their territories are usually defined with some detail and are potentially playable nations, while "empty" or "blank" territory which is ripe for colonial expansion was inhabited by people who had patterns of land use and systems of government which did not register with a Eurocentric concept of sovereignty. An infamous example from history was the British and White Settler Australian legal understanding of Australia as a "Terra Nullius," an empty land which was used to deny the sovereign rights of the Indigenous Australian and Torres Strait Island people in Australian courts until the 1990s.[27]

The state is an age-old organization with much history, although it is usually defined through modern notions such as law, citizenship and its responsibilities to its citizens.[28] States, nations and nation-states are inherently intertwined.[29] A nation is centered on the idea of collective cultural heritage, linguistic unity or a sense of shared identity amongst the members, while the state is an institution defined mainly by its use of force, the legitimacy of the institution, the presence of institutional bodies to operate government tasks and control over a territory.[30] A nation-state embodies a concept that is a state defined by nation. But at what point does nationhood come into being?[31] This realization may be tied to a national conscience, a national identity, a nation-formation process or some ancestral connection. Smith argues that the nation is manifested through the creation of a collective name, myths/memoirs of communal history, common laws and customs, shared public culture and a historic territory.[32] However, defining a nation by race, language, religion or geography is problematic given the constant integration, fragmentation and transformation of beliefs, people and cultures.[33] While white settler histories acknowledge that some indigenous tribes did have significant political and

25. Janice Thomson, "State Sovereignty in International Relations: Bridging the Gap between Theory and Empirical Research," *International Studies Quarterly* 39.2 (1995): 213-214.
26. Max Weber, *Politics as a Vocation* (Fortress, 1968), 1.
27. Stuart Banner, "Why Terra Nullius? Anthropology and property law in early Australia," *Law and History Review* 23.1 (2005): 95-131.
28. Global Policy Forum, "What Is a 'State'?"
29. James Paul, "Nations and States Part 1: Nations and States—What's the Difference?," *Global Policy*, https://www.globalpolicy.org/component/content/article/172/30345.html; Peter Ravn Rasmussen, "Nations or States: An Attempt at Definition," *Nations, States and Politics*, http://www.scholiast.org/nations/whatisanation.html.
30. Rasmussen, "Nations or States."
31. Walker Conner, "When Is a Nation?," *Ethnic and Racial Studies* 13.1 (1990): 93; Anthony Smith, "When Is a Nation," *Geopolitics* 7.2 (2002): 5.
32. Smith, "When Is a Nation," 17.
33. Ernest Renan, "What is a Nation?," in Ernest Renan, *Qu'est-ce qu'une nation?*, trans. Ethan Rundell (Presses-Pocket, 1992).

administrative bodies, they also claim that they lacked a hierarchy of authority or formal government.[34] This approach to understanding indigenous nationhood also reflects how *EUIV* depicts indigenous nations with no sovereignty or government, and thus as territories rather than states.

Some indigenous tribes are documented as having systems that are closer to the Eurocentric notion of sovereignty and statehood. Historically a number of the Torres Strait Islanders of Australia had ownership of residential land and areas of gardens that could be passed down from generation to generation.[35] One island in particular had fetish priests who ruled over other islanders through fear of black magic. Europeans that documented the island's way of life saw the fetish priests as a type of hereditary government that could control others and had the capacity to enforce their own laws.[36] The extent to which Torres Strait Islanders exerted control over their lands, was crucial in the robust recognition of indigenous title in Australian courts in the 1990s.

The core challenge of working with *EUIV* to mod indigenous perspectives is that the game uses the sovereign nation-state as a fundamental actor and driver of history. These concepts—nation, state and sovereignty—have done a great deal of harm indigenous people and indigenous culture, as they are the conceptual tools that European colonial powers and white settlers used to justify displace Indigenous people from their lands and institute new forms of colonial governance that ignored traditional rights and native title. *EUIV* offers very little scope to challenge these perspectives, particularly without disrupting the drive to be "realistic,"[37] which could potentially just mean that "Indigenous Peoples of Oceania" is creating a richer experience for a simulation of colonialism.

CONCLUSION

Some strategy games, such as *EUIV*, have made some effort to portray indigenous people as autonomous people with rich cultural heritage through aesthetics, gameplay, written text and historical narratives. However, this has largely been achieved through targeted expansion packs to the game which provide finer grained detail on regional indigenous cultures, a measure that upholds the relegation of indigenous history to a secondary tier vis-à-vis the central European-focused storyline. Thus, there is a strong case for *EUIV* to include more indigenous content given that it increases the entertainment and educational value of the game for all of its players, as well as the profitability of the game to the developers and publishers. Furthermore, there is considerable scope for players to create their own game content through mods, as Rhett's "Indigenous People of Oceania" mod did. This process also adds to the player experience and profitability of *EUIV*. Through fuller and more detailed depictions of indigenous people, non-indigenous players may become better informed about otherwise unfamiliar indigenous histories. There is also potential for mods of these games to be used as expressive tools by indigenous people to portray their own perspectives on history. But it is here that the crucial problem arises: the central place of Eurocentric concepts such as nation, state and sovereignty in the design of games like *EUIV*. Modding *EUIV* from the indigenous perspective necessarily involves positioning indigenous culture in relation to the concepts of nation, state and sovereignty that were used by European colonial powers and white settlers to justify displacing indigenous people from their land by violence or other means.

34. Mervyn Meggitt, "Indigenous Forms of Government among the Australian Aborigines," *Bijdragen tot de taal-, land-en volkenkunde* 1 (1964): 163-180.
35. Jeremy Beckett, *Torres Strait Islanders: Custom and Colonialism* (Cambridge University Press, 1990), 115-116.
36. Ibid., 116.
37. Adrienne Shaw, "The Tyranny of Realism: Historical Representation and the Politics of Representation in Assassin s Creed III," *Loading...The Journal of the Canadian Game Studies Association* 9.14 (2015): 20.

ACKNOWLEDGEMENTS

We would like to acknowledge the Torres Strait Islander community in Queensland, Australia. We would also like to thank Jakub Majewski for his detailed feedback on early drafts of this chapter.

WORKS CITED

Apperley, Thomas. "Modding the historians' code: Historical verisimilitude and the counterfactual imagination." In *Playing with the Past: Videogames and the Simulation of History,* edited by Matthew Kapell and Andrew Elliot, 185-198. New York: Bloomsbury, 2013.

—. "Counterfactual Communities: Strategy Games, Paratexts and the Player's Experience of History. *Open Library of the Humanities,* 4.1 (2018): 1-22.

Apperley, Thomas and Chris Walsh. "What Digital Games and Literacy Have in Common: A Heuristic for Understanding Pupils' Gaming Literacy," *Literacy* 46.3 (2012): 115-122.

Banner, Stuart. "Why Terra Nullius? Anthropology and property law in early Australia." *Law and History Review* 23.1 (2005): 95-131.

Beckett, Jeremy. *Torres Strait Islanders: Custom and Colonialism*. Cambridge University Press, 1990.

Bembeneck, Emily Joy. "Phantasms of Rome: Video Games and Cultural Identity." In *Playing with the Past: Digital Games and the Simulation of History,* edited by Matthew Kapell and Andrew Elliott, 77-90. Bloomsbury, 2013.

Chapman, Adam. *Digital Games as History: How Videogames Represent the Past and Offer Access to Historical Practice*. Routledge, 2016.

Connor, Walker. "When Is a Nation?"" *Ethnic and Racial Studies* 13.1 (1990): 92-103.

Corntassel, Jeff. "Who Is Indigenous? 'Peoplehood' and Ethnonationalist Approaches to Rearticulating Indigenous Identity." *Nationalism and Ethnic Politics* 9.1 (2003): 75-100.

Dillon, Beth A. "Signifying the West: Colonialist Design in *Age of Empires III: The WarChiefs*." *Eludamos. Journal for Computer Game Culture* 2.1 (2008): 129-144.

Ehrmann, Markus. "The Status and Rights of Indigenous Peoples." *New Zealand Universities Law Review* 14.37 (1990): 463-496.

El-Nasr, Magy Seif and Brian K Smith. "Learning through Game Modding." *Computers in Entertainment (CIE)* 4.1 (2006): 1-20.

EUIV Wiki. "Modding," http://www.eu4wiki.com/Moddinghttp://www.eu4wiki.com/Modding.

Global Policy Forum. "What Is a 'State'?" *Global Policy Forum,* https://www.globalpolicy.org/nations-a-states/what-is-a-state.html.

Gurr, Ted Robert. *Peoples Versus States: Minorities at Risk in the New Century*. U.S. Institute of Peace Press, 2000.

Hassig, Ross. *Aztec Warfare: Imperial Expansion and Political Control*. University of Oklahoma Press, 1995.

History.com. "Native American Cultures." *A&E Networks*, http://www.history.com/topics/native-american-history/native-american-cultures.

HOI4 Wiki. "Modding—Hearts of Iron 4 Wiki," http://www.hoi4wiki.com/Modding.

Lameman, Beth Aileen, Jason E Lewis and Skawennati Fragnito. "Skins 1.0: A Curriculum for Designing Games with First Nations Youth." *Proceedings of the International Academic Conference on the Future of Game Design and Technology* (2010), 105-112.

LaPensée, Elizabeth. "Video Games Encourage Indigenous Cultural Expression." *The Conversation*, 22 March, 2017.

Majewski, Jakub. "Oldest Culture, Newest Medium: What Emerges from the Clash?" *Proceedings of Digital Games Research Association of Australia 2016 National Conference: Tensions*, Swinburne University of Technology, Melbourne (November 2016).

Meggitt, Mervyn J. "Indigenous Forms of Government among the Australian Aborigines." *Bijdragen tot de taal-, land-en volkenkunde.*1ste Afl (1964): 163-80.

Monterrat, Baptiste, Elise Lavoué and Sébastien George. "Learning Game 2.0: Support for Game Modding as a Learning Activity." *Proceedings of the 6th European Conference on Games Based Learning*, (2012): 340-347.

Mukherjee, Souvik. *Video Games and Storytelling: Reading Games and Playing Books*. Palgrave, 2015.

—. "Playing Subaltern: Video Games and Postcolonialism." *Games and Culture* 13.5 (2016): 1-17.

Murray, Padmini Ray and Chris Hand. "Making Culture: Locating the Digital Humanities in India." *Visible Language* 49.3 (2015): 141-155.

National Aboriginal and Islander Health Organisation. "Sovereignty," www.kooriweb.org/foley/news/story8.html.

Paradox Interactive. "Paradox Celebrates International Women's Day with DLC." Paradox Interactive, http://www.europauniversalis4.com/news/paradox-celebrates-international-women's-day-dlc.

Paul, James A. "Nations and States Part 1: Nations and States—What's the Difference?," *Global Policy*, https://www.globalpolicy.org/component/content/article/172/30345.html.

Pobłocki, Kacper. "Becoming-State." *Focaal-European Journal of Anthropology* 39 (2002): 163-77.

Rasmussen, Peter Ravn. "Nations or States: An Attempt at Definition." *Nations, States and Politics*, http://www.scholiast.org/nations/whatisanation.html.

Renan, Ernest. "What is a Nation?." In Ernest Renan, *Qu'est-ce qu'une nation?*, translated by Ethan Rundell. Presses-Pocket, 1992.

Scacchi, Walt. "Computer Game Mods, Modders, Modding, and the Mod Scene." *First Monday* 15.5 (2010).

Shaw, Adrienne. "The Tyranny of Realism: Historical representation and the politics of representation in Assassin's Creed III." *Loading... The Journal of the Canadian Game Studies Association* 9.14 (2015): 4-24.

Smith, Anthony D. "When Is a Nation." *Geopolitics* 7.2 (2002): 5-32.

Thomson, Janice E. "State Sovereignty in International Relations: Bridging the Gap between Theory and Empirical Research." *International Studies Quarterly* 39.2 (1995): 213-33.

Tragula, Trin. "Eu4 – Development Diary – 2nd of May 2017." Paradox Interactive, last modified 2 May 2017, https://forum.paradoxplaza.com/forum/index.php?threads/eu4-development-diary-2nd-of-may-2017.1018557/.

United Nations Permanent Forum on Indigenous Issues. "Fact Sheet: Who Are Indigenous Peoples?." United Nations Permanent Forum on Indigenous Issues, 2006, https://www.un.org/esa/socdev/unpfii/documents/5session_factsheet1.pdf.

Uricchio, William. "Simulation, History, and Computer Games." In *Handbook of Computer Game Studies*, edited by Joost Raessens and Jeffrey Goldstein, 327-338. MIT Press, 2005.

Weber, Max. *Politics as a Vocation*. Fortress Press, 1968.

Wilmer, Franke. *The Indigenous Voice in World Politics: Since Time Immemorial*. Sage, 1993.

Yucel, Ibrahim, Joseph Zupko and Magy Seif El-Nasr. "IT Education, Girls and Game Modding." *Interactive Technology and Smart Education* 3.2 (2006): 143-56.

LUDOGRAPHY

Blizzard. *Warcraft III: Reign of Chaos*. Blizzard, 2002.

Ensemble Studios. *Age of Empires*. Microsoft, 1997.

—. *Age of Empires III: The WarChiefs*. Microsoft Game Studios, 2006.

Firaxis Games. *Sid Meier's Civilization IV*. 2K Games, 2005.

Krome. *Ty the Tasmanian Tiger*. Electronic Arts, 2002.

Loban, Rhett "Indigenous People of Oceania Mod." *Europa Universalis IV* [mod], https://forum.paradoxplaza.com/forum/index.php?threads/mod-indigenous-people-of-oceania.902625/.

NIL Entertainment. *Survival Island 3: Australia Story*. NIL Entertainment, 2015.

Paradox Development Studios. Clausewitz Maya Exporter. Paradox Interactive, 2016.

—. *Europa Universalis IV*. Paradox Interactive, 2013.

—. *Europa Universalis IV: Conquest of Paradise*. Paradox Interactive, 2014.

—. *Europa Universalis IV: El Dorado*. Paradox Interactive, 2015.

—. *Hearts of Iron IV*. Paradox Interactive, 2016.

SCE San Diego Studio. *The Mark of Kri*. Sony Computer Entertainment, 2002.

Upper One Games. *Never Alone*. E-Line Media, 2014.

Xylozi, zitres and Vauvin. "A Song of Ice and Fire Mod" *Europa Universalis IV* [mod].

DIGITAL MASKS AND LUCHA LIBRE

VISUAL SUBJECTIFICATION AND ALLEGORY OF MEXICO IN VIDEO GAMES

DANIEL CALLEROS VILLARREAL

Hay hombres que luchan un día y son buenos.
Hay hombres que luchan un año y son mejores.
Hay quienes luchan muchos años y son muy buenos.
Pero los hay quienes luchan todos los domingos...
¡Esos son los chidos!

-Botellita de Jerez

Based on their conditions of production and loci of enunciation, video games are often treated as cultural objects that pertain exclusively to the global north. As with other mass media, the representational nature of video games is instrumental in the articulation of collective identities, providing spaces and elements that further define subjectivities.[1] However, as stated in Phillip Penix-Tadsen's introduction to this anthology, it is imperative to resort to interdisciplinary lenses that integrate perspectives from the periphery in order to open up the possibility to focus on cultural aspects previously ignored or marginalized.[2] While video games are a space in which identities, both central and peripheral, can be constructed, the representational elements employed in the articulation of said identities is skewed towards dominant normative notions of gender and race.[3] In his work on cultural ludology, Penix-Tadsen has identified the range of representations of Latin Americans in three categories: contras, tomb raiders and *luchadores*.[4] However, he also argues that it is imperative to reexamine how the cultural context in which video games are played can affect interpretation and forge diverse structures that guide meaning-formation processes in markets outside of the global north.[5] In a similar light, William Nericcio brings up the need to revisit representations of Mexicans across different media objects in order to better understand their origin and social impact, thus creating spaces of discussion that allow for deeper readings.[6] Taking up this task, this article scrutinizes the digital presence of the *lucha libre* [Mexican professional wrestling] mask in order to demonstrate how an essentializing representational practice also offers the possibility for the reappropriation of symbolic objects through the negotiation of cultural elements in the process of designing, marketing and playing video games.

Taking into consideration the complex power relations within the representation of Other subjects and the production of meaning through player interaction with video games, this chapter analyzes the visual and narrative construction of the Mexican subjects represented through the image of

1. Imma Tubella, "Television, the Internet, and the Construction of Identity," in *The Network Society: A Cross-Cultural Perspective*, ed. Manuel Castells (Edward Elgar, 2004).
2. Lev Manovich, *The Language of New Media* (MIT Press, 2002).
3. Jon Dovey and Helen W. Kennedy, *Game Cultures: Computer Games as New Media* (Open University Press, 2006).
4. Phillip Penix-Tadsen, "Latin American Ludology: Why We Should Take Video Games Seriously (and When We Shouldn't)," *Latin American Research Review* 48.1 (2013): 174-90.
5. Phillip Penix-Tadsen, *Cultural Code: Video Games and Latin America* (MIT Press, 2016).
6. William Nericcio, *Tex[t]-Mex: Seductive Hallucinations of the "Mexican" in America* (University of Texas Press, 2007).

the *luchador* [wrestler], from its historical and textual significations to the branching onto other mediations. As a point of departure, this article argues the importance of the lucha libre mask as a symbolic token for Mexico and for video game designers in general. From there, the focus will shift to the many appearances of luchadores from the earliest games to the eighth generation titles (meaning games for consoles released since 2012, including Sony's PlayStation 4, Microsoft's Xbox One and Nintendo's Wii U), highlighting criteria in the articulation of the characters and the cultural value assigned to the mask. Finally, this chapter analyzes the ways in which the peripheral culture enters the center to gain prominence and, in some cases, transform the video game into a digital interactive text through which didactic and persuasive cultural experiences, as well as self-representation, are possible.

"MASKED" CULTURE, MEN IN TIGHTS AND REPRESENTATIONAL FETISHES

In Mexico, the lucha libre mask is present in every conceivable social space and evokes a network of meanings engrained in the social imaginary. In the same manner, the symbolism of lucha libre has become a trope for Mexico in the global north and is used recurrently as a representational technique when it comes to the articulation of Mexican identities. Lucha libre and its iconography serve the purpose of synthesizing complex cultural contexts into simplified symbolic systems embedded in gamespace, facilitating the process of cultural representation for game designers. In other words, the lucha libre mask serves as a stereotyping fetish through which networks of historical, political and cultural discourses can be projected. In the terms of Homi Bhabha, when a stereotype is [re]articulated the represented peripheral identities reflect the identity of the center. Thus, the articulation of the Other through a fetishized image is a discursive construction that controls the identity of the represented group based on a dominant ideological framework. However, the representational fetish also has an ambivalence that creates fissures that allow for the disavowal of the stereotyping discourse.[7]

Although the remediation of cultural objects for representational purposes in digital media can divest them of their cultural value,[8] this practice also allows the gamer to easily identify images, characters and rhetorical constructs.[9] As a cultural motif, the lucha libre mask possesses basic characteristics through which recognizable digital identities are articulated. Based on its deep roots in the Mexican social imaginary, lucha libre has become a synecdoche of Mexican popular culture as a sporting practice and as a spectacle. Through the mask, Levi argues, it is possible to evoke allusions of Mexico and its cultural iconography.[10] Hence, the luchador *enmascarado* [masked wrestler] has become a trope for Mexico across mediatized representations in Latin America and the United States. The luchador is the product of a meaning-formation process accentuated by the visual aspects of a masked-faceless body. However, it simultaneously allows the integration of symbolic elements to create a character because "the mask helps to foreground some elements of performance and to mute others."[11] The mask is, therefore, a tool through which meaning articulation and objectifying processes are synchronized.

In Mexico, the *máscara* seeps into social spaces beyond the wrestling ring: musicians compose songs for luchadores or feature them in their music videos, enmascarados fulfill the role of comic book characters, television personalities, action movie heroes and even real-life activists who fight for a variety of social issues that range from animal cruelty and pollution to housing practices and

7. Homi Bhabha, *The Location of Culture* (Routledge, 2004).
8. Geoff King and Tanya Krzywinska, *Tomb Raiders and Space Invaders: Videogame Forms and Contexts* (I. B. Tauris, 2006).
9. Rachael Hutchinson, "Performing the Self: Subverting the Binary in Combat Games," *Games and Culture* 2.4 (2007): 283-99.
10. Heather Levi, *The World of Lucha Libre: Secrets, Revelations, and Mexican National Identity* (Duke University Press, 2008).
11. Levi, *The World of Lucha Libre*, 113.

gay rights.[12] The lucha libre mask has provided Mexicans with a cultural mechanism to enhance performative elements and create their own heroes. While Batman and Superman fought to keep safe their respective urban centers in the United States, Mexico's protection rested on El Santo's shoulders. Mexican intellectuals Octavio Paz and Samuel Ramos regarded this luchador, characterized by his trademark silver-lamé mask and his graciousness in the ring, as a new archetype that provided a new form of national masculinity. For his fans, however, El Santo was an influential presence that provided entertainment and taught them values that helped them deal with life in the growing urban centers of mid-20th-century Mexico.[13] In 1952, through the pen of Mexican artist José Guadalupe Cruz, el Santo's iconic mask went from the wrestling ring to the pages of his own comic book, *Santo, Emascarado de Plata*, which would be published for three and a half decades. In the same year, El Santo along with another luchador—Huracán Ramírez—kicked off the genre of luchador films, low-budget movies in which enmascarados would fight the evil in the shape of Martians, insane scientists and a mishmash of monsters.

El Santo and the luchadores that starred in the approximately 150 films released from the early 1950s to the mid-1990s became cultural icons not only in Mexico, but also became internationally recognizable.[14] Luchadores have also been featured prominently in American popular culture. For instance, the fictitious character Ángel de la Plata from Guillermo del Toro's cable television show *The Strain* (20th Television, 2014) is clearly based on El Santo and the luchador films of the 1960s. Other popular culture texts expressly created around the luchador include TV shows like Cartoon Network's *¡Mucha lucha!* (Warner Bros., 2002) and Rob Zombie's *The Haunted World of El Superbeasto* (Film Roman, 2009). It is not difficult to see how the luchador has become an easily recognizable symbol and why it has been mediated across platform outlets, also materializing in the digital world.

THE DIGITALIZATION OF THE MASK: A HISTORICAL OVERVIEW OF LUCHADORES IN VIDEO GAMES

The first video game representation of a Mexican character as a luchador appeared in the late 80s in the first wrestling title for the Nintendo Entertainment System (NES), *Pro Wrestling* (Nintendo, 1986). It was a masked wrestler named Star Man who wore a bright pink mask adorned with a purple star and whose listed origin read: "Mexico?" His *moveset*—the term referring to the collection of attacks and techniques a character has available, each of which is triggered by a specific control command programed by the developers—included flashy aerial techniques, characteristic of the lucha libre style. In 1990, the NES added *Tecmo World Wrestling* (Tecmo, 1989) to their game lineup. Said title included combatants representing countries around the globe. From Mexico hailed El Tigre, a luchador sporting a tiger-themed mask and matching cape. Those familiar with New Japan Pro-Wrestling (NJPW) and All Japan Pro Wrestling (AJPW) would notice the glaring similarities between El Tigre and famed Japanese wrestler Tiger Mask. However, to gamers who had no previous exposure to NJPW or AJPW, El Tigre could evoke the image of a *cuāuhocēlōtl*, an Aztec jaguar warrior. Three years later, another Mexican character arrived in an arcade game titled *Saturday Night Slam Masters* (*SNSM*) (Capcom, 1993), from Acapulco, Mexico: El Stingray (see Image 1.6.1). Unlike El Tigre, however, El Stingray was based on the real-life wrestler Lizmark, an actual Mexican luchador. The design of this *SNSM* character was faithful to its inspiration down to the costume color palette, his physical attributes and his presumed city of origin.

Beyond wrestling games alone, luchadores represent Mexican subjects in other video game genres. In

12. "Super Barrio," *Hemispheric Institute: Instituto Hemisférico de Performance & Política*, 16 October 2014, http://hemisphericinstitute.org/journal/1_1/sb.html.
13. Anne Rubenstein, "El Santo's Strange Career," *The Mexico Reader: History, Culture, Politics* (Duke University Press, 2002).
14. Carlos Monsiváis and Gabriel Rodríguez, *Lucha Libre: Masked Superstars of Mexican Wrestling* (Trilce, 2005).

Image 1.6.1. Mexican characters in early wrestling computer games. From left to right: Pro Wrestling (1987), Temco World Wrestling (1990) and Saturday Night Slam Masters (1993).

the action-adventure title *Saints Row: The Third* (THQ, 2011), the player encounters a group known as "Luchadores," a criminal organization whose members wear wrestling masks (see Image 1.6.2). Their leader is Killbane, an American man who fled to Mexico after killing an opponent in a wrestling match. During his time south of the border, Killbane adopted a luchador mask and returned to the fictional city of Steelport in the United States to command a criminal ring of drug trafficking, gambling and arms dealing. Although the gang members' nationalities are revealed as non-Mexican in some cases and not specified in others, their origins are rendered irrelevant, since they all are "Mexicanized" through the use of the lucha libre mask.

In the fighting genre, video game designers and developers recurrently resort to the luchador trope in order to personify Mexican characters. In this type of game, the digital subjects' nationalities are often referenced, integrating them in different narrative spheres that range from in-game stories and iconography to promotional campaigns built around specific characters' based on their country of origin,[15] The *Street Fighter* (*SF*) (Capcom, 1987-), *Tekken* (Namco, 1994-) and *The King of Fighters* (*KoF*) (SNK, 1994-) franchises represent an important collection of titles in the genre based on their longevity, influence in other games, remediation in other popular culture texts and their economic and critical success worldwide.[16] Although the games have a faithful consumer base spread wide outside of their loci of production, most of the selectable characters represented are depicted as American or Japanese. Of the more than 220 characters that have populated the rosters of these games since the early 90s, fourteen are Latin American: five Brazilians, a Colombian who lives in Brazil and seven Mexicans. Although Japanese and American characters are portrayed in a rather diversified manner—law enforcement officers, soldiers, mercenaries, secret agents, martial artists, boxers, movie stars, athletes, musicians, Casanovas, businessmen, etc.—Brazilians have a tendency to be capoeira practitioners and Mexicans are usually depicted as luchadores. With the exception of *Street Fighter*'s T. Hawk—an indigenous man from an undetermined region in the Arizona-Sonora desert—all the other Mexicans have a strong association with lucha libre. After T. Hawk flopped as a character, *SF* publisher Capcom went back to the drawing board and came up with El Fuerte, a Mexican wrestler reminiscent of both iconic luchador El Santo and Nacho from the American comedy film *Nacho Libre* (Paramount, 2006).

15. See "KOF14 Developers Interview by Famitsu, pt2," *Mad Man's Café*, 23 August 2017, http://www.mmcafe.com/news/posts/10212.html.
16. "Capcom Platinum Titles," *Capcom*, 24 February 2016, http://www.capcom.co.jp/ir/english/business/million.html; see also "Game Database," *VGChartz.com*, 13 May 2015, http://www.vgchartz.com/gamedb/.

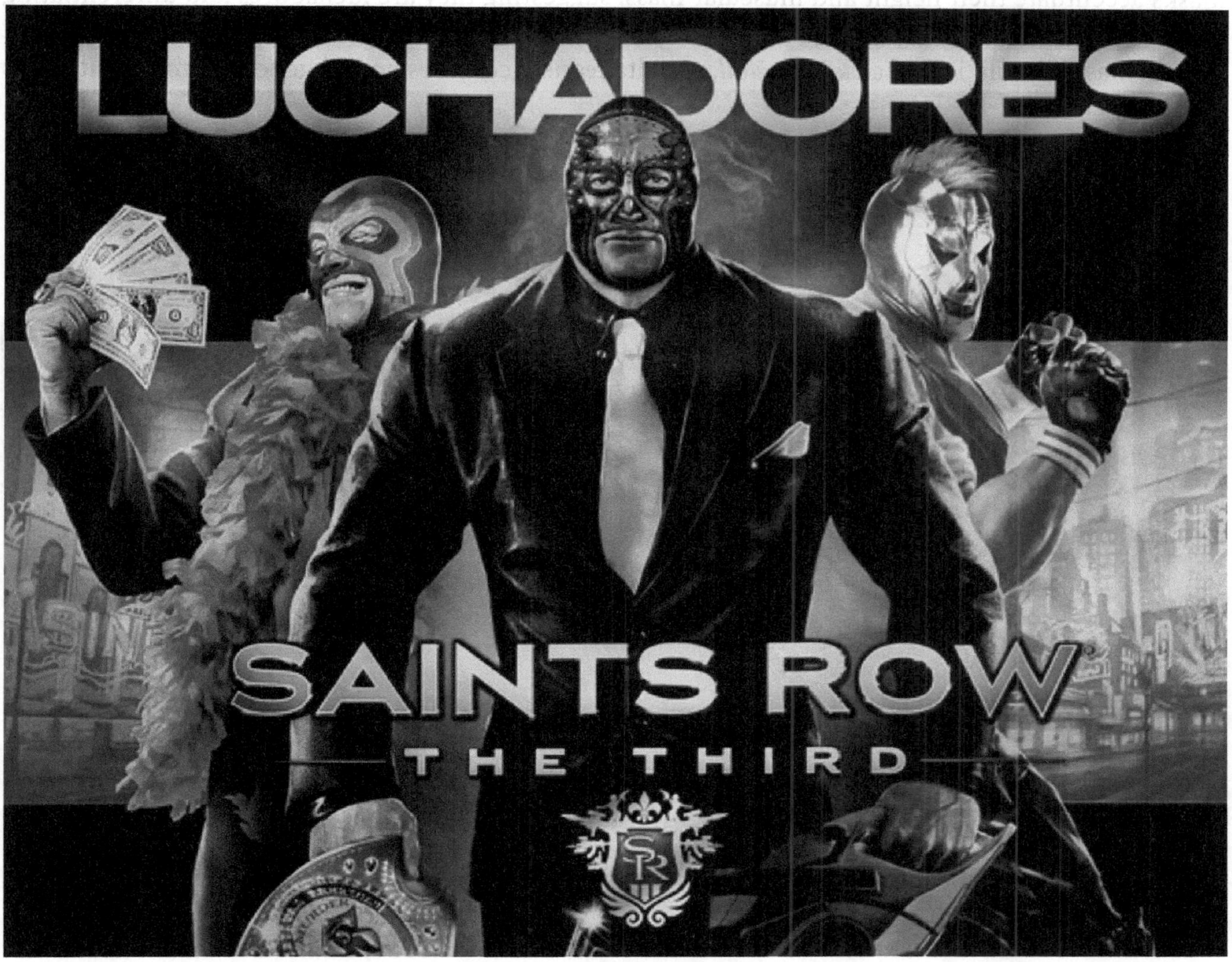

Image 1.6.2. "Luchadores," one of the gangs behind the criminal activity in Saints Row: The Third.

In Namco's *Tekken* series there have been two Mexican characters: King and Armor King, both of whom use realistic feline wrestling masks. The *KoF* saga has three Mexican characters in its ranks: Ángel,[17] Tizoc,[18] and *Ramón;*[19] Successive Characters: Ramon," *The King of Fighters Official Web Site*, 19 June 2016, http://kofaniv.snkplaymore.co.jp/english/character/index.php?num=ramon; see also "Team Mexico: Ramón," *The King of Fighters XIV Official Website*, 22 June 2016, https://www.snkplaymore.co.jp/us/games/kof-xiv/characters/ramon.php. the latter two are luchadores. The Mexican wrestlers in these fighting games are encoded through the articulation of recognizable signifiers. In *Mythologies*, Roland Barthes argued that "[t]he physique of the wrestlers [...] constitutes a basic sign, which like a seed contains the whole fight [...] The different strata of meaning throw light on each other, and form the most intelligible of spectacles."[20] *Tekken*'s King and Armor King's bodies as well as *KoF* 's Tizoc's physique—robust men wearing boots and tights—are in themselves signifiers that allow them to pass as wrestlers. However, their

17. "KOF Successive Characters: Angel," *The King of Fighters Official Web Site*, 19 June 2016, http://kofaniv.snk-corp.co.jp/english/character/index.php?num=angel; see also "Team Mexico: Ángel," *The King of Fighters XIV Official Website*, 22 June 2016, https://www.snkplaymore.co.jp/us/games/kof-xiv/characters/angel.php.

18. In *KoF XIV* (2016) Tizoc appears under his alter ego persona: The King of Dinosaurs. However, it is made clear through in-game narratives that The King of Dinosaurs is, in fact, Tizoc, the same man who would wrestle under the moniker of "The Griffon Mask." See "*KOF* Successive Characters: Tizoc," *The King of Fighters Official Web Site*, 19 June 2016, http://kofaniv.snkplaymore.co.jp/english/character/index.php?num=tizoc; see also "Team Mexico: King of Dinosaurs," *The King of Fighters XIV Official Website*, 22 June 2016, https://www.snkplaymore.co.jp/us/games/kof-xiv/characters/kod.php.

19. "*KOF*

20. Roland Barthes, *Mythologies* (Noonday, 1957), 18.

masks accentuate their height and muscular mass, suggesting they are luchadores and differentiating them from American and Japanese wrestlers. These characters' visual construction, whether or not intended as a simulation of a *cuāuhocēlōtl*, simultaneously conjures an indigenous component to his identity (see Image 1.6.3).

Image 1.6.3. King (left) and Armor King (right) about to suplex Kazuya in Tekken Tag Tournament 2.

DETERRITORIALIZATION AND LUCHA LIBRE: WHEN MEXICAN CULTURE ENTERS GAMESPACE

The juxtaposition of lucha libre and a pre-Hispanic past, as well as the dynamics of representation and cultural negotiation, cannot be seen more clearly than in the "metroidvania" game *Guacamelee!* (Drinkbox Studios, 2013), developed by Toronto-based company Drinkbox Studios. The game is themed around the world of lucha libre and its symbology, and from the beginning of the game, images of luchadores are scattered throughout the world of *Guacamelee!*

Soon after the beginning of the game, Carlos Calaca kills Juan Aguacate, sending him to the world of the dead, which turns out to be an alternate version of the world of the living. The action serves to introduce another trope of Mexican culture: el Día de los Muertos. Shortly after his death, Juan meets a masked luchadora by the name of Tostada, who announces that "The Mask" has chosen him to put a stop to the chaos Calaca has generated. Juan then transforms into "Luchador," an evil-fighting enmascarado, complete with bleeding heart tattoos, tights, wrestling boots and a championship belt. As an anthropological object, that the unworn mask is in itself an entity of its own, with the potential to project preconceived meanings and power.[21] While Juan was swiftly defeated with a single attack earlier, Luchador gained immeasurable strength by wearing The Mask.

Although *Guacamelee!* was developed by a Canadian studio, it materializes the vision of the Mexican-

21. John Emigh, *Masked Performance: The Play of Self and Other in Ritual and Theatre* (University of Pennsylvania Press, 1996), xviii.

Image 1.6.4. Fervor for the luchador image in Guacamelee!

born artist and illustrator Augusto Quijano, who wanted to create a game where the luchador would serve as the heroic figure in a digital world saturated with references from his own cultural experiences.[22] Eduardo Marisca argues that *Guacamelee!* provides the gamer with an unequivocal experience of the dynamic nature of cultural negotiation. He says the game presents culture as being "permanently under redesign," suggesting an "open, complex system, rather than a closed, defined set of traditions."[23]

Lucha libre has also been the vehicle for Mexican video game designers to internationalize their product. *Lucha Libre AAA: Héroes del Ring* (Konami, 2010), developed by Mexican studio Immersion Software and Graphics (then known as Slang), is to date the only video game widely distributed through a major transnational publisher. Although the studio director, Federico Beyer, had Latin America in mind as the primary market for the title,[24] the game ended up providing gamers in the global north with a cultural context that distinguished and differentiated lucha libre from traditional American wrestling. The game expanded on the traditional mechanics of the wrestling genre. Beyond the introduction of actual luchadores and a basic creation mode where the gamer can design masks and outfits for their characters, *Héroes del Ring* provides a historical—though, not necessarily accurate—overview of the cultural practices and traditions surrounding lucha libre. Penix-Tadsen argues that this title offers "the player an opportunity for the acquisition of contextualized cultural knowledge through the process of play."[25] The player selects a luchador and advances through the storylines by winning matches and completing specific in-game tasks. Periodically, the game displays documentary-style videos where luchadores explain the nuances of lucha libre as a Mexican cultural phenomenon. When it comes to technologically advanced cultural objects in which Latin American subjects are represented, it is generally assumed that they are products of the global north and have

22. Augusto Quijano, "The Art of Making Guacamelee! From Folklore to Finish," Presentation at Game Developers Conference, 2014, http://www.gdcvault.com/play/1020419/The-Art-of-Making-Guacamelee.
23. Eduardo Marisca, "Developing Game Worlds: Gaming, Technology and Innovation in Peru," Master's Thesis, Massachusetts Institute of Technology, 2014, 142.
24. Brandon Sheffield, "Q&A: Federico Beyer On Targeting Latino Market with Slang, Lucha Libre," *Gamasutra*, 9 June 2010, http://www.gamasutra.com/view/news/119723/QA_Frederico_Beyer_On_Targeting_Latino_Market_With_Slang_Lucha_Libre.php.
25. Penix-Tadsen, *Cultural Code*, 42.

little cultural significance from a Latin American perspective. However, it is possible to see that the cultural dynamics that come into play in the creation of these are not as unilateral as once thought, particularly when clearly recognizable symbols—such as the lucha libre mask—are involved.[26] That is to say, these cultural objects serve as a clear example illustration how media products from the global north are influenced and modified by localized cultural practices that originate in the different markets in which said media products circulate, including the global south.[27]

ONE, TWO, THREE: GAME OVER?

García Canclini argues that globalization diminishes the importance of foundational myths and national boundaries to give way to electronic media as the primary source of cultural identity.[28] In the same way in which García Canclini questions how local cultural identities are maintained while they are simultaneously exposed to globalization, it is imperative to explore the dynamics in which disembedded cultural objects are reintroduced into their original locales. The video game (re)produces and projects an essentialized and fixed representation of otherness without allowing for a space to disavow the representation from within the mass culture object itself. While it is possible to undermine the stereotype by accentuating the fissures in the hegemonic discourse that shaped it,[29] the most effective practice comes in the form of gamer interaction with the video game. In other words, the players "do not merely consume a pre-established piece of media, but instead are active participants in the creation of their experience through interaction with the underlying code during gameplay."[30] Even though the cybertyping of the Mexican subjects in video games occurs within a representational system that conditions the used images and their annexed meanings, the intended interpretation does not necessarily reconcile with the meaning produced within different social contexts when the gamer plays the game and experiences the animations, iconography and narrative.

Furthermore, in the cutthroat industry of video games, technological advancement and polished graphics do not guarantee commercial success, as gamers are more attracted to immersive stories, gameplay and replayability. Hence, even when it could appear that the consumers do not have an impact on the shaping of video game titles, game developers are actively researching methods through which they better appeal to their consumer base. For example, when gamers considered that Capcom had not included enough Latin American fighters in their crossover game *Street Fighter X Tekken* (Capcom, 2012), Don Ramón—a character from the popular TV show *El Chavo del Ocho* (Televisa, 1971)—made its way into the roster of the PC version of the game. As Thaiane Olivera, José Messias and Diego Amaral argue in their chapter in this anthology, *modding* (or software modification) serves "encourage the emergence of affective communities and the subversion of representations in the pop culture by inserting local references," showing that video games are not fixed cultural objects and can be transformed to accommodate the desires of players from different markets. In *The King of Fighters XIV* (SNK, 2016), SNK rendered a localized stage for Team Mexico: The Dynamite Ring, a lucha libre ring surrounded by *calaveras* and other Day of the Dead decorations in a recreation of a colonial plaza in Guanajuato, México. With *Tekken*, Namco decided to allow gamers to visually customize their characters. Among the graphic elements available for King, the gamer can add a championship belt and an alternate mask, which replaces the realistic jaguar mask with a more traditional, feline-themed *máscara*.

26. Néstor García Canclini, *Consumidores y ciudadanos: Conflictos multiculturales de la globalización* (Grijalbo, 1995).
27. Yuri Takhteyev, *Coding Places: Software Practice in a South American City* (MIT Press, 2012).
28. García Canclini, *Consumidores y ciudadanos*, 95.
29. Bhabha, *The Location of Culture*.
30. Gordon Calleja, *In-Game: From Immersion to Incorporation* (MIT Press, 2011), 55

James Paul Gee has argued that game designers must follow certain principles in use of symbolic materials: "To understand or produce any word, symbol, image, or artifact in a given semiotic domain, a person must be able to situate the meaning of that word, symbol, image, or artifact within embodied experiences of action, interaction in or about the domain."[31] In this respect, the lucha libre mask is a cultural object that circulates materially and symbolically, metonymically representing Mexico across media platforms. While the lucha libre mask is intended to serve as a representational fetish that is easily recognizable and through which specific national identities can be articulated, it is also an important symbolic object that enables cultural negotiation in the world of video games.

WORKS CITED

Barthes, Roland. *Mythologies*. Noonday, 1957.

Bhabha, Homi K. *The Location of Culture*. Routledge, 2004.

Bolter, Jay David and Richard Grusin. *Remediation: Understanding New Media*. MIT Press, 1999.

Calleja, Gordon. *In-Game: From Immersion to Incorporation*. MIT Press, 2011.

Cervera, Humberto and Quesnel, Jacinto. "Mexico." In *Video Games Around the World*, edited by Mark J. P. Wolf. MIT Press, 2015.

Crawford, Chris. *The Art of Computer Game Design*. Osborne/McGraw-Hill, 1984.

Dovey, Jon and Helen W. Kennedy. *Game Cultures: Computer Games as New Media*. Open University Press, 2006.

Emigh, John. *Masked Performance: The Play of Self and Other in Ritual and Theatre*. University of Pennsylvania Press, 1996.

Frasca, Gonzalo. "Ludology Meets Narratology: Similitude and Differences between (Video) Games and Narrative." *Ludology.org.*, 1999, http://www.ludology.org/articles/ludology.htm.

—. "Simulation versus Narrative: Introduction to Ludology." In *The Video Game Theory Reader*, edited by Mark J. P. Wolf and Bernard Perron, 221-236. Routledge, 2003.

Galloway, Alexander R. *Gaming: Essays on Algorithmic Culture*. University of Minnesota Press, 2006.

García Canclini, Néstor. *Consumidores y ciudadanos: Conflictos multiculturales de la globalización*. Grijalbo, 1995.

Gee, James Paul. "Semiotic Domains: Is Playing Video Games a 'Waste of Time'?." In *The Game Design Reader: A Rules of Play Anthology*, edited by Katie Salen and Eric Zimmerman. MIT Press, 2006.

Hutchinson, Rachael. "Performing the Self: Subverting the Binary in Combat Games." *Games and Culture* 2.4 (2007): 283-99.

King, Geoff and Tanya Krzywinska. *Tomb Raiders and Space Invaders: Videogame Forms and Contexts*. I. B. Tauris, 2006.

31. James Paul Gee, "Semiotic Domains: Is Playing Video Games a 'Waste of Time'?," in *The Game Design Reader: A Rules of Play Anthology*, eds. Katie Salen and Eric Zimmerman (MIT Press, 2006), 240.

Levi, Heather. *The World of Lucha Libre: Secrets, Revelations, and Mexican National Identity.* Duke University Press, 2008.

Manovich, Lev. *The Language of New Media*. MIT Press, 2002.

Marisca, Eduardo. "Developing Game Worlds: Gaming, Technology and Innovation in Peru." Master's Thesis, Massachusetts Institute of Technology, 2014, http://cmsw.mit.edu/wp/wp-content/uploads/2016/06/233509575-Eduardo-Marisca-Developing-Game-Worlds-Gaming-Technology-and-Innovation-in-Peru.pdf.

McAllister, Ken S. *Game Work: Language, Power, and Computer Game Culture*. University of Alabama Press, 2004.

Monsiváis, Carlos and Gabriel Rodríguez. *Lucha Libre: Masked Superstars of Mexican Wrestling*. Trilce, 2005.

Nakamura, Lisa. *Cybertypes: Race, Ethnicity, and Identity on the Internet*. Routledge, 2002.

Nericcio, William Anthony. *Tex{t}-Mex: Seductive Hallucinations of the "Mexican" in America*. University of Texas Press, 2007.

Newman, James. *Videogames*. Routledge, 2004.

Ohmann, Richard M. *Selling Culture: Magazines, Markets, and Class at the Turn of the Century*. Verso, 1996.

Penix-Tadsen, Phillip. *Cultural Code: Video Games and Latin America*. MIT Press, 2016.

—. "Latin American Ludology: Why We Should Take Video Games Seriously (and When We Shouldn't)." *Latin American Research Review* 48.1 (2013): 174-190.

Rubenstein, Anne. "El Santo's Strange Career." In *The Mexico Reader: History, Culture, Politics*, edited by Gilbert M. Joseph and Timothy J. Henderson. Duke University Press, 2002.

Takhteyev, Yuri. *Coding Places: Software Practice in a South American City*. MIT Press, 2012.

Tubella, Imma. "Television, the Internet, and the Construction of Identity." *The Network Society: A Cross-Cultural Perspective*, edited by Manuel Castells. Edward Elgar, 2004.

Wark, McKinzie. *GAM3R 7H3ORY*. Harvard University Press, 2007.

Wilde, Tyler. "The Worst Street Fighter Characters Ever." *Game Radar*, 21 March 2008, http://www.gamesradar.com/the-worst-street-fighter-characters-ever/2/.

Wolf, Mark J. P. *The Medium of the Video Game*. University of Texas Press, 2001.

LUDOGRAPHY

Backbone. *Super Street Fighter II Turbo HD Remix*. Capcom, 2008.

Brezzasoft. *The King of Fighters 2001*. SNK, 2001.

Capcom. *Saturday Night Slam Masters*. Capcom, 1993.

—. *Street Fighter Alpha 3*. Capcom, 1998.

—. *Street Fighter II*. Capcom, 1991.

—. *Street Fighter IV*. Capcom, 2009.

—. *Super Street Fighter II*. Capcom, 1993.

—. *Super Street Fighter II Turbo*. Capcom, 1994.

—. *Super Street Fighter IV*. Capcom, 2010.

—. *Super Street Fighter IV: Arcade Edition*. Capcom, 2011.

—. *Street Fighter X Tekken*. Capcom, 2012.

Drinkbox Studios. *Guacamelee!*. Drinkbox Studios, 2013.

Namco. *Tekken*. Namco Bandai, 1994.

—. *Tekken 2*. Namco, 1996.

—. *Tekken 3*. Namco, 1998.

—. *Tekken 4*. Namco, 2002.

—. *Tekken 5: Dark Resurrection*. Namco, 2007.

—. *Tekken Tag Tournament*. Namco, 2002.

Namco Bandai. *Tekken 6*. Namco Bandai, 2009.

—. *Tekken Revolution*. Namco Bandai, 2013.

—. *Tekken Tag Tournament 2*. Namco Bandai, 2012.

Nintendo. *Pro Wrestling*. Nintendo, 1987.

SNK. *Art of Fighting 3: The Path of the Warrior*. SNK, 2006. =

—. *Garou: Mark of the Wolves*. SNK, 1999.

—. *The King of Fighters '94*. SNK, 1994.

—. *The King of Fighters 2000*. SNK, 2000.

—. *The King of Fighters 2002*. Playmore, 2002.

—. *The King of Fighters XIV*. SNK, 2016.

SNK Playmore. *The King of Fighters 2002: Unlimited Match*. SNK Playmore, 2009.

—. *The King of Fighters Neowave.* SNK Playmore, 2005.

—. *The King of Fighters 2003.* SNK Playmore, 2003.

—. *The King of Fighters XI.* SNK Playmore, 2007.

—. *The King of Fighters XIII.* SNK Playmore, 2010.

Temco. *Temco World Wrestling.* Temco, 1990.

Volition. *Saints Row: The Third.* THQ, 2011.

PART TWO: GAMING COMMUNITIES AND SUBCULTURES

NOT WAITING FOR OTHER PLAYERS ANYMORE

GAMING IN THE MIDDLE EAST BETWEEN ASSIGNATION, RESISTANCE AND NORMALIZATION

PIERRE-ALAIN CLÉMENT

In the last decade, ludology has expanded its object of analysis, mirroring an expansion in the worldwide use of gaming technologies. Though they are sometimes thought of as a product of pop culture produced and consumed in the industrialized countries of the global north, video games have been used extensively in regions sometimes characterized as peripheral or semi-peripheral, including Latin America, Africa, the Middle East and Asia. These regions have been the field of actual wars and thus actual propaganda from which topoi have been integrated into the products of global pop culture: movies, television series and more recently, video games. The many representations of the Self and the Other in American video games have been extensively studied by scholars who have analyzed popular stereotypes of the United States[1] or Latin America[2] used by mainstream game producers.

Today, video games are increasingly produced and consumed in the "global south," This qualification requires definition. Often considered as "peripheral" regions and countries to a global "Western"[3] (and Japanese) core because of the (economic or military) power gap between the two, this dichotomy is of little help when analyzing global popular culture artifacts like video games: gamers from different minorities do not see themselves as outsiders from video game culture.[4] Rather, the qualification is a metaphor for societies having experienced colonialism—and may still struggle with neocolonialism—without defining them above all by their dominated condition.[5] The study of popular culture in dominated countries doubles the risk of analytical asymmetry (a dominated object appropriated by dominated societies). This asymmetry is characterized by two equally problematic biases: populism (celebrating popular culture as more authentic while being blind to the domination relations that shaped it) and *miserabilism* (considering the poor's culture as a poor culture, necessarily wanting in comparison to the legitimate culture).[6]

This increase of production and consumption has taken place in all the parts of the global south, including Africa, Asia and South America[7]—and the Middle East is no exception. This has led to the

1. Gagnon Frédérick, "'Invading Your Hearts and Minds': Call of Duty and the (Re)Writing of Militarism in U.S. Digital Games and Popular Culture," *European Journal of American Studies* 5.3 (2010).
2. Phillip Penix-Tadsen, "Latin American Ludology: Why We Should Take Video Games Seriously (and When We Shouldn't)," *Latin American Research Review* 48.1 (2013).
3. Understood here as strictly European countries, the United States, Canada, Australia and New Zealand. This represents the countries which are industrialized, from Christian heritage and have a mostly white population. These countries are politically and economically dominant at the global level and are associated with a history of imperialistic or racist policies, including the Atlantic slave trade, colonization and post-colonial conflicts.
4. See Phillip Penix-Tadsen, "Introduction: Video Games and the Global South," in this volume.
5. Ibid.
6. Claude Grignon and Jean-Claude Passeron, *Le Savant et le populaire. Misérabilisme et populisme en sociologie et en littérature* (Le Seuil, 1989).
7. See the following chapters in this volume: Jules Skotnes-Brown, "Colonized Play: Racism, Sexism and Colonial Legacies in the Dota 2 South Africa Gaming Community"; Rebecca Yvonne Bayeck, "The Emerging African Video Game Industry: An Analysis of the Narratives of Games Developed in Cameroon and Nigeria"; Nicola Pallitt, Muya Koloko and Anja Venter, "Whose 'Game Culture' is It, Anyway? Exploring Children's Gameplay across Cape Town"; Souvik Mukherjee, "Replaying the Digital Divide: Video Games in India"; José Messias, Diego Amaral and Thaiane Oliveira, "Playing Beyond Precariousness: The Political Aspect of Brazilian Modding in Pro Evolution Soccer"; Daniel Calleros Villareal, "Digital Masks and Lucha Libre: Visual Subjectification and Allegory of Mexico in Video Games"; and Jerjes Loayza, "Ludic Solidarity and Sociality: An Analysis of the Impact of Dota 2 on Lima's Youth."

development of several strategies to mitigate negative stereotypes conveyed by Western games and to offer an endogenous narrative. One has been to reverse the roles usually attributed to Western soldiers and Arab-Muslim fighters. The other has been to offer a specifically Muslim experience, where Islam—as a religion and culture—is positively depicted rather than merely serving as a counter-narrative.[8]

While perspectives on ludology continue to expand, still relatively few studies have focused on gaming practices in countries from the global south.[9] This may be attributed to several theoretical and practical issues: the relatively lower impact of these countries on the global game industry, language barriers and practices that make circulation difficult to measure, including piracy, modding and variations in internet connectivity. However, internet access is increasing across the Middle East, and as was observed in the widespread use of social networks during the Arab Spring, the specific ways people in this region create and use digital products deserve to be further explored.

This chapter aims at providing a basic exploratory framework for understanding current video game practices in the Middle East.[10] It will first describe the current state of the field and the theoretical tools useful for approaching video games in the Middle East from an academic perspective. Next, the chapter will review the results of current research, drawing on a holistic approach to the examination of the objects of pop culture in their four primary dimensions: their context of their production, their content, their audience and the recoding operated by the audience.[11] These results will be analyzed to the light of recent data of online gaming and internet usage practices in the region.

MIDDLE EASTERN LUDOLOGY: FROM A LACK OF SYSTEMATIC ASSESSMENT TO A POSTCOLONIAL THEORETICAL FRAMEWORK

As a result of the scarcity of the field of ludology in and on the Middle East, this chapter remains an exploratory study. Within this specific subfield, there is relatively little information to build upon, due in part to a gap in knowledge, the lack of a constituted field and a relatively minute object of study.[12] Structured scientific knowledge on the subject is still wanting, as evidenced in measurable data such as Google Scholar searches. A search with the keywords "'Middle East' 'video games'" yields roughly 14,000 results. It bears comparing to the results of similar searches on other popular culture artifacts: "'Middle East' 'internet'" (444,000), "'Middle East' 'television'" (221,000), "'Middle East' 'radio'" (219,000), (205,000), "'Middle East' 'movie'" (64,000), "'Middle East' 'social media'" (38,000) or "'Middle East' 'rap'" (32,000). Still, more niche items yield fewer results, including 'comics' (9,000), 'pop music' (7,000) and 'porn' (7,000). These numbers are dwarfed by those of similar searches regarding the United States, one of the most widely studied countries and societies within media studies and other fields. The search shows approximately nine times more results, with 120,000 for "'United States 'video games.'"[13] Seeking to go beyond decontextualized analyses

8. Pierre-Alain Clément and Barthélémy Courmont, "When Geopolitics Meets the Game Industry. A Study of Arabic Video Games and What They Teach Us," *Hemispheres* 29.1 (2014).
9. Among seminal works figure Phillip Penix-Tadsen, "Latin American Ludology" and Souvik Mukherjee, *Videogames and Postcolonialism: Empire Plays Back* (Palgrave Macmillan, 2017).
10. Understood here as the 22 member states of the Arab League.
11. Harold Hinds, "A Holistic Approach to the Study of Popular Culture: Context, Text, Audience, and Recoding," in *Popular Culture Theory and Methodology*, eds. Harold Hinds, Marilyn Motz and Angela Nelson (University of Wisconsin Press, 2006).
12. Foundational works include: Helga Tawil-Souri, "The Political Battlefield of Pro-Arab Video Games on Palestinian Screens," *Comparative Studies of South Asia, Africa and the Middle East* 27.3 (2007); Vít Šisler, "Digital Arabs: Representation in Video Games," *European Journal of Cultural Studies* 11.2 (2008); Šisler, "Palestine in Pixels: The Holy Land, Arab-Israeli Conflict, and Reality Construction in Video Games," *Middle East Journal of Culture and Communication* 2.2 (2009a); Šisler, "Videogame Development in the Middle East: Iran, the Arab World, and Beyond," in *Gaming Globally: Production, Play, and Place*, eds. Nina Huntemann and Ben Aslinger (Palgrave Macmillan, 2013); Ahmad Ahmadi, "Iran," in *Video Games Around the World*, ed. Mark J. P. Wolf (MIT Press, 2015); Mohammed Ibahrine, "Video Games as Civilizational Configurations," in *Islamism and Cultural Expression in the Arab World*, ed. Abir Hamdar and Lindsey Moore (Routledge, 2015); Radwan Kasmiya, "Arab World," in *Video Games Around the World*, ed. Mark J. P. Wolf (MIT Press, 2015).
13. Not surprisingly, industrialized or emerging regions and countries yield more results with this search: Japan (53,000), China (46,000), India (31,000), Mexico (27,000),

of popular culture products focused on the "text," Hinds promotes a holistic approach in which the context of production of the object, the audience it reaches and the feedback it receives from consumers are equally important aspects.[14] Middle Eastern ludology has laid ground for the analysis of these four aspects.

The context of gaming in the Middle East has only just begun to be systematically appraised. The founding work in this regard is Šisler's 2013 article categorizing the environmental constraints for the gaming industry as legal and social conditions shaping the editors' business models and games content.[15] Unsurprisingly, content is the main focus: representations of Arabs and Muslims have been the most studied theme,[16] especially in comparison to Western games representations.[17] Other analyses emphasize the specific cultural message transmitted by many games.[18] More precisely, representations of Arab or Muslims in Western games have been widely covered,[19] along with the negative attitudes towards Arabs and Muslims they could strengthen,[20] or the reduced bias a "serious game" could induce.[21]

The intensification of stereotypes seems to be an inherent aspect of video games: "we must accept that games are fundamentally reductive in nature."[22] This means that, within any culture, game designers don't create stereotypes on their own but reflect more vividly widely held (false) representations, though games "seem to exploit these stereotypes and clichés in a more apparent manner than other forms of media."[23] Reichmuth and Werning attribute this to the fact that, as a form of "neglected media," games, video or of other kind, suffer from "a lack of cultural prestige and scientific coverage" and are "seldom accepted as culturally relevant."[24] This has led to a stereotypical or even offensive treatment of many regions of the global south, like India.[25] In the case of the Middle East, Western games have often versed into Orientalism,[26] or as Radwan Kasmiya put it, a view of the Middle East focused on "the Crusades, oil and terrorism."[27] (Kasmiya is the former CEO of Syrian developer Afkar Media, which released several of the most professionally-made games in the region, and founder

Korea (25,000), Brazil (19,000) and Russia (17,000). However, other regions or countries of the global south covered in this book yield as much or less results: South Africa (14,000), Latin America (10,000), Caribbean (10,000) and Nigeria (6,000). The countries of the Middle East yielding the most results are Iraq (15,000) and Iran (10,000).

14. Hinds, "A Holistic Approach to the Study of Popular Culture."
15. Šisler, "Videogame Development in the Middle East."
16. Alexander Galloway, "Social Realism in Gaming," *Game Studies* 4.1 (2004); Šisler, "Digital Arabs"; Šisler, "Palestine in Pixels"; Vít Šisler and Ebrahim Mohseni, "Revolution Reloaded: Spaces of Encounter and Resistance in Iranian Video Games," in *Place, Space, and Mediated Communication: Exploring Context Collapse*, eds. Carolyn Marvin and Hong Sun-ha (Routledge, 2017).
17. David Machin and Usama Suleiman, "Arab and American Computer War Games: The Influence of a Global Technology on Discourse," *Critical Discourse Studies* 3.1 (2006); Helga Tawil-Souri, "The Political Battlefield of Pro-Arab Video Games on Palestinian Screens."
18. Krystina Derrickson, "Second Life and The Sacred: Islamic Space in a Virtual World," in *Digital Islam*, online platform edited by Šisler, 2008, http://www.digitalislam.eu/article.do?articleId=1877; Heidi Campbell, "Islamogaming: Digital Dignity via Alternative Storytellers," in *Halos and Avatars: Playing Video Games with God*, ed. Craig Detweiler (Westminster John Knox Press, 2010).
19. Ibrahim Marashi, "The Depiction of Arabs in Combat Video Games," paper presented at the Beirut Institute of Media Arts, Lebanese American University, 5-9 November 2001; Dean Chan, "Playing with Race: The Ethics of Racialized Representations in e-Games," *International Review of Information Ethics* 4.12 (2005); Anna C. Everett, "Serious Play: Playing with Race in Contemporary Gaming Culture," in *Handbook of Video Game Studies*, eds. Joost Raessens and Jeffrey Goldstein, (MIT Press, 2005); David Leonard, "Not a Hater, Just Keepin' it Real: The Importance of Race- and Gender-based Game Studies," *Games and Culture* 1.1 (2006); David Machin and Suleiman, Usama, "Arab and American Computer War Games"; Philipp Reichmuth and Stefan Werning, "Pixel Pashas, Digital Djinns," *ISIM Review* 18 (2006); Johan Höglund, "Electronic Empire: Orientalism Revisited in the Military Shooter," *Game Studies* 8.1 (2008); Anandam Kavoori, "Gaming, Terrorism and the Right to Communicate," *Global Media Journal* 7.13 (2008); Majed Balela and Darren Mundy, "Analysing Cultural Heritage and its Representation in Video Games," paper presented at Digital Games Research Association, Hilversum: The Netherlands, 2015; and Mohammed Ibahrine, "Video games as civilizational configurations."
20. Muniba Saleem, "Effects of Stereotypic Video Game Portrayals on Implicit and Explicit Attitudes," Master of Science Thesis, Iowa State University, 2008; Muniba Saleem and Craig Anderson, "Arabs as Terrorists: Effects of Stereotypes within Violent Contexts on Attitudes, Perceptions, and Affect," *Psychology of Violence* 3.1 (2013).
21. Saleem Alhabash and Kevin Wise, "PeaceMaker: Changing Students' Attitudes Toward Palestinians and Israelis Through Video Game Play," *International Journal of Communication* 6 (2012); Cleotilde Gonzalez, Lelyn Saner and Laurie Eisenberg, "Learning to Stand in the Other's Shoes: A Computer Video Game Experience of the Israeli–Palestinian Conflict," *Social Science Computer Review* 31.2 (2013).
22. Penix-Tadsen, "Latin American Ludology," 180.
23. Šisler, "Digital Arabs," 204.
24. Reichmuth and Werning, "Pixel Pashas, Digital Djinns," 47.
25. See, in this volume: Souvik Mukherjee, "Replaying the Digital Divide: Video Games in India."
26. Edward Said, *Orientalism* (Routledge & Kegan Paul, 1978).
27. Quoted by Ed Halter, "Islamogaming: Looking for Videogames in the Muslim World," *Computer Gaming World*, September 2006.

of Falafel Games.) With this treatment, there are two types of Middle East: a fantasy Middle East, focused on the exoticism of timeless tribal societies and a contemporary Middle East, focused on the threat of anti-Western or anti-Semitic terrorists. This issue can be compounded or alleviated by genre. First-person shooter (FPS) games tend to polarize identifications: the player is a hero "killing" dehumanized enemies. On the other hand, the balance of factions required in real-time strategy (RTS) games tends to present different groups as equally appealing. Thus, in games such as *Sid Meier's Civilization* (Microprose, 1991), "the in-game description of many features of Islamic civilization is unique for its correctness and sensitivity,"[28] a precision that can be expected by RTS players who want to "explore and roleplay alternative realities," or "try to 'accurately' roleplay history attempting to recreate historical empires or nations."[29]

Nevertheless, as Penix-Tadsen has argued, the medium itself requires some simplification for the sake of readability for the player.[30] In narrative media, such stereotypes serve a purpose: to draw the player's attention to the gameplay, the scenario, characters, etc., by providing a familiar semiotic context that requires minimal interpretation. This is why so many games that involve fighting use monsters: the dehumanizing process necessary to facilitate the act of "killing" is already done.[31] Problems arise, however, when games create realistic portrayals involving real-life human groups as the player's enemies. Things are even further complicated when Western games depict a Western hero fighting enemies belonging to the global south, echoing actual imperialistic, colonial and postcolonial conflicts led by the former against the latter as well as current neocolonial economic and political domination. But to date, Middle Eastern self-representations have attracted far less critical attention.

In terms of audience reception, modding and recoding practices in the Middle East, there are even fewer studies still. Analyses of how players receive and appropriate the games and their messages have been conducted in Palestine,[32] Iran,[33] in the Arab world in general,[34] in the West[35] and online.[36] Recoding remains the least-studied facet of Middle Eastern gaming. Tracing how consumers' practices can feedback to producers is difficult in and of itself, however it has shown how the increased weight of Middle Eastern markets (and Arab or Muslim consumers in the West) has incited Western developers to adopt a more sensitive approach when depicting Arabs and Muslims.[37]

The field of ludology in the Middle East has faced several notable obstacles in its path to development as a discipline. The first obstacle is the difficulty of accessing the field: the authoritarian context prevailing in most of the region and the persistence of language barriers are considerable hindrances, including for this author.[38] Plus, as might be expected from popular culture practices in impoverished or relatively impoverished contexts, gaming has spread throughout the Middle East primarily through the black market,[39] leading to a gap in first-hand data and a weak reliability of official numbers

28. Šisler, "Digital Arabs," 210.
29. See Rhett Loban and Thomas Apperley, "Eurocentric Values at Play: Modding the Colonial from the Indigenous Perspective," in this volume.
30. Penix-Tadsen, "Latin American Ludology," 180.
31. Mukherjee, *Videogames and Postcolonialism*, 55.
32. Tawil-Souri, "The Political Battlefield of Pro-Arab Video Games on Palestinian Screens."
33. Hamid Allahverdipour, Mohsen Bazargan, Abdollah Farhadinasab and Babak Moeini, "Correlates of Video Games Playing Among Adolescents in an Islamic Country," *Bio Med Central Public Health* 10.286 (May 2010); Šisler, "Playing Muslim Hero: Construction of Identity in Video Games," in *Digital Religion: Understanding Religious Practice in New Media Worlds*, ed. Heidi Campbell (Routledge, 2012).
34. Šisler, "Video Games, Video Clips, and Islam: New Media and the Communication of Values," in *Muslim Societies in the Age of Mass Consumption*, ed. Johanna Pink (Cambridge Scholars Publishing, 2009b); Shaw, "Identity, Identification, and Media Representation in Video Game Play."
35. Pam Nilan, *Muslim Youth in the Diaspora: Challenging Extremism through Popular Culture* (Routledge, 2017).
36. Ahmed Al-Rawi, "Video Games, Terrorism, and ISIS's Jihad 3.0," *Terrorism and Political Violence* 17.1 (2016).
37. Šisler, "Video Games, Video Clips, and Islam."
38. For more insight on the methodological and ethical issues of such fields, see Vincent Romani, "Enquêter dans les Territoires palestiniens. Comprendre un quotidien au-delà de la violence immediate," *Revue française de science politique* 57.1 (2007) and Carolyn Nordstrom and Antonius Robben, eds., *Fieldwork under Fire: Contemporary Studies of Violence and Survival* (University of California Press, 1995).
39. Šisler, "Videogame Development in the Middle East," 251.

regarding this market. The second obstacle to the expansion of Middle Eastern game studies the relative lack of interest in this field: while established, ludology in itself is still sometimes considered as illegitimate by those considering popular culture as lacking in prestige. Meanwhile, contemporary studies of Middle East are focused on phenomena related to political violence, specifically its protagonists and causes.[40] Other studies deal with representations of Arabs and Muslims in Western games rather than games made in the region.[41] As a result, studies on the subject of gaming practices among the population of the Middle East are relatively scarce.[42] A third obstacle to the academic analysis of gaming in the Middle East is the fact that the region does not have as prolific a gaming industry as North America, Europe or Japan. On *Digital Islam*, the online platform dedicated to research on the subject he first developed, Vit Šisler records some 26 Arab video games, without any claims to exhaustiveness.[43] This is in stark contrast to the American or British gaming industries, which have grossed several times more than their respective movie industries for over a decade.[44]

In spite of these hurdles, Middle Eastern ludology is relevant to Middle Eastern studies for the same reasons Penix-Tadsen defends Latin American ludology: due to video games' "massive dispersion and consumption, participatory cultural simulation, the remediation of existing expressive traditions, and the capacity to have a profound impact on the way an ever-growing portion of the population sees our world," in other words, "games today are lived experiences, deeply affecting the way the world understands [Middle Eastern] culture and the way [Middle Easterners] understand themselves."[45] Moreover, in authoritarian contexts, digital tools can become a useful way to bypass the monitoring of expressions of dissent. This was notably the case before and during the Arab Spring when activists used social media to attract international heed and apply pressure on the dictatorial regimes under which they lived.[46] For these reasons, developing ludology in the Middle East will allow us to further develop our critical understanding of a neglected but important aspect of the cultural representations in the region's societies.

In short, current literature on gaming and the Middle East has primarily focused on representations of Arabs and Muslims in Western games. With the development of an endogenous gaming scene, video games and Middle East specialists have begun studying self-representations by analyzing game content and audience reception in the region. Only recently have contextual and recoding studies emerged, showing evidence of an increasingly mature field. In this regard, a postcolonial theoretical framework is increasingly useful: it allows to articulate how individuals in subaltern societies deal with former and current colonial domination, a type of domination that is frequently incorporated into the economic context of production and the cultural messages transmitted by video games. Within such a framework, the postcolonial concept of mimicry developed by Frantz Fanon and Homi Bhabha is useful: it is understood by the former as the dehumanizing tendency of the subaltern to mimic the dominant; and by the latter as a more ambivalent process in which the dominant is also

40. Romani, "Enquêter dans les Territoires palestiniens," 30.

41. Šisler, "Videogame Development in the Middle East," 252.

42. Tawil-Souri, "The Political Battlefield of Pro-Arab Video Games on Palestinian Screens."

43. See the following list: http://www.digitalislam.eu/findInSection.do?sectionId=1115&limit=50. Over time, the list has expanded from 15 and currently includes 160 games related to the Middle East. They were published between 1983 and 2012 (5.5 a year), including 26 "Middle Eastern and Islamic" games between 2001 and 2012 (two per year).

44. Trevir Nath, "Investing in Video Games: This Industry Pulls In More Revenue Than Movies, Music," *Bloomberg*, 13 June 2016 Tom Chatfield, "Videogames Now Outperform Hollywood Movies," *The Guardian*, 27 September 2009. This is hardly a novelty: during the so-called "golden age of video games" in the 1980's, the home gaming revenues equaled those of pop music and Hollywood, and the arcade gaming revenues were their double; see Everett Rogers and Judith Larsen, *Silicon Valley Fever: Growth of High-Technology Culture* (Basic Books, 1984), 263.

45. Penix-Tadsen, "Latin American Ludology," 185.

46. Margaret Keck and Kathryn Sikkink, *Activists Beyond Borders* (Cornell University Press, 1998); Ethan Zuckerman, "Meet the Bridgebloggers," *Public Choice* 134 (2008); Marc Lynch, "After Egypt: The Limits and Promise of Online Challenges to the Authoritarian Arab State," *Perspectives on Politics* 9.2 (2011). For a dissenting view, arguing that authoritarian regimes use the Internet to control the population, see Evgeny Morozov, *The Net Delusion: the Dark Side of Internet Freedom* (Public Affairs, 2011).

modified by its domination, in a form of hybridization.[47] Bhabha's complex definition is particularly relevant to gaming in the Middle East. Indeed, as the next section will demonstrate, the region is replete with contradictory perspectives on mimicry. On the one hand, there are strategies of distinction by producers, who have to negotiate between colonial representations in Western games, historical and geopolitical domination, and authoritarian regimes. On the other hand, consumers mimic to a large extant global trends in game consumption, participating in a complex relationship with stereotyped depictions in Western games which are popular, while also appropriating the medium and adapting it to local audiences.

VIDEO GAMES IN THE MIDDLE EAST: DISTINCTION IN PRODUCTION, MIMESIS IN CONSUMPTION

Furthering the holistic approach described by Hinds, this section is drawing a summary portrait of contemporary gaming in the region in the four dimensions he outlined: context, text, audience and recoding.[48] Before proceeding, it is crucial to emphasize the global approach adopted here should not conceal the extensive diversity of a region comprised of 22 countries on two continents, home to close to 400 million people practicing multiple religions, speaking various languages, having distinct histories and ranking very differently with regard to myriad political, economic and social factors. The main reason to deal the region as a whole is because of similar traits—such as mostly Muslim societies and mostly authoritarian regimes—as well as the region's treatment as a homogenous, one-dimensional monolith by Western game developers.

The context of the Middle East today is marked by the contradictory forces of political and social constraints and technological evolution. The gaming industry in the region is still in an early stage, even if it is growing. Like the relative lack of formal scholarship, the scarcity of locally-produced games is the result of several structural obstacles. Most importantly, production is hindered by a number of legal issues. The market is "flooded with cheap pirated games" according to Kasmiya, meaning local gamers get their hands on Western games not long after, or even before, they're released on the legal market, and for a couple of dollars.[49] The piracy rate for Middle East and Africa has been constant in the 2010 close to 60%, with only Israel, Qatar, the United Arab Emirates and Saudi Arabia scoring below 50%.[50] With many Arab countries having adopted no laws or joined any treaty to protect intellectual property, the market looks like a "pool full of sharks" to Kasmiya,[51] where games priced over 10 dollars are not sold.[52] This prevents the growth of developers and editors: with 40 people at its peak, Afkar Media is the region's largest game development company to date.[53]

This situation gives little incentive to foreign companies to localize their games or even mitigate their losses to piracy. The Middle East and Africa is the second-to-last out of six regions in terms of commercial value lost to piracy, at approximately US$3.7 billion in 2015.[54] Also, Šisler evokes technological hurdles caused by geopolitical tensions: "due to US technology embargoes, developers often can't legitimately buy engines, middle-ware and other development software."[55] This leads to games lagging in quality, even for "indie" games: *Unearthed: Trail of Ibn Battuta* (Semaphore, 2013),

47. Mukherjee, *Videogames and Postcolonialism*, 17, 59-60.
48. Hinds, "A Holistic Approach to the Study of Popular Culture," 2006.
49. Kasmiya, "Arab World," 30; see also Vit Šisler and Ebrahim Mohseni, "Revolution Reloaded: Spaces of Encounter and Resistance in Iranian Video Games," in *Place, Space, and Mediated Communication: Exploring Context Collapse*, eds. Carolyn Marvin and Hong Sun-ha (Routledge, 2017).
50. Business Software Alliance, *Seizing Opportunity Through License Compliance – BSA Global Software Survey*, May 2016, http://globalstudy.bsa.org/2016/: 7.
51. Quoted in Halter, "Islamogaming."
52. Games for Change, "Interview with Radwan Kasmiya of Afkar Media," *Games for Change*, 12 November 2010, http://www.gamesforchange.org/blog/2010/11/12/592/.
53. Halter, "Islamogaming."
54. Business Software Alliance, *Seizing Opportunity Through License Compliance*, 7.
55. Šisler, "Videogame Development in the Middle East," 201.

Saudi developer Semaphore's first game, which is often cited by critics of Middle Eastern game development, has been panned for its bugs, poor gameplay and animations, even though its developers used the relatively advanced Unity engine.[56] This also leads to creative developing: *Quest for Bush* (Al Qaeda, 2006) is a mod of the American *Quest for Saddam* (Petrilla Entertainment, 2003); *Special Force 2* (Hezbollah, 2006) is believed to be a *Far Cry* mod; *The Clanging of the Swords* (or *Salil al-Sawarem*, unknown, 2014), a game produced by Islamic State sympathizers is a mod of *Grand Theft Auto V*.[57] Interestingly, in spite of the militant groups' tech-savviness, especially in their magazines and videos, they still lag behind the most-advanced and popular games (the so-called "AAA games"). For example the initial *Special Force* (Hezbollah, 2003) was released in four languages (Arabic, English, French and Farsi), whereas the second opus was only released in Arabic; by the same token, Islamic state's "game" appears to be a game trailer (not even a mod) made to attract media attention, calling into questioning their intention to produce a real game in the first place.[58] When AAA games require budgets in the hundreds of thousands of dollars to make, these groups cannot compete. That may be why they reoriented their video game activities to the production of trailers and "let's play" videos (recorded while the player plays the game), which are far easier to copy from existing games.[59]

A further hindrance to the Middle Eastern game development is the prevalence of authoritarian regimes, many of which try to minimize Western cultural influence, placing constraints on developers. The richest or more active states have recognized video games as a tool to increase their influence. Thus, the United Arab Emirates (UAE), Saudi Arabia and Iran have subsidized production for reasons both international—presenting a positive image of Islam through a modern medium—as well as national—strengthening cohesion through religion.[60] In the other countries of the region, private entrepreneurs join spiritual and economic motivations to fund games which encourage Islamic values. Thus developers still have to take into account social norms and expectations and produce games highlighting "three common basic cultural values: collectivism, honor and hospitality."[61] These cultural requirements have been institutionalized with the creation of the Entertainment Software Rating Association by Iran and the UAE in 2010, on the model of the U.S. Entertainment Software Rating Board (ESRB) and the Pan European Game Information (PEGI) systems.

Technology has also had an impact on regional game development. Increased access to the Internet has allowed for the possibility of bypassing some censorship measures and decreasing production costs. On the global level since 2016, mobile gaming has been generating more revenue than the former largest segment, PC gaming, and Middle Eastern developers have adopted this trend too.[62] The growth of the mobile gaming segment is promoted by lower development costs, lower consumer prices and a profitable freemium business model that helps to mitigate piracy. As a result, one of the greatest recent successes in regional game development in terms of free and paid downloads has been the Lebanese game *Pou* (Paul Salameh, 2013), which has also gained popularity in Europe.[63] Kasmiya left Syria in 2011 to establish Falafel Games, a massive multiplayer online developer of mobile strategy

56. Kasmiya, "Arab World"; Balela and Mundy, "Analysing Cultural Heritage and its representation in Video Games."
57. However, now only a trailer and online videos of it exist. The game doesn't seem to have ever been released or even made. See Pam Nilan, *Muslim Youth in the Diaspora*, 123.
58. Miron Lakomy, "Let's Play a Video Game: Jihadi Propaganda in the World of Electronic Entertainment," *Studies in Conflict & Terrorism*, 2017, 10-18; Al-Rawi, "Video Games, Terrorism, and ISIS's Jihad 3.0," 7.
59. Lakomy, "Let's Play a Video Game," 24-25.
60. Šisler and Mohseni, "Revolution Reloaded: Spaces of Encounter and Resistance in Iranian Video Games."
61. Ibid.
62. Newzoo, "The Global Games Market Reaches $99.6 Billion in 2016, Mobile Generating 37%," *Newzoo*, 21 April 2016, https://newzoo.com/insights/articles/global-games-market-reaches-99-6-billion-2016-mobile-generating-37/.
63. Kasmiya, "Arab World," 33.

games based in Lebanon and China. To date, Falafal has managed to raise several million dollars of funds from regional venture capital investors based in Lebanon, Saudi Arabia and the UAE.[64] Other succeeding companies producing web browser games are Emirati Tahadi and Jordanian Maktoob, in which Yahoo invested after the latter's first successes.[65]

As a fledgling industry, Middle Eastern game development is reacting to global dynamics in terms of its content, gameplay and business models. The most common depictions of the region are being made by others, and therefore Middle Eastern developers struggle to voice an autonomous discourse. By and large, they adopt three approaches to the stereotypical depictions of the Middle East and its people that are prominent in video games: avoidance, transgression and subversion. Avoidance characterizes the large portion of regional production, especially in the early years, that has been dedicated to educational games directed towards young children that teach religious and cultural norms in a way that is little affected by the global dynamics of the industry.

Transgression has been the most spectacular, and perhaps the best-known, way in which Middle Eastern game developers have responded to dominant in-game stereotypes of the region. Games that attempt to transgress these depictions by reversing their hierarchical taxonomies includes *Stone Throwers* (or *Rumah al-Hijara*, Damascus online, 2000); *Special Force* (Hezbollah, 2003); the educational *Children of Jerusalem* (or *Fata al-Quds*, Hezbollah, 2004); the FPS *Special Force 2: Tale of the Truthful Pledge*; *Quest for Bush*,the game produced by an Al Qaeda-affiliated media company;[66] *Night of Bush Capturing* (or *Laylat al-Qabd ala Bush*, Global Islamic Media Front, 2006), *Special Operation* (or *Amaliyat-e Vizhe*, Iranian Student Union, 2007) and the Islamic state presumptive game *The Clanging of the Swords*. These games reverse the polarities of player identification usually found in games—in them, the player has to fight against Israeli soldiers; to save a nuclear scientist abducted by American forces or to kill the final boss portrayed as former president Bush. Thus these games react to other games or real-life events, but they also produce relatively little innovation and their quality remains low. Some of them are mods of U.S. games indeed, but not in the sense of "epistemic disobedience" against "industry mandates of standardization."[67] Rather, these games could be more precisely read as a form of trolling, which is indeed a strategic form of communication used as such by many militant groups.[68]

Parallel to this trend, more ambitious developers have favored subversion over transgression. They have tried both to deconstruct stereotypes and to affirm a specific identity beyond the confrontations between the East and West or the global north and south. As Kasmiya has stated, the point is not to "make 'anti-GI Joe' games" but rather to "make games that speak truths that are hidden behind louder voices."[69] These games seeks to re-appropriate Muslim, Arab or Persian identity, refusing to frontally confront the stereotypes common in the West in favor of highlighting the cultural aspects deemed a source of pride and civilizational progress in the Arab-Muslim world,[70] providing a sense

64. K.O, "Falafel Games lève 2,6 millions de dollars supplémentaires," *l'Orient–le Jour*, 19 October 2016.
65. Kasmiya, "Arab World," 32.
66. Ibahrine also mentions two games supposedly made by Al Qaeda: a 2009 Tetris-like puzzle game featuring the Twin Towers and in 2013 *Call of Jihad: Scourge of the Infidels*, a *Call of Duty*-like first-person shooter; see Mohammed Ibahrine, "Video Games as Civilizational Configurations," in *Islamism and Cultural Expression in the Arab World*, eds. Abir Hamdar and Lindsey Moore (Routledge, 2015): 213-214. In fact, these games do not exist, as they are hoaxes invented by parody websites, the former by Faking News, an Indian news satire site (http://www.fakingnews.firstpost.com/world/al-qaida-launches-video-game-to-celebrate-8th-anniversary-of-911-159) and the latter by *Duffel Blog*, an American military news satire site (http://www.duffelblog.com/2013/06/call-of-jihad-video-game/).
67. See José Messias, Diego Amaral and Thaiane Oliveira, "Playing Beyond Precariousness: The Political Aspect of Brazilian Modding in Pro Evolution Soccer," in this volume.
68. Al-Rawi, "Video Games, Terrorism, and ISIS's Jihad 3.0."
69. Games for Change, "Interview with Radwan Kasmiya of Afkar Media."
70. Clément and Courmont, "When Geopolitics Meets the Game Industry," 2014.

of "digital dignity."[71] This can be understood as subversion, as these games do not try to produce a mirror image of stereotyped Arab-Muslims; they are rather stepping aside and explore other things their producers think are relevant to share with the world: "what emerges from the Middle Eastern game production is a story of 'hybridization' and cross-cultural exchange rather than 'authenticity.'"[72] This trend testifies of a maturing field, switching from a defensive, identity-driven and avenging form of production to one that engages with the global industry.

While Middle Eastern game designers show signs of innovation, the region's gaming audience generally imitates global habits. Games like *Quraish* (Afkar Media, 2007) fared well: it "has been positively received by Arab gamers and has sold more than 50,000 copies."[73] But imitation is the main trait of the Middle Eastern gaming scene. Indeed, as an emerging scene, "a 'mainstream' Arab, Iranian or Pakistani gaming culture does not yet exist—or, more precisely, it consists primarily of the consumption of 'Western' games, albeit in new contexts and social settings."[74] This is confirmed by an epidemiological study conducted in Iran suggest similar consumptions and psychological impacts. From a sample of 444 Iranian middle schoolers, half of respondents had played "intensely violent" games. The authors mention several game series without specifying the individual titles: the British series of games *Driver* (Reflections, 1999) and *Grand Theft Auto* (Rockstar, 1997); the American series of games *Mortal Kombat* (Acclaim, 1992) and *Prince of Persia* (Brøderbund, 1989); and the Japanese series of games *Dead or Alive* (Team Ninja, 1996) and *Resident Evil* (Capcom, 1996). This study draws a "relationship between video game playing and mental health outcomes, with 'moderate' gamers faring best [while] 'excessive' gamers showed mild increases in problematic behaviors [and] non-gamers showed the worst outcomes."[75] This imitative approach to gaming can lead to some cognitive dissonance when Arab or Muslims play games depicting them in negative stereotypes. In a qualitative survey on how these gamers cope with such portrayals, Nilan found that they usually respond by distancing themselves from the content, or by highlighting its fictional nature and entertaining purpose.[76]

The YouTube scene reflects this mimetic stance in the Middle East vis-à-vis global game culture, which can also observed with regard to other dimensions of pop culture. Following "Comedy and Entertainment," "Tech and Gaming" channels get the most YouTube views throughout the region, averaging between 149,000 and 322,000 views and between 352,000 and 871,000 followers for the top five channels.[77]Reine Farhat, "What Are Users in the Arab World Watching on YouTube? (Infographic)," *Wamda*, 19 March 2014, https://www.wamda.com/2014/03/what-did-users-in-the-middle-east-watch-on-youtube-this-year. These five channels all come from Saudi Arabia, a country producing 25% of the "Tech and Gaming" content, Oman and Kuwait outputting 18% each. These results are obviously explained by internet access, which is considerably higher in wealthier countries. They are also almost all in Arabic, as is 93% of YouTube content from the region, showing that in spite of imitating Western patterns of game consumption, Arab gamers have appropriated the medium for purposes specific to the regional audience. Such a phenomenon appeared in South America, another prolific source of stereotypes for Western games, where the emergence of local producers led to a "boom in self-representation" which is maybe "just one of the first steps in the evolution of gaming as a global phenomenon."[78] In this

71. Šisler, "Digital Arabs," 213-214.
72. Šisler, "Videogame Development in the Middle East."
73. Ibid.
74. Ibid.
75. Allahverdipour, Bazargan, Farhadinasab and Moeini, "Correlates of Video Games Playing Among Adolescents in an Islamic Country," 3, 5.
76. Nilan, Muslim Youth in the Diaspora, 104-126.
77.
78. See Phillip Penix-Tadsen, "Introduction: Video Games and the Global South," in this volume.

regard, signals of appropriation of the medium, like the recent success of Tamatem, one of the largest Arabic speaking mobile games publisher, in raising US$2.5 million, may be a signal of increasing empowerment by local actors.[79]

Recoding is probably the most difficult process to trace in pop culture, but it represents one way in which Middle Eastern players "play back" against popular stereotypes, pushing for more diverse and accurate representations. Following up on the previous sections of this chapter, modding and recoding practices help to verify some of the hypotheses presented. First, more culturally-sensitive games are to be expected from modding communities. Public scandals like #Gamergate and the campaign of harassment against Anita Sarkeesian have led to some introspection regarding how games treat masculinity as well as female and homosexual players. In the same way, Arabs and Muslims living in Western countries and playing Western games can be expected to have the resources to voice concern against blatant stereotypes. If games offering a radically different take on these societies are unlikely, companies fearing commercial backlash are more likely to produce more nuanced games. Second, a desire for increased realism is likely to lead to more balanced portrayals. In FPS and RTS games in which all factions are playable, the "good vs. evil" narrative gives way to more dispassionate depictions. This has long been observable in historical war games offering the possibility to play as part of factions such as the Nazis. Recently, gamers have pushed realism further in the aptly named *Project Reality*, a *Battlefield 2* (Electronic Arts, 2005) mod that includes, among other factions, the "Middle East Coalition," the "Syrian Rebels," the "Taliban," the "Iraqi Insurgents" and the "African Resistance Fighters." Finally, gaming in the age of the internet will induce diversification with unclear consequences. The internet allows a multiplicity of producers (states, militant groups, activists, individuals) to generate a diversity of content, from ISIS propaganda to memes mocking ISIS propaganda. This can lead to polarization, as consumers are prone to restrict themselves to media validating their pre-existing beliefs, an effect particularly salient online. But this can also lead to positive familiarization, as the effects of increased exposure can increase consumers' favorability to cross-cultural content, through the psychological mere-exposure effect.

CONCLUSION

As can be seen in the examples analyzed above, Middle Eastern game developers and modders use multiple strategies of distinction, first to subvert Western stereotypes and second to bypass or endorse Middle Eastern political and cultural constraints. On the contrary, on the consumer side, similarities with the West are strong, in spite of an irreducible distance caused by widespread Orientalist depictions in popular Western games. Mimetic adoption of globally popular games and game genres by gamers of the region is probably due to the marketing acumen of Western games, which are capable of entertaining—and being sold to—people all over the world. This is leading Middle Eastern gamers to develop various strategies to deal with the cognitive dissonance between emotional entertainment and intellectual discomfort.

The Middle East thus shares three out of the four key factors characterizing gaming in the global south referenced in Penix-Tadsen's introduction to this anthology: except for the absence of a "longstanding game culture," the region indeed shares a "set of historical obstacles and affordances," a "legacy of cultural representation" shaped in the global north and "a conflicted official perspective" on the medium. Thus only time distinguishes the Middle East from the rest of the global south, which allows to make predictions with comparable societies in the south. Today, the Middle Eastern

79. Wamda, "Tamatem Raises $ 2.5M to Localize Mobile Games for the MENA Market," *Wamda*, 2 February 2018, https://www.wamda.com/2018/02/tamatem-raises-25m-localize-mobile-games-mena-market.

gaming scene can be described as a scene struggling to exist autonomously. Looking West to the roots of the medium, Middle Eastern producers are the most active in their responses, since they are consciously rejecting the assignation to be the "usual suspects" of stereotyped antagonists. They do this through diverse practices of resistance, notably by distinguishing themselves from the most frowned-upon "excesses" of Western games: sexualization, violence and individualism. With regard to their own authoritarian regimes, the producers are far less engaged due of their vulnerability to state repression or their adhesion to a given regime's orientation. But nevertheless gamers, in their mimetic consumption of Western games, exhibit behaviors whose effects are far less subversive in nature. For this reason, in their struggle against assignation at the hands of stereotypes or state manipulation, stakeholders in Middle Eastern gaming are adopting behaviors of resistance or normalization that may well contribute to their emancipation from internal and external forces of domination.

WORKS CITED

Ahmadi, Ahmad. "Iran." In *Video Games Around the World*, edited by Mark J. P. Wolf. MIT Press, 2015.

Alhabash, Saleem and Kevin Wise. "*PeaceMaker*: Changing Students' Attitudes Toward Palestinians and Israelis Through Video Game Play." *International Journal of Communication* 6 (2012).

Allahverdipour, Hamid, Mohsen Bazargan, Abdollah Farhadinasab and Babak Moeini. "Correlates of Video Games Playing Among Adolescents in an Islamic Country." *Bio Med Central Public Health* 10.286, May 2010.

Al-Rawi, Ahmed. "Video Games, Terrorism, and ISIS's Jihad 3.0." *Terrorism and Political Violence* 17.1 (2016).

Balela, Majed and Darren Mundy. "Analysing Cultural Heritage and its Representation in Video Games." Paper presented at Digital Games Research Association, Hilversum: The Netherlands, 2015.

Business Software Alliance. *Seizing Opportunity Through License Compliance–BSA Global Software Survey*, May 2016, http://globalstudy.bsa.org/2016/

Campbell, Heidi. "Islamogaming: Digital Dignity via Alternative Storytellers." In *Halos and Avatars: Playing Video Games with God*, edited by Craig Detweiler. Westminster John Knox Press, 2010.

Chan, Dean. "Playing with Race: The Ethics of Racialized Representations in e-Games." *International Review of Information Ethics* 4.12 (2005).

Chatfield, Tom. "Videogames Now Outperform Hollywood movies." *The Guardian*, 27 September 2009, https://www.theguardian.com/technology/gamesblog/2009/sep/27/videogames-hollywood.

Clément, Pierre-Alain and Barthélémy Courmont. "When Geopolitics Meets the Game Industry. A Study of Arabic Video Games and What They Teach Us." *Hemispheres* 29.1 (2014).

Derrickson, Krystina. "Second Life and The Sacred: Islamic Space in a Virtual World." In *Digital Islam*, online platform edited by Vít Šisler, 2008, http://www.digitalislam.eu/article.do?articleId=1877.

Everett, Adrienne. "Serious Play: Playing with Race in Contemporary Gaming Culture." In *Handbook of Video Game Studies*, edited by Joost Raessens and Jeffrey Goldstein. MIT Press, 2005.

Farhat, Reine. "What Are Users in the Arab World Watching on YouTube? [Infographic]." *Wamda*, 19 March 2014, https://www.wamda.com/2014/03/what-did-users-in-the-middle-east-watch-on-youtube-this-year.

Gagnon, Frédérick. "'Invading Your Hearts and Minds': *Call of Duty* and the (Re)Writing of Militarism in U.S. Digital Games and Popular Culture." *European Journal of American Studies* 5.3 (2010).

Galloway, Alexander. "Social Realism in Gaming." *Game Studies* 4.1 (2004).

Games for Change. "Interview with Radwan Kasmiya of Afkar Media." *Games for Change*, 12 November 2010, http://www.gamesforchange.org/blog/2010/11/12/592/.

Gonzalez, Cleotilde, Lelyn Saner and Laurie Eisenberg. "Learning to Stand in the Other's Shoes: A Computer Video Game Experience of the Israeli–Palestinian Conflict." *Social Science Computer Review* 31.2 (2013).

Grignon, Claude and Jean-Claude Passeron. *Le Savant et le populaire. Misérabilisme et populisme en sociologie et en littérature*. Le Seuil, 1989.

Halter, Ed. "Islamogaming: Looking for Videogames in the Muslim World." *Computer Gaming World*, September 2006, http://eddostern.com/texts/Islamogaming.pdf.

Hinds, Harold. "A Holistic Approach to the Study of Popular Culture: Context, Text, Audience, and Recoding." In *Popular Culture Theory and Methodology*, edited by Harold Hinds, Marilyn Motz and Angela Nelson. University of Wisconsin Press, 2006.

Höglund, Johan. "Electronic Empire: Orientalism Revisited in the Military Shooter." *Game Studies* 8.1 (2008).

Ibahrine, Mohammed. "Video Games as Civilizational Configurations." In *Islamism and Cultural Expression in the Arab World*, edited by Abir Hamdar and Lindsey Moore, Routledge, 2015.

Kasmiya, Radwan. "Arab World." In *Video Games Around the World*, edited by Mark J. P. Wolf. MIT Press, 2015.

Kavoori, Anandam. "Gaming, Terrorism and the Right to Communicate." *Global Media Journal* 7.13 (2008).

Keck, Margaret and Kathryn Sikkink. *Activists Beyond Borders*. Cornell University Press, 1998.

K.O. "Falafel Games lève 2,6 millions de dollars supplémentaires." *l'Orient–le Jour*, 19 October 2016, https://www.lorientlejour.com/article/1013412/falafel-games-leve-26-millions-de-dollars-supplementaires.html.

Lakomy, Miron. "Let's Play a Video Game: Jihadi Propaganda in the World of Electronic Entertainment." *Studies in Conflict & Terrorism* (2017).

Leonard, David. "Not a Hater, Just Keepin' it Real: The Importance of Race- and Gender-based Game Studies." *Games and Culture* 1.1 (2006).

Lynch, Marc. "After Egypt: The Limits and Promise of Online Challenges to the Authoritarian Arab State." *Perspectives on Politics* 9.2 (2011).

Machin, David and Usama Suleiman. "Arab and American Computer War Games: The Influence of a Global Technology on Discourse." *Critical Discourse Studies* 3.1 (2006).

Marashi, Ibrahim. "The Depiction of Arabs in Combat Video Games." Paper presented at the Beirut Institute of Media Arts, Lebanese American University, 5-9 November 2001.

Morozov, Evgeny. *The Net Delusion: The Dark Side of Internet Freedom*. Public Affairs, 2011.

Mukherjee, Souvik. *Videogames and Postcolonialism: Empire Plays Back*. Palgrave Macmillan, 2017.

Nath, Trevir. "Investing in Video Games: This Industry Pulls In More Revenue Than Movies, Music." *Bloomberg*, 13 June 2016, http://www.nasdaq.com/article/investing-in-video-games-this-industry-pulls-in-more-revenue-than-movies-music-cm634585.

Newzoo. "The Global Games Market Reaches $99.6 Billion in 2016, Mobile Generating 37%." *Newzoo*, 21 April 2016, https://newzoo.com/insights/articles/global-games-market-reaches-99-6-billion-2016-mobile-generating-37/.

Nilan, Pam. *Muslim Youth in the Diaspora. Challenging Extremism through Popular Culture*. Routledge, 2017.

Nordstrom, Carolyn and Antonius Robben, eds. *Fieldwork under Fire. Contemporary Studies of Violence and Survival*. University of California Press, 1995.

Penix-Tadsen Phillip. "Latin American Ludology: Why We Should Take Video Games Seriously (and When We Shouldn't)." *Latin American Research Review* 48.1 (2013).

Reichmuth, Philipp and Stefan Werning. "Pixel Pashas, Digital Djinns." *ISIM Review* 18 (2006), https://core.ac.uk/download/pdf/15604749.pdf.

Rogers, Everett and Judith Larsen. *Silicon Valley Fever: Growth of High-Technology Culture*. Basic Books, 1984.

Romani, Vincent. "Enquêter dans les Territoires palestiniens. Comprendre un quotidien au-delà de la violence immediate." *Revue française de science politique* 57.1 (2007).

Said, Edward. *Orientalism*. Routledge and Kegan Paul, 1978.

Saleem, Muniba. "Effects of Stereotypic Video Game Portrayals on Implicit and Explicit Attitudes." Master of Science Thesis, Iowa State University, 2008.

Saleem, Muniba and Craig Anderson. "Arabs as Terrorists: Effects of Stereotypes within Violent Contexts on Attitudes, Perceptions, and Affect." *Psychology of Violence* 3.1 (2013).

Shaw, Adrienne. "Identity, Identification, and Media Representation in Video Game Play: An Audience Reception Study." Ph.D. Dissertation, University of Pennsylvania, 2010.

Šisler, Vít. "Digital Arabs: Representation in Video Games." *European Journal of Cultural Studies* 11.2 (2008).

—. "Palestine in Pixels: The Holy Land, Arab-Israeli Conflict, and Reality Construction in Video Games." *Middle East Journal of Culture and Communication* 2.2 (2009a).

—. "Video Games, Video Clips, and Islam: New Media and the Communication of Values." In *Muslim Societies in the Age of Mass Consumption*, edited by Johanna Pink. Cambridge Scholars Publishing, 2009b.

—. "Playing Muslim Hero: Construction of Identity in Video Games." In *Digital Religion: Understanding Religious Practice in New Media Worlds*, edited by Heidi Campbell. Routledge, 2012.

—. "Videogame Development in the Middle East: Iran, the Arab World, and Beyond." In *Gaming Globally: Production, Play, and Place*, edited by Nina Huntemann and Ben Aslinger. Palgrave Macmillan, 2013.

—. "From *Kuma\War* to *Quraish*: Representations of Islam in Arab and American Video Games." In *Playing with Religion in Digital Games*, edited by Heidi Campbell and Gregory Price Grieve. Indiana University Press, 2014.

Šisler, Vít and Ebrahim Mohseni. "Revolution Reloaded: Spaces of Encounter and Resistance in Iranian Video Games." In *Place, Space, and Mediated Communication: Exploring Context Collapse*, edited by Carolyn Marvin and Hong Sun-ha. Routledge, 2017.

Tawil-Souri, Helga. "The Political Battlefield of Pro-Arab Video Games on Palestinian Screens." *Comparative Studies of South Asia, Africa and the Middle East* 27.3 (2007).

Wamda. "Tamatem raises $ 2.5M to localize mobile games for the MENA market." *Wamda*, 2 February 2018, https://www.wamda.com/2018/02/tamatem-raises-25m-localize-mobile-games-mena-market.

Zuckerman, Ethan. "Meet the Bridgebloggers." *Public Choice* 134 (2008).

NATIONAL CULTURES AND DIGITAL SPACE

INTERPERSONAL COMMUNICATION IN WORLD OF WARCRAFT, FROM LATIN TO NORTH AMERICA

VERÓNICA VALDIVIA MEDINA

VIDEO GAMES AS CULTURAL OBJECTS

In order to analyze elements of a social reality, we must understand that such phenomena involve not only isolated social relations, but also the contexts, material and technological elements that mediate those relations.[1] Therefore, technological objects stimulate and constitute a form of "cultural narration" in our daily lives.[2] But the types of media in which this cultural narration occurs—such as video games—can be highly complex, and thus it is important to examine the ways these technologies are constructed, not just in terms of their primary function as objects of play, entertainment or communication, but also the kinds of meaning associated with them and, perhaps just as importantly, the different purposes they fulfill in everyday life. Other scholars have paved the way for this critical trajectory, including Paul Du Gay et al.,whose work shows how the use of the Sony Walkman affects users' interactions with their surroundings,[3] as well as Heather A. Horst and Daniel Miller's research, which shows how people appropriate artefacts like cellphones based on characteristics particular to their national contexts and cultural backgrounds, putting them to use in unique ways.[4] To paraphrase Adrienne Shaw, it is important to study video games in their cultural contexts rather than merely analyzing them as a form of culture.[5] Among other reasons, this is because the video game medium is characterized by communication and negotiation amidst players,[6] who bring with them a certain context and *habitus*.[7] Therefore, the creation and consumption of technologies such as video games involves a continual process of feedback and modification, allowing games to be adapted to the reality in which their players are living.

As a result, it is key to consider video games' role as a form of contemporary cultural narration, in particular since the advent of massively multiplayer online (MMO) games. Once play goes online, gaming ceases to be an isolated activity in which the player interacts exclusively with the machine, and involves an increasing element of interpersonal interaction as online players come together and create collective spaces for gathering. Even if human interactions can be realistically simulated by machines, as shown by Sherry Turkle's analysis of technological toys like Sony's AIBO robot dog, the Furby and others,[8] we have to consider the difference between them, as interactions with machines are based on pre-programmed responses, and hence they are not willfully reciprocal. In other words, all

1. Author's Note: I would like to thank all the people who contributed in one way or another to the development of this article, especially Claudio Ramos Zincke.

2. Ian Woodward, "Material Culture and Narrative: Fusing Myth, Materiality, and Meaning," in *Material Culture and Technology in Everyday Life: Ethnographic Approaches*, ed. Phillip Vannini (Peter Lang, 2009), 60.

3. Paul du Gay et al., *Doing Cultural Studies: The Story of the Sony Walkman* (Sage, 1997), 84-113.

4. Heather A. Horst and Daniel Miller, *The Cell Phone: An Anthropology of Communication* (Berg, 2006), 81-136.

5. Adrienne Shaw, "What is Video Game Culture? Cultural Studies and Game Studies," *Games and Culture* 5.4 (2010): 416.

6. Anne Mette Thourhauge, "The Rules of the Game—The Rules of the Player," *Games and Culture* 8.6 (2013): 389.

7. According to Pierre Bourdieu, habitus can be define as a "systems of durable, transposable dispositions, structured structures predisposed to function as structuring structures, that is, as principles which generate and organize practices and representations that can be objectively adapted to their outcomes without presupposing a conscious aiming at ends or an express mastery of the operations necessary in order to attain them." See Bourdieu, *The Logic of Practice* (Stanford University Press, 1992).

8. Sherry Turkle, *Alone Together: Why We Expect More From Technology and Less From Each Other* (Basic Books, 2011), 35-66.

contact with the game and all dialogues produced have been pre-programmed, as opposed to human interactions, in which there is a degree of free will, since the person can decide how to respond to other players' communicative cues and whether to keep interacting with them or not. With artificial intelligence, robot toys or game software, on the contrary, the object is obligated to interact upon the user's demand. In online games, a player interacts with a number of real individuals, which not only makes player communications unpredictable and variable, but also increases the importance of interpersonal communication for success in the game.

This chapter focuses on *World of Warcraft* (Blizzard, 2004), a game that reached its peak number of users in 2010 with 12 million subscriptions worldwide. In light of this massive quantity of players spread across different geographical regions, it is important to consider: Is this collective space constructed in the same way across different regions? Do we have the same gaming experience, regardless of geographical locale? Do players in the global south experience *WoW* differently than those in the global north? And in what ways do players integrate elements of their national cultures into the gaming experience? While important research has already shed light on certain aspects of the experience of playing *WoW*, such as conflicts and relationships that are generated therein, or transformations in the player experience in modes such as the PvE (player-versus-Environment) "end-game," up to now research has yet to examine how aspects of one's regional culture are integrated in *WoW*, which can profoundly affect the experience of the game.[9]

RELEVANCE AND METHODOLOGY

This chapter focuses on the new spaces of socialization that have been generated by virtual platforms like MMOs. As Dmitri Williams has argued, virtual communities—online video games among them—have taken the place of public squares, taverns and other previously-dominant social spaces and meeting places outside the household and workplace.[10] Moreover, social interactions between players do not just take place within the game, but rather interpersonal communication is extended and expanded upon through other media and platforms. This shows why the division between "virtual reality" and "real life" cannot be sustained, as a number of studies have argued.[11] Scholarship also demonstrates that online games are fundamentally social experiences,[12] in which relationships are developed based on shared interests and common objectives.[13] Therefore, players' approaches to *WoW* and other MMOs can be associated with factors such as age,[14] nationality[15] and commitment, as it sometimes can be confused with relations of production.[16]

In this chapter, I use an auto-ethnographic approach to analyze *WoW* from the perspective of my own experience of the game as a 23-year-old female Chilean player.[17] In video games in general, as well

9. For an analysis of conflicts and relationships among players, see Bonnie Nardi, *My Life as a Night Elf Priest: An Anthropological Account of* World of Warcraft (University of Michigan Press, 2010); Lauren B. Collister, "Surveillance and Community: Language Policy and Empowerment in a World of Warcraft Guild," *Surveillance & Society* 12.3 (2014): 337-348; and Nickolas Jordan, "World of Warcraft: A Family Therapist's Journey into Scapegoated Culture," *The Qualitative Report* 19 (2014): 1-19. For an examination of PvE play, see Mark Chen, "Communication, Coordination and Camaraderie in World of Warcraft," *Games and Culture* 4.1 (2009): 47-73; and Alex Golub, "Being in the World (of Warcraft): Raiding, Realism and Knowledge Production in a Massively Multiplayer Online Game," *Anthropological Quarterly* 83.1 (2010): 17-46.
10. Dmitri Williams, "Why Game Studies Now? Gamers Don't Bowl Alone," *Games and Culture* 1.1 (2006): 14.
11. See, for example, Sima Forghani, et al., "MMORPG Worlds: On the Construction of Social Reality in World of Warcraft," *Living Virtually: Researching New Worlds*, ed. Don Heider (Peter Lang, 2006), 67-92; Vili Lehdonvirta, "Virtual Worlds Don't Exist: Questioning the Dichotomous Approach in MMO Studies," *Game Studies* 10.1 (2010); and Golub, "Being in the World (of Warcraft)."
12. Torill Elvira Mortesen, "WoW Is the New MUD: Social Gaming From Text to Video," *Games and Culture* 1.4 (2006): 404.
13. Margaret de Larios and John T. Lang, "Pluralistic Ignorance in Virtually Assembled Peers: The Case of World of Warcraft," *Games and Culture* 9.2 (2014): 107.
14. Thorsten Quandt, Helmut Grueninger and Jeffrey Wimmer, "The Gray Haired Gaming Generation: Findings from an Explorative Interview Study on Older Computer Gamers," *Games and Culture* 4.1 (2009): 43-45.
15. T. L. Taylor, "Does WoW Change Everything?: How PvP Server, Multinational Player Base and Surveillance Mod Scene Caused Me Pause," *Games and Culture* 1.4 (2006): 1-20.
16. Nick Yee, "The Labor of Fun: How Video Games Blur the Boundaries of Work and Play," *Games and Culture* 1.1 (2006): 68-71.
17. Using guidelines regarding auto-ethnography elaborated by Atkinson (2011), Denzin and Lincoln (2002) and O'Riordan (2014).

as *WoW* in particular, innumerable factors work in concert to develop a complex reality that can be perceived by playing a game, which generally exceeds that domain, evidencing a cultural dimension to game's meaning that cannot be grasped through a "close reading" of the game in isolation. Therefore, this chapter is based on data collected from two high-population *WoW* servers, one in Latin America (Us-Ragnaros) and one in North America (Us-Thrall), both in the Eastern Standard Time Zone (UTC -5).[18] In order to gather relevant information, I created avatars to engage in gameplay on both servers, recorded observational and analytical notes, made note of conversations among players in the game's chat rooms, intervened or proposed certain topics of conversation for comparative purposes and recorded information over more than 228 hours (9 days) of gameplay between September and December of 2015. Observations for this chapter focused particularly on the public discussion boards such as "General," "Trade" and "Looking for Group," as well as analysis of the guilds to which my characters belonged.

INTERPERSONAL COMMUNICATION IN *WOW*, FROM LATIN TO NORTH AMERICA

It is difficult to translate the experience of player communication in *WoW* into a linear written form, as in-game interactions lack non-verbal communication and involve multiple, simultaneous conversations registered in the same chat dialogue box, all of which are programmed to disappear after two minutes have passed, or if there are more than eight new messages from players. While communication—from the coordination of activities to the exchange of goods—is an important part of the game, the everyday conversations that players have while playing are not a core element of gameplay. Players have access to these chats in the main hubs of the game—places to rest, where goods can be exchanged or tasks can be completed (see Image 2.2.1). The lower left corner of the screen is the default space for the in-game chat dialogues, though this interface can also be customized according to the user's preferences.

On these servers,gender, a user's class or race cannot be verified, and therefore players generally do not know whom they are addressing when emitting judgments or opinions. In this space of anonymity, people can make statements without experiencing the same social retaliation that might occur in an environment with their own acquaintances or one involving direct personal contact, as is also reflected in Jules Skotnes-Brown's work in this anthology. This does not mean, however, that the construction of this space is neutral: as elaborated in the work of Lisa Nakamura, gender, class, race and other factors impact the experience of online interaction.[19] Moreover, most players share some characteristics, such as the masculine gender, and these commonalities determine the norms of behavior inside the game, which is also complemented with each player's own national culture brought into the game as they have different expectations or cultural norms.

Many *WoW* players, even those with shared characteristics, do not participate actively in the chats available. This could be explained, at least in part, by the dynamics of communication typical to the online gaming context: a light and playful conversational environment where everything and everyone—even, and especially, sensitive topics— can be derided or insulted, which causes some players to keep their distance. A language-based analysis is crucial for understanding these chats, not only because of their frequent use of slang, gaming abbreviations and online chat lingo, but also because of what is considered acceptable or not within a given community, i.e., the ways normativity

18. Data from Blizzard Entertainment, Inc. show 303,418 players on the North American server and 314,840 players on the South American server analyzed in this chapter (2015).

19. See Lisa Nakamura, *Digitizing Race: Visual Cultures of the Internet* (University of Minnesota Press, 2008); and Lisa Nakamura, *Cybertypes: Race, Ethnicity, and Identity on the Internet* (Routledge, 2002).

Image 2.2.1. Visualization of chat dialogue boxes, World of Warcraft.

is conveyed through language. Therefore, having described the basics of the *WoW* interface, which is essentially the same for players in the Latin and players in the North, the following section will take a closer look upon the differences between servers, analyzing the cultural factors these differences reflect, as well as exploring player actions that could be seen as a cultural appropriation of the gaming experience by analyzing three themes that were often brought up in both servers: 1) Recruitment and the demand for guilds, 2) Interpersonal relationships and 3) Political discussion.

Recruiting and Demands of the Guilds

An important part of the interpersonal communication in *WoW* is produced in their open channels, where they often use them to recruit players or look up for guilds. As T. L. Taylor has demonstrated, guilds are the primary formal organization in the game, constituted of different associations of people whose avatars take on diverse objectives in *WoW*. To recruit players, guilds sometimes place conditions on new members with regard to their schedule, level of progression in the game or possession of a requisite item level, role or class. The data for this chapter included a total of 88 announcements for Latin American guilds and 119 announcements on the North American server, which were analyzed to determine the specific characteristics of the most sought-after players and guilds in each region.

Player characteristics have a defining role in guild selection and membership. Aside from the basic characteristics of guild announcements, such as the guild's appeal to either casual or hardcore players, guilds use a number of criteria to filter through potential members and make decisions regarding new applicants. For both Latin American and the North American servers (as determined by Blizzard's designations), I distinguish data using categories related to both the domain of the game (referred to the player's experience and their knowledge of the class and role they play) and to player's personality (such as responsibility, commitment, sense of humor, among other attributes). The few guilds that demanded certain characteristics of their members on either server tended to value personality characteristics more those related to the game domain, though players interested in completing raids always sought players with a higher ranking (see Table 2.2.1).

	Total characteristics referenced	Characteristics related to game domain		Characteristics related to player personality	
North American	119	15	12.6%	22	18.5%
Latin American	88	21	23.9%	39	44.3%

Table 2.2.1. Distribution of game domain and player characteristics among WoW guild announcements

The most notable difference between servers were the specific personality characteristics sought by guilds: Latin American groups frequently aimed for properties like punctuality, while North American guilds often looked for fun players with a sense of humor. There were also particularities to both servers—on one hand, there were ten announcements on the North American server from guilds seeking mature players featuring an age condition (18 , 21 and 30), and even one guild that required player interviews before inviting them to join. On the other hand, on the Latin American server there were guilds searching for players or guilds with certain nationalities, possibly because regional slang and national dialects can create barriers among the Latin American players, impeding communication. Nationality was also an object of humor, as players would frequently ridicule the slang of certain countries during their chats with other players on the Latin American server.

Recruitment strategies and new player orientation practices also differed considerably between the South American and North American servers. One observation regarding recruitment was that, for players who had not completed the latest content or were just starting the latest raid, Latin American guilds offered the experience of "learning on the go" or the idea of "growing together," while on the North American server, some guilds tended to offer to sell their services in exchange of gold (375k) so the person could access in-game rewards. This practice is further publicized when guilds document their time taken for each task. This is a difference that impacts not only the individual player experience, but the ways of a given server views the game itself.

Guilds tended to offer a pleasant and stress-free community on both servers. Offers promising such an environment were more prevalent on the North American server than those seeking certain player characteristics, and there were also "atypical" guilds seeking out-of-the-ordinary experience—for instance, playing old content/earlier expansions of the game while staying under their maximum ranking in the announcements of two guilds; or unusual, humorous announcements that seemed to be aimed at a particular audience (six guilds). On the other hand, on the Latin American server there was a guild whose announcement stated that there was "a lot of bullying," the only case in which a guild was publicized based on an attribute that is largely considered negative.

Interpersonal Relationships

When players dedicate a considerable portion of their time to playing *WoW* and interacting with

other players, they can develop interpersonal relationships of friendship, love or animosity, including connections that are built in-game, relationships established prior to the game and new bonds with other players that evolve through the shared experience of online gameplay. These dynamics provide the basis for the construction of interpersonal relationships as well as the foundations for entire communities on the same servers: among these communities, player's responses and questions about the game may be scrutinized or comments about a player's personal affairs may be asked, establishing the particular dynamics for the dialogue that will develop in that community—whether more friendly or more hostile—as well as the types of exchanges that can take place within the parameters of a given domain.
Community and friendship were highly valued on the South American and North American WoW server alike. Preparation for this chapter included extensive analysis of public chats, focusing specifically on dialogues seeking to establish friendships rather than those developing existing relationships or associations. Among the Latin American community, there was a greater disposition toward creating and maintaining friendships by acknowledging fellow players and making friendly gestures—such as wishing a fellow player a good weekend or expressing concern rather than insults. Meanwhile, the North American community was more susceptible to conflict due to a greater presence of "trolls" creating a hostile environment, bringing about a greater frequency of insults and aggressive comments in public chats, with other players often responding with even greater hostility to the player(s) who initiated the conflict. This was clear in the public chat, as some players marginalize certain type of people who have only recently started playing the game or who are overly sensitive by using insults, ironic comments or plainly stating that they were not welcome. Since these communications took place in the context of a public chat (not in a raid, battleground or dungeon), they did not revolve around any challenge or objective in which the less-experienced player could negatively impact other players' performance.

Hostility among the Latin American community, however, was primarily directed toward certain characters or prototypes of players. During the period of observation, there was one player (mentioned 421 times in the chat logs) who clearly participated in "trolling," which Claire Hardarker would define as deliberate provocation of others to incite conflict, high emotional reactions and disturbance in others for the troll's own amusement. This player, who identified himself as male but described himself with contradictory statements, participated very frequently in the period of observation, using misogynist language and slurs and making ignorant statements on sensitive subjects such as Venezuela's political situation. On a number of occasions, other players declared that they were going to report him to Blizzard's moderators for hostile language. The presence of hostility toward this troll was notable in the content of some of his and his interlocutors' statements.

Players frequently made open requests for friends or partners (always women), both seriously and in jest, using *WoW*'s in-game chats. In general, requests by players on the American server were seeking romantic relationships more often than friendship. When seeking a partner, players would sometimes offer gold (the in-game currency) or request a girlfriend with a webcam (as one particular player did on 13 occasions). The North American community requested friendship and partners with less frequency than on the Latin American server, but each player tended to make more friendship requests overall. One reason men were more frequently found looking for female partners, and women were observed participating less frequently overall in such searches, is likely because women are a minority on these servers, which is explained by Clara Fernández Vara and Adrienne Shaw as they elucidate how the industry of video games is perceived as a masculine one where women are misrepresented or their bodies are emphasized based on their sexual qualities, creating a cycle where the industry creates video games that are unappealing to women.[20] Nick Yee even argues that it is the social and cultural constraint for women who enter these spaces that explains the lower percentage of female in the MMO population.[21] Additionally, the ethnography done in *WoW* by Jenny Sudén and Malin Svenigsson, showed how women were conceived as fineries or an additional aesthetic of the game and not players on the same level as men.[22] This is complemented with the studies of Jesse Fox, Wai Yen Tang, Jeffrey H. Kuznekoff and Lindsey M. Rose who showed how the treatment in online games is condition by gender as findings indicate more negative and severe comments towards women.[23] On the Latin American server, women represented a total of 29.8% of players, while on the North American server they made up 36.5%.[24] As a result, an extreme form of toxic masculinity has appropriated many of these chats, which may well have resulted in the relatively low female participation in these dialogues. The gender gap between players is evidenced in the use of sexually-connoted language and the fact that some players even go so far as to "pay" for a girlfriend. Thus on both servers, the gameplay experience took place in a sexualized environment dominated by aggression and toxicity, reinforcing the male-dominated communication in the in-game chats, where some concerns were commented on differently according to the perceived gender of the communicator, likely contributing to a lower proportion of women playing on *WoW*'s servers and chatting in the game's dialogue boxes.

Among hostile interactions, one tendency that was observed almost exclusively on the Latin American server was the use of homophobic slurs as insults or provocations against other players, some of whom went so far as to assert that homosexuality constitutes a sin by a player, without any other player comments reacting against this viewpoint. Just because several Latin American countries—Argentina, Uruguay, Mexico and Brazil—have taken a leading role by legalizing same-sex marriage, this does not mean that there is more respect toward the subject in Latin America's virtual spaces, where homosexuality is used as the basis for abuse and insults. For example, when one player asked a question about his love life, nearly all the responses were aimed at making fun of the situation was in, telling him to explain to his parents why he didn't have a girlfriend yet and making various references of coming out of the closet. Even though this occasion did not involve abusive language used against a homosexual player, male homosexuality was used as an insult and a way to make fun of others. On the North American server, on the other hand—both Canada and the United States have legal marriage for partners of the same sex—these jokes or insults registered with less frequency (three cases were observed in all, none of which were in reference to a particular individual). Other characteristics used as the basis for insults included age (being a child or adolescent), illiteracy and, with less frequency, mental disability, the latter of which was observed only on the North American server. Given the parameters of the *WoW* platform, it is possible that the rapidity of the messages produced in these chats requires players to express themselves with relatively little thought, favoring the types of simplistic and discriminatory insults that are commonplace in many online (and offline) cultures, and certainly in both the South American and North American *WoW* servers.

At times, the very presence of female players on the *WoW* servers could be a contentious subject. As there was a lower percentage of women in the servers, in many instances when a player declared

20. See Shaw, "What is Video Game Culture?" and Clara Fernández Vara, "La problemática representación de la mujer en los videojuegos y su relación con la industria," *Revista de Estudios de Juventud* 106 (2014): 93-108.
21. Yee, "The Labor of Fun."
22. Jenny Sundén and Malin Sveningsson, *Gender and Sexuality in Online Game Cultures* (Routledge, 2012).
23. See Jesse Fox and Wai Yen Tang, "Women's Experiences with General and Sexual Harassment in Online Video Games: Rumination, Organizational Responsiveness, Withdrawal, and Coping Strategies," *New Media & Society* (2016): 1-18; and Jeffrey H. Kuznekoff and Lindsey M. Rose, "Communication in Multiplayer Gaming: Examining Player Responses to Gender Cues," *New Media & Society* 15. 4 (2013): 541-556.
24. Data provided by Blizzard Entertainment, Inc. (2015)

herself to be female, other players tended not to believe her. For example, when a player self-identified as female on the North American server, another player responded, "women are a myth," which was echoed by another player's denial that the player could be female, stating that "girls in wow are guys in real life." On this particular occasion, another player responded by saying it was a pathetic attitude, and an additional player agreed. On the other hand, players on the Latin American server expressed their doubt even more aggressively, labeling these female players transsexual, calling them "easy" or implying that they had male genitals. One of the particularly interesting points among these interactions, in terms of the language used by the players, is that Latin American players were consistently more aggressive and blunt than those on the North American *WoW* server. Likewise, nobody intervened to defend the player who had claimed to be female, nor did the player whose sexuality was being questioned express indignation or any similar reaction, all of which helped to validate this type of speech within the community.

In the open chats included in the *WoW* interface—namely the General Chat and the Trade Chat, which, unlike private chat rooms, are accessible to all players—the only normative enforcement for the use of language comes from reporting an individual player for breaking the game's Terms of Service, which include provisions prohibiting verbal abuse, bullying and harassment. However, in the grand scheme of the game, due to the high number of players engaged in gameplay on densely-populated servers, reporting individual players has very little effect on the climate for interpersonal communication overall. Still, the game does provide a set of tools designed to allow players to mute specific other players, leave certain chats or censor mature language by replacing terms of offensive words with asterisks. Players are allowed to create, curate and moderate custom chats as well, and each guild also has its own intra-guild chat. Each of these layers of player-to-player communication expands the possibilities for collaboration and community-building among participants, as Lauren Collister shows in her research on guild policies and mechanisms for maintaining safe spaces.[25]

The type of misogynist dialogue described above was manifested on repeated occasions in which women and their bodies were sexualized and conventional gender roles were reinforced, making *WoW*'s chats sexist spaces dominated by insults that relegate women with the domestic sphere and objectify them sexually. In the public chats, there was such a common tendency to eroticize the female body that players were expected to partake in it regardless of their own sex or sexual orientation as it is what most people in the community like. The hyper-sexualization of women could be observed in recurrent jokes and insults that involved references to players' mothers, and in the case of Latin American servers, their sisters as well. This did not imply that women could not participate in the discussion, but rather that they would have to adapt to the way the environment had been constructed, including the language patterns and topics of discussion sustained within these chats. Thus, the invitation to female players may exist, but certain conditions still apply, and a woman's decision to participate might be heavily conditioned by the topics and dynamics of the discussions taking place.

Political Discussions

Political topics were a regular part of the interactions between players on the *WoW* chats, whether they were making fun of future presidential candidates on the North American server—Donald Trump was mentioned 108 times in the dialogue registers, while Bernie Sanders was mentioned 27 times and George and Jeb Bush were mentioned 19 times—or discussing the political situation in

25. The nature of these compartmentalized channels exceeds the scope of this particular investigation; see Collister, "Surveillance and Community."

Venezuela and other countries on the Latin American server—Venezuela was mentioned 41 times, president Nicolás Maduro was mentioned 20 times and Argentina was mentioned 12 times, including references that were not related to political discussion as such, but rather to nationalistic rivalries. Overall, participation in political discussion on the Latin American server was lower than on the North American server—consider, for example, that like the United States, Argentina was also in the midst of a presidential election year. As mentioned above, the types of dialogue observed in the game were not necessarily the most profound or detailed, particularly given that they were situated in a space where communication is reduced to short, typed chats in which everything was generally taken lightly. Indeed, exhibiting seriousness in a discussion or showing sensitivity towards certain topics could even provoke rejection from active participants in the *WoW* communications channels. Therefore, it is important to examine the nature of the political discussions that arise in these sorts of environments in order to understand why players argue about politics when they have very little chance of arriving at consensus or reaching a political compromise, let alone taking political action of any sort.

Because the servers have different compositions, the political conversations observed in both cases were radically distinct: the Latin American servers are populated by players from all the Spanish-speaking countries of Latin America, while the North American servers are populated by a far more homogeneous player base in terms of nationality. On the one hand, Latin American dialogues were filled with various provocations based on players' nationalities or expressing certain longstanding rivalries among countries, for example making fun of the fact that Bolivia is landlocked as a consequence of the War of the Pacific, or that the Falkland Islands are not part of Argentina's territory due to British occupation. When political discussion did arise, it was usually related to countries in South America (in addition to Mexico, which was mentioned seven times). Moreover, the comments on this server made less frequent reference to outside events than on the North American server: the Chilean earthquake of September 16, 2015 was mentioned as a news item as well as a subject of mockery, in one player's joking comment that there was a tsunami alert in effect for Bolivia. Even if these dialogues frequently began with the purpose of provoking conflict, they tended to end in a peaceful manner. When making light of the situation in Venezuela, for example, some players—who were not necessarily Venezuelan, but demonstrated their solidarity—intervened, disagreeing with the derisive comments and proclaiming the need to show respect regarding a sensitive matter. This policing of communications from within the players on the Latin American server nurtures a less hostile and fragmented community relative to the North American server. Political topics were mostly referenced anecdotally, by players sharing information about current living conditions in their own countries, without delving into more profound or larger-scale political arguments.

On the North American *WoW* server, on the other hand, rivalries regularly developed surrounding a variety of contingent topics within the dialogues, such as the use of drugs, freedom of expression, the Paris attacks of 13 November 2015 or foreign policy issues affecting the United States such as the conflicts with Russia and Syria, even if this discussion was generally superficial. There was a common denominator of participants instigating conflict through comments or statements whose sole purpose was to stir fights on sensitive subjects, including declarations such as "white males are the cause of school shootings" or "Obama did sandy hook." When referencing presidential candidates on the North American server, mockery and irony provided the guiding ethos for these channels—even the candidates themselves were the subject of derision, while on the Latin American server, the mention of candidates and leaders seemed inclined to produce conflict, but with a more serious tone. In conclusion, on both servers the same logic of association that appeared within the construction of the community was reproduced on the political front. Within this realm, no major differentiation seems to be present between servers, with the exception of what is discussed, or how dialogues are used: on the North American server, political figures are an excuse to spread a playful dialogue, while on the Latin American server, politics are used more to produce conflicts and less as the subject of jokes.

CONCLUSION: THE IMPACT OF NATIONAL CULTURE ON THE EXPERIENCE OF *WOW*

The public spaces of communication in both Latin American and North American *WoW* servers develop certain behavioral norms that are bolstered by factors including the condition of anonymity and the male-dominated game environment. Dialogues developed in the chats should not simply be taken at face value, as they are also a constantly filled of mockery and playful jeering. Differentiation between regions takes place at their margins: on the North American server, players make fun of presidential candidates, while on the Latin American server, while there is space for sharing personal experiences, these are also the subject of frequent mockery from other players.

Since both Latin American and North American *WoW* servers feature the same software and chat tools, use the same game rules and have a majority of male players, there are similarities in the construction of online interactions within this space—such as a relative lack of reflection and a relative prominence of argumentation in the dialogues, as well as the persistent sexualization of women, among others. Although there are characteristics that can lead to a construction of a homogenous gaming experience across servers in distinct geographical locations, differentiation occurs nevertheless as the game is appropriated by gaming populations of diverse cultural backgrounds, precisely because the appropriation of the game is also a product of the player's prior socialization within the realm of *WoW*.

At least preliminarily, it can be shown that the experience of *WoW* differs between Latin American and North American servers with regard to the treatment of politics, gender relations and personal events. For instance, the Latin American server tended to have a friendlier atmosphere among players and presents hostility only towards certain individuals ("trolls"). However, women were frequently excluded given the misogynist discourse produced and reproduced in these spaces. On the other hand, the North American server was home to a disjointed community in which player interactions were notably more individualized and aggressive when discussing others' opinions. Yet at the same time, players on the North American server were more respectful in relation to other subjects, for instance vocally rejecting verbal violence towards women and mockery of homosexuality, both of which were persistent on the Latin American server.

The approximation towards the experience of the game appears to be different between the Latin and the North American servers. The types of available guilds are different as on the one hand, the North America server offers a mature atmosphere (selecting players by age criteria); and on the other hand, the Latin American server offers guilds with specific nationalities. Furthermore, there are two different perspectives on the game for players who have not started or are beginning to play the last content of the game: an experiential viewpoint (Latin American) and another that seeks effectiveness (North American), hinting the cultural dispositions that affect conceptions of the game.

These are not the only aspects that could be observed in terms of appropriation of the experience of the game, and other factors may influence or produce differentiation between servers. Further research could follow up on the interpersonal relationships in the game that are produced within chats or social guilds, or analyze how culturally and nationally determined characteristics are integrated to the experience of the end-game (PvE/PvP), where players have a greater commitment. There is a more wholly constructed relationship between the characters of the game, and players are exposed to more engaging and demanding environments, where certain types of gameplay performance are expected. Likewise, further research could be developed on the level of commitment and immersion that exists while playing the game: What type of leisure are we seeking in our free time? Why do we choose to play on this platform rather than face-to-face? What consequences does this bring? Finally, this chapter points to emergent questions regarding the dynamic of anonymity: In what ways do people express or perform their gender, race or class in these games? Do they act differently dependent on their personal and cultural identity? Under what circumstances do players accentuate their gender, race and class backgrounds? Is there still a degree of discrimination when players know each other better? These questions point to the relevance of continued research on video games—particularly MMOs—as they constitute an important burgeoning space for socialization.

WORKS CITED

Atkinson, Paul, et al. *Handbook of Ethnography*. Sage, 2011.

Chen, Mark. "Communication, Coordination and Camaraderie in World of Warcraft." *Games and Culture* 4.1 (2009): 47-73.

Collister, Lauren B. "Surveillance and Community: Language Policy and Empowerment in a World of Warcraft Guild." *Surveillance & Society* 12.3 (2014): 337-348.

De Larios, Margaret and John T. Lang. "Pluralistic Ignorance in Virtually Assembled Peers: The Case of World of Warcraft." *Games and Culture* 9.2 (2014): 102-121.

Denzin, Norman K. and Yvonna Lincoln. *Handbook of Qualitative Research*, 2nd ed. Sage, 2002.

Du Gay, Paul, et al. *Doing Cultural Studies: The Story of the Sony Walkman*. Sage, 1997.

Fernández Vara, Clara. "La problemática representación de la mujer en los videojuegos y su relación con la industria." *Revista de Estudios de Juventud* 106 (2014): 93-108.

Forghani, Sima, et al. "MMORPG Worlds: On the Construction of Social Reality in World of Warcraft." In *Living Virtually: Researching New Worlds*, edited by Don Heider, 67-92. Peter Lang, 2006.

Fox, Jesse and Wai Yen Tang. "Women's Experiences with General and Sexual Harassment in Online Video Games: Rumination, Organizational Responsiveness, Withdrawal, and Coping Strategies." *New Media & Society* (2016): 1-18.

Golub, Alex. "Being in the World (of Warcraft): Raiding, Realism and Knowledge Production in a Massively Multiplayer Online Game." *Anthropological Quarterly* 83.1 (2010): 17-46.

Hardaker, Claire. "Trolling in Asynchronous Computer-Mediated Communication: From User Discussions to Academic Definitions." *Journal of Politeness Research* 6 (2010): 215–242.

Horst, Heather, A. and Daniel Miller. *The Cell Phone: An Anthropology of Communication*. Berg, 2006.

Jordan, Nickolas. "World of Warcraft: A Family Therapist's Journey into Scapegoated Culture." *The Qualitative Report* 19 (2014): 1-19.

Kuznekoff, Jeffrey H. and Lindsey M. Rose. "Communication in Multiplayer Gaming: Examining Player Responses to Gender Cues." *New Media & Society* 15.4 (2013): 541-556.

Lehdonvirta, Vili. "Virtual Worlds Don't Exist: Questioning the Dichotomous Approach in MMO Studies," *Game Studies* 10.1 (2010), http://gamestudies.org/1001/articles/lehdonvirta.

Mortesen, Torill Elvira. "WoW Is the New MUD: Social Gaming From Text to Video." *Games and Culture* 1.4 (2006): 397-413.

Mette Thorhauge, Anne. "The Rules of the Game—The Rules of the Player," *Games and Culture*, 8.6 (2013): 371-391.

Nakamura, Lisa. *Digitizing Race: Visual Cultures of the Internet.* University of Minnesota Press, 2008.

Nakamura, Lisa. *Cybertypes: Race, Ethnicity, and Identity on the Internet.* Routledge, 2002.

Nardi, Bonnie. *My Life as a Night Elf Priest: An Anthropological Account of World of Warcraft.* University of Michigan Press, 2010.

O Riordan, Niamh. "Autoethnography: Proposing a New Method for Information System Research." European Conference on Information Systems (ECIS), Tel Aviv, Israel, June 9-11, 2014.

Quandt, Thorsten, Helmut Grueninger and Jeffrey Wimmer. "The Gray Haired Gaming Generation: Findings from an Explorative Interview Study on Older Computer Gamers." *Games and Culture* 4.1 (2009): 27-46.

Shaw, Adrienne. "What is Video Game Culture? Cultural Studies and Game Studies." *Games and Culture* 5.4 (2010): 403-424.

—. *Gaming at the Edge: Sexuality and Gender at the Margins of Gamer Culture.* University of Minnesota Press, 2015.

Sundén, Jenny and Malin Sveningsson. *Gender and Sexuality in Online Game Cultures.* Routledge, 2012.

Taylor, T. L. "Does WoW Change Everything?: How PvP Server, Multinational Player Base and Surveillance Mod Scene Caused Me Pause." *Games and Culture* 1.4 (2006): 1-20.

Turkle, Sherry. *Alone Together: Why We Expect More From Technology and Less From Each Other.* Basic Books, 2011.

Williams, Dmitri. "Why Game Studies Now? Gamers Don't Bowl Alone." *Games and Culture* 1.1 (2006): 13-16.

Woodward, Ian. "Material Culture and Narrative: Fusing Myth, Materiality, and Meaning." In *Material Culture and Technology in Everyday Life: Ethnographic Approaches,* edited by Phillip Vannini, 59-72. Peter Lang, 2009.

Yee, Nick. "The Labor of Fun: How Video Games Blur the Boundaries of Work and Play." *Games and Culture* 1.1 (2006): 68-71.

Yee, Nick. "Maps of digital desires: Exploring the Topography of Gender and Play in Online Games." In *Beyond Barbie and Mortal Kombat: New Perspectives on Gender and Gaming*, edited by Yasmin B. Kafai, Carrie Heeter, Jill Denner and Jennifer Y. Sun, 83-96. MIT Press, 2008.

COLONIZED PLAY

RACISM, SEXISM AND COLONIAL LEGACIES IN THE DOTA 2 SOUTH AFRICA GAMING COMMUNITY

JULES SKOTNES-BROWN

Video games, it has often been argued, are products of an unequal world in which the aftermath of colonialism continues to perpetuate inequalities in the global south.[1] From the production of computers in southeast Asia, to the mining of coltan in the Democratic Republic of Congo, to the narratives, rules and visual regimes of mainstream games, a link between past and present imperialism and video gaming has been made. Such studies have, however, paid less attention to the link between video games, colonialism and gaming communities in the global south. In South Africa, despite slow internet rollouts and disproportionately expensive computer systems, various lively gaming communities exist—particularly in the case of one of the most popular computer games, *Dota 2* (Valve Corporation, 2013). In a relatively new democracy, where the wounds of apartheid and colonialism are still fresh, it is perhaps unsurprising that some gaming communities in South Africa are plagued by racism and sexism. The extent to which this is the case in the *Dota 2* South Africa community, however, is staggering—female players are often belittled and ridiculed, while racial slurs, including words that are punishable by fine or imprisonment, are commonplace.[2]

Several essays in this volume have drawn attention to how the legacies of colonialism have shaped present-day video gaming. Mainstream video games, saturated with orientalist representations of the other, imperialist politics which take the nation state as the only legitimate political unit and rules which normalize colonial conquest have inhibited the development of postcolonial game cultures.[3] *Dota 2* in South Africa can be regarded as a part of this trend.

This paper thus differs considerably from Jerjes Loayza's analysis of professional *Dota 2* players in Lima, Peru. His ethnographic study, which focuses on gaming at LANs and internet cafes, finds social and ludic "interface between the physical and virtual worlds."[4] My study, contrastingly, shows how a virtual environment in which actions have no consequences has become a space where racism, perverse historical nostalgia, and aggressive masculinity are allowed to fester amid widespread national attempts to rid the country of such colonial legacies.[5]

To demonstrate this, I analyze the *Dota 2* South Africa community as a product of the close connection between gaming and colonialism, a history of colonial thinking in South Africa, as well as the visual regime, rules and narrative of *Dota 2* itself. Multiplayer video games are valuable historical sources:

1. See for example, Patrick Crogan, *Gameplay Mode: War, Simulation, and Technoculture* (University of Minnesota Press, 2011); Nick Dyer-Witheford and Greig de Peuter, *Games of Empire* (University of Minnesota Press, 2009); Walter Mignolo, *Local Histories/Global Designs: Coloniality, Subaltern Knowledges, and Border Thinking* (Princeton University Press, 2012); and Souvik Mukherjee, *Videogames and Postcolonialism: Empire Plays Back* (Palgrave Macmillan, 2017).
2. Reuters, "South African Woman Jailed in Landmark Ruling for Racist Rant," *The Guardian*, 28 March 2018, https://www.theguardian.com/world/2018/mar/28/south-african-woman-jailed-in-landmark-ruling-for-racist-rant.
3. SeeSouvik Mukherjee, "Replying the Digital Divide: Videogames in India"; Bushra Alfaraj, "Arab Gamers: An Identity Inclusivity Study"; and Rhett Loban and Thomas Apperley, "Eurocentric Values at Play: Modding the Colonial from the Indigenous Perspective," in this volume.
4. See, Jerjes Loayza, "Ludic Solidarity and Sociality: The Impact of Dota 2 on Lima's Youth," in this volume.
5. While this chapter focuses primarily on race, it also includes a brief discussion of gender dynamics among player communities.

their rules and narratives are traces of cultures and ideologies, but they are simultaneously spaces in which cultural and social interactions take place. Within their virtual environments, there are several levels at which social interactions play out, which provide the organizational structure of the remainder of this chapter. Firstly, there are broader *global, structural and generic factors*—ideological dimensions to video game genres and practice which influence which groups of people play video games, and why. Secondly, there are *regional historical and cultural forces* which mediate such social interactions. And thirdly, the *rules and visual regimes* of individual video games influence how players interact with them, and with each other.

GLOBAL, STRUCTURAL AND GENERIC FACTORS: GAMES OF EMPIRE

Claudio Fogu and Wulf Kansteiner have both argued that virtual worlds will fundamentally change the production of historical consciousness. Since, as many gamers can confirm, powerful and cherished memories are produced in virtual spaces, these worlds will not only produce new histories, but change the way we think about history.[6] Such thinking will, no doubt, be influenced by the fact that many video games remain saturated with colonial tropes which romanticize classification and conquest. As Henry Jenkins has pointed out, part of the appeal of video games is their status as new frontiers. In an era when physical space has been thoroughly explored, virtual spaces harken back to the romance of the colonial frontier—as new regions to discover and conquer.[7] Such conquest is not just psycho-symbolic, but also sensitive to the legacies of colonialism and underdevelopment. Since most mainstream video games are produced and disseminated in the "developed" world, they are spaces in which primarily ex-colonial nations can continue to "conquer" the "other," even in postcolonial periods.[8] Such colonial narratives often promote a still widely prevalent Western brand of historical consciousness which depicts the history of colonialism as one of "white man's burden"—as a benevolent process of taming the wild frontier through sword and scripture or, more recently, drones and democracy.

For example, in many popular action-adventure or FPS games, the European or American white male avatar is thrust into a realm of chaos and disorder, and tasked with bringing civilization to the land—either through ridding the "noble savage" of evil and depravity, or through intervening in conflict on foreign soil.[9] In sandbox-building games such as *Minecraft*, the player arrives, like Robinson Crusoe, into a *terra nullius* and encourages him to "improve" this land—by clearing jungles, draining marshes, building infrastructure and mining minerals. Its inhabitants—hostile monsters or local villagers—appear simply as obstacles in the path of development, or as resources to exploit. In the map-based interfaces of strategy games, entire regions are transformed into dehumanized tracts of land and resources, ripe for exploitation.[10] Cartography, in the history of European colonialism, has been argued as a means by which to render land "legible"—that is, to point out its essential resources, enable their exploitation and minimize any competition to this supply of resources, such as the local

6. Claudio Fogu, "Digitising Historical Consciousness," *History and Theory* 47 (2009): 103-121; Wulf Kansteiner, "Alternate Worlds and Invented Communities: History and Historical Consciousness in the Age of Interactive Media," in *Manifestos for History*, eds. Keith Jenkins, Sue Morgan, Alun Munslow (Routledge, 2007): 131-148.
7. Quoted in David Leonard, "An Untapped Field: Exploring the World of Virtual Sports Gaming," in *Handbook of Sports and Media*, eds. Arthur Raney and Jennings Bryant (Lawrence Erlbaum Associates, 2006): 433.
8. Jules Skotnes-Brown, "Redrawing the Magic Circle: Video Games, Imperial Conquest, and Shifting Concepts of Play," Honours Thesis, University of Cape Town, 2015, 34.
9. Ryan Lizardi, "Repelling the Invasion of the 'Other': Post-Apocalyptic Alien Shooter Videogames Addressing Contemporary Cultural Attitudes," *Eludamos: Journal for Computer Game Culture* 3.2 (2009): 295-308; Johan Höglund, "Electronic Empire: Orientalism Revisited in the Military Shooter," *Game Studies* 8.1 (2008), http://gamestudies.org/0801/articles/hoeglund.
10. See Rhett Loban and Thomas Apperley's chapter "Eurocentric Values at Play" in this volume for a more in-depth analysis of this. See also Rebecca Mir and Trevor Owens, "Modeling Indigenous Peoples: Unpacking Ideology in Sid Meier's Colonization," in *Playing With the Past: Digital Games and Simulations of History*, eds. Matthew Kapell and Andrew Elliot (Bloomsbury, 2013): 92; and Shoshana Magnet, "Playing at Colonization: Interpreting Imaginary Landscapes in the Video Game Tropico," *Journal of Communication Enquiry* 30.2 (2006): 143.

population.[11] Many strategy game maps operate under the same logic. Last of all, in most role-playing games (RPGs),[12] playable characters are created based on biopolitical constructs of race through the linking of *physical* and *intellectual* attributes with racial types.

Take, for example, the discursive strategy visible in the following two descriptions. The first is from *Baldur's Gate II* (Bioware, 2000):

> Half-orcs are born from the union of human and orc parents. They are as tall as humans, but a little heavier due to their muscular builds. Their greenish pigmentation, sloping forehead, jutting jaw, prominent teeth, and coarse body hair make their lineage plain for all to see. In the Sword Coast, half-orcs are tolerated, as unlike in the north the local people haven't had centuries of warfare with orc kind. Half-orcs are known for their great strength.[13]

Compare this to an account of an African skull cited in Josiah Nott and George Gliddon's *Indigenous Races of the Earth* (1868):

> The front of the head, including the forehead and face, is compressed laterally [...] The bony substance is denser and harder; the sides of the skull thicker, and the whole weight consequently more considerable. The bony apparatus employed in mastication, and in forming receptacles for the organs of sense, is larger, stronger, and more advantageously constructed for powerful effect, than in the races where more extensive use of experience and reason, and greater civilization, supply the place of animal strength [...] the intellectual part is lessened, the animal organs are enlarged.[14]

Between these two depictions, we see similarities with regard to the treatment of racial physiognomy—both "races" are described as having sloping foreheads, flat faces, prominent jaws and enlarged teeth. Similarly, half-orcs receive a penalty to intelligence, and a bonus to strength. This makes a sense of Foucauldian biopower tangible within the game, as such classification controls the way each race can interact with the world: Half-Orcs by virtue of race are incapable of studying magic, but can excel as warriors.[15] Because the genre, in many ways, remains indebted to Dungeons and Dragons, and classic isometric-perspective RPGs of the 1980s and 1990s, like *Baldur's Gate* itself, such is the same in many other RPGs as well. In *Skyrim* (Bethesda Softworks, 2011), for example, the Khajit receive racial bonuses to stealth, lock-picking and pick-pocketing—making them racially apt thieves—in what almost seems to be a silent citation of the notorious British "Criminal Tribes" Act (1871) in India, wherein the British developed a penal system to control people believed to be hereditarily prone to crime.[16]

The effect of all this is that many game narrative and rule systems remain influenced by nineteenth and twentieth-century European visions of race, land and conquest. In such games, the white man is needed to liberate the "native" from her "primitive" lifestyle, land exists primarily for resource exploitation and development and racial classification is not only a biological norm, but certain races need to live according to their strengths—whether intellect, or bestial power. It is perhaps not surprising then, that video games tend not to be particularly inclusive with regard to protagonists. For David Dietrich, because many role-playing games do not "allow for the creation of avatars with a

11. James Scott, *Seeing Like a State: How Certain Schemes to Improve the Human Condition Have Failed* (Yale University Press, 1998): 1.
12. The role-playing games I have in mind are those that allow the player to construct an avatar from a multiplicity of fictional (or real) races, all with different physical and intellectual attributes.
13. James Ohlen and Ray Muzkya, *Baldurs' Gate* (Bioware, 1998), Character Creation Screen.
14. Joseph Nott and George Gliddon, *Indigenous Races of the Earth* (Trubner & Co., 1868): 325.
15. Michel Foucault, *The Birth of Biopolitics: Lectures at the College de France, 1978-79*, trans. Graham Burchell (Palgrave Macmillan, 1999): 317-325; Michel Foucault, "Society Must Be Defended," in *Lectures at the College de France, 1975-76*, eds. Mauro Bertani and Allesandro Fortana, trans. David Macey (Picador, 2003): 239-263.
16. For a good discussion of The Criminal Tribes Act, see Andrew Major, "State and Criminal Tribes in Colonial Punjab: Surveillance, Control and Reclamation of the 'Dangerous Classes,'" *Modern Asian Studies* 33.3 (1999): 662.

non-white racial appearance," this results in the construction of all-white virtual spaces, "contributing to the creation of a virtual 'white habitus.'"[17] The repeated attacks from "hardcore" gamers launched against those who attempt to diversify game communities—exemplified by the #Gamergate scandal of 2014—seem only to confirm such observations.[18] Clearly, there is a structural problem associated with "hardcore" gaming as a hobby: many communities seek isolation and the maintenance of spaces of imperial nostalgia.

REGIONAL HISTORICAL AND CULTURAL FORCES: RACISM, SOUTH AFRICAN IDENTITY POLITICS AND THE *DOTA 2* SOUTH AFRICA FACEBOOK GROUP CONTROVERSY (2014-2016)

As Penix-Tadsen has argued, video games both create culture, and draw upon culture as a narratological, visual or ludological resource.[19] Similarly, the *Dota 2* South Africa gaming community is influenced both by game environments and by broader South African national political, cultural and economic identities. The current state of South African identity politics and cultural problems of racism is strongly reflected in the *Dota 2* community. Having only emerged from an institutionalized racist police state in 1994, South Africa is still battling with the historical legacies of apartheid. In mid-2014, the South African Human Rights Commission reported a spike of cases of racism, with over 500 cases in court in that year alone. From 2013 to 2014, 45% of the commission's complaints were race-related.[20] This problem both coincided with and culminated in the 2015-2016 Rhodes Must Fall Student Movement, described as a reawakening of the radical youth.[21] This movement, which has now split into smaller groups, aimed for the decolonization of knowledge production, and the transformation of instruction to promote greater black visibility and participation.

Since 2014, the South African press, public and courts have increasingly targeted racist individuals to make an example of them in an attempt to eliminate visible forms of racism. In contrast to a series of shocking examples of physical violence,[22] one of the most highly publicized of these cases was an offense that took place in a closed, somewhat private space—real estate salesperson Penny Sparrow's Facebook profile. In early January 2016, Sparrow referred to black people as "monkeys" in an inflammatory Facebook post about litter on beaches. She was tried in court and fined, what is in South Africa an incredible sum of R150,000 ($12,500, or slightly less than a school teacher's yearly salary) for hate speech.[23]

This cultural and political anti-racism campaign, emerging in the face of widespread national discussions about systemic racism and the myth of the South African "Rainbow Nation," is thus alert to transgression in both virtual and physical spaces and seems to have had a degree of success

17. David Dietrich, "Avatars of Whiteness: Racial Expression in Video Game Characters," *Sociological Enquiry* 82.1 (2013): 82-105.
18. For an interesting analysis of #Gamergate and the necessity of cultural campaigns to disrupt hyper-masculine gaming culture, see Sarah Evans and Elyse Janish, "#INeedDiverseGames: How the Queer Backlash to GamerGate Enables Nonbinary Coalition," *QED* 2 (2015): 125-150.
19. Phillip Penix-Tadsen, *Cultural Code: Video Games and Latin America* (MIT Press, 2016), 1-26.
20. "SAHRC: Spike in racism-related incidents in SA," *News 24*, 31 August 2014, http://www.news24.com/SouthAfrica/News/SAHRC-probed-over-500-racism-cases-20140731.
21. Rebecca Hodes, "'The Rhodes statue must fall': UCT's radical rebirth," *Daily Maverick*, 13 March 2015, https://www.dailymaverick.co.za/article/2015-03-13-the-rhodes-statue-must-fall-ucts-radical-rebirth/#.
22. See for example, the case of Djavan Arrigone, who urinated on a taxi driver: Sue Segar, "I Don't Care if I Pee on a Black Man," *IOL News*, 15 November 2014, http://www.iol.co.za/news/crime-courts/i-dont-care-if-i-pee-on-a-black-man-1780859; Tammy Peterson, "Ex-Model Gets 200 Hours Community Service for Urinating on Taxi Driver," *News 24*, 30 September 2016, http://www.news24.com/SouthAfrica/News/ex-model-gets-200-hours-community-service-for-urinating-on-taxi-driver-20160930; Tammy Peterson, "Model Should Be Jailed for Racist Comments, Urinating on Me – Taxi Driver," *News 24*, 30 September 2016, http://www.news24.com/SouthAfrica/News/model-should-be-jailed-for-racist-comments-urinating-on-me-taxi-driver-20160930. See also the case of Tim Osrin, who assaulted a domestic worker: Masa Kekana, "Assault Victim Not Ready to Testify Against Swimming Coach," *Eyewitness News*, 13 October 2015, http://ewn.co.za/2015/10/13/Assault-victim-not-ready-to-testify-against-CT-swimming-coach; Kieran Legg, "Tim Osrin 'Ready to Plead Guilty'," *IOL News*, 28 November 2014, http://www.iol.co.za/news/crime-courts/tim-osrin-ready-to-plead-guilty-1787632.
23. Taschica Pillay, "Penny Sparrow Ordered to Pay R150,000 for Racist Facebook Rant," *Times Live*, 10 June 2016, http://www.timeslive.co.za/local/2016/06/10/Penny-Sparrow-ordered-to-pay-R150,000-for-racist-Facebook-rant.

in asserting that both violent actions and racist comments in digital social media speech are unacceptable and will be met with consequences.

RULES, RACISM AND *DOTA 2*

Before proceeding with a discussion of racism in the *Dota 2* South Africa community, a brief description of *Dota 2*'s game rules is necessary. Described as a hybrid of soccer and chess, *Dota 2* is a multiplayer online battle arena (MOBA), a game which pits two teams of five players against each other.[24] These players can choose from more than one hundred heroes—units that grow progressively stronger as the game goes on, each taking on a different role. The goal of the game is to destroy the enemy team's "ancient"—a large, fortified structure. In this chapter, I am less interested in the game infrastructure in and of itself, and more focused on how the game's design impacts player communities. However, it is beyond this chapter's scope to analyze the *Dota 2* South African gaming community in its entirety, which would be a colossal task. Rather, my research is derived from interactions within the game's infrastructure (for example, game-developed chatrooms) as well as news articles and exchanges recorded on two similarly-named Facebook groups, "DOTA 2 South Africa" and "Dota 2 South Africa."[25]

To some extent, the South African anti-racism campaign has spread to the *Dota 2* South Africa community, however it has failed to serve as a deterrent to racism. The frontier-like virtual environment has become a space in which normal social rules, norms and etiquette do not apply: games' virtual worlds have offered socially unacceptable racism a "safe space" in which to fester. My personal experiences with the game plainly testify to this fact: during my seven years of playing the original *Warcraft III* (Blizzard, 2002) mod (*DoTA: Allstars*) and four years of playing *Dota 2* in South Africa, I have witnessed countless examples of racism and sexism, and I am not alone in such observations.[26] Chat logs including racial slurs, as well as graphic descriptions of gendered violence have been reproduced on numerous occasions in the two Facebook groups, as well as on other websites.[27] With only one exception, this use of banned hate speech has drawn very little press-publicity. In January 2014, player RapingNinja hurled racist insults at player Strider, on account of his partner being black.[28] Unlike the Penny Sparrow affair, whose monkey insult is light relative to the language used in this case, there was no trial, fine or forced apology. In fact, despite some players claiming to have discovered his identity, nothing happened beyond a few concerned writers penning their opinions.[29]

In the wake of this 2014 incident, serious, concerned discussion began in the first Facebook group, "DOTA 2 South Africa," with players detailing their experience of racism and the problems within the community. Some players considered the discussion to be somewhat productive, but within a few hours, the entire thread was deleted by a group administrator: *Dota* was "just a game" and the online

24. Valve Corporation, *Free to Play* (Documentary Film), https://www.youtube.com/watch?v=UjZYMI1zB9s.

25. As of December 2018, "DOTA 2 South Africa" (https://www.facebook.com/groups/dota2southafrica/) has 4173 members, and "Dota 2 South Africa" (https://www.facebook.com/groups/dota2sa/) has 1646.

26. I have agonized over whether to include examples of such racism and sexism in this paper or not, and in the end, decided against it. To reproduce the unacceptable speech characteristic of the *Dota 2* South Africa gaming community would be to perpetuate second-order violence.

27. There is, for example, a dedicated website for naming and shaming such racists. See "SA Gaming Racists: Name & Shame," *Youth Inspired Ascension*, http://www.yialife.co.za/2013/12/sa-gaming-racists-name-shame/.

28. Gavin Mannion, "Racism Continues in the Local DOTA 2 Scene," *Critical Hit Gaming*, 29 January 2014, http://www.criticalhit.net/gaming/racism-continues-in-the-local-dota-2-scene/.

29. See Gavin Mannion, "Racism Is a Real Problem in Local eSports," *Critical Hit Gaming*, 27 January 2014, at http://www.criticalhit.net/gaming/racism-is-a-real-problem-in-local-esports/. This problem has continued to plague the community until present; see "Radical Racism in South African Gaming" (reader-submitted think piece), *My News 24*, 17 April 2015, http://www.news24.com/MyNews24/Radical-Racism-in-South-African-Gaming-20150417. In 2016, the issue reached mainstream media, but has still not commanded a great deal of attention; see Alex Michley, "Racism Alive in Online Games," *The Citizen*, 22 January 2016, http://citizen.co.za/news/south-africa/956306/racism-alive-in-online-games-2/.

world a hostile, offensive place, rendering the issue insignificant. Two years later, little seemed to have changed. In a poll conducted on 24 November 2016, seventy-two percent of the respondents thought that the issue should not be discussed on the group.[30]

In response, a new Facebook group was created on 28 January 2014 to enable productive discussions of communal racism.[31] Like in the physical world, players began posting screenshots of examples of racism on the Facebook group. While these well-meaning players were trying to discourage racism by asserting it as unacceptable speech, this strategy did not have the desired effect. Largely, the problem persists, with complaints about racism continuously cropping up online. Valve (the game developer) has implemented a system in which players are able to report other abusive players. Players deemed worthy of punishment are put in a 'low-priority' matchmaking pool until they win a certain number of games, depending on the severity of the offense. Valve does not appear to enforce a sufficiently punitive anti-racism policy and it is very difficult to identify people from their Steam profiles and prosecute them under anti-racism laws. Similarly, because video game playing (unlike Facebook use) is largely considered a leisurely and marginal activity, use of hate speech among gamers is not an issue that has been condemned by the broader non-gaming public.

It may be easy to assume here that this racism is only a result of a country battling with its own legacies of colonialism and apartheid—legacies which, under the shroud of anonymity, amidst the frontier-like virtual environment, bubble to the surface. Some psychological research has corroborated this interpretation, suggesting that since the internet is perceived as an anonymous, often lawless and hostile place, this promotes toxic behavior.[32] For some gamers, the more perverse or violent such behavior, the greater the psychological reward. It may also be easy to explain this problem as a result of general invisibility outside the player community and limited black visibility within the community. Perhaps because of economic and infrastructural inequality on racial lines, perhaps because of the nature of the community, there seem to be few black players by comparison with white players. No research has yet been conducted as to what these demographics are in the case of *Dota 2*, but Walton and Pallitt's 2012 study on video games and inequality in South Africa suggests that, by and large, console and computer gaming platforms are primarily accessible in (predominantly white) middle class homes.[33]

Yet not all multiplayer gaming communities in South Africa have the same racism problem as the *Dota 2* community. Hence, it is essential to ask what it is about the game rules and environment of *Dota 2* itself that encourages such *visible* racism to thrive—especially given the strong connection between mainstream gaming, colonial tropes and racial discourse.

VISUAL REGIMES: AGGRESSIVE MASCULINITY AND THE NORMALIZATION OF WHITENESS

Several ludic features of *Dota 2* promote a toxic, aggressive space in which suppressed social prejudices can emerge. Firstly, the game is characterized by a highly stressful, hostile environment. Long respawn timers mean that when a player flounders and dies, the outcome can be disastrous and directly result in a loss. Hence, because teamwork is critical, one player's mistake can cost the entire game. Psychological studies have argued such a social environment often generates extreme anger and frustration.[34] Secondly, the game promotes and affirms aggressive masculinity. Players are

30. Interestingly, this poll was conducted on the second Facebook group—which had originally been founded with the intent of facilitating productive discussions of race and racism.

31. The group's foundational post is available here: https://www.facebook.com/groups/dota2sa/permalink/274043846086669/.

32. John Suler, "The Online Disinhibition Effect," *CyberPsychology & Behavior* 7.3 (2004): 321-326.

33. Marion Walton and Nicola Pallitt, "'Grand Theft South Africa': Games, Literacyand Inequality in Consumer Childhoods," *Language and Education* 26.4 (2012): 347-361.

rewarded for killing other players through killstreaks, a booming, empowering kill announcement voice reverberates in all the other players' ears, and the more one kills, the more powerful one becomes. The game is thus a site at which players are psychically interpellated to exert coercive, violent power over one another. Thirdly, there is an abusive, militaristic hierarchy of roles within the game. Certain players take on subordinate "support" roles, who exist solely to serve "core," or "carry" players—to prevent them from being killed, to set up engagements in which they can thrive and to be their eyes and ears on the map. Ignorance of this, deliberate or not, can be extremely frustrating for players in core/essential roles, who believe they are entitled to subservient support. Yet, the game does not actively enforce any of these roles or rules. Rather, players take this task upon themselves and, in doing so, often resort to rage, insults or passive aggression. Valve has been battling since the initial release of the game to address this toxicity problem, and has had little success. The game infrastructure psychologically rewards individual excellence through kill to death ratios, and an economy based on claiming bounties for killed enemies. It punishes failure through monetary-penalties for dying. Yet it simultaneously requires teamwork to procure a victory, and this often involves support players sacrificing themselves for core players. Support players, who earn virtually no in-game money, and end up with poor kill to death ratios, and become an easy target for attack. Such an environment provides fertile ground in which suppressed social prejudices can manifest.

Dota 2's visual regime contributes to this environment. Like many games, the avatars appear to be constructed with a predominantly white male audience in mind, and create a caricature of sexualized femininity. All fourteen female humanoid characters at the time of writing are conventionally attractive or sexualized in some way, with the exception of Medusa (whose backstory is, notably, about her loss of beauty) and Legion Commander, who will be discussed shortly. While some male humanoid characters are sexualized, there is a plurality of look—from plump Pudge, to veiled Sven or Dragon Knight, to conventionally handsome Omniknight or roguish Kunkka. Further, characters of color are woefully underrepresented. Out of twenty-five "human-based" characters (characters based on real-world races) only two are black. The first, Chen, is a support hero—a character that sits at the bottom of the in-game hierarchy, and is expected help the core heroes generate income. The second, Legion Commander, is a notable deviation from the game's racial and gendered norm.[35] This black female core hero, styled as a powerful front-line feudal general, was introduced on 26 January 2014. Interestingly, she is also the only hero whose gender was changed in the transition from the original *DoTA Warcraft III* mod, to the standalone *Dota 2*. This change was likely an attempt to diversify the game and bodes well for future development.[36] However, for now, there is still obvious racial underrepresentation, and most female characters remain highly sexualized. This has the effect of normalizing the white heterosexual male, and places diversity on his terms.[37]

In the face of a ruleset that generates anger, frustration and toxicity, a visual regime designed to appeal

34. Megan Hughes and Johann Louw, "Playing Games: The Salience of Social Cues and Group Norms in Eliciting Aggressive Behaviour," *South African Journal of Psychology* 43.2 (2013): 252-262.

35. Some players have made efforts to discuss this problem. See for example the following thread, where the concern is dismissed as "Fuckin sjws": https://www.reddit.com/r/DotA2/comments/4i8qyq/why_is_there_only_black_hero_in_dota_serious/.

36. *DoTA Allstars* was originally a mod for *World of Warcraft III* (Blizzard, 2002), which became more popular than the game itself. Legion Commander from the original mod was a pompous moustachioed racist white man whose voiced dialogue exhibited a disdain for any non-human races. For a discussion of this, see "The Turn of the Tide: International eSports and the Undercurrency in Dota 2," in Stephanie Boluk and Patrick LeMieux, *Metagaming: Playing, Competing, Spectating, Cheating, Trading, Making, and Breaking Videogames* (University of Minneapolis Press, 2017).

37. *Dota 2*'s considerable and fast-growing support base in China also appears to be encouraging the game developers to diversify the game. In 2014, the game developers introduced a New Bloom festival in-game event in commemoration of the Chinese New Year. In the same year, hero "Ember Spirit" (although still somewhat fitting Said's discussion of orientalism) was introduced, and styled as a feudal Taoist "Asian" soldier. In 2017, Sun Wokong, a mythological Song dynasty (900-1279) character was introduced into the game as a new hero. Such attempts at diversity are a step in the right direction, which will hopefully in future include the African continent as well. I am indebted to Stephanie Boluk for this observation.

to a white-hetero-male player and affirm his agency, it is not surprising that the game in South Africa at least, remains a space of racism, sexism and colonial nostalgia.

CONCLUSION

To conclude, I argue that there are three factors that have created a toxic, racist culture in the *Dota 2* South Africa community. Firstly, a broader structural problem associated with online "hardcore" video gaming—that it is largely considered a white hobby, and many mainstream games affirm a colonialism-friendly conception of historical consciousness. Secondly, South Africa's cultural and political history has created an environment in which racist attitudes exist and are largely suppressed in public. However, such attitudes emerge in the "safe spaces" provided by anonymity and the nature of online gaming as a wild-west-style frontier. Thirdly, the rules and visual regime of *Dota 2* appeal to white aggressive-masculinity and affirm unconscious desires for power in a country where certain communities feel disempowered and emasculated by the *perceived* loss of white minority power through affirmative action.[38] This constructs spaces of perverse historical nostalgia and discourages the formation of inclusive gaming communities.

Clearly, this points to a degree of feedback between game cultures, national identities and historical consciousness. Since other essays in this volume have treated virtual and physical spaces as porous or imbricated, the pertinent question is to what extent these game spaces translate suppressed racism into *visible* racism in physical spaces.[39] That is, does the creation and maintenance of virtual racist spaces encourage unacceptable behavior in the physical world? And lastly, given the vast temporal, emotional and financial investments the game demands, how many people who previously may not have held racist attitudes, or may have suppressed them, are being indoctrinated into this racist culture and perpetuating it in other spheres of society?

These are important questions, and it is essential that we keep asking them. With that said, and on a slightly more positive note, in an era when progressive forces appear to be crumbling under the vanguard of racism, sexism, islamophobia, homophobia and transphobia—as exemplified by leaders like Donald Trump—video games actually have the potential to challenge and subvert such ideologies. Since games are spaces that can mold historical consciousness as well as create and reinforce social norms, they are also spaces that can act as forces to re-forge such norms when game infrastructure is critically re-examined and the legacies of colonialism and apartheid are rejected. It is a dual responsibility of gaming communities to expose intolerant players, and for developers to reimagine the role they play in fostering such intolerance.

WORKS CITED

Boluk, Stephanie and Patrick LeMieux. *Metagaming: Playing, Competing, Spectating, Cheating, Trading, Making, and Breaking Videogames*. University of Minneapolis Press, 2017.

Dietrich, David. "Avatars of Whiteness: Racial Expression in Video Game Characters." *Sociological Enquiry* 82.1 (2013): 82-105

Evans, Sarah and Elyse Janish. "#INeedDiverseGames: How the Queer Backlash to GamerGate Enables Nonbinary Coalition." *QED* 2 (2015): 125-150.

38. Economic data does not support this perception. See Anna Orthofer, "Wealth inequality in South Africa," *REDI3x3 Working Paper* 15 (2016): 20-21.
39. See Jerjes Loayza, "Ludic Solidarity and Sociality" and Verónica Valdivia Medina, "National Cultures and Digital Space: The Case of World of Warcraft," in this volume.

Fogu, Claudio. "Digitising Historical Consciousness." *History and Theory* 47 (2009): 103-121

Foucault, Michel. *The Birth of Biopolitics: Lectures at the College de France, 1978-79*, translated by Graham Burchell. Palgrave Macmillan, 1999.

—. *"Society Must Be Defended."* In *Lectures at the College de France, 1975-76*, edited by Mauro Bertani and Allesandro Fortana, translated by David Macey, 239-263. Picador, 2003.

Höglund, Johan. "Electronic Empire: Orientalism Revisited in the Military Shooter." *Game Studies* 8.1 (2008), http://gamestudies.org/0801/articles/hoeglund.

Hughes, Megan and Johann Louw. "Playing Games: The Salience of Social Cues and Group Norms in Eliciting Aggressive Behavior." *South African Journal of Psychology* 43.2 (2013): 252-262

Hodes, Rebecca. "'The Rhodes statue must fall': UCT's radical rebirth." *Daily Maverick*, 13 March 2015, https://www.dailymaverick.co.za/article/2015-03-13-the-rhodes-statue-must-fall-ucts-radical-rebirth/#.

Kansteiner, Wulf. "Alternate Worlds and Invented Communities: History and Historical Consciousness in the Age of Interactive Media." In *Manifestos for History*, eds. Keith Jenkins, Sue Morgan and Alun Munslow, 131-148. Routledge, 2007.

Kekana, Masa. "Assault Victim Not Ready to Testify Against Swimming Coach." *Eyewitness News*, 13 October 2015, http://ewn.co.za/2015/10/13/Assault-victim-not-ready-to-testify-against-CT-swimming-coach.

Leonard, David J. "'Live in Your World, Play in Ours': Race, Video Games, and Consuming the Other." *Studies in Media & Information Literacy Education* 3.4 (2003): 1-8.

—. "An Untapped Field: Exploring the World of Virtual Sports Gaming." In *Handbook of Sports and Media*, edited by Arthur Raney and Jennings Bryant, 393-407. Lawrence Erlbaum Associates, 2006.

Lizardi, Ryan. "Repelling the Invasion of the 'Other': Post-Apocalyptic Alien Shooter Videogames Addressing Contemporary Cultural Attitudes." *Eludamos: Journal for Computer Game Culture* 3.2 (2009): 295-308.

Magnet, Shoshana. "Playing at Colonization: Interpreting Imaginary Landscapes in the Video Game *Tropico*." *Journal of Communication Enquiry* 30.2 (2006): 142-162.

Major, Andrew. "State and Criminal Tribes in Colonial Punjab: Surveillance, Control and Reclamation of the 'Dangerous Classes." *Modern Asian Studies* 33.3 (1999): 657-688.

Mannion, Gavin. "Racism Is a Real Problem in Local eSports." *Critical Hit Gaming*, 27 January 2014, http://www.criticalhit.net/gaming/racism-is-a-real-problem-in-local-esports/.

Mannion, Gavin. "Racism Continues in the Local *DOTA 2* Scene." *Critical Hit Gaming*, 29 January 2014, http://www.criticalhit.net/gaming/racism-continues-in-the-local-dota-2-scene/.

Michley, Alex. "Racism Alive in Online Games." *The Citizen*, 22 January 2016, http://citizen.co.za/news/south-africa/956306/racism-alive-in-online-games-2/.

Mir, Rebecca and Trevor Owens. "Modeling Indigenous Peoples: Unpacking Ideology in *Sid Meier's Colonization*." In *Playing With the Past: Digital Games and Simulations of History,* edited by Matthew Kapell and Andrew Elliot, 91-106. Bloomsbury, 2013.

Mulvey, Laura. "Visual Pleasure and Narrative Cinema." *Screen* 16.3 (1975): 6-18.

Nott, Joseph and George Gliddon. *Indigenous Races of the Earth.* Trubner & Co, 1868.

Ohlen, James and Ray Muzkya. *Baldurs' Gate*. Bioware, 1998.

Orthofer, Anna. "Wealth inequality in South Africa." *REDI3x3 Working Paper* 15 (2016): 1-50

Penix-Tadsen, Phillip. *Cultural Code: Video Games and Latin America*. MIT Press, 2016.

Peterson, Tammy. "Ex-Model Gets 200 Hours Community Service for Urinating on Taxi Driver." *News 24,* 30 September 2016, http://www.news24.com/SouthAfrica/News/ex-model-gets-200-hours-community-service-for-urinating-on-taxi-driver-20160930.

Peterson, Tammy. "Model Should Be Jailed for Racist Comments, Urinating on Me – Taxi Driver." *News 24,* 30 September 2016, http://www.news24.com/SouthAfrica/News/model-should-be-jailed-for-racist-comments-urinating-on-me-taxi-driver-20160930.

Pieterse, Jan. *White on Black: Images of Africa and Blacks in Western Popular Culture*. Yale University Press, 1995.

Pillay, Taschica. "Penny Sparrow Ordered to Pay R150,000 for Racist Facebook Rant." *Times Live,* 10 June 2016, http://www.timeslive.co.za/local/2016/06/10/Penny-Sparrow-ordered-to-pay-R150,000-for-racist-Facebook-rant.

"Radical Racism in South African Gaming" (reader-submitted think piece), *My News 24,* 17 April 2015, http://www.news24.com/MyNews24/Radical-Racism-in-South-African-Gaming-20150417.

Reuters, "South African Woman Jailed in Landmark Ruling for Racist Rant." *The Guardian,* 28 March 2018, https://www.theguardian.com/world/2018/mar/28/south-african-woman-jailed-in-landmark-ruling-for-racist-rant.

"SAHRC: Spike in Racism-Related Incidents in SA." *News 24,* 31 August 2014, http://www.news24.com/SouthAfrica/News/SAHRC-probed-over-500-racism-cases-20140731.

Sassen, Saskia. "Towards a Sociology of Information Technology." *Current Sociology* 50.3 (2002): 365-388.

Segar, Sue. "I Don't Care if I Pee on a Black Man." *IOL News,* 15 November 2014, http://www.iol.co.za/news/crime-courts/i-dont-care-if-i-pee-on-a-black-man-1780859.

Suler, John. "The Online Disinhibition Effect." *CyberPsychology & Behavior* 7.3 (2004): 321-326.

Scott, James. *Seeing Like a State: How Certain Schemes to Improve the Human Condition Have Failed.* Yale University Press, 1998.

Skotnes-Brown, Jules. *Redrawing the Magic Circle: Video Games, Imperial Conquest, and Shifting Concepts of Play*. Undergraduate Thesis, University of Cape Town, 2015.

Valve Corporation. *Free to Play*. Documentary Film, 2014, https://www.youtube.com/watch?v=UjZYMI1zB9s.

Chidester, David. *Savage Systems*. University of Virginia Press, 1996.

Walton, Marion and Nicola Pallitt. "Grand Theft South Africa: Games, Literacy and Inequality in Consumer Childhoods." *Language and Education* 26.4 (2012): 347-361.

LUDIC SOLIDARITY AND SOCIALITY

THE IMPACT OF DOTA 2 ON LIMA'S YOUTH

JERJES LOAYZA

INTRODUCTION: UNDERSTANDING VIDEO GAMES AND YOUTH IN LIMA, PERU

Today's young generations are coming up in a world of technological reason that is continually redefining discourse and behavior, making socialization take on multiple forms across virtual platforms that multiply our connections and links to one another. Some would argue that our society is becoming less intelligent, with a marked division between the uninformed, ignorant masses and a cluster of experts who manage the knowledge and productive resources under the current economic model,[1] while others maintain that our access to new spaces through computerized and mediated communication enables increased participation in public debate, a more diverse set of voices and a better platform for cultural and political expression than in pre-digital society.[2] Rather than representing an irreconcilable divide, these two perspectives reflect a non-dogmatic debate that is open to multiple positions. Thus, communication technologies have allowed for the development of decentralized political practices in contemporary settings where politics has been transformed by expanded dynamics that exceed the conventional limits of political institutions.[3]

Undoubtedly, the development of new forms of narrative and communication changes things into something different from what they used to be, and in that process certain versions of the present take precedence over others.[4] However, this perspective could also be seen as a defensive reaction to the fear that a loss of shared identity might result in the total disappearance of society as a signifying social system.[5] Howard Rheingold takes umbrage with such a pessimist vision, arguing that these media offer consumers the power to create, publish, broadcast and debate their points of view.[6] But the question explored in this chapter is whether, in a post-human era,[7] contemporary consumers have the knowledge necessary to use these powerful instruments without abandoning our biological bodies or sacrificing essential values such as human dignity.

Ultimately, it is difficult to avoid a binary logic that hinders the analysis of subjects like the diminished, damaged and denied bodies that encounter positive feedback in the virtual realm, allowing them to forget their dissatisfaction with a social atmosphere characterized by denial and disapproval.[8] The artificiality of the body no longer runs counter to nature, but rather everything is

1. Antoni Brey, Daniel Innerarity and Goncal Mayos, *La sociedad de la ignorancia [Ignorance Society]*, (Infonomia, 2009).
2. Douglas Kellner, *Cultura mediática, estudios culturales, identidad y política entre lo moderno y lo posmoderno [Media Culture, Cultural Studies, Identity and Politics between the Modern and the Postmodern]*, (Akal, 2011).
3. Carlos Valderrama, "Sociedad de la información. Hegemonía, reduccionismo tecnológico y resistencias" ["Information Society: Hegemony, Technological Reductionism and Resistence"], *Nómadas* 36 (2012): 13-25.
4. Adolfo Estalella, "Ensamblajes de esperanza. Una etnografía del bloguear apasionado" ["Assemblies for Hope: An Ethnography of Dispassionate Blogging"], *Revista de Athenea Digital* 12 (2012): 161-174.
5. Miguel Fernández-Carrión, "Control social en la sociedad red" ["Social Control in Network Society"], *Revista Entelequia* 3 (2007): 146
6. Howard Rheingold, *Multitudes inteligentes, la próxima revolución social [Intelligent Multitudes: The Next Social Revolution]* (Gedisa, 2004).
7. Katherine Hayles, *How We Became Posthuman: Virtual Bodies in Cybernetics, Literature, and Informatics* (University of Chicago Press, 1999).
8. Arturo Rico, "Un filosofar desde el cuerpo para la sociedad de la información" ["A Philosophy of the Body for Information Society"]. *Comunicación y sociedad* 24 (2015): 243-264.

part of the same organism, leading to the abandonment of the limitations of the body and transferal to a cybernetic plane.[9] Both respect and recognition remain utterly essential in spaces where intersubjective relationships are neither physical nor virtual, but irreducibly syncretic.

This integrated perspective on the relationship between gaming and everyday life characterizes this chapter's approach to the topic of video game play, which takes interactive technologies as a sort of persistent interface between the physical and virtual worlds. The chapter focuses on how video game spaces can facilitate interaction and inter-generational support, exploring the impact and consequences of virtual play on the overall life of players. This is done by analyzing the practices of young patrons of particular public LAN centers—establishments made to serve gamers and other internet users by renting out access to a high-speed Local Area Network in their computer labs/cafés—located in areas of Lima frequented by college students. The online game chosen for this study was *Dota 2* (Valve, 2013; also referred to as *Dota*), due to its massive popularity over the past several years, both internationally and among Peruvian gamers in particular. These *Dota* players refer to themselves as *doteros*, the term that will be used for the remainder of this chapter. What is remarkable about these doteros' particular practices is their preference for shared common spaces for social gameplay, which allow them more easily and flexibly coordinate each element of gameplay with the rest of the team.

This chapter uses the framework of virtual ethnography, which approaches the internet as an object in people's everyday lives and a site for community formation by examining the ways it is used, interpreted and reinterpreted by particular audiences.[10] Following the guidelines for data collection established by T. L. Taylor's scholarship on virtual ethnography,[11] research for this chapter included Interviews and short biographies of the members of the player group, as well as audiovisual recordings of several gameplay sessions that were published on a private Facebook group, in which players commented on the videos of their earlier play. Finally, the players involved in the study provided commentary on the final version of the chapter. This method connects symbolic interactionism, an interpretive focus, with research on participatory action, a critical focus. This type of work aims to incorporate participants as protagonists and critical authors of their own experiences.

The five players chosen for this chapter played together on a team they named *Last Resort*. The team's successes and achievements from 2013-2014 earned them popularity and prestige among *Dota 2* players in the city of Lima. To give a sense of the chosen subjects' context, it is worth sketching out some of the general traits of average gamers in Lima that can be observed in the major LAN centers where they gather: the players are almost entirely male; consumers range in age from 17 to 23; and finally, it is notable that the majority of them are in their last two years of high school and first three years of college, meaning they are circulating in a sort of liminal space of collective identity. The author of this chapter was able to establish a friendly relationship with each member of the team in 2014 thanks to an earlier friendship with Jacoby, a leading member who facilitated connections between the researcher and the group. Table 2.4.1 reviews each player's basic data. Analyzing the data collected, it can be seen that the ritual of online video game play has expanded completely beyond all rational expectations, becoming a common space for shared identities and the reinforcement of positive emotions in ludic contexts.[12] Each member of the participating team agreed that their

9. Sebastian Gómez, "TECNO-BÍOS: una aproximación bopolítica a la relación cuerpo – máquina en el contexto cibercultural contemporáneo" ["TECHNO-BIOS: A Biopolitical Approach to the Body-Machine Relationship in the Contemporary Cybercultural Context"], *Aisthesis* 52 (2012): 342-368.
10. Christine Hine, *Virtual Ethnography* (Sage, 2000): 64.
11. T. L. Taylor, *Play Between Worlds: Exploring Online Game Culture* (MIT Press, 2009).
12. Regarding "Zone of residence in Lima": the Lima metropolitan area contains a total of 43 districts, which can be divided into four socio-economic zones: Lima Norte, Lima Sur, Lima Este and Lima Centro. Lima began to expand around 1950, increasing its urban radius beyond what had been Lima Centro. Due to their

capacity for establishing friendly ties improved as they became more and more fully integrated into the team.

Name	**Sex**	**Age**	**District**	**Current level of studies**	**Zone of residence in Lima**
Víctor	M	20	Santa Anita	University	Este
Taz	M	21	Jesús María	University	Centro
Humita	M	16	Los Olivos	High School	Norte
The Situation	M	19	Los Olivos	High School	Norte
Jacoby	M	19	Los Olivos	University	Norte

Table 2.4.1. Basic data on the members of Last Resort, the Dota team interviewed for this chapter.

PC GAMING ONLINE: THE *DOTA* PHENOMENON IN LIMA

Over the past several decades, video games have largely been reduced to a single-player experience. Shared games have been limited to mutual, timed competitions, as in the case of sports, fighting or racing games. But after 2009, when the console generation led by Microsoft's Xbox 360 and Sony's PlayStation 3 began to fully take advantage of online play, thousands of players across the globe were motivated by their competitive nature to connect to the web and share virtual spaces, allowing them to forge relationships and ties based on ludic commitment in order to secure their status as players among the many others across the globe.[13] While earlier computer games had already explored the possibility of bringing together players from different geographical locations, over the past decade, the city of Lima has seen a proliferation in the number of LAN centers, which have brought together the types of young people that in the past would have been stereotyped as problematic video game addicts. As established in the introduction to the this anthology, the rapid growth in online video game play has been a global phenomenon that has reached beyond social and economic divisions. Peru, as this chapter shows, was no exception.

However, these shared gaming spaces were laying the groundwork for something new: friendly face-to-face experiences were constructed upon the foundation of virtual experiences situated in real LAN centers. Unlike online connections in the privacy of one's home, where players generally stuck to conversations about game objectives, LAN centers fostered more complex connections and friendships due to the co-presence of the play experience. The stigmas that once reduced players to isolated and antisocial stereotypes started to fade away through these friendly gaming encounters, whose participants began to form dedicated player communities. Research by scholars such as Jansz and Martens has shown that LAN Centers were preferred due to the way they allow players to communicate with one another mid-game.[14] Cole and Griffiths refer to this as a feeling of being "more themselves," laying the groundwork for behaving without inhibitions or fear of being judged for one's

disproportionate growth, these zones began to be known pejoratively as *barriadas*, and later *conos*, before they came to be known under their current denomination as *zonas*.

13. Jerjes Loayza, "Sensibilidades y videojuegos en línea: un análisis de la frontera entre lo real y lo virtual en América Latina," *Austral* 20 (2011): 19-40.

14. Jeroen Jansz and Lonneke Martens, "Gaming at a LAN event: the social context of playing video games," *New Media & Society* 7.3 (2005): 333-355.

appearance.[15] Likewise, other analyses have offered further evidence of LAN centers' importance, such as Penix-Tadsen's research on cybercafés in Latin America[16] and Swalwell's long-term analysis of the Australasian case from 1999 to 2008.[17] As these researchers' work shows, LAN centers have frequently provided important links to socialization due to their capacity to bring their members closer together.

The popularity of online games played on PCs has generated continual growth in the population of players of multiplayer games, which in Peru's case have proven especially attractive to younger players in particular. However, at the same time, game rentals for consoles such as the Xbox One and PlayStation 4 have declined in Peru, due to the popularity of PC games that make room for ludic experiences within a shared physical space (see Image 2.4.1). On devices other than PCs, users' desire to win can sweep them away to a ludic exile where they can enjoy themselves without needing to look for other collaborators outside of their own comfort zones. PCs, however, act as an intermediary by establishing a bridge that connects users of diverse types and interests. For Latour, intermediaries are capable of overflowing the boundaries of the roles for which they were created, producing new possibilities with every step.[18] This is why LAN centers can be found in districts throughout the capital city regardless of the area's socioeconomic class or status: they enable young people to make meaningful connections with their peers.

Image 2.4.1. An online PC gaming center located in the popular Arenales mall, Lince district, city of Lima, 2014. This locale is a very popular site for gaming meetups, as it was one of the city's first.

In this context, the *Dota* phenomenon has brought together numerous players under a single umbrella

15. Helena Cole and Mark D. Griffiths, "Social Interactions in Massively Multiplayer Online Role-Playing Gamers," *Cyberpsychology & Behavior* 10.4 (2007): 582.
16. Phillip Penix-Tadsen, *Cultural Code: Video Games and Latin America* (MIT Press, 2016): 51-53.
17. Melanie Swalwell, "Lan Gaming Groups: Snapshots from an Australasian Case Study, 1999-2008," *Gaming Cultures and Place in Asia-Pacific*, ed. Larissa Hjorth and Dean Chan (Routledge, 2009): 117-136.
18. Bruno Latour, *Reensamblar lo social [Reassembling the Social]* (Manantial, 2008).

(see Image 2.4.2). To use Beavis, Nixon and Atkinson's terminology, these spaces are characterized not only by their liminal nature but also for tolerance for ambiguity and capacity for enabling hybrid practices.[19] These types of online games bring together gamers in shared physical spaces, to battle teams from the same LAN center or from other locations in the city. They yell, they get angry, they burst out in laughter, they experience all sorts of sensations, and at times they stop to look around at their companions before returning to their seats. After a few hours, at the end of the match, they reminisce about the greatest moments and prepare to partake in some other sort of activity.

Image 2.4.2. Last Resort team members during an online competition against adversaries from the city of El Callao, 2013. CyberPlaza mall, Cercado district, city of Lima.

The *Dota* phenomenon brings together hundreds of young people across multiple LAN centers in Lima. It is usually played in teams of five doteros, and is won by those with the most well-defined strategy, as well as the most well-balanced group play. The number of players on a team can vary from one to five, however five-player teams are usually used in tournaments and for all competitive battles. Last Resort's fifth team member would vary depending on the demands and duties of each gamer, and therefore this spot was always reserved for a free player who may not necessarily belong to the team, but would join them on occasion to offer support. Jacoby explains each team member's role: the *Support* buys items that help everyone and has the primary duty of protecting the Hard-Carry until they can collect the items necessary to win the game; the *Semi-Carry* takes the center position, attacking and destabilizing the other team; and the *Hard-Carry* travels with these supporters while taking charge of "farming" and securing as much gold as possible in order to purchase large items that will allow them to defeat the other team. Each match lasts approximately 20 minutes to an hour, depending on the balance of skills between teams. There is no time limit, and the match ends when one of the teams surrenders and their base is destroyed.

19. Catherine Beavis, Helen Nixon and Stephen Atkinson. "LAN Cafés: Cafés, Places of Gathering or Sites of Informal Teaching and Learning?," *Education, Communication & Information* 5.1 (2005): 41-60.

Throughout Peru, there are groups of doteros with great potential, some of whom have even won international competitions. In the context of Lima, these teams don't just play to win: they also make considerable financial wagers. Added to this is the effervescence of the side-by-side ludic experience with the rest of the team, which reinforces friendly ties that transcend the space of the LAN center itself. According to Beavis, Nixon and Atkinson, LAN centers are transitory and ephemeral spaces that fulfill certain functions according to particular and specific conditions that are in constant flux.[20] As Trepte, Reinecke and Juechems have argued, offline social support reinforces the clan through shared activities that go beyond gameplay.[21] Thus, the LAN center exceeds its primary functional purposes and becomes a sort of context for social integration among these peers. In this way, mediators like PCs—and more specifically the video games played on them—function as processes rather than finished products, in more of a simultaneous and plural than a linear fashion, meaning we are dealing with technological mediators that are, to a greater or lesser degree, ludic distractors: they are the ritualized basis for social exchange among their members, which will always be developed hand-in-hand with the emotions and sensibilities that are shared by their players in real time.[22]

In order to examine the particular case analyzed in this chapter, the author joined a series of matches and tournaments from 2012 to 2013 along with the Last Resort team, consisting of Jacoby, Taz, The Situation, Víctor and Humita.[23] In addition, interviews were conducted with two former players. Analyzing the interactive experience of playing *Dota* means examining the particular attraction that this product has for its players. Víctor recalls his days as a dotero:

> In my own lifetime, *Dota* has turned 14 years old. I still remember back when I started in 10th grade! My friends and I would go to these internet centers where we played LAN and I can remember clearly that the owner of the place himself installed the game, which was the newest and greatest at the time, with all its impressive graphics and resolution, telling us, "Kids, I just brought you *Dota*." We started playing it, even though it was kind of hard to adapt to the game since it's a strategy game based on character choice.[24]

It is always difficult to get started, but when it comes to online PC games like *Dota*, there are friends that can help doteros feel more sure of themselves. This is abundantly apparent in the concerns expressed by Jaime Durán and Santiago Nieto, who observe that most users learn to play without the help of other humans, dabbling in a personal and solitary activity or limiting themselves to contact only with people who are already in the virtual space.[25] However, this perspective does not take into account that there are spaces in which the virtual and the real are highly permeable spheres.

Jacoby recalls his early days: "I got into playing Dota at an internet café because of my friends. It seemed really boring at first, but little by little I started to like it and get the hang of it—because it took a lot of skill and strategy." Jacoby's capabilities demonstrate that the types digital divides that are emerging as problems in the present day have less to do with technological platforms, and more to do with social relations. Marín and Gonzales argue that this divide is fundamentally cognitive, operating in the minds of individuals who are accustomed to the practice of symbolic skills, which are qualitatively different than instrumental skills.[26] Jacoby and his friends developed their capabilities in

20. Ibid.
21. Sabine Trepte, Leonard Reinecke and Keno Juechems, "The social side of gaming: How playing online computer games creates online and offline social support," *Computers in Human Behavior* 28.3 (2012): 837.
22. Marshall McLuhan, *La galaxia de Gutenberg* [*The Guttenberg Galaxy*] (Planeta, 1985).
23. At the players' request, their actual in-game pseudonyms are used in this chapter.
24. Unless otherwise noted, all team member quotations are cited from the author's field journal, 2013.
25. Jaime Durán and Santiago Nieto, *Mujer, sexualidad, internet y política: los nuevos electores latinoamericanos* [*Women, Sexuality, the Internet and Politics: New Latin American Voters*] (Fondo de Cultura Económica, 2006).

proportion with the game, a virtual mediator with the capacity to transform its users, who ceased to be isolated players and crossed over from a simulated dotero gameworld into a real, physical space.

Taz, a talented dotero who belonged to several important leagues and was also Jacoby's partner, explains that his early days playing *Counter-Strike* (Valve, 2000)[27] got him started on the path to playing *Dota*: "I was playing Counter-Strike online until a friend showed me how to play Dota for like a month, then I got hooked on playing and little by little I got better. I liked the game in general—all of my friends used to play and I used to watch and I enjoyed it all." Friendship became an important shared foundation for becoming a dotero, running counter to an individualist logic or rationale for gaming. The Situation, another member of Last Resort, reiterates the importance of friendship in his game choice: "My friends didn't make me play, it's just that my friends and I were always doing things together—if we weren't playing ball we were playing Dota with each other, and I was one of the few friends that kept playing not just for fun, but to learn more." These affective networks built around gaming do not contradict a supposedly entangled offline world or seemingly fleeting virtual networks,[28] but rather these distinctions tend to fade away in young people's social practices.

Playing *Dota* thus represents a way of sharing time together, of increasing group integration, encouraging greater team confidence, strengthening team instincts and the affective ties that characterize this practice. It is notable that this social space is crucial to the process of socialization through which these young people develop a notion of the social "self" and the generalized "other" that give structure to their personalities.[29] Being a dotero means combining virtual acts and real contexts, brought together in a vibrant, youthful identity that moves beyond this dichotomy and sees such experiences as an inseparably combined whole. This could be seen as the *Blade Runner* syndrome, which Carles Feixa and Yanko González use as a way of describing young people's wavering "between the will to break free and obedience to the adults who raised them, while they are at the same time thrust into artificial worlds such as online communities and different configurations of large-scale adolescent networks."[30] This allusion allows us to comprehend the way in which the networked foundations for an online game like *Dota* enable the development of a logic of socialization in which younger players seek to affirm their self-identities as part of constantly-self-renewing urban tribes capacitated by technological mediators that have become the circuits where young people's rites of passage take place. This is a means of compensating for the adult-centered exclusion with which they are faced on the job and in social environments due to their supposed lack of experience.

MULTIPLAYER CONNECTIVITY: TOWARD NEW AFFECTIVE COMMUNITIES

The interviews conducted for this chapter show that players are willing to give up a number of responsibilities in other areas of their lives due to their desire to play at every available moment. Each of the interviewees missed school at least once a month in order to play. One ex-dotero explains: "I got to the point of going to *dotear*[31] after leaving school with my friends, to the point where we started to skip classes. My friends' and my grade averages in high school went down. We had been good students, but some of us almost failed the year." Working and studying were the motivations that

26. Isidro Marín and Ramón González-Piñal, "Relaciones sociales en la sociedad de la información, hacia una noción de la intersubjetividad digital" ["Social Relations in Information Society: Toward a Notion of Digital Intersubjectivity"], *Prisma social* 6 (2011): 1-18.
27. Counter-Strike is another online PC game with a large number of players. While it cannot compare to the Dota phenomenon, it dominated PC gaming at the height of its popularity. It is still played today, with a number of fans placing it in second after Dota on their lists of favorite games.
28. Asur Fuente, Juan Herrero and Enrique Gracia, "Internet y apoyo social, sociabilidad online y ajuste psicosocial en la sociedad de la información" ["The Internet and Social Support, Online Sociability and Psychological Adjustment in Information Society"], *Acción psicológica* 1 (2010): 9-15.
29. George Mead, *Espíritu, persona y sociedad* [*Mind, Self and Society*] (Paidós Studio, 1990).
30. Yanko Gonzalez and Carles Feixa, *La construcción histórica de la juventud en América Latina: bohemios, rockanroleros y revolucionarios* [*The Historical Construction of Youth in Latin America: Bohemians, Rock-and-Rollers and Revolutionaries*] (Cuarto Propio, 2013): 111.
31. A recently coined neologism in Spanish, the verb "dotear" means "to play Dota."

ultimately drove these ex-doteros from their deep play practices. The current doteros in Last Resort are conscious of carefully scheduling their time so that they do not have to miss classes, which for two of them are now at the university level. However, back in his early days, Jacoby would "play hooky" by going to locales far from his home community in the Los Olivos district on the north side of Lima.

Initially, each member of Last Resort, as well as each of the ex-doteros, played the game in their own homes. Asked about the importance of sharing the same physical space, Taz replied: "It's best when everyone is playing together, that's the most ideal situation. But the missions just start out one step at a time, and if someone connects from their house and we play, it could still turn out fine, but it's not like when we're all together because things just turn out better. We can talk so that we get more combos." While Taz is conscious that the team cannot get together all the time, he prizes matches played face-to-face in common spaces over those played remotely online.

While playing with a group from home means finding a moment when everyone is available at the same time, it is even harder to get together physically due to the greater investment of time and effort required. The ideal situation for Jacoby also centers on dialogue with the rest of the team: "I mean, I can go either way—playing at the crib is comfortable, but when you play LAN with everyone else right next to you it's like there's more confidence, and you can point out the mistakes right that very second and stuff like that." Indeed, as shown in Sondgrass, Lacy, Dengah and Fagan's research, playing *World of Warcraft* with real-life friends allows players to transfer their online achievements and experiences to offline social networks, allowing them to overcome real-life conflicts and competitors.[32] After settling on *Dota* as his game of choice, Jacoby began to enjoy it in its entirety, identifying himself as part of a first-person plural, unlike many home console gamers.

> My friends and I started to play in the internet café in my neighborhood with our pals in 2009. We would play for fun from 4:00 to 8:00 in the evening, and it went on like that for a year. After a couple of months, another group of five buddies showed up and told us that to play we had to bet, and of course we accepted. I remember we won, and we felt really superior. Little by little more people started to show up and we would usually win with ease.

Dota is a video game that involves sports-like *roles* in a manner reminiscent of a soccer game among friends. Thinking back on his gaming days, one ex-dotero explained: "I started to distance myself from Dota a little bit, but I would get anxious for vacation to come so I could go back to the cybercafé. I had to pass all my classes to avoid going to summer school, and I did that. I was undefeated, and I would dedicate hours to playing at home, then I'd lie and say I was going to play ball so I could go get together with my friends and keep playing Dota on LAN." Although Víctor resorted to lying to be able to go out with his friends and play video games, the parallel he draws between the soccer ball and the PC holds true: it is the object that provides the pretense the group needs to come together, interact and exchange experiences through shared play.

These new social networks thus become potential sources of mutual support, especially given their potential benefits for individuals with difficulty in face-to-face social interactions, or those at risk of social isolation and exclusion.[33] Thus we can see how cooperation—which in its best manifestations has provided the origin for the greatest works of human civilization—goes beyond the foul ends that authors such as Rheingold so feared.[34] Indeed, as Reer and Krämer have established, one important

32. Jeffrey G. Snodgrass, Michael G. Lacy, HJ Francois Dengah II and Jesse Fagan, "Enhancing One Life Rather than Living Two: Playing MMOs with Offline Friends," *Computers in Human Behavior* 27.3 (2011): 1211-1222.
33. Fuente, Herrero and Gracia, "Internet y apoyo social, sociabilidad online y ajuste psicosocial en la sociedad de la información," 13
34. Howard Rheingold, *Multitudes inteligentes, la próxima revolución social* [*Intelligent Multitudes: The Next Social Revolution*] (Gedisa, 2004).

effect of this video game genre is establishing offline links among members, enhancing their social capital through physical proximity, familiarity, ongoing communication and enrichment of friendship among players.[35] As Swalwell argues in her research on LAN centers, these locations cannot compete with the comfort of home, even if one's home has very high internet connection speeds, because players prefer face-to-face interaction: for them, there is nothing better than "being there," and for this reason it is hard to imagine LAN centers disappearing any time in the near future.[36] We are dealing with spaces that enable deeply-rooted and highly structured socialization among each of the clan's members.

When questioned about their favorite memories of their experiences as *Dota* players, the members of Last Resort cited friendship as the most salient value, showing that these networks are capable of "renovating communities through the strengthening of ties that connect us to the non-immediate social world while they simultaneously expand our power in that world."[37] The Situation explains:

> There were a lot of things, but the thing I remember most was when my friends and I stayed up all night in a cybercafé and played *Dota* almost all night long, and in some way I felt happy, because after that we would talk to each other every day about how to improve our game, and that brought us together even more, since we were alsofriends online. I would say that the best thing is how you get to know someone better by playing the game with them, because in the game you express yourself in a certain, more free way, I'd say, but emotions take place not only during gameplay, but also outside of the game. We would think back on what we had played so we could correct our mistakes, and even though sometimes we would criticize each other, it all brought us closer together and allowed us to grow as a team.

A good team is one that is able to help its players rise above their differences through the amicable trust they are able to share with one another, as well as the ability to criticize one another without feeling shamed by those critiques, though it may mean being insulted. The Situation was one of those most frequently criticized by Jacoby during one training, but unlike Taz, who would reply with anger to every criticism, The Situation would keep quiet. Was he bothered by this habit? The Situation replied in a cheerful tone: "Well, if that insult were coming from somebody I didn't know and didn't trust, I'd be uncomfortable with that person doing it and it would bother me, but with Jacoby we've known each other for a long time, and if he insults me, I insult him back twice as badly and we just keep going on like that." Insults, shouts and complaints during gameplay appeared to have little consequence, other than to help drive the team toward victory.

Due to the mutual trust between all the members of Last Resort, which was the result of all of those post-*Dota* get-togethers, they felt free to insult one another and be insulted without experiencing further frustration. This was reflected in their responses to a video of a team training match, displayed for team members only through the Facebook group. Jacoby had been the most hot-tempered, and upon seeing the video he reflected: "It's better not to shout, even if I'm the team member most prone to rage and I usually shout at people myself. But I've learned to control myself and to be more tolerant over the past month, because it can freak out other players and it's better if they're calm. I'm the one who usually gets the most frustrated when things don't go my way, but I'm getting better." Indeed, these types of insults and other forms of criticism between teammates are forbidden during official tournament play.

35. Felix Reer and Nicole C. Krämer, "Underlying Factors of Social Capital Acquisition in the Context of Online-Gaming: Comparing *World of Warcraft* and *Counter-Strike*," *Computers in Human Behavior* 36 (2014): 179-189.
36. Swalwell, "Lan Gaming Groups," 133.
37. Peter Kollock and Marc Smith, *Comunidades en el ciberespacio [Communities in Cyberspace]* (UOC, 2003): 20.

For Taz, shouts and derogatory comments during training are to be expected, however "it's different in a tournament—we don't talk at all—it's different." It's important to feel safe, and if one cannot find safety on a team, the slightest trace of mental weakness during a tournament can end up hurting the group. Jacoby explains it in this way:

> It's tough to beat the first-class players.[38] I've played a few times against them, and we put up a fight, but experience always wins in the end. And I think it's a psychological thing, because your team isn't as famous as theirs, and they're well known, and people support them, and if you do something wrong they insult you or they follow behind you talking trash. Half the time those people end up getting tilted[39] and the other players that know them don't say anything to them, so they end up screwing everything up.

As Nussbaum has explained, emotions tend to connect us to elements that we may consider essential to our wellbeing, but which are not completely within our own control. This is why "emotion registers that sensation of vulnerability and imperfect control: if there is no emotion, we have the right to say that there are no complete or total judgments."[40] In contexts of trust and friendship, these conflicts are forms of what Joaquín Linne has referred to as *multimidad* or "multi-intimacy," meaning links that reveal new configurations of subjectivity, public and private life that exhibit certain intimate content as part of their performances of self-presentation.[41]

Jacoby also shared, by way of his gaming experience, how threats can arise in relation to bad relations between team members: "I made three good friends on that team, but unfortunately I didn't get along that well with one of them because he felt some sort of rivalry or something, and he and I would always have conflicts. I didn't like him and he didn't like me." According to Jacoby, this person tainted the group's harmony. The dotero context allows for no fragmentation, because it could end up doing the group in and putting an end to not only their shared victories, but also the friendships gained, which are the result of the key social element of *Dota* play, the factor most frequently cited by team members. As The Situation explained, this game allows players to get to know one another, sharing in a lived experience that allows them to do away with more formal appearances, letting out their most intense jubilation along with their most spiteful rage. This is explained in an image posted on one of the doteros' Facebook walls, which includes the following caption:

> Thanks to *Dota*: I Learned basic English; I de-stress and have fun in a healthy way; I have greater musical appreciation; I am free from the vices that are common to other young people; I exercise my mind much more than by watching TV; I have made great friends; I feed my imagination; I challenge my skills; I never get bored; I challenge my mental abilities, my reflexes, etc.; I've acquired a new appreciation for technological art, etc.[42]

One of the most highly-rated comments on the image states: "Dota is super-sketchy, even more so if you play in *pubs*."[43] Stress could add to the fragmentation of the team, however unlike with other single-player video games, doteros can turn to mutual encouragement from their clan, an important form of emotional support that can correlate to their success in tournaments. This is why, for The

38. Here, Jacoby is referring to the highest competitive level in Dota, out of three levels: the weakest is Low Skill, characterized by those who play just for fun, of whom there are many in the local cybercafés. The second level is Mid Skill, where doteros with a longer history of playing as well as those who play at more regular intervals can be found. Finally, first place is occupied by High Skill players, who are always the ones to compete in tournaments, ending up as finalists in many of them. The names of the teams and their members are nationally and internationally known, thanks to regular online tournaments.
39. Getting "tilted" is gaming terminology for experiencing feelings of fear, anger or insecurity, which cause the player to make constant mistakes.
40. Martha Nussbaum, *Paisajes del pensamiento* [*Upheavals of Thought*] (Paidós, 2008): 66.
41. Joaquín Linne, "La 'multimidad': performances íntimas en Facebook de adolescentes de Buenos Aires" ["'Multi-Intimacy': Intimate Performances by Buenos Aires Adolescents on Facebook"], *Estudios Sociológicos* 100 (2016): 65-84.
42. Quoted from Jacoby's Facebook wall, December 2013.
43. Pubs are play sessions meant just for relaxation, where no money or tournament position is in play. In Dota tournament games, one can clearly see the doteros' intense mutual respect and the ways they take care of their fellow team members. In a high-stakes game, there is no room for insults or distractions.

Situation, winning and conquering is not just something you do for the sake of winning, for him "it's about spending time with your friends," as he stated on one occasion when congratulated on a win.

As a final reflection, *Dota* demonstrates how *non-place* is linked to *place*, to use Marc Augé's terminology.[44] The non-place is constituted by virtual online networks of play, which could make for a cold space of selfish, individualist behaviors. However, it is linked to the place constituted through interactions among players, not only in LAN centers, but also outside of them, where they collectively partake in a variety of activities in different spaces of socialization that unify their members, bringing them closer to forms of face-to-face coexistence:

> With them, I learned to play a different way that was more competitive—it wasn't just for fun, it was the feeling of beating people who've played longer than you and taking their five *soles* every game, that was great. It was awesome cracking ourselves up afterward and seeing where we'd messed up while we'd eat some burgers and sodas. Since we would always bet people who played on normal level and higher, we would win some and lose some.

When Taz reflects on his future with *Dota*, he observes: "I treat it like a work/game and I plan to play it for many years until I reach my potential." When all is said and done, the best thing for Taz has to do with "good friendships, and also some serious trash talk, plus money or prizes like a new mouse or something like that." Although Taz seems to enjoy himself even more when faced with the challenge of continually improving his performance, friendship and ludic sociality are fundamental elements of any good team. This is echoed by past and present doteros, who have experienced intense moments of collective effervescence. Who said video games were bad for you?

CONCLUSION: LUDIC SOLIDARITY AND SOCIALITY IN *DOTA*

An ethnographic review of the most active groups of doteros on social media showed a large number of memes that laud the virtues of the game, with thousands of "likes" and comments. The photos published there have been shared an average of 300 to 500 times among the whole *Dota* community. Many of these memes are used by players to make fun of themselves, their excesses and their defects. In the same way, through face-to-face connections they come to deal with moments of stress, learning to withstand insults as long as they are backed by a desire to collaborate and the shared goal of improving as a team.

The video games in these LAN centers fulfill a vitally important social function: far from isolating them, they bring young people together around their computers to build friendships in the time before, during and after their gameplay sessions. Socialization makes games like *Dota* intermediaries, agents who transcend their makers, allowing players to use simulations as a pretext for playing pertinent roles through ludic rituals that prepare their participants for contexts in which they will have control over their own lives, learning to make collective and shared decisions.

The group of friends with whom one shares and collaborates in video game play can function as a key cornerstone, allowing communities of gamers to enrich the meaning of their interactions and further strengthening their social ties. Today, four years after the research for this chapter began, Jacoby still misses being able to give himself over completely to playing *Dota* at the LAN center: "I wish I were 16 years old again and I could just play, with no responsibilities. When you're losing and you come back, it makes you yell and feel alive!" Nowadays, The Situation and Jacoby continue to play together, although they know nothing of Humita, for whom Jacoby shows concern: "he was my buddy and I

44. Marc Augé, *Los no lugares, espacios de anonimato* [*Non-Places: Introduction to an Anthropology of Supermodernity*] (Gedisa, 1998).

miss him." In contexts like the LAN centers where Last Resort, other teams of Peruvian doteros and other players across the globe get together to play and form lasting relationships, gamers are not just surrounded by their team members, but by friends for life.

Translated from the Spanish by Phillip Penix-Tadsen

WORKS CITED

Augé, Marc. *Los no lugares, espacios de anonimato* [*Non-Places: Introduction to an Anthropology of Supermodernity*]. Gedisa, 1998.

Beavis, Catherine, Helen Nixon and Stephen Atkinson. "LAN Cafés: Cafés, Places of Gathering or Sites of Informal Teaching and Learning?." *Education, Communication & Information* 5.1 (2005): 41-60.

Brey, Antoni, Daniel Innerarity and Goncal Mayos. *La sociedad de la ignorancia* [*Ignorance Society*]. Infonomia, 2009.

Cole, Helena and Mark D. Griffiths. "Social Interactions in Massively Multiplayer Online Role-Playing Gamers." *Cyberpsychology & Behavior* 10.4 (2007): 575-583.

Durán, Jaime and Santiago Nieto. *Mujer, sexualidad, internet y política: los nuevos electores latinoamericanos* [*Women, Sexuality, the Internet and Politics: New Latin American Voters*]. Fondo de Cultura Económica, 2006.

Estalella, Aldofo. "Ensamblajes de esperanza. Una etnografía del bloguear apasionado." ["Assemblies for Hope: An Ethnography of Dispassionate Blogging"]. *Revista de Athenea Digital* 12 (2012): 161-174.

Fernández-Carrión, Miguel. "Control social en la sociedad red" ["Social Control in Network Society"]. *Revista Entelequia* 3 (2007): 141-157.

Fuente, Asur, Juan Herrero and Enrique Gracia. "Internet y apoyo social, sociabilidad online y ajuste psicosocial en la sociedad de la información" ["The Internet and Social Support, Online Sociability and Psychological Adjustment in Information Society"]. *Acción psicológica* 1 (2010): 9-15.

Gómez, Sebastian. "TECNO-BÍOS: una aproximación bopolítica a la relación cuerpo – maquina en el contexto cibercultural contemporáneo" ["TECHNO-BIOS: A Biopolitical Approach to the Body-Machine Relationship in the Contemporary Cybercultural Context"]. *Aisthesis* 52 (2012): 342-368.

Gonzalez, Yanko and Carles Feixa. *La construcción histórica de la juventud en América Latina: bohemios, rockanroleros y revolucionarios* [*The Historical Construction of Youth in Latin America: Bohemians, Rock-and-Rollers and Revolutionaries*]. Cuarto Propio, 2013.

Hayles, N. Katherine. *How We Became Posthuman. Virtual Bodies in Cybernetics, Literature, and Informatics.* University of Chicago Press, 1999.

Hine, Christine. *Etnografía virtual* [*Virtual Ethnography*]. UOC, 2004.

Jansz, Jeroen, and Lonneke Martens. "Gaming at a LAN Event: The Social Context of Playing Video Games." *New Media & Society* 7.3 (2005): 333-355.

Kellner, Douglas. *Cultura mediática, estudios culturales, identidad y política entre lo moderno y lo posmoderno* [*Media Culture, Cultural Studies, Identity and Politics between the Modern and the Postmodern*]. Akal, 2011.

Kollock, Peter and Marc Smith. *Comunidades en el ciberespacio* [*Communities in Cyberspace*]. UOC, 2003.

Latour, Bruno. *Reensamblar lo social* [*Reassembling the Social*]. Manantial, 2008.

Linne, Joaquín. "La 'multimidad': performances íntimas en Facebook de adolescentes de Buenos Aires" ["'Multimidad': Intimate Performances by Buenos Aires Adolescents on Facebook"]. *Estudios Sociológicos* 100 (2016): 65-84.

Loayza, Jerjes. "Sensibilidades y videojuegos en línea: un análisis de la frontera entre lo real y lo virtual en América Latina" ["Sensibilities and Online Video Games: An Analysis of the Frontier between the Virtual and the Real in Latin America]. *Austral* 20 (2011): 19-40.

Marín, Isidro y Ramón González-Piñal. "Relaciones sociales en la sociedad de la información, hacia una noción de la intersubjetividad digital" ["Social Relations in Information Society: Toward a Notion of Digital Intersubjectivity"]. *Prisma Social* 6 (2011): 1-18.

McLuhan, Marshall. *La galaxia de Gutenberg* [*The Guttenberg Galaxy*]. Planeta, 1985.

Mead, George. *Espíritu, persona y sociedad* [*Mind, Self and Society*]. Paidós, 1990.

Nussbaum, Martha. *Paisajes del pensamiento* [*Upheavals of Thought*]. Paidós, 2008.

Penix-Tadsen, Phillip. *Cultural Code: Video Games and Latin America*. MIT Press, 2016.

Reer, Felix and Nicole C. Krämer. "Underlying Factors of Social Capital Acquisition in the Context of Online-Gaming: Comparing *World of Warcraft* and *Counter-Strike*." *Computers in Human Behavior* 36 (2014): 179-189.

Rheingold, Howard. *Multitudes inteligentes, la próxima revolución social* [*Intelligent Multitudes: The Next Social Revolution*]. Gedisa, 2004.

Rico, Arturo. "Un filosofar desde el cuerpo para la sociedad de la información" ["A Philosophy of the Body for Information Society"]. *Comunicación y sociedad* 24 (2015): 243-26

Snodgrass, Jeffrey G., Michael G. Lacy, HJ Francois Dengah II and Jesse Fagan. "Enhancing One Life Rather than Living Two: Playing MMOs with Offline Friends." *Computers in Human Behavior* 27.3 (2011): 1211-1222.

Swalwell, Melanie. "Lan Gaming Groups: Snapshots from an Australasian Case Study, 1999-2008." In *Gaming Cultures and Place in Asia-Pacific*, edited by Larissa Hjorth and Dean Chan, 117-136. Routledge, 2009.

Taylor, T. L. *Play Between Worlds: Exploring Online Game Culture*. MIT Press, 2009.

Trepte, Sabine, Leonard Reinecke and Keno Juechems. "The Social Side of Gaming: How Playing Online Computer Games Creates Online and Offline Social Support." *Computers in Human Behavior* 28.3 (2012): 832-839.

Valderrama, Carlos. "Sociedad de la información. Hegemonía, reduccionismo tecnológico y resistencias" ["Information Society: Hegemony, Technological Reductionism and Resistence"]. *Nómadas* 36 (2012): 13-25.

ARAB GAMERS

AN IDENTITY INCLUSIVITY STUDY

BUSHRA ALFARAJ

Gamers are not immune to the sociopolitical realities of today's world, and this is reflected within video game narrative and design. Minorities who regularly face adversity may not relate to their core or sub-identities in their favorite video games—and that is if those identities are represented to begin with. There is an issue of game developers relying on stereotypes and having little to no association with the identities they are stereotyping.[1] As the diversity of gamer culture proves the stereotype of the "typical gamer" to be inaccurate, developers should consider creating relatable content for these gamers, who are far more complex than various media make them out to be.

Arabs and their culture have a history of being misrepresented by non-Arabs in mainstream media, and video games are no exception. Non-Arab storytellers may not know everything about Arabs in great detail, but this lack of knowledge should not be an excuse to ignore the fact that the historically rich Arab world is home to twenty-two countries encompassing multiple racial and religious groups, and that Arabs are as diverse and complex as other ethnicities.[2] Hussein Ibrahim has summarized the issue, explaining that it leaves us with inaccurate, unrelatable portrayals, which are often apathetically accepted as evidence of the status quo. Nevertheless, this indifference has not erased the reality that Arabs are far more diverse than the stereotypes with which we are often bombarded.[3]

Ibrahim's research also demonstrates that gamers react differently to seeing their identities being mis- or underrepresented, hence it is of the utmost importance that these representations be judged from the perspective of those whose identities are being depicted. Therefore, I bring to this chapter my own perspective as a female Arab gamer, as well as the perspectives of 81 gamers who are either ethnically Arab or have some firsthand association with Arab culture, with whom I conducted interviews focused on collecting qualitative data between March and May 2016.

The goal of gathering this data is twofold: First, to show the diverse responses of individual gamers with opinions on this subject matter, thus proving that real-life Arabs seldom hold true to stereotypes or monolithic categorizations; and second, to provide documentation of an underrepresented group of gamers as a contribution to discussions of intersectionality in digital media. Whether interview participants were indifferent or outraged by the state of Arab representations in video games, their opinions play an integral role in reflecting how complex identities and sub-identities can be. The primary findings of interview data are as follows:

1. Ibrahim Hussein, "What It's Like to Always Play the Bad Guy: On the Portrayal of Arabs in Online Shooters," in *The State of Play: Creators and Critics on Video Game Culture*, eds. Linus Larsson and Daniel Goldberg (Seven Stories Press, 2015).
2. B. Wingeld and M. Karaman, "Arab Stereotypes and American Educators," in *Beyond Heroes and Holidays: A Practical Guide to K-12 Multicultural, Anti-Racist Education and Staff Organization*, eds. Enid Lee, Deborah Menkart and Margo Okazawa-Ray (Teaching for Change, 2002).
3. Vít Šisler, "Digital Arabs: Representation in video games," *European Journal of Cultural Studies* 11.2 (2008): 203-220.

1. Arab players overwhelmingly report that Arabs are either underrepresented or misrepresented in video games.
2. Arab participants of more privileged gender or sexual orientation expressed restrictions on what constitutes acceptable representation in video games, in particular expressing trepidation regarding what they consider to be morally questionable content in video games.
3. Participants were largely in favor of non-Arab game developers collaborating with Arab developers and consultants.

To maintain anonymity, each participant is identified by their initials or an alias of their choice throughout this chapter. The first question participants were asked was how strongly they identified with their Arab background, on a scale from 1 to 10; this question did not require any explanation beyond the numerical value, but a few did briefly explicate that they identify as a full 10 simply for having Arab ancestry, or answered with lower numbers for reasons not related to biological or ethnic factors.

One of the most frequent responses to Arab representations was that of indifference. A Saudi participant under the pseudonym Quillcannon said that he "barely" identified as Arab despite being born and raised in his home country, and that seeing accurate balanced portrayals of Arabs in video games was of no importance to him. He cited games such as *Dying Light* (Warner Bros., 2015) and *Sly Cooper: Thieves in Time* (Sony, 2013), suggesting that the former represents Arabs positively while the latter does so negatively, but ultimately concluded that the representations in both games simply "amused" him:

> Arabs are represented in games [...] just as inaccurately as any other ethnic group or culture [...] This is to be expected when any individual [...] tries to encapsulate the experience of another background with which they are not familiar. Make no mistake: I am absolutely fine with inaccurate representation of Arabs in videogames, because it means people get to express themselves however they please. It also means I get to enjoy seeing my culture from [...] different viewpoints; something that could never happen if every developer [...] followed an exact recipe to accurate Arab representation.[4]

While I intentionally used open-ended terms such as "positive," "negative" and "accurate" in the interviews, a few participants delved more deeply into the semantics while explaining their answers. Algerian gamer HK (who identified as a 5/10 on the scale), explained that, to him, "accurate images of Arabs" can mean one of two things, and his response to each case is different: "Is it important to me that Arabs aren't portrayed as backwards and uneducated people? Yes, absolutely it is. Is it important to me that video games try to capture Arab culture? No, not really."[5] HK cited *Civilization IV* (Firaxis Games, 2005) as a game that portrays Arabs positively, highlighting the historical accuracy of its narrative and crediting the developers for their recognition of "the impact that our history had on modern math and science, and that definitely made my happy and gave me a rare (and short-lived) sense of pride of our people."[6] HK stated multiple times that the relatively limited scope of representations of Arabs in games makes it difficult to construct a valid opinion, but even brief encounters with positive or balanced representations can have an impact on gamers, invoking a sense of pride even when if their affinity to their culture is not that strong to begin with.

Thus, even when participants are indifferent to representations of Arab culture in games, the few positive representations they do encounter reinforce and remind them of the positive qualities of

4. Quillcanon, email interview, 2016.
5. HK, email interview, 2016.
6. Ibid.

their backgrounds. On the other hand, it comes as no surprise that some participants would not take strong offense to the lacking or stereotypical depictions of Arabs in games. Research by Adrienne Shaw on underrepresented groups in video games has shown that it is possible for a person belonging to a minority group to enjoy a game regardless of how inaccurately that aspect of their identity is portrayed in that game—however, for many players whose identities are under- or misrepresented in the games they play, encountering a positive portrayal is still "nice when it happens."[7]

While the previous participants were indifferent to Arab representation in games, others felt stronger feelings of discontent and concern. Algerian game developer AG, who introduced himself as very well-informed in how games are produced, traced his frustration at lacking Arab representations to mainstream developers:

> They make me feel sad. Mainly sad from the side of game designers being all about money, or the project manager…to be like we need to make money! "Yes, we will make an FPS game…and it's obvious that it has to involve Arabs. You know, everybody hates Arabs, so why not make the enemy an Arab, shoot them down… Shoot thousands of them!" It makes me feel sad. It makes me feel like they have such a bad imagination, trying to come up with a storyline that doesn't involve…portraying any of the stereotypes as a bad race.[8]

Possessing direct knowledge on game development, his frustration comes from knowing how feasible it is to create non-stereotypical content, yet financial concerns seem to matter more to producers. This brings us to an important notion that Anna Anthropy has tackled in her work: the mainstream game industry settling for creative stagnation in order to comfortably target a mainstream audience for profit rather than take a more innovative approach to representation in games.[9]

LH, a Lebanese game designer based in Spain, shared her experience working on a project designing a scene that took place in the room of a young girl from China. It was important for her to make the room as authentic as possible, by researching what a young Chinese girl's room might look like. With her professional and ethnic background in mind, she elaborated further on what makes Arab stereotypes in games problematic:

> No one is going to feel good about the negative representations, you know? I mean, even for example, like in *Uncharted* [Naughty Dog, 2011], you know the antagonist is like…he wasn't bad, he was Egyptian, it was really funny, like the things that he said, you know? But when…that is the only representation that you see, like a bad person and they're always the antagonist or the terrorist or whatever, you get bored of it [….] Like […] that pushes the whole stereotype and stuff, and it's just like come on, *laughs* we are more than that.[10]

The data also shows that the effects stereotypes have on gamers are in online environments quite notable. Emirati gamer FY said that she limits her gaming to offline games because "online people who are playing sometimes ruin the experience."[11] While she does not mention being personally targeted in an online game, she recounted a time when she was playing *Call of Duty* (Activision, 2003-) and witnessed a fellow Arab being harassed by other players:

> I stopped playing online They called another player names, and abused him emotionally [it] was *Call of Duty* […] and players first did not know he was an arab until he spoke or something and then they started to call

7. Adrienne Shaw. *Identity, Identification, and Media Representation in Video Game Play: An Audience Reception Study*, Ph.D. Dissertation, University of Pennsylvania (2010): 191.
8. AG, Google Hangouts interview, 2016.
9. Anna Anthropy, *Rise of the Videogame Zinesters: How Freaks, Amateurs, Artists, Dreamers, Dropouts, Queers, Housewives, and People Like You Are Taking Back An Art Form* (Seven Stories Press, 2012): 5-8.
10. LH, Skype Interview, 2016.
11. FY, email interview, 2016.

> him names like "Camel F***er" or "Go F*** your sister and mother" It was just horrible I don't remember details as I just logged off and felt sorry for such closed minded people.[12]

Sometimes, simply being recognized as Arab in an online game is enough to trigger others to begin harassing that player. American-born Syrian gamer FH explained that the stereotypes in games and media are so prevalent, they influence players of games that do not even contain Arab references. He shared the story of one such instance on the browser-based, unofficial fan game *Pokémon Showdown* (Guangcong Luo, 2011):

> I was matched with a player who had a Forretress [a species of Pokemon] with the nickname "Allahu Akbar" ["God is great" in Arabic], but with the actual Arabic text [...] Forretress sometimes is able to learn the move "Explosion," which knocks out the Pokemon that uses it but does a lot of damage to the opposing Pokemon as well... because I was able to read the text, I figured that based on stereotypes, this player probably did have the move on his Forretress. And unfortunately, I was correct [...] I pointed this out to the player after the move occurred in the chat, and I think he responded with "lol" or something similar... even though I won, I thought that it was pretty dumb that I was able to do so by essentially predicting someone else to be racist. I wanted to type in the chat "Dude not cool" or something like that. Nothing too accusatory [...] I just wanted to point out that it wasn't funny to me.[13]

The few non-Arabs in our pool of participants also showed dismay to the repetitive stereotypes of Arabs in video games, including Musti, a Pakistani who grew up in the United Arab Emirates:

> I hate to see it. It is unfair and crude the way they are portrayed. It is one thing to get the clothing and the character design right, but what is the point when that character is acting in a negative manner or follows the same stereotype that we are sick of. Too many times have I found myself saying "Oh look, an Arab terrorist looking character how original..." Can I please have an Arab looking Counter-Terrorist for once? How much more stereotypical do you have to be with the sunglasses, cigarette pack in the front pocket and Arab headdress around your neck.[14]

Compare this with an observation from a Kuwaiti gamer and developer:

> Mrs.Q8GEEK: I simply haven't encountered enough Arab characters in games, and often when I do, I think of them the same way I think of Disney's *Aladdin* [1992]: it's just a fantasy world constructed to suit the views of the writers, producers, or designers.

Mrs.Q8GEEK is not necessarily critical of the developers, as she attributes their intentions to game design decisions, however she does state that the representations have failed to meet her expectations by being limited to stereotypes with which she does not associate. Perhaps such flat depictions cause less direct harm than those of menacing terrorists, but they are rooted in the same pigeonholing of Arabs through an Orientalist lens.[15]

Very few participants referred to Orientalism[16] by name in their interviews when describing how they believe the mainstream developers perceive Arabs. Among them was Saudi gamer Echo, who sees a lack of interest or research on the mainstream developers' side as the root of a lack of depth in cultural depictions, asking, "Should we go back to the idea of orientalism? [...] We Arabs have a direct experience with our own culture. Mainstream game developers however, do not. They [...] do not care, and/or don't have reliable sources to gather info."[17]

12. Ibid.
13. FH, email interview, 2016.
14. Musti, email interview, 2016.
15. Mrs.Q8GEEK, email interview, 2016.
16. Edward Said, *Orientalism* (Vintage Books, 1994).

For identity group experiencing microaggressions, it is not uncommon for individuals to have more lenient reactions. Nevertheless, this does not invalidate responses that demonstrate discontent with the depictions in question.

Some participants said that the relative influence of news and films is arguably more powerful than video games, and would blame the preexisting notions of Arabs by non-Arab gamers and developers on non-game media. Kuwaiti gamer AWN shared online gaming scenarios where non-Arab gamers would express surprise at his ethnicity. He took offense that their expectations of an Arab would be so different from themselves:

> When I ask them why were they surprised, the answers are more or less similar "because you think and speak like us." Some give a slightly offensive but understandable answer such as "I didn't expect someone from your side of the world to have such a Western way of thinking," which is offensive because they affiliated progress, development and growth to the west and nowhere else, which is the media's fault, frankly speaking.[14]

To have others give backhanded compliments, classifying Arabs as progressive by Western standards, seems to link to the larger picture of what the Western media has satirized as Arab, as opposed to the sophisticated Western hero.

Another finding from the data gathered for this chapter is that the more marginalized Arab gamers are, the more likely they are to be harmed by the current state of affairs in the gaming world. For example, AK is an Egyptian developer who identifies as gay. He emphasizes how important it is to him to see diversely accurate representations of Arabs in games and other media, as the current stereotypes in Hollywood of aggressive heterosexual Arab men have a personal effect on his identity and what people expect from him as a male, as an Arab and as an Arab male:

> I think [accurate portrayals are] important as a gay and as Arabian. For example when I arrived at US, all people expect me straight (can't be gay) because games and movies show arabs as these [...] tough people. Even in gay community they profile me as the strong alpha male [...] I got harassed from someone yesterday and he used that (the idea about me being arabian and being terrorist).[18]

This serves as another reminder that the more intertwined a minority identity is, the more likely they are to be discriminated against.

To some participants, there was a belief that Arabs are to blame for the lack of creative narratives in media, thus did not point the blame entirely on non-Arab game developers. Emirati developer Asatiir expressed that Arabs do not export enough narratives that would appeal to people beyond the Arab region:

> I think Arabs are unexplored enough, we've yet to have our culture or folklore portrayed in a light similar to, say, Victorian England, Feudal Japan or Norse Viking or even Medieval Europe. Arab culture is as rich a story-telling setting as the mentioned settings.... Who can you blame for this lack of attention though? Most of the folklore in the region is fragmented, historians only cover the Arab golden age of enlightenment, and anything older is just clumped together as pre-islamic dark ages ... without any documentation to fall back on.[19]

Participants have different perspectives on what is stereotypical, and their genre preferences naturally

17. AWN, email interview, 2016.
18. AK, email interview, 2016.
19. Asatiir, WhatsApp interview, 2016.

influence the kind of exposure they see of Arabs in video games. Characters such as Rashid from *Street Fighter* (Capcom, 2016) and Altaïr from *Assassin's Creed* (Ubisoft, 2007) were frequently cited by participants as positive Arab representations.

Jordanian gamer Lovidore plays a variety of genres, and cited the entire *Call of Duty* franchise as one that depicts Arabs negatively, as well as *Counter Strike: Condition Zero* (Valve, 2004) and *Battlefield 3* (EA, 2011). When asked how he felt about the portrayals in those games, Lovidore replied, "Sad. Sad and mad. Seriously." However, he was pleased with representations in other games, such as Rashid from *Street Fighter V*. He shared his thoughts on why he considers Rashid to be a positive portrayal:

> Well, he's actually a strong character in *Street Fighter V*. People actually like playing him, and I like that...They took the traditional style of Arab dress and merged it with futuristic gadgets to make for a nice, dare I say, steam punk-esque look? It's nice for a change rather than having himself blow up because of his disgruntled view of western foreign politics.[20]

Lovidore is not the only one with a critical view of the gaming world's embrace of Arab cultures. AS is an Egyptian gamer who mostly plays online games, and finds that the personalities of Arab players on those platforms often gives non-Arab gamers a bad impression of them, which also connects to the common sentiment among interview participants of "Arabs blaming Arabs":

> This is kind of [...] disastrous, but yeah [...] the majority of online gamers [...] in a game called Conquest [...] is swarmed with Arabs. And the majority of these Arabs are Egyptians. Cool? Yeah. And they are the most famous scammers on this game [...] When I'm training with someone and he'd be like "ah nice raid. Where are you from?" From Egypt. "Oh my God. An Arab. I'm out."[21]

While he shared this anecdote in a humorous tone, he was certainly frustrated that enough online Arab gamers have brought negative attention to themselves.

It is important to look at the role privilege plays in the Arab gamer community across different identity groups. Systemic privilege exists in the Arab world and works similarly to Western or white privilege, where cisgendered, heterosexual, able-bodied males have the most straightforward access to first-class treatment. For the purpose of this study, I have narrowed the definition of "Arab privilege" to heterosexual, male, religious Arabs. While many male participants stated their support for seeing more representations of women in games, others provided indifferent responses. As for Arab LGBTQ representation, we received an array of opinions ranging from enthusiasm to indifference to absolute disapproval, from straight male and female participants alike. With intersectionality and privilege in mind, it is worth considering how Elisabeth Hayes describes the prioritization of male and female gamer perspectives: "To better understand women's and men's orientations toward gaming, we need to take into account the complexity of people's identities, not just gender alone, but its interplay with and enactment in combination with personal histories and cultural factors that play out different in individuals' lives."[22] This intersectional perspective is helpful for understanding the diverse responses of different Arab gamers.

Near the end of their interviews, participants were asked for their opinions on the representations of Arab men, women and LGBTQ characters, respectively, and then answered a hypothetical question asking how to present Arabs in a diverse way. DW, a Saudi male, could not recall a single Arab LGBTQ representation in any games. When asked if he believed this identity group should have

20. Lovidore, email interview, 2016.
21. AS, Skype interview, 2016.
22. Elisabeth Hayes, "Gendered Identity at Play: Case Studies of Two Women Playing Morrowind," *Games and Culture* 2.1 (2007): 23-48.

representation, he replied, "That is a powder keg. If you an Arab gamer you probably wouldn't care if a game is developed by non-arabs if it had any LGBT content. The censors might care if it got through their channels but these guys hate fun. It could go catastrophic if media, public opinion or clergy paid attention to it."[23] DW highlights the difficult dilemmas faced by game developers and publishers in the Arab world.

Syrian gamer Doom is among many participants who noticed a decline in Arab representations based on gender and sexuality. Throughout his interview, he exhibited an apathetic and mostly cynical attitude toward the current state of Arab representations: "Usually [an Arab man is represented as] either a terrorist or someone with a backwards way of thinking [...] I do not recall seeing an Arab Woman in a video game [...] Have not run into [Arab LGBTQ representations] either... video game companies want what sells, I want Arabs to be portrayed the way they are, normal."[24] For Doom and many other players, "normalcy" is defined as representing Arabs as diversely as possible without any question of their ethnicity. This emerged as many participants stated that having "normal" Arabs in a video game is an ideal means of presenting diversity. Despite his cynicism, Doom ended his interview commenting that he believes there has been some improvement in the representations of Arabs in video games recently, although still thinks that the game industry has a long way to go before it achieves accurate portrayals of Arabs.

LAZ from Oman made similar observations of how representations decline based on gender identity and sexual orientation. She expressed how important it is for Arab characters to be "normal," and said she would like to see greater diversity in the representation of Arab identity in games, noting that Arab men are represented as:

> War criminals, enemies, and terrorists. If they're in AAA games. It's hard to determine what Arabs should be presented as in games, as race shouldn't equate to better or worse treatment. Having an Arab as an important protagonist would be really cool if the protag was well-thought out and studied for... I've yet to come across Arab women in games. I don't think I've ever seen or heard of Arab LGBTQ characters in video games. That is upsetting, I would like to see a character like that.[25]

While representations of Arab women are scarcer than their male counterparts, some gamers have encountered them. Most participants confirmed that Arab women are portrayed—as Sudanese-Austrian participant MESB succinctly describes it—either blatantly sexualized or rendered as passive beings. Simply put, Arab women are often exoticized in video games. He offered heavily critical analyses of representations of Arabs in games and other media, many of which trace back to Orientalism, explaining that the representation of Arab women in games follows "mostly one of two orientalist tropes: oversexualised in belly dancer outfits, or as hapless background props with no agency."[26] MESB's comment confirms not only the ethnic stereotypes to which Arab women are subjected, but the gender-related ones as well. The representation of women is focused almost entirely on their sexuality and physical appearance, coupled with their dependency on the presumably male protagonist. The representations of Arab women have fallen victim to this trend overall, in addition to their ethnicity becoming a plot device. In the data on existing representations of Arab women, I found the ironic burqa-clad versus belly-dancer trope to be a recurring theme among participants, where the belly-dancer trope seemed to outnumber the fully covered Muslim-Arab woman.[27]

23. DW, email interview, 2016.
24. Doom, email interview, 2016.
25. LAZ, email interview, 2016.
26. MESB, email interview, 2016.
27. Šisler, "Digital Arabs."

Badoor, who has written critical analyses on Arab character representation in online forums, shared his thoughts on how he has seen Arab women depicted in games:

> Arab Women representation tends to come hand in hand with a sexualization aspect.... There are quite a few belly-dancer tropes whenever an Arab woman is represented, because it's a very convenient representation that both shows that she's "Arab" and also get her to show some skin because she's a woman and women tend to get objectified in media.[28]

The concept of designing Arab women as belly-dancers to appeal to the male gaze does not appeal to all men. Iblis, who identifies as a pansexual Arab, said he was unhappy with the female Arab belly-dancer trope.

> [Arabs] are represented as strangely alien or as if we came out of the *A Thousand and One Nights* stories, where the women are all clad in belly-dancer or [sex] slave outfits. The game [*Subway Surfers: Arabia* (Kiloo Games, 2012)] showed a very stereotypical image of the Arab world, as if it were something out of the *Aladdin* movie. Not to mention that the game presented a horrible character named Amira; she was depicted in...clothes that indicate her being an Oriental belly-dancer.[29]

Sylvia Chan-Malik illustrates the problem with these repetitive stereotypes of exotic Asian women: "On the one hand, it might seem like it might be a tongue-in-cheek portrayal of those types of images, but on the other hand you have to be in on the joke. My question is: Are we all in on the joke, and are we all laughing?"[30] This response addresses both racial and gender concerns when it comes to portraying minority groups in popular culture, specifically in American media that reach audiences overseas as well as within the United States. The rhetorical question "are we all laughing?" is applicable to portrayals of Arab women through an Orientalist lens, a misguided perspective through which many women in the Asian continent have been viewed.[31]

In the same way representations of non-privileged Arabs in video games tend to be less frequent, enthusiasm for the representation of minority Arabs was somewhat uneven. There were 13 female participants and 68 male ones, for all of whom it was optional to disclose their sexual orientation before commencing the interview; one identified as pansexual, two identified as gay, a few identified as straight and the rest did not provide an answer. While being a straight Arab male does not make someone homophobic by default, there were heterosexual participants who were not supportive of representations of Arab LGBTQ groups in video games. For example, Hamada, a male Saudi gamer, left the interview sections about female Arab and LGBTQ characters in games blank, and did not provide answers until I followed up with him. He then explained: "I have never played a game that has Arab women in it. I am not opposed to women characters being in games, but if it's an Arab woman then she must be represented in a respectful way. Although, representing Arab characters in a positive way should be focused on boys only, because the presence of girls isn't that important anyway."[32]

Hamada's statement that the presence of girls in these games is of little importance demonstrates that his notion of a good game is limited to what an adult male audience wants. While his was the only response that excluded women gamers as audience members, and though a few other male participants held relatively more progressive views regarding the portrayal of Arab women,

28. Badoor, email interview, 2016.
29. Iblis, email interview (translated from Arabic), 2016.
30. Sylvia Chan-Malik, "Cultural and Literary Production of Muslim America," in *The Cambridge Companion to American Islam*, eds. Juliane Hammer and Omid Safi (Cambridge University Press, 2013).
31. *Slaying the Dragon: Reloaded,* directed by Elaine H. Kim (2011).
32. Hamada, email interview (translated from Arabic), 2016.

they all shared some notion that Arab women are, by default, practicing Muslims who would dress modestly—a standard these specific participants seem to have for Arab women. While it is debatable how and when designing modest or immodest attire for women in games matters, the perspective of these male gamers comes off as chauvinistic, and fails to recognize that games are as important to female gamers as they are to male ones.

Furthermore, Hamada, along with several others, drew the line at the prospect of LGBTQ representations in games. A common trend among male participants was that they "did not mind" seeing representations of Arab women. They also did not always dictate that the women be dressed a certain way. Presumably Muslim participants would often bring up the *hijab* (the headscarf worn by some Muslim women) and say that it did not have to be worn by an Arab woman in order for her to be an accurate representation of an Arab female. However, the *hijab* was a common indicator that the woman in question would be Muslim. Whether these men fully supported or "did not mind" seeing Arab women, the latter frequently tended to be less favorable when it came to representations of Arab LGBTQ groups.

Female participants who had not seen representations of their gender were all in favor of those representations. However, not all of these participants were supportive of LGBTQ representations, and gave their reasons as conservatively religious ones. For instance, Saudi gamer SMH says that Arab women are not represented fairly in video games, but rather are depicted:

> like they dont have a personality and have zero value and scared and like she cant do anything without a male [...] Yes they should [be represented differently] because Arab women are smart and courageous and caring and are nothing like the way [the developers] they show them.[33]

After SMH sent in her responses and left the question on Arab LGBTQ representations blank, I followed up, asking if she intentionally did not answer the question, and added that I would like to learn her stance on seeing representations of LGBTQ Arabs:

> I didn't answer [...] because i don't remember playing a game that included arab LGBTQ characters ... Well im against it and i hope there wont be any LGBTQ arabs and the reason is because its *haram* [Arabic word for *sin* or *forbidden*] and its not acceptable in the society and if there was a game trust me most of the arabs wont buy it and it wont be allowed to be sold in the markets.[34]

While supportive of seeing more female representations, she did not wish the same for non-heteronormative depictions. This brings us back to the concept of the privileged Arab who does not wish nor bother to use their status to uplift less privileged groups within their community.

A pattern of responses showed that there is a dichotomization of Arab LGBTQ representations among some participants, such as those who were against LBGTQ representations were those who seemed to refuse to believe that LGBTQ groups even exist within Arab nations and culture. Jordanian gamer Maverick said he was in favor of seeing varied representations of women "because not every Arab woman is veiled." However, his stance on LGBTQ Arab representations was quite different: "I have a bit of an unapologetic opinion regarding the LGBTQ community so I would definitely be upset if there's such reference, especially to an Arab as the whole deviation from the human nature isn't

33. SMH, email interview (translated from Arabic), 2016.
34. Ibid.

really something Arabs were ever known for."[35] MS shared Maverick's opposition to prospects of Arab LGBTQ representations:

> I think that's one of the most important problems that we will face in their [Western] games. They develop to make this new standard, this new Arabian standards [...] When we play their game, after this period of time, we will face a problem. Also, when our kids plays these games, maybe they know or they practice some things we are not [...] we do not need this.[36]

Likewise, XxIGamerGirlxX expressed a similarly prohibitive stance with regard to the representation of LGBTQ Arabs in games:

> Naturally I am against it. We wouldn't accept it from non-Arabs, let alone from Arabs. I am opposed to this because first of all, it is known that most Arabs are Muslims, and Islam forbids this kind of thing. I can't imagine any Arab country that would promote games with homosexual representations of Arabs.[37]

Using pronouns such as "we" and "us" to claim that Arabs are, by default, heteronormative, led me to the conclusion that these opinions come from privileged and conservative gamers. Emphasizing this theme is important because it shows us mutual issues shared by underrepresented gamer groups with more "mainstream" ones. In this case, privileged straight Arab gamers are alienating people from their same ethnic background because they do not accept their sexual orientation—ironic, given that the former group often craves acceptance from non-Arab groups in general.

While the Muslim-Arab gamers who showed disapproval of LGBTQ representations did not consider the possibility of other Arabs who might identify as gay, whether coming from a religious background or not, lack of LGBTQ inclusivity within the Arab world does not go unnoticed by gamers who are allies to this group. Generalizing that "most Arabs are Muslim" also excludes Arabs who follow religions other than Islam or simply do not subscribe to any faith. Joe, a Christian Lebanese-Canadian developer, pointed out that the intolerance toward homosexuality and other sexual orientations is the product of generational and educational gaps within certain Arab communities, rather than the product of conservative religious practices alone:

> [Homosexuality is] not an accepted idea over there, and usually not by the young generation, just by the older generation... The young generation really doesn't care. And I think also it depends on the young generation, where they actually studied... So... usually educated people probably won't have that much of an issue with them.[38]

He did, however, show some concern when asked if he believed there should be transparency in portraying Arab LGBTQ groups in games, explaining, "I don't think any company wants to start the first storm... I've played a lot of games where the characters are gays, or in movies for example, if a character is gay. I really don't care about it."[39] This brings us back to DW's quote earlier in this section, where he predicted the ramifications of Arab developers hoping to integrate LGBTQ Arabs in their games: "And if you are an Arab Dev... You are just playing with fire. Though I have to say a lot of artists and game Devs are impressionable.... And don't really notice or even think about it that they are making characters with LGBT traits that are subtle."[40] While a significant number of participants were torn between opposition and apathy when it came to representing Arab LGBTQ characters in

35. Maverick, email interview, 2016.
36. MS, Skype interview, 2016.
37. XxIGamerGirlxX, email interview (translated from Arabic), 2016.
38. Joe, Skype interview, 2016.
39. Ibid.
40. DW, email interview, 2016.

games, others were very supportive of the concept. Privileged or not, they mostly believed that Arab diversity cannot be achieved by annihilating unprivileged identities, even if many other Arabs are less than receptive to these depictions.

One of the most supportive and inclusive responses to the prospect of Arab LGBTQ and women characters came from Sharifa, a straight Egyptian-American gamer. She was among the few participants who were aware of an upcoming game by an Arab game company, titled *Saudi Girls Revolution* (NA3AM, not yet released):

> DUDE! [...] I'm really glad that you're asking this. This game is going to be about eight Arab women [...] One of them is gay! I am so excited to see this character revealed [...] and I like cannot wait for the lesbian character. Her name is Hessa, I think? [..]. Having any character that is not cis-gendered and is also Arab or Muslim, I think it's great! Because it shows that we're the same! Like your struggles are our struggles, and our struggles are your struggles, and our struggles are not different! IT'S SO EXCITING.[41]

To exude such eagerness to seeing multiple Arab women in a game, including a lesbian character, shows that intersecting identities are indeed scarce. Throughout her interview, Sharifa emphasized how important it is to have varied and diverse representations of Arabs in games.

In the final part of the interview, participants were asked to imagine themselves as cultural consultants, and were asked how Arabs could be portrayed non-stereotypically in games. The response of Saudi gamer Rakatash summarized the feelings of many participants:

> ...Just get Arab screenwriters? Or...travel to some Arab country and really observe it from there, and then get the story from there... the whole region is quite huge. I mean, being Saudi... if there are Arabs in the game ... usually, the Arab equates Gulf. Which is either a Saudi or an Emirati or a Kuwaiti... someone wearing a *thobe* and a *shmagh*. Or an accent. If it's about war, it's probably Iraq. But you don't see Moroccans, you don't see Egyptians, you don't see Sudanese, you don't see Syrians, or Lebanese... so it's kind of a bit skewed...but if you want to accurately portray a region or an Arab character, you either zoom into that...spot, where it's not just an Arab.... I mean, if I were Moroccan, I would feel like I'm kind of left out.[42]

Many respondents echoed these suggestions of travel, research and normalcy as ways to improve the depiction of Arab culture in video games.

Participants were also strongly in favor of having Arab developers and consultants on game design teams in order to improve representation. Moon, an Algerian-American, said he believes in the potential of implementing Arab folklore in order to create a game that presents Arabs in their diversity. When asked if this meant assigning the developers Arabic literature as part of the research for their games, he replied:

> Oh God, no. I wouldn't actually tell them to do that. I would read the books; I would tell them what to do. They're not gonna read [...] they're too busy coding [...] I would obviously go back to folklore [...] A fantasy setting. If that wasn't the genre, then I would simply want Arabs in general to be portrayed in like a kind of fairer manner [...][43]

Responses that favored having a designated consultant seem to indicate a realization that not all developers have the capacity or motivation to conduct research beyond aesthetic and design purposes.

41. Sharifa, Skype interview, 2016.
42. Rakatash, Google Hangouts interview, 2016.
43. Moon, Skype interview, 2016.

It should do more good to a development team's status to have a professional consultant in the long run, rather than publish inaccurate content that harms their reputation and audiences in the long run.

The characters Shaheen from *Tekken 7* (Bandai Namco, 2017) and Rashid from *Street Fighter V* (Capcom, 2016) were frequently cited as positive examples of Arab characters in video games. Belonging to fairly recent video game releases, participants who cited them seemed mostly familiar with the process the developers took in involving their Arab fans in the character design process. In their responses on this final topic, many participants observed that the stereotypes of Arab people in video games may be on the decline.

Qatari gamer FAN is hopeful that more developers will continue to ditch stereotypical characterizations: "Luckily, the games we love show us appreciation from time to time. The *Tekken* dev team and *Street Fighter* dev team worked hard with the Saudi community to represent characters from their country well. Hopefully more of that will happen."[44] FAN had ranked his identity as an Arab as being an 8, and elaborated how he would have given a lower number had he been asked the question even two years ago. He also stated that, to him, seeing accurate representations of Arabs "slowly becomes more and more important every day."[45]

Returning to the three primary findings of this research after interview analysis, we will see that a total of nine themes have manifested from the interviews:

1. The acknowledgement of lacking representation is independent of ethnic identity
    - Blame is distributed between game developers, mainstream media and Arabs blaming themselves
    - Different game genres and online communities influence exposure and perceptions of Arabs in video games
2. Arab privilege plays an important role in inclusivity
    - In video games, representations of Arabs decline starting from men to women to LBGTQ groups
    - Arab gamers' advocacy toward non-privileged Arab representations is intermittent, often tracing back to a participant's awareness of their own privilege
3. Game developers can and should employ measures to improve Arab representations
    - Employing Arabs developers and consultants
    - Request for developers to familiarize Themselves with Arab identities

Despite many of the mixed responses that manifested from these interviews, it is noteworthy that one constant was the idea that portrayals of Arab culture in video games are gradually improving. Titles including *Overwatch* (Blizzard, 2016) and *Assassin's Creed Origins* (Ubisoft, 2017) have been positively received by Arab gamers on social media. I was also struck by the following message, sent to me by a participant as I was wrapping up my research: "It's super interesting how everyone thinks of

44. FAN, email interview, 2016.
45. Ibid.

themselves as victims. But can't be bothered to think of the others (whom are going through the same difficulties)."[46]

I was not expecting participants to necessarily reevaluate their agenda throughout the course of the interviews, regardless, reflections such as the aforementioned one imply the importance of addressing these issues. It shows an innate tendency to neglect intersectional inclusivity, and that critical thinking is a positive step forward.

There are far too many nuances to cover within the scope of this chapter, which was always a given as I began this research conceding that everyone is a complex individual. I truly believe that the participants, no matter what their respective stances are in regards to gatekeeping representations, have reflected the complexity of Arab gamer identities. As with any industry, video games are bursting with as much potential as there exists capacity for improvement.

WORKS CITED

Anthropy, Anna. *Rise of the Videogame Zinesters: How Freaks, Amateurs, Artists, Dreamers, Dropouts, Queers, Housewives, and People Like You Are Taking Back An Art Form*. Seven Stories Press, 2012.

Chan-Malik, Sylvia. "Cultural and Literary Production of Muslim America." In *The Cambridge Companion to American Islam*, edited by Juliane Hammer and Omid Safi. Cambridge University Press, 2013.

Hayes, Elisabeth. "Gendered Identity at Play: Case Studies of Two Women Playing *Morrowind*." *Games and Culture* 2.1 (2007): 23-48.

Hussein, Ibrahim. "What It's Like to Always Play the Bad Guy: On the Portrayal of Arabs in Online Shooters." In *The State of Play: Creators and Critics on Video Game Culture*, edited by Linus Larsson and Daniel Goldberg. Seven Stories Press, 2015.

Shaw, Adrienne. "Identity, Identification, and Media Representation in Video Game Play: An Audience Reception Study." Ph.D. Dissertation, University of Pennsylvania, 2010.

Said, Edward. *Orientalism*. Vintage Books, 1994.

Šisler, Vít. "Digital Arabs: Representation in video games." *European Journal of Cultural Studies* 11.2 (2008): 203-220.

Wingeld, B. and M. Karaman. "Arab Stereotypes and American Educators." In *Beyond Heroes and Holidays: A Practical Guide to K-12 Multicultural, Anti-Racist Education and Staff Organization*, edited by Enid Lee, Deborah Menkart and Margo Okazawa-Ray. Teaching for Change, 2002.

46. AAM2, email, 2016.

ESPORTS GAMERS IN CHINA

CAREER, LIFESTYLE AND PUBLIC DISCOURSE AMONG PROFESSIONAL LEAGUE OF LEGENDS COMPETITORS

BORIS PUN, YIYI YIN, AND ANTHONY FUNG

INTRODUCTION: THE RISE OF GAMING IN CHINA

The term "eSports" has recently become one of the most-frequently-searched internet keywords in China.[1] A portmanteau of the terms "electronic" and "sports," eSports carries a positive connotation at the lexical level, implying professional game playing as a form of organized sport and situating video games within the bigger picture of sports studies. The "e" in eSports refers not only to the electronic format of the sports in question, but also implies a relationship to the more complex socio-cultural context of virtual space and digital activities, encouraging public perceptions of gaming as a professional endeavor. In China, eSports seems an inevitable dimension of the progress of modernization. In many respects, China's emergence as a global power appears unstoppable, with the country's businesses having recently risen to challenge the dominant forces in a number of industries. Video games, characterized by researchers such as T. L. Taylor and Sue Schneider as one of the most appealing forms of entertainment for young consumers and global investors alike, perfectly illustrate this growing global dominance: China is now recognized as the largest national video game market in the world as well as the most potent challenger to the previously-dominant market, the United States.[2] In a 2018 report by investment researcher Newzoo, China was projected to reach US$37.9 billion in annual revenue, putting it at the top of all global game markets.[3] A 2016 report from the China Game Publishers Association highlights the astonishing fact that China's online gaming industry brought in a total of US$16.5 billion that year, with more than 566 million active mobile users consuming online games.[4] These data illustrate the prosperity that the Chinese game market has experienced as the state has begun open up its cultural policies. The significant economic impact of China's emerging game market is of particular interest to academics due to several latent factors that have catalyzed the abrupt rise of the Chinese video game market, making up its formula for success.

Although limited in scope, previous academic research has focused on different factors related to the topic of China's emerging gaming industry. For example, Yong and Downing, whose work is recognized as the one of the key structured studies analyzing the emerging Chinese game industry, have examined public perceptions of virtual gaming.[5] Fung and Liao have also highlighted the impact of cultural policy on the economics of the game industry in China, discussing how the market has expanded and gaming culture has grown to include more players, promoters and game companies.[6]

1. The authors wish to acknowledge the Research Grant Council, HKSAR government through the Research Grant Fund (Project no. CUHK14617716), whose support was key to this project's completion.

2. T. L. Taylor, *Raising the Stakes: E-sports and the Professionalization of Computer Gaming* (MIT Press, 2012); Sue Schneider, "Social Gaming and Online Gambling," *Gaming Law Review and Economics* 16.12 (2012): 711-712.

3. See Newzoo, "Top 100 Countries/Markets by Game Revenues," *Newzoo*, 2018, https://newzoo.com/insights/rankings/top-100-countries-by-game-revenues/.

4. See Consulate General of the Kingdom of the Netherlands, Guangzhou, China, "China: Top Sector Games," 2014, https://www.rvo.nl/sites/default/files/2014/12/china-top-sector-games-opportunity-report-cg-gz-20141023.pdf.

5. Yong Cao and John D. H. Downing, "The Realities of Virtual Play: Video Games and their Industry in China," *Media, Culture & Society* 30.4 (2008): 515-529.

Research conducted by Dal Yong Jin, Larissa Hjorth and Dean Chan have explored gaming culture in Asia and how electronic games' transition to mobile devices has triggered massive growth in the popularity of gaming throughout Asia.[7] Still, relatively little research has focused on how game users, including both common players and professionals, have participated in sustaining or transforming perceptions of gaming culture in the regional context. How do gaming professionals develop careers in eSports and related entertainment businesses, such as livestreaming? How do players deal with social pressure in order to succeed as professional gamers? How does the growth of the Chinese video game market illustrate the ways economics can serve as a driving force behind political change? And what cultural and societal transformations can result from governmental changes to cultural policy in response to economic concerns? This chapter responds to gaps in existing research by exploring the development of eSports in China since the loosening of restrictions on imported media and controls over public discourse in 2009, pointing to cultural policy as the most significant factor in bringing about China's gaming boom.

Research for this chapter was based on two methods. First, textual analysis was used to examine public discourse on eSports in China collected from major news web sites and search engines, which evidenced the impact of the significant distinctions in the Chinese government's posture toward public discourse in cultural policy drafted before and after 2009, helping to sketch a general portrait of how professional gaming has been officially conceptualized. Second, participatory observation was used to understand professional gamers' lifestyles behind the masks of their public images and beyond the uproar surrounding their glorious victories. These methods point to the conclusion that, in response to the enormous revenues of the video game market, public discourse regarding "gaming" has refocused on the discussion of eSports and pro-gamers in China, while amateur gaming is still widely regarded in a negative light.[8] This analysis helps explain how gaming culture, which had been perceived in the past as vulgar, violent, non-productive and lacking in cultural sophistication, became one of the most prominent emerging sectors of the entertainment business in China, as well as the key role cultural policy played in this transformation. To understand the changing landscape of Chinese gaming, it is essential to take into account the polarization of public discourse on gaming, which is the focus of this chapter.

GAMING IN CHINA PRIOR TO 2009: GOVERNMENT POLICY, PUBLIC DISCOURSE AND MORAL PANIC

As mentioned above, 2009 was a watershed year for the Chinese gaming market, while prior to 2009 there were a number of strict policies and regulations that prevented the growth of gaming businesses. The year 2004 marks a turning point for governmental censorship of gaming content through the implementation of cultural policy in China, with the publication of the "Government Notice Prohibiting the Broadcast of Television Shows on Video Games" by the State Administration of Radio, Film and Television of People's Republic of China (hereafter SARFT). However, the "censorship war" between game companies, game users and the Chinese government has been going on since the very onset of video gaming in China, when arcade games entered the Chinese market in the 1980s following its post-Mao opening and reform drives. As Yong Cao and John D. H. Downing have suggested, at that time privately-owned arcades featuring coin-operated games from the U.S. and Japan began to have a significant impact on youth entertainment culture in China, and gaming soon earned a negative reputation as a threat luring children to addictive lifestyles.[9] This widespread

6. Anthony Y. H. Fung and Sara Xueting Liao, "China," in *Video Games Around the World*, ed. Mark J. P. Wolf (MIT Press, 2015): 119-135.
7. Dal Yong Jin, "Mobile Gaming in Asia: Politics, Culture and Emerging Technologies," in *Mobile Communication in Asia: Local Insights, Global Implications*, ed. Sun Sun Lim (Springer, 2016); *Gaming Cultures and Place in Asia-Pacific*, eds. Larissa Hjorth and Dean Chan (Routledge, 2009).
8. "Pro-gamer" is the term most frequently used in China for eSports professionals.
9. Cao and Downing, "The Realities of Virtual Play."

public stereotype led to a push for the establishment of governmental regulations controlling the importation of game consoles. Tracing back to policies like the 1990 "Government Notice Strengthening the Regulation of Billiards and Video Games"[10] and the 1992 "Government Notice Prohibiting Gambling in the Use of Video Games,"[11] as well as further legislation strengthening regulations on commercial video gaming businesses and internet cafés in 1996 and 1998, the state has sought to hinder the development of gaming in Chinese society for the purpose of "protecting the ideological thinking and morality of young people."[12] During this period of time, many foreign games were banned and could not be imported to China, while domestic games received official warnings requiring publishers to modify game content related to the depiction of violence and sex to make it more "healthy."[13] Local television broadcasting companies were also forbidden to produce programs about digital gaming.[14] These measures clearly reflect China's official viewpoint prior to 2009, which treated video games and gaming as a problematic social ill or as a dangerous form of cultural importation, without recognizing the strengths and potentialities of the medium.

The Chinese news media fanned the flames of this negative public discourse, helping to hinder the development of gaming at that time. As in several other countries in global south, the Chinese government maintains complete control over all forms of publication in order to ensure the strict adherence of all publications and broadcasts to party ideology. Looking back at Chinese news media from this period of time, it is common to find articles labelling video games as a form of "heroin targeting children" or a "threat to public wellbeing."[15] Other news reports commonly associated gaming with other societal taboos like crime, violence, juvenile delinquency, lack of education and gambling. In at least one case, governmental restrictions on gaming were formulated in response to a major news story, namely a 2002 fire at an internet café in Beijing, an act of malicious arson that left 25 dead and 12 injured. The case attracted national attention, culminating with Beijing Mayor Qi Liu's announcement cutting support for further development of internet cafés, prohibiting their business permits and shutting down all such establishments in existence at that time. Not long afterwards, this policy would be executed on a national scale.

This overwhelmingly negative public discourse on gaming in Chinese society led to a state of "moral panic," which Stanley Cohen has defined as a kind of exaggerated social reaction through which "a condition, episode, person or group of persons emerges to become defined as a threat to societal values and interests."[16] More recent research by scholars such as David Garland and Sean Hier characterizes moral panic as a tactic frequently provoked by the elite or dominant classes, who use it when their own interests are threatened as a means of controlling the mediated distribution of information in support of grassroots organizations.[17] In the case of China, gaming has been "demonized" through association to "online addiction" or "digital addiction," perceived as a sickness with potentially long-lasting and even fatal consequences. This viewpoint is reflected in the Abstinence Center of Internet Addiction, established in 2006 by Yongxin Yang, a self-proclaimed medical therapist who applies electroshock to heal those who suffer from "digital addiction."[18]

10. Ministry of Culture of the People Republic of China (hereafter MCPRC) and Ministry of Public Security of the People's Republic of China (hereafter MPS).
11. See MCPRC and MPS, 9 December 1992.
12. Fung and Liao, "China."
13. Controls on internet and gaming content got even stricter under the "Regulation on Publishing of Digital Publication" in 2008 and the "Administration of Software Production" in 2009, which limited certain issues and ideologies, along with visual practices that could give rise to violence and sexual arousal, or those that could be judged to go against dominant Chinese ideologies.
14. Xinhua Net, "Announcement from SARFT: Forbidding Broadcasting Programs about Computer Online Game," 2004, http://news.xinhuanet.com/zhengfu/2004-04/21/content_1432492.html.
15. Zhouxiang Lu, "From E-Heroin to E-Sports: The Development of Competitive Gaming in China," *The International Journal of the History of Sport* 33.18 (2016): 2186-2206.
16. Stanley Cohen, *Folk Devils and Moral Panics: The Creation of the Mods and Rockers* (Paladin, 1973).
17. David Garland, "On the Concept of Moral Panic," *Crime Media Culture* 4.1 (2008): 9- 30; Sean Hier, "Thinking beyond Moral Panic: Risk, Responsibility, and the Politics of Moralization," *Theoretical Criminology* 12.2 (2008): 173-190.

Hundreds of parents have sent their children to this center to seek treatment, where "patients" were treated inhumanely and punished with detention, electroshock, starvation and other forms of physical, verbal and mental abuse. It was not long before an "addicted" youth was beaten to death, ten hours after entering a secured camp in Nanning in 2009. Discussions regarding abstinence centers bloomed all over the country, and as a result, the moral panic surrounding gaming then began to decrease.

THE DAWN OF A NEW (GAMING) ERA: ECONOMICS, CULTURAL POLICY AND ESPORTS IN CHINA AFTER 2009

In 2009, a number of blockbuster multiplayer online battle arena video games including *League of Legends* (Riot games, 2009; hereafter *LoL*) and the new All Pick version of *Dota 2* (Valve, 2013) sparked enthusiasm for the development of a more competitive gaming culture, connecting China to global cultural and economic trends in gaming. The pool of online gamers and gaming revenues alike have expanded sharply with the loosening of official policies toward games, such as granting official governmental approval for the importation and distribution of Western games like *Dota 2* and *LoL*. Since then, the Chinese government has begun to reconsider and even redefine gaming as an important cultural industry with economic potential, as evidenced in 2011 by the "12th Five-Year Plan for the Development of National Economy and Society," which names the cultural industries—including film, animation, comics and video games—as the most important sphere for further development.

One renowned example of China's intensive devotion of resources to the cultural industries is the "quota policy," by which Western game publishers are permitted to distribute their games only through vendors affiliated with one of the China-based gaming agencies.[19] As a consequence, some of the world's most popular games—including *LoL, Dota 2, Starcraft* (Blizzard, 1998) and *Minecraft* (Mojang, 2009)—are franchised in China through national publishers Tencent and NetEase, who receive a significant portion of the games' national revenues. On the one hand, this policy aims to protect Chinese game developers, especially those belonging to the Chinese Cultural Cluster, which is a specific technological zone in which the Chinese government situates various companies and supplementary infrastructure for running cultural business; on the other hand, it helps strengthen China's soft power by promoting the development of more domestic games using funds raised through the commissioning and taxation of vendors and gaming agencies.[20] This policy has helped local game companies develop rapidly, improved social views on participation in the game industry and increased overall domestic revenues and employment opportunities in this sector.

However, this improvement in social perspectives on gaming has focused only on professional gameplay, while recent public discourse related to amateur gamers remains negative. For instance, the news media has published stories that paint gaming in a negative light, such as "Game-Addicted Adult Stole to Buy Gaming Equipment,"[21] "18-year-old Girl Raped and Impregnated after Meeting In-Game Friends"[22] and "Young Video Game Addict in Hangzhou Stole from Villagers."[23] As can easily be seen in these headlines, the news has tended to link playing video games with crime or other negative behaviors. Meanwhile, the government has passed a series of measures maintaining prohibitions on

18. W. Q. He and T. J. Ma, "The Development of Chinese Online Games Industry and the Stigmatization," Paper presented at the 2017 Chinese DiGRA Conference, Hong Kong, 2017.
19. Peichi Chung and Anthony Fung, "Internet Development and the Commercialization of Online Gaming in China," in *Gaming Globally: Production, Play, and Place*, eds. Nina Huntemann and Ben Aslinger (Palgrave Macmillan, 2013): 233-250.
20. Anthony Fung and John Erni, "Cultural Clusters and Cultural Industries in China," *Inter-Asia Cultural Studies* 14.4 (2013): 644-656.
21. *Chutian Daily*, 11 May 2017.
22. *Dayue Net*, 8 April 2017.
23. *Mass Net*, 9 May 2017.

internet cafés and controlling the content of the imported games, especially those that include sexual and criminal content. Obviously, negative public discourse on gaming has still continued to exist after 2009.

The emergence of eSports has helped gaming professionals shake social critiques of their gaming behavior. Due to its competitive nature, eSports is similar to traditional sporting competition in terms of satisfying people's enthusiasm for play, risk-taking and excitement. Borowy and Jin reviewed the historical commercialization and spectacularization of the digital game industry from the era of arcades in the 1980s through the 21st century, arguing that eSports was originally born in the tradition of spectator sports.[24] On the one hand, eSports stimulate and engage fans by offering them a public and spectacularized representation of professional gaming lifestyles. On the other hand, the commercialized format of eSports leads to potential economic benefits, including jobs not only in competitive gaming, but also in related areas. The social view of gaming has thus shifted from viewing it purely as a form of entertainment to understanding it as a professional occupation, leading to greater public acceptance of gaming as a potential entryway into a productive career path. Therefore, with the aid of the national government, the public discourse surrounding video games has shifted toward a positive depiction of eSports. National news stories such as the "Report on Chinese eSports, January-March 2017" predict that the market value of Chinese eSports could soon reach 70 billion RMB (US$11 billion).[25] Meanwhile, once the MSPRC named eSports as one of the country's top cultural development projects, Chinese society as a whole gradually began to express a more positive attitude toward the industry. More recently, several educational institutions, including three universities and colleges in Sichuan, have begun to establish eSports-related courses.

The differentiation between "gaming" and "eSports" in Chinese public discourse is abundantly clear, and it leads to our next concern: even while eSports has been reframed in public discourse as a component of China's cultural industries and professional landscape, amateur gaming is still devalued as a waste of time and money. Given this status, it is important to consider how current professional gamers have undergone changes in their identity, social status and cultural position during their transformation from amateur players to professional gamers.

LEGENDS OF CHINESE ESPORTS: MYTHS AND REALITIES OF PROFESSIONAL GAMER LIFESTYLES

To answer the questions mentioned above, we chose to focus this chapter's research on the *LoL*-focused Team WE, since they are one of the oldest and most famous eSports teams in China, and thus a paradigmatic case for understanding the world of Chinese professional gaming as a whole. The online participatory observation for this chapter began at the start of the summer season of the Chinese *LoL* Professional League (LPL) in May 2016, along with offline participatory observation of the regional qualifying game for the 2016 *LoL* World Championship and 2017 LPL finals. The observations provided insight into the ways professional gamers act before and after competition, as well as how they relate to their fans through online communication after failing in competition, in the face of social pressures to maintain their professional gaming careers.

As mentioned above, the data collected from gaming-related news outlets in China reflect a clear differentiation in the depiction of professional competitive gamers versus common game players. According to research on eSports in other countries by Ivo van Hilvoorde and Niek Pot, conditions

24. Michael Borowy, "Pioneering ESport: The Experience Economy and the Marketing of Early 1980s Arcade Gaming Contests." *International Journal of Communication* 7 (2013): 21.
25. "2017中国电竞发展报告," 13 July 2017, http://data.lmtw.com/yjbg/yeneibg/201707/146841.html.

for professional gamers in China, as elsewhere, are extremely strict and competitive: players are generally 15-30 years old, and the career of pro gamers usually lasts for only about seven-to-ten years.[26] This leads to the circulation of trade secrets and the development of particular practices within player communities. For example, one professional player interviewed for this chapter reported that every career gamer needed a fast average number of clicks-per-minute (CPM) on the keyboard. For pro-gamers, the basic requirement is 200 CPM, while outstanding players usually have to reach over 300 CPM through either talent or practice. Some Korean players have reported tying sandbags or weights to their wrists to train their muscles. Professional gamers also need to keep up with every software update to be competitive, and to develop their gaming strategies through repeated viewing of other teams' tournament play.

For professional gamers, every tournament has a potential impact on their popularity and value, which pushes them to fight for scores and ranking, even to the extent of playing all day long to earn those scores. Hong Kong-based player Gear points out that he would practice immediately after waking up in the morning, and kept practicing until midnight: "I spent all day on gaming without really knowing what I was doing."[27] Gear is now a professional gamer whose daily life is fully arranged and regulated by the team manager, including a strict daily schedule that requires him to play practice matches at 2pm, 4pm and 7pm, then review the matches with a coach and an analyst at 9pm. In addition to the effort dedicated to practice on an individual level, professional gamers need to learn different theories and strategies related to any number of situations that could potentially arise during competition. They also need to play practice matches with teammates to improve teamwork and collaborative dynamics. These types of intensive training regiments have created a number of career opportunities, including positions for game analysts, game designers, team managers, video anchors, coaches, judges and others. Retired professional gamers may turn to jobs like these as a way of continuing their eSports careers while helping new players by sharing skills and experience. This echoes the research of Seo Yu-ri and Sang-Uk Jung,[28] who have shown how computer games can go beyond the solitary nature of gaming and bring about concrete changes to social practices and the cultural landscape.

Each year, twelve LPL teams attend two seasons of tournaments, including the spring and summer split. Usually by August, three teams, including the champion of the summer split, the team with highest season score and the champion of the Regional Qualifying competition, attend the *LoL* World Championship. During the regular season, there are seven-to-eight tournaments held in Shanghai each week. The tournaments are regularly held from 5pm to 9pm on weekdays, and from 3pm to 7pm on weekends. There are two-to-three matches daily, playing Best of Three (BO3) per match, meaning each team has to participate in more than five games per week.

One of the top-performing and also the most controversial gaming teams in the LPL is Team WE, who won their first championship in 2012, in the fifth tournament of the IGN ProLeague series. As their prominence grew, the team's pro-gamers began to face higher expectations and ultimately greater social and financial pressures. LPL tournaments are regularly held in broadcast studios with the capacity to accommodate live audiences numbering in the hundreds. Meanwhile, each LPL team has its own team bunker in Shanghai, which is basically a dwelling house where team managers, coaches and pro-gamers all live and train together. As a result, pro-gamers from other provinces in China frequently suffer from homesickness and preoccupations related to prolonged stays in an

26. Ivo van Hilvoorde and Niek Pot, "Embodiment and Fundamental Motor Skills in eSports," *Sport, Ethics and Philosophy* 10.1 (2016): 14-27.
27. "19歲電競選手月薪2萬, 靠打機搵食, 父母反對," *Apple Daily*, 30 August 2016, https://hk.finance.appledaily.com/finance/daily/article/20160830/19753793.
28. Yuri Seo and Sang-Uk Jung, "Beyond Solitary Play in Computer Games: The Social Practices of eSports," *Journal of Consumer Culture* 16.3 (2016): 635-655.

unknown and unfamiliar urban locale. To sustain their lives and keep a positive outlook, they rely upon their in-game ranking and performance, which in turn leads to an extremely high degree of devotion to the craft among Chinese pro-gamers.

Being a pro-gamer in China means much more than just making a living through gaming, and implies demands to be presentable, charming and interactive in order to satisfy the expectations of fans. As fan reception is one of the most significant factors in assessing the success of a gaming team, nowadays each LPL team uses its Weibo social network account to announce news, report game results and, most importantly, to interact with fans. On the team's social networking profiles, each and every post is an act requiring thorough consideration and careful editing. The primary function of these narratives is to reduce the isolation between the pro-gamers and fans and to form an emotional bond. This can be especially notable after a team faces a loss. For example, one of the posts on Team WE's Weibo account, posted by the team's commander after a loss in the Regional Qualifier in 2016, explains: "I opened Weibo on my way back. Many friends left messages to me, saying that they were crying and sad tonight. I also hear from others in passing that while most people were watching the game happily backstage, Su was hiding in the corner, with tears ruining her make-up."[29]

Social media posts such as this point to the reactions of several parties after the loss, with terms like "crying," "sad" and "tears" illustrating the feelings of sorrow that establish an affective relation between pro-gamers and fans as the former attempt to earn the forgiveness of the latter for their losses and the disappointment they have caused. They also show the serious effort put into image management, and how Chinese pro-gamers' job definitions have expanded beyond their original status as gaming professional to that of gaming idols, demonstrating the uniqueness of the demands on their lifestyles vis-à-vis those that face pro-gamers in other counties.

THE EFFECTS OF CHINESE PROFESSIONAL GAMERS' CONVERSION INTO CULTURAL ICONS

1. Market First, Play Later

The schedules of Chinese pro-gamers in famous organizations like Team WE are packed not just with training and competition, but also with the various commercial and marketing tasks involved in seeking sponsorship and increasing public exposure. The venue and promotional materials (see Image 2.6.1) help illustrate how pro-gamers, who often privately characterize themselves as shy gaming nerds, have to portray themselves as superstars and publicly perform their coolness, which can involve increasing fan awareness and appreciation through acts such as giving hugs, signing autographs or posing for photographs using the Korean heart sign, a hand gesture commonly used by cultural icons in Korea and elsewhere to display the message of love for their admirers. The functions Chinese pro-gamers perform in public correspond to the expectations for idols or celebrities in other spheres of popular culture. Thus in the eyes of fans, pro-gamers are regarded as the true idols of the game industry and of game culture in general.

2. Don't Speak, Just Play

Given the fact that non-gaming activities are generally managed and organized by team managers who are responsible for maintaining the team's public image and marketing value, it could logically be expected that the team members, who are under constant supervision, would not be permitted to take

29. WE_Smallorc, "今年结束了，总得说点啥吧," 29 August 2016, https://www.famulei.com/p/485130.

Image 2.6.1. Team WE's venue for fans gathering before the LPL tournament in 2017.

part in any "unauthorized" interview or other business function. Still, the state media is sometimes granted opportunities to interview pro-gamers, since official attention can serve both as a promotion of the gaming team and as a form of political propaganda promoting China's national image. Image 2.6.2 shows the transcript of an interview in *China Daily* with a member of another prominent organization, Team RNG, explaining that "he is honored to participate in competitive gaming at the global level, and will try his very best to win for the country."[30]

Meanwhile, fans frequently revel in celebrations of the off-stage and off-screen lives of pro-gamers in China. For example, after the 2016 LPL final, in which Team WE won the Nanjing-based tournament, hundreds of fans gathered around the back door of the arena where the team was about to be picked up. The fans hands were filled with supportive signs and glow sticks as they awaited the team's appearance. After 30 minutes, the players finally came out of the door, at which point the crowds went crazy, chanting "WE! WE!" until the bus left. During these five minutes, the players simply got on the bus, without any interactions with fans. Every outward communication by the pro-gamers is strictly controlled, and the messages and information transmitted to the audience have already been manipulated by other power-players, for example the team managers and the team's chief sponsors.

30. China Daily Weibo, "对话RNG成员严君泽：亚运会，我准备好了！," 16 July 2018, https://www.weibo.com/1663072851/Gqcluhsgf?from=page_1002061663072851_profile&wvr=6&mod=weibotime; image translation: "'China Daily Interview with RNG Player Letme: I am Ready for the Olympics.' China national gaming member Letme was interviewed by China Daily, and exclaimed he was honored to wear the national gaming team uniform and represent China in worldwide competition: 'I will win the game for the glory of homeland.'"

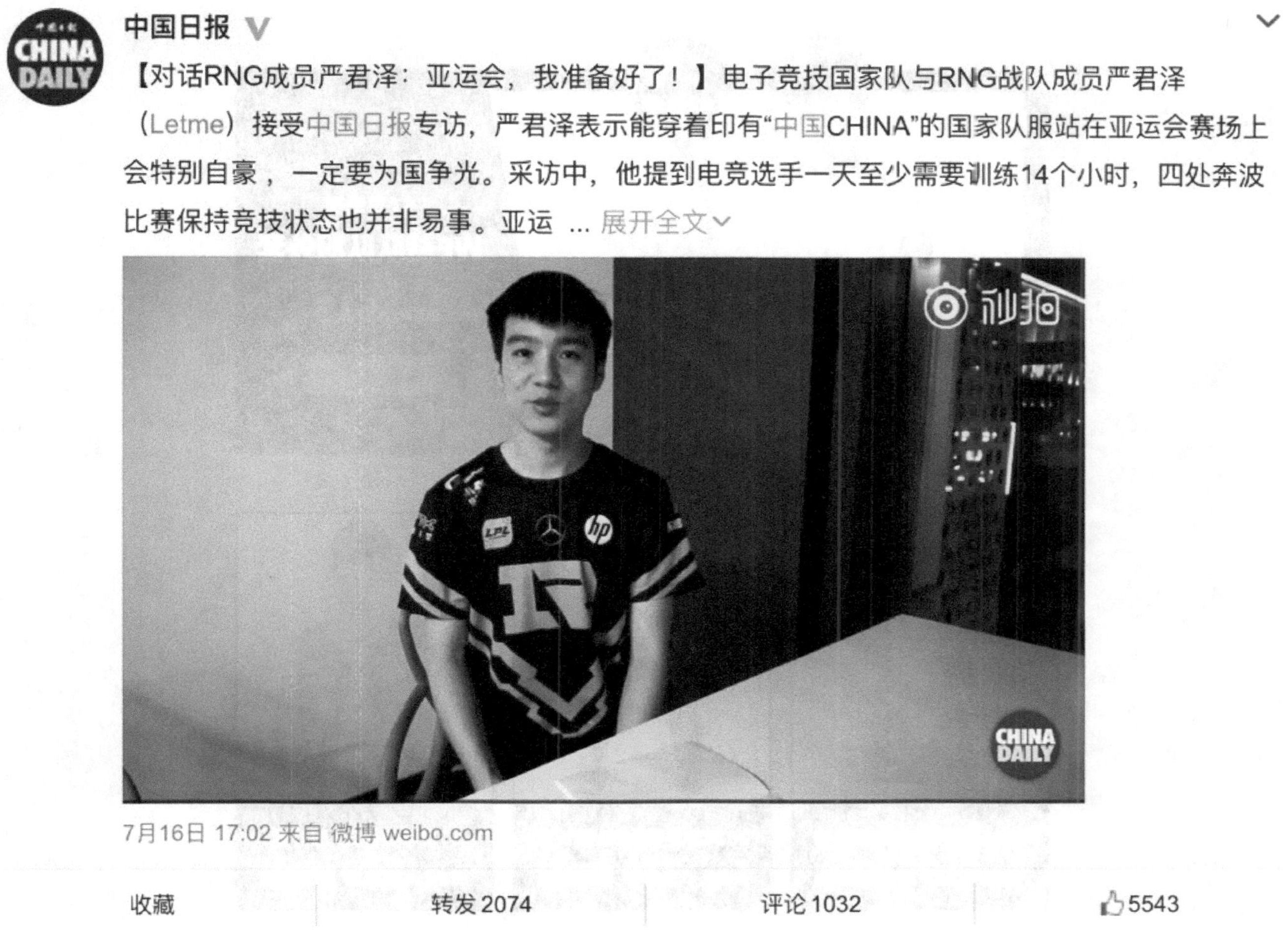

Image 2.6.2. Screen capture of a news thread on weibo.com.

3. Keeping up Appearances

Pro-gamers also need to put significant effort into maintaining the appearance of their faces and bodies, as their personal charisma can be as significant a factor as their gaming techniques in generating fan support and sales of merchandise related to the players and teams. In Image 2.6.3, a screen capture of Team WE's online store, demonstrates how pro-gamers, in full make-up, are required to act as fashion models to sell team jackets with their names and other similar products. According to interviews conducted for this chapter, pro-gamers can receive considerable commissions if they promote a hot-selling product, while those with lagging sales record may be classified as less valuable to the business, which can be a deciding factor in the signing or extension of team contracts.

This is highly unusual when compared to the cases of players of games like *World of Warcraft* and *Dota 2* analyzed in other chapters of the present anthology, such as Verónica Valdiva Medina's work on *WoW* in Chile and Jules Skotnes–Brown or Jerjes Loayza's work on *Dota 2* in South Africa and Peru, respectively. Unlike gamers in other countries, Chinese pro-gamers in a competitive setting just step onto the stage, sit down and start playing. Two teams occupy the two sides on the stage, while the center of the stage is dominated by a large screen displaying the gameplay. When the competition ends, the winner goes to shake hands with the loser, and then goes to the middle of the stage to take a bow. The only conversation, or rather the only chance for the audience to communicate with

Image 2.6.3. The e-shop of Team WE on Taobao, featuring players as models.

the players, comes during the short interviews that follow these competitions, in which the host frequently invites one player from the winning team to answer a few questions from the audience.

4. Public Life and Private Matters

Due to the commercialization of eSports, pro-gamers today have become idolized figures in the eyes of fans. Their performance and even their personal relationships have thus become the focus of online gossip or the subject of critique on social networks. One example is the case of player retirement. At the end of 2014, the captain of Team WE, Weixiao, announced his plans to withdraw from professional competition. Weixiao was one of the best players in the world, and was responsible for China's first *LoL* World Championship win. During his last year of professional competition, when his old teammates had all left the team, Weixiao was not able to build on his past successes and lead the team to a better place. Despite having been such a high-performing player in the past, he became the target of online criticism from fans due to his poor performance. During the entire season, the most common comment under his Weibo was "Retire and go sell snacks!"[31] In his retirement announcement, Weixiao wrote: "I am a competitive and ambitious person, but I've been through a lot. I think it's time to give up… I'm not defeated, but I have decided to leave."[32] His explanation

31. Selling snacks online is one common career taken on by previous pro-gamers following retirement in China.
32. Weixiao, "。," 31 August 2014, https://www.weibo.com/p/1001603749754428380601.

made clear that his retirement was not about a losing record in competition (defeat), but rather his disappointment in the face of continued online abuse that, ironically, came mainly from fans who had previously acted as some of his most vocal supporters.

Since the value of pro-gamers in the fans' viewpoint is largely related to their performance in competition, they frequently face online abuse when they make mistakes during gameplay, especially if any non-gaming-related factors are seen as intervening in their performance. One such instance is illustrated in Image 2.6.4: during the summer season of 2017, a player known as Condi went to his girlfriend's place for the weekend and his girlfriend posted a photo on her Weibo account, saying that they had enjoyed a lunch together at home. The following week, the player in question performed poorly and lost the game. Immediately afterward, fans began to express their fierce anger at the player for "being romantic" and "not focusing on practicing." They started to criticize the player and his girlfriend on Weibo, accusing the girl of inappropriate behavior in private life. One fan even expressed his wish that the couple would "die together." This story ended when the girlfriend closed her Weibo account, and the team manager offered an online explanation. Image 2.6.4 is a screen capture of the discussion on Team WE's official Weibo account, in which a fan explains, "I would not criticize him if he did not go to find his girlfriend before the competition. I can forgive him if he is just not good enough, but I cannot bear it now as he lost for other reasons other than the game."[33] For this same reason, a Team WE fan drafted a thread with the title "Being a noob is a crime in eSports" (in Chinese 電子競技，菜是原罪),[34] criticizing players and attributing their in-game losses to their private lives.

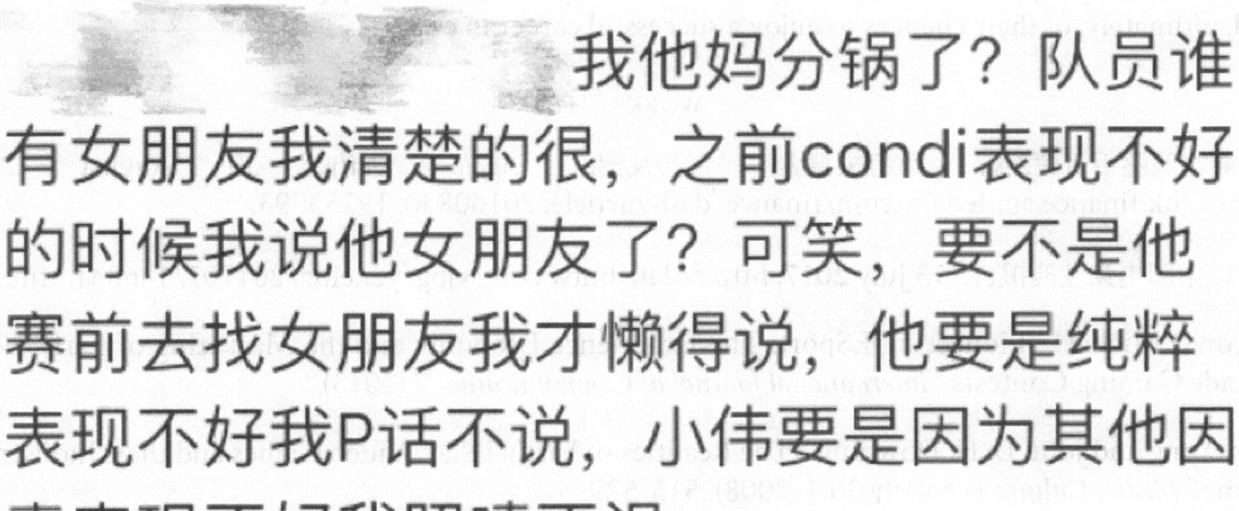
我他妈分锅了？队员谁有女朋友我清楚的很，之前condi表现不好的时候我说他女朋友了？可笑，要不是他赛前去找女朋友我才懒得说，他要是纯粹表现不好我P话不说，小伟要是因为其他因素表现不好我照喷不误

共42条回复 >

Image 2.6.4. A fan criticizing pro-gamer Condi on Team WE's official Weibo account.

33. Team WE Weibo, 17 August 2017, https://www.weibo.com/u/5870389740?profile_ftype=1&is_all=1&is_search=1&key_word=风花雪月#1549770094891; image translation: "I know pretty well about which [players] dates a girl and which ones don't. Did I blame Condi [the player] last time when he didn't hang out with his girlfriend? I can forgive him if he just played badly for a game. I wouldn't blame him here if he hadn't played with his girlfriend before the competition."
34. fx.weico.net, 12 September 2017, https://fx.weico.net/share/57335980.html?weibo_id=4283391816120881.

CONCLUSION: THE TRANSFORMATION OF GAMING IN CHINA, FROM SOCIAL ILL TO CAREER PATH

This chapter analyzes two major facets of eSports gaming in China. The first half illustrates the change in public discourse surrounding gaming, from its perception as a form of "digital heroin harming the lives of youth" in the past to the current view of gaming as "a professional avenue with a bright future." This contrast in public opinion, in turn, highlights how cultural policy has played an important role in bringing about change by providing education, career training and job opportunities after retirement, as well as by promoting gaming culture through the loosening of restrictions on imports and making an effort to fight negative stereotypes surrounding games and gaming in China. The second half of the chapter separates myths about the practices of pro-gamers in China from the difficult realities of the lifestyles they must take on, particularly when compared with pro-gamers in other countries, showing how the idolized view of pro-gamers in China can differ significantly from the realities of professional players' lives. Pro-gamers must pay constant attention to functions unrelated to their gameplay abilities in order to maintain audience support and comply with commercial interests, while at the same time all of their outward communication is strictly limited and controlled. Pro-gamers are also vulnerable to online abuse, due in part to the large population of players in Chinese, Taiwanese and Korean gaming communities who see themselves as skillful and potentially capable of doing a better job than existing pro-gamers who have earned renown in eSports. Indeed, now more than ever there are many Taiwanese and Korean players coming to China to seek their fortunes in professional gaming, as many Chinese game teams are openly recruiting players and offering highly competitive salaries. In such an environment, pro-gamers in China are easily replaceable, and their performance in gaming is the only guarantee of their popularity and, ultimately, of their chances to enjoy a successful career in eSports.

WORKS CITED

"19歲電競選手月薪2萬, 靠打機搵食, 父母反對." *Apple Daily*, 30 August 2016, https://hk.finance.appledaily.com/finance/daily/article/20160830/19753793.

"2017中国电竞发展报告." 13 July 2017, http://data.lmtw.com/yjbg/yeneibg/201707/146841.html.

Borowy, Michael. "Pioneering ESport: The Experience Economy and the Marketing of Early 1980s Arcade Gaming Contests." *International Journal of Communication* 7 (2013).

Cao, Yong and John D. H. Downing. "The Realities of Virtual Play: Video Games and their Industry in China." *Media, Culture & Society* 30.4 (2008): 515-529.

China Daily Weibo. "对话RNG成员严君泽：亚运会，我准备好了！." 16 July 2018, https://www.weibo.com/1663072851/GqcIuhsgf?from=page_1002061663072851_profile&wvr=6&mod=weibotime.

Chung, Peichi and Anthony Fung. "Internet Development and the Commercialization of Online Gaming in China." In *Gaming Globally: Production, Play, and Place*, edited by Ben Aslinger and Nina B. Huntemann. Palgrave Macmillan, 2013.

Cohen, Stanley. *Folk Devils and Moral Panics: The Creation of the Mods and Rockers.* Paladin, 1973.

Consulate General of the Kingdom of the Netherlands, Guangzhou, China. "China: Top Sector

Games," 2014, https://www.rvo.nl/sites/default/files/2014/12/china-top-sector-games-opportunity-report-cg-gz-20141023.pdf.

Fung, Anthony and John Erni. "Cultural Clusters and Cultural Industries in China." *Inter-Asia Cultural Studies* 14.4 (2013): 644-656.

Fung, Anthony Y. H. and Sara Xueting Liao. "China." In *Video Games Around the World*, edited by Mark J. P. Wolf. MIT Press, 2015: 119-135.

fx.weico.net. 12 September 2017, https://fx.weico.net/share/57335980.html?weibo_id=4283391816120881.

Garland, David. "On the Concept of Moral Panic." *Crime Media Culture* 4.1 (2008): 9- 30.

Hier, Sean. "Thinking beyond Moral Panic: Risk, Responsibility, and the Politics of Moralization." *Theoretical Criminology* 12.2 (2008): 173-190.

Hilvoorde, Ivo van and Niek Pot. "Embodiment and Fundamental Motor Skills in eSports." *Sport, Ethics and Philosophy* 10.1 (2016): 14-27.

Hjorth, Larissa, and Dean Chan, eds. *Gaming Cultures and Place in Asia-Pacific*. Routledge, 2009.

Jin, Dal Yong. "Mobile Gaming in Asia: Politics, Culture and Emerging Technologies." *Mobile Communication in Asia: Local Insights, Global Implications*, edited by Sun Sun Lim. Springer, 2016.

Lu, Zhouxiang. "From E-Heroin to E-Sports: The Development of Competitive Gaming in China." *The International Journal of the History of Sport* 33.18 (2016): 2186-2206.

Newzoo. "Top 100 Countries/Markets by Game Revenues," 2018, https://newzoo.com/insights/rankings/top-100-countries-by-game-revenues/.

Schneider, Sue. "Social Gaming and Online Gambling." *Gaming Law Review and Economics* 16.12 (2012): 711-712.

Seo, Yuri and Sang-Uk Jung. "Beyond Solitary Play in Computer Games: The Social Practices of eSports." *Journal of Consumer Culture* 16.3 (2016): 635-655.

Taylor, T. L. *Raising the Stakes: E-sports and the Professionalization of Computer Gaming*. MIT Press, 2012.

Team WE Weibo. 17 August 2017, https://www.weibo.com/u/5870389740?profile_ftype=1&is_all=1&is_search=1&key_word=风花雪月#1549770094891.

WE_Smallorc. "今年结束了，总得说点啥吧." 29 August 2016, https://www.famulei.com/p/485130.

Weixiao. "。." 31 August 2014, https://www.weibo.com/p/1001603749754428380601.

Xinhua Net. "Announcement from SARFT: Forbidding Broadcasting Programs about Computer Online Game," 2004, http://news.xinhuanet.com/zhengfu/2004-04/21/content_1432492.html.

PART THREE: CIRCULATION OF GAMES AND GAME CULTURE

DIGITAL GAMING'S SOUTH-SOUTH CONNECTION

THOMAS APPERLEY

Digital games are a site of intercultural contact, and while this intercultural contact isn't necessarily welcomed by some players, others are willing to undertake considerable constraints on their activities just have the chance to play with another person in an overseas location.[1] Other intercultural elements of the digital games industry and aesthetic of digital games have been noted in previous scholarship by Mia Consalvo, which pinpoints their hybrid origin,[2] produced through the cultural and technological mingling of corporate Japan and the U.S. This chapter develops the notion that digital games are a site of intercultural communication by considering them as a part of the wider landscape of communication infrastructures that both facilitate communication across cultural, linguistic and national boundaries and shape the "content and form of contemporary media."[3] The global south has functioned as the "periphery" to various "centers" of network infrastructures that are located in the global north, where digital games are often produced and published.[4] This exploration of the way digital gaming directly connects the nations of the global south, enabling south-south connections, adds to the welcome growth of work on digital game production and consumption in the global south, and outside the English-speaking world, more generally.[5]

This chapter reports on data from a "situated" comparative ethnographic project, involving long-term participant observation and interviews with select participants. The project was conducted between March 2005 and February 2006 in research sites in Melbourne, Australia and Caracas, Venezuela.[6] The two field sites were both commercial cybercafés in which among other activities, people used to conduct network gaming, both on the local-area networks (LANs) in the cafes and with people in remote locations. The Caracas field site was Cybercafé Ávila, a small café with 11 working PC computers, placed close together in cramped conditions. The internet speed was relatively fast, the main technical issue was the age and capacity of the computers, only two of the computers had specifications which meant it was possible to play contemporary AAA new releases like *The Sims 2* (Maxis, 2004). Cybercafé Ávila was located on a residential street in the area of Caracas called San Bernardino, just north and east of the more well-known, historic La Candelaria neighborhood. This area of was largely developed by European immigrants during Venezuela's era of post-World War II prosperity.[7]

1. Tae-Jin Yoon and Hyejung Cheon, "Game Playing as Transnational Cultural Practice: A Case Study of Chinese Gamers and Korean MMORPGs," *International Journal of Cultural Studies* 17.5 (2014): 469-483.
2. Mia Consalvo, "Console Video Games and Global Corporations: Creating a Hybrid Culture," *New Media & Society* 8.1 (2006): 117-137.
3. Lisa Parks and Nicole Starosielski, "Introduction," *Signal Traffic: Critical Studies of Media Infrastructures* (Illinois University Press, 2015): 1.
4. Steven Kline, Nick Dyer-Witheford and Greig de Peuter, *Digital/Play: The Interaction of Technology, Culture and Marketing* (McGill/Queen's University Press, 2003).
5. Thomas Apperley, *Global Rhythms: Play and Counterplay from the Situated to the Global* (Institute of Network Cultures, 2010); Dal Yong Jin, *Korea's Online Gaming Empire* (MIT Press, 2010); Larissa Hjorth and Dean Chan, *Gaming Cultures and Place in the Asia-Pacific* (Routledge, 2009); Nina Huntemann and Ben Aslinger, *Gaming Globally: Production, Play, and Place* (Palgrave, 2013); Bjarke Liboriussen and Paul Martin, "Regional Game Studies," *Game Studies* 16.1 (2016); Phillip Penix-Tadsen, *Cultural Code: Video Games and Latin America* (MIT Press, 2016); Mark J. P. Wolf, *Video Games Around the World* (MIT Press, 2015).
6. I have previously written about other aspects of this fieldwork in: Thomas Apperley, "Venezuela," in *Video Games Around the World*, ed. Mark J. P. Wolf (MIT Press, 2015); and Thomas Apperley, "Digital Gaming, Social Inclusion, and the Right to Play: A Case Study of a Venezuelan Cybercafé," in *The Routledge Companion to Digital Ethnography*, eds. Larissa Hjorth, Heather Horst, Anne Galloway and Genevieve Bell (Routledge, 2017).

The Melbourne site was Cydus, a medium-sized cybercafé located close to the central commercial district. Cydus was composed of two adjacent rooms, each with approximately 30 computers. One room was set up as a more generic cybercafé, catering to backpackers, tourists and international students, and the other was focused on gaming. Cydus had a relatively fast internet connection that was superior to many people's domestic connections, which meant that in 2005-2006 people often went there to play *World of Warcraft* (Blizzard, 2004), rather than playing from home. Cydus was situated across from the Queen Victoria Market, a high-profile tourist destination, and is proximate to many restaurants, bars and backpacker-style tourist accommodations. The area is readily accessible from the city center and from the student housing around the University of Melbourne and RMIT University to the north and east, as well as the gentrified suburb of North Melbourne. This area of Melbourne has a high proportion of immigrants, who are predominantly Cantonese speaking.[8]

The large proportion of international students living in the area around Cydus, mainly from China, Taiwan, Singapore and Malaysia, created a demand for networked games that were popular in East and Southeast Asia. As noted by Will Balmford, et al. in this volume, this cohort of players used gaming to stay connected with home during their periods of study in Australia. Notable were popular South Korean-made "freemium" massively multiplayer online (MMO) games like *Fly For Fun* (Webzen, 2005) and *Ragnarok Online* (Gravity, 2003) and the pay-to-play *ROSE Online* (TriggerSoft, 2005). The café also stocked prepaid game cards for *Ragnarok Online* so that players could purchase items using microtransactions in the Kafra Shop. These games were installed on the same computers alongside more standard (to the Anglophone world) networked games such as *City of Heroes* (Cryptic Studios, 2004), *Defense of the Ancients* (Blizzard, 2003) and *World of Warcraft*. International students played these games and others, and Australian locals also played some of the South Korean games, most notably *Fly For Fun*. But it was the international students that choose to play these games deliberately to reconnect themselves with people in other countries, making the cross-cultural and transnational context of networked gameplay apparent.

Cybercafé Ávila operated as a part of Venezuela's substantial informal or "gray" economy. It was an off-the-books small business,[9] which offered miscellaneous digital network services, including computer repair, pirated software, software training, CD and DVD burning and printing. The eleven computers in the cafe were not standardized, and had different games installed on them according to their capacities. They were constantly being upgraded and repaired, often by transferring parts from other computers, making Cybercafé Ávila a locally-maintained, neighborhood "DIY" type of infrastructure, operating with a frugal ingenuity similar to many local cybercafés throughout the global south.[10] One computer was so old it was used for MSN and Yahoo! "chat" only, however most of the computers had *The Sims 2, Grand Theft Auto: Vice City* (Rockstar Games, 2002) and *Age of Empires II: The Conquerors* (Ensemble Studios, 2009) installed. The South Korean MMO *MU Online* (Webzen, 2002) and the German MMO *Tibia* (CipSoft, 1997) were also installed on most computers, but they were very rarely played. But the suite of games available in Cybercafé Ávila was more varied than that at Cydus, not just because they weren't constricted by copyright issues, but also because they were responsive to individual requests from regular customers, who were often also friends and neighbors. This meant each computer would have different games installed depending on past use, which would eventually be removed if they weren't subsequently played by other customers.

7. Apperley, *Global Rhythms*, 57-62.
8. Ibid., 62-65.
9. Jairo Lugo and Tony Sampson, "E-Informality in Venezuela: The 'Other Path' of Technology," *Bulletin of Latin American Research* 27.1(2008), 102-118.
10. Padmini Ray Murray and Chris Hand, "Making Culture: Locating the Digital Humanities in India," *Visible Language: The Journal of Visual Communication Research* 49.3 (2015): 141.

The most striking similarity between the desktops of computers in Cydus and Cybercafé Ávila was the game *GunBound: World Champion* (Softnyx, 2005; *Gunbound* hereafter), which was then in beta. *GunBound* was developed by the Seoul-based, South Korean company Softnyx. The beta was released in 2003, and it was launched in South Korea, Indonesia and China later that year. Each portal had a localized servers and was translated into local languages, while an "International" English-language portal was also established. By March 2005, when the fieldwork in Cybercafé Ávila began, *GunBound* already had portals connecting players to local servers in China, Indonesia, Japan, Taiwan, the Philippines and Vietnam. It also had a specific Spanish-language "Latino" portal. The game was officially launched over 2005-2006. In North America it was available through the ijji online gaming portal as *GunBound Revolution* (Softnyx, 2006) from 2006-2009. Since 2009 the game has only been available through Softnyx servers. In July 2017, *GunBound* was released as a free mobile game, retitled as *GunBoundM* and available through iTunes and Android.[11]

This chapter will first explicate the features of *GunBound*, as played on the International portal, which made it a feature that Cydus and Cybercafé Ávila have in common, with reference to the structure of the game, salient elements of the practices of players, technical aspects of how the game is served locally and internationally and the in-game virtual economy. Then, the chapter will shift to examine how the technical infrastructure of *GunBound* and the social networks, knowledges and practices of players facilitate south-south connections through gaming.

THE APPEAL OF GUNBOUND: WORLD CHAMPION

Playing *GunBound* extends outside of the game environment because of the important preparatory steps taken before the players enter the game environment and begin team-based combat. The main steps are:

- Avatar customization. Each player controlled a Manhwa (Korean print comic/cartoon aesthetic similar to Manga) style avatar, which they initially chose, then customized from templates. The avatar could be further customized by purchasing Avatar Items at the Avatar Store using one of *GunBound*'s two in-game currencies. Avatar Items could be purely aesthetic, or might also have an in-game effect.
- Vehicle selection. During combat, each avatar used one of sixteen vehicles (which were discussed as "mobiles" in the cyber café) with mounted guns. While the vehicle could be changed from game to game, it was fixed once combat had begun. Each vehicle came with specific strengths and weaknesses that created environmental advantages and disadvantages. Some vehicles required very specific tactics, which were difficult to master.

This wide range of potential choices meant that this ostensibly simple *Worms*-like 2D game had sophisticated nuances which demanded that players developed a large repertoire of skills and knowledge in order to play *GunBound* effectively.

These variables also establish several areas of mastery within the overarching game that make it so that players with different interests, levels of skill and gaming backgrounds can accumulate, share and display their gaming capital.[12] With gaming capital, Consalvo defines a specific form of "social capital,"[13] which is developed through experience, and by gaining skills and knowledge of digital

11. Alex Walker, "Gunbound Is Back As A Mobile Game," *Kotaku Australia*, 5 July 2017, https://www.kotaku.com.au/2017/07/gunbound-is-back-as-a-mobile-game/.
12. Mia Consalvo, *Cheating: Gaining Advantage in Videogames* (MIT Press, 2007).
13. Pierre Bourdieu, *Distinction: A Social Critique of the Judgement of Taste* (Routledge, 1984).

games. Gaming capital suggests that the player's experience of digital play is not just limited to interactions with a piece of software. Rather, digital play also imbricates players in larger circuits of meaning through both the integration of information from other sources and interactions with other players.[14] The accumulation of gaming capital often involves developing a suite of secondary skills in order to display one's prowess among the community of players. These can range from minor technical knowledges, such as how to take a screenshot or upload a video to YouTube;[15] through to relatively advanced traditional literacies found in text walkthroughs and creative writing inspired by digital games, like the after-action report;[16] to more technical activities such as modding, level design and the creation of machinima.[17] This chapter suggests that it is also important to consider how the nebulous skills and knowledges indicated by gaming capital underpin the integration of transnational infrastructures into the everyday experience of digital game players.

The significance of the cybercafé in the production and sharing of gaming capital with *GunBound* was notably different between the two fieldwork locations. In Cybercafé Ávila, the location, was itself, an incredibly important site for sharing information between players in a manner similar to that outlined by Jerjes Loayza in his chapter in this volume, dealing with more recent observations from a cybercafé in Lima, Peru. The exchanges in Cybercafé Ávila also suggested that competition and cooperation were imbricated in these spaces (see Pierre-Alain Clèment's chapter this volume). In Cydus, playing *GunBound* did not involve other people in the café, it was played across the network with players in other locations.

The *GunBound* avatars are persistent and remain tied to each player's account. After the game, each winning player is rewarded with "gold," the in-game currency. This meant that, as players became more experienced and acquired more gold, the time spent shopping for items for their avatar became lengthier. Shopping was much less time-dependent than playing, which meant that people often took their time deciding on their next purchases. The Avatar Shop has many items with different in-game effects that players often required advice, either from a *GunBound* walkthrough, FAQ or forum, or in some cases from other players in the cybercafé. These Avatar Items could enable special tactics that would shape future iterations of play, so consulting among teammates on purchases was also common. This meant that playing *GunBound* wasn't just about the actual moments of the game, but an ongoing consideration of how to re-invest winnings from the game into producing more effective avatars. For those playing in the global south where personal computers are less common, having an account where avatar purchases can be stored allows the meaningful development of an avatar in a way which players might not otherwise have access to through an AAA commercial game. This is because AAA commercial games traditionally rely on players being able to save games and return to the same computer to reload them.

Players must also choose a "bot" or vehicle for the avatar to use. This vehicle can be changed from game to game, and each of the sixteen possibilities has three individualized weapons, each with their own unique trajectories, range and effects, as well as specific strengths and vulnerabilities. The player's familiarity and skill with the game was particularly salient when choosing the vehicle, because the vehicle selected had a large impact on the player's affordances within the game and their potential role within a team. Some vehicles were considered to be good ones for novices to learn the game,

14. Thomas Apperley, "Understanding digital games as educational technologies," in *Popular Culture, Pedagogy and Teacher Education: International Perspectives*, eds. Phil Benson and Alice Chik (Routledge, 2014), 46.
15. Chris Walsh and Thomas Apperley, "Researching Digital Game Players: Gameplay and Gaming Capital," in *Proceedings of IADIS International Conference Gaming 2008: Design for Engaging Experience and Social Interaction*, eds. Y. Xiao and E. Ten Thij (Amsterdam: IADIS, 2008): 99-102.
16. Souvik Muhkerjee, "Videogames as 'Minor Literature': Reading Videogame Stories through Paratexts," *GRAMMA: Journal of Theory and Criticism* 23 (2016): 60-75.
17. Thomas Apperley and Catherine Beavis, "A Model for Critical Games Literacy," *e-Learning & Digital Media* 10.1 (2013): 1-12.

while others were considered to be so difficult to use effectively that they were only appropriate for expert players. Novice players were directed toward vehicles like the "ArmorMobile" and "Grub," because the aim of their primary weapons is less affected by "forces" (each turn in *GunBound* is shaped by one of eleven "forces"), while accurate aim is required with a few of the available vehicles, like the "Boomer" and "NakMachine," making them difficult even for experienced players to use effectively. Choosing a vehicle also requires much consideration and consultation, because in team play (the majority of *GunBound* play is team vs. team) the combinations that the abilities of the various vehicles would create when used together is salient. The usefulness of particular vehicles was dependent on the tactical approach planned. Coordinating the vehicles was relatively important for success in the game, and the process facilitated contact between players in the same team, both locally and across networks. When ongoing discussion and negotiation is necessary to successfully play a game, it can enable intercultural contact, even across language barriers, due to the highly functional nature of the communication.

During this selection and configuration process the players also had access to several in-game messaging channels. To begin playing, one player must first set up the game by opening and naming a "room." Then other players can join the "room" either as team members or opponents. This usually involves a short wait, as more players joined from various other locations. If the "room" took too long to fill, some players might leave in order to pursue solo or one-on-one play, which had much shorter wait times.

The play of *GunBound* involves the players in short but intense turns that cycle around the participants. Each lasts for a maximum of thirty seconds and each game has between two and eight players, so the turns could be as infrequent as every four minutes, creating the possibility of using time within the game for other activities. Often team members having taken their turn would begin to discuss tactics, or exchange other light-hearted banter and "smack talk." Some players would use the gap between their turns to conduct a brief flurry of chat exchanges using MSN or Yahoo! Messenger. The turn-based play of *GunBound* established a rhythm of intensive competitive play, interspersed with waiting and reflective pre-game decision-making around avatar purchases and vehicle selection suited the social milieus of Cydus and Cybercafé Ávila. Players that were setting up games or waiting for them to start would discuss *GunBound* or more general topics. In this socialization, *GunBound* was sometimes neglected as players got distracted by other activities and overlooked their commitments to their teams. By leaving space for socialization, *GunBound* was structured in a way that facilitated intercultural contact in order to fill the awkward silences of the waiting periods in the game.

The servers within the International portal were organized by level of avatar, according to the way that avatar abilities could be used. First, servers are designated as "beginner," "free" and "newb-free": beginner servers are closed to avatars above the required level, while free servers are open to all avatars and the newb-free serves have a required minimum avatar level to enter. Second, servers are divided into those which were "avatar on" and "avatar off" servers: in the "avatar off" servers the Avatar Items purchased for avatars were "turned off," while they still appeared as a part of the avatar's appearance the made no change to the power and abilities of the avatar; conversely, in the "avatar on" servers these purchased Avatar Items are fully operational. This categorization of servers creates many different contexts of competitive play. The divisions between servers created by limits on avatar levels, allows newer players to choose to avoid being grossly underpowered, and likewise experienced players to make sure they find suitably challenging opponents. The division between "avatar off" and "avatar on" servers created a way for players to excel based on skill or on a combination of skill and experience, a factor which is crucial for engaging players from a variety of socio-economic backgrounds.

The virtual economy of *GunBound* was a freemium game, a distribution model that was pioneered by South Korean MMOs at the time. In this model *GunBound* was made freely available to download and play, with publisher profits derived by making small in-game purchases called microtransactions available to players. To counter the perceived unfairness of microtransactions, the international portal for *GunBound* includes two key levelers that make it possible for all freemium players to enjoy the game on a more-or-less equal footing with those players who use microtransactions. First, by having "avatar off" servers that rendered all purchased Avatar Items inoperable, players could compete on an equal footing in the game based purely on knowledge and ability, without interference from economic inequality. Second, because of the dual-currency virtual economy with a set exchange rate, players with different economic backgrounds are also able to compete more equally in the "avatar on" servers. The items at the Avatar Shop can be both purchased with "gold" that is won during play, and with "gcoin" microtransactions with real money. Many items at the Avatar Shop are only available to those players who have access to "gcoin," but because of the possibility of controlled exchange between the virtual currencies, which means that "gcoin" can be purchased using "gold," even if this requires a substantial investment in time from the players purchasing "gcoin." How gaming capital is understood across these contexts is varied, but because of the construction of the virtual economy there is always a space for players who are invested in a competition that based on pure skill and performance and action, without being impacted by economic disparity. The emergence of such models in commercial game design is of great significance to gamers in the global south as it removes issues of cost and digital rights management which have effectively kept players in many areas in local silos, unable to play in official competition or servers.

In Venezuela, the focus was on purchasing Avatar Items that had in-game effects, while purchasing a cosmetic item was considered a waste of money. However, for some players using Avatar Items to personalize their avatar was equally as important as purchasing items with in-game effects. In Australia, if the economic dimensions of the game were discussed at all, the main issue that arose was a general distaste for microtransactions. One interview participant who admitted that her boyfriend had made microtransactions on her behalf, carefully emphasized that the items only customized her avatar's appearance. In part the disdain was caused by the preference in both Cybercafé Ávila and Cydus was for playing in the "avatar off" servers. How players used Avatar Items in the expression of gaming capital through their avatar was considered important. While microtransactions were not regarded as "cheating," using microtransactions to purchase gcoin-only Avatar Items was regarded as not understanding the game's "spirit." Of course *GunBound* is characterized by a wide variety of attitudes towards play among its players, but a significant element of gamers respect the ideal of equal competition between players in disparate locations. This ties their gaming capital to an ability to understand the structural issues of negotiating uneven infrastructures, both from a point of privilege and as underprivileged users.

SOUTH-SOUTH CONNECTIONS ON *GUNBOUND*'S INTERNATIONAL PORTAL

The International portal was favored at both Cybercafé Ávila and Cydus because people believed that more skilled players congregated on that portal. Playing on local or regional portals was not seen as a good choice for serious players who wanted a challenge and to develop their skills through competition. However, playing on local portals was justified in particular circumstances. For example, the Latino portal was often used by group of friends playing together in Cybercafé Ávila, as they were "just playing for fun" and wanted to be able to include more novice players who would find a Spanish-language interface more usable. At Cydus, one interview participant described how she would play practice games with her friends on a local portal before shifting to play on the International portal. The importance of the International portal for *GunBound* players again illustrates how gaming capital was closely tied to global access. While people may choose to play *GunBound* for a variety of reasons, including "making do" with it, it was possible to "make do" with it because the game was able to connect people around the world on even terms across uneven infrastructures.

National identity was also important on the International portal. In both fieldwork sites some players were deeply invested in identifying their avatar as belonging to a player from a particular nationality, or in some cases, linguistic background. Nationality was asserted with one or more of many items available for purchase with "gold" or "gcoin" in the form of a flag or other national symbol, e.g., a Panda. Establishing language identity required the deliberate deployment of language in the game. While national identity was often a source of pride, it also encouraged rivalry between players which mimicked existing prejudices. In her chapter in this volume, Verónica Valdivia Medina observes that Venezuelans were the most universally reviled Latino players on the servers she observed; likewise, in the fieldwork for the present chapter, Venezuelan players often mocked players from other countries, particularly the people of Colombian descent among them in Cydus. National languages were also used to open new channels for cheating, by using an ostensibly public space to conduct private chat as well as, unsurprisingly, in "smack talk." For these reasons, many other network games such as *Tibia*—but not *GunBound*—enforced linguistic conformity in their public chat channels, although players could address each other in whatever language they chose in their private talk. This openness to different languages was a part of the appeal of *GunBound*, as players did not feel excluded from the game even if they were in a linguistic or cultural minority on the portal in which they were playing.

While public communication in the International portal was in English by default, this was not policed, and many different languages mingled in the chat channel. The design of *GunBound* meant that joining a game did not require complex communication, and could be managed through software by both the joining player and the person who had set up the "room." Speaking different languages mainly inhibited the sociality that took place between players during the game while they were waiting for their turn. During play, what was typed into the chat channel by the player also appeared in a cartoon balloon over their avatar's head. This resonated with the Manhwa aesthetic found in other aspects of *GunBound*, and had a performative element that was endorsed by many players at Cybercafé Ávila and Cydus; likewise, in the wider culture of players, it was an element of the game that was often celebrated online in various player-productions.[18] Emphasis in the performance was on the timing and execution of an appropriate comment, so that it would appear in response to something which had just occurred in the game: the death of a team member, hitting an enemy, a new environmental force, etc. The most celebrated performances were when the player made a comment which appeared after their vehicle had been destroyed and their avatar was eliminated but was still in the process of being airlifted from the gamespace. At this moment, managing to time a snide remark to the opposing team or a word of encouragement to remaining team members was admired.

The South Korean origin of *GunBound* is salient. Although it was published in multiple locations in local languages, it had a recognizable origin in South Korea. In part this is from the clear Manhwa aesthetic, but also from its association with a suite of popular freemium South Korean MMOs that used a similar payment model, such as *ROSE Online, Fly for Fun, Ragnarok Online, Hero Online* and *MU*

18. Apperley, *Global Rhythms*, 112.

Online. Games like these pioneered freemium in the global market, at a time when MMORPGs were at their peak popularity globally, exemplified by the global popularity of the South Korean MMORPG *Lineage II*.[19] As many regulars at Cydus were international students that still had strong ties to the regions where these games were popular, they were familiar with and receptive to them. Staff in Cydus recognized that this type of game had a cache with their regulars and made sure that they kept up with key developments. In this way the cohort of international students in Melbourne, also described by Balmford, et al. in this volume, who used gaming as a way to connect to home, influence tastes in gaming more generally by opening local players to new repertoires of games. For example, the South Korean MMO *ROSE Online*, which was released in December 2005 during the fieldwork period, was installed on every computer in the cafe on the day of its release, making it a significant event for all regulars, not just international students.

In Cybercafé Ávila, rather than connecting a mobile population of gamers back to networks from their home countries, people were attuned to gaming developments originating in South Korea other reasons. In Venezuela, South Korea in general had a large cultural cachet, particularly in terms of luxury cars and appliances, the latter of which were often sold in dedicated *Corea* stores that stocked a range of appliances from Daewoo, Hyundai, LG and Samsung. In addition to this generally positive disposition towards South Korean products, the relative graphic simplicity of games like *MU Online* and *GunBound* allowed them to function effectively on the local infrastructure, characterized by low GPU computers and fluctuations in network speed. The freemium model that many South Korean games used also suited the economic situation of many of the players at Cybercafé Ávila, who had no access to the credit cards which were essential for many subscription-based games. *GunBound*, in particular, mitigated many of the issues of being a free-to-play player alongside others who used microtransactions by having a fixed exchange rate between the earned "gold" currency and the purchased "gcoin" currency.

At Cydus, *GunBound* players often played with people located in the Asia-Pacific, while in Cybercafé Ávila, they tended to play with people in other Spanish-speaking Latin American countries, or occasionally with people in North America. As Balmford, et al. have also demonstrated in this volume, the role of international students is crucial in facilitating the connection between Australia and the Asia-Pacific. The fieldwork in Cydus further suggests that connection was also strengthened by the synchronized time zones of Australia and Southeast and East Asia. Australia shares time zones with China, Hong Kong, Indonesia, Japan, Malaysia, Philippines, Singapore, South Korea and Taiwan, along with many other countries in the Asia-Pacifc. This means that from Cydus, it was relatively easy to play with people from these countries, as no special effort was required to find a time to play which was mutually suitable since the daily rhythms of work, study, leisure and sleep were roughly synchronous. At Cybercafé Ávila this was also true, as the networks were more regionally oriented within North and South America, sharing several synchronized time zones: Venezuela is 30 minutes ahead of EST (Eastern Standard Time), putting it in roughly the same time zone as Bolivia, Chile, Colombia, Cuba, Ecuador, Peru, the populous east coast of the United States and the Canadian provinces of Ontario and Québec.

The proliferation of local *GunBound* portals might suggest a splintering of players into multiple local and regional communities. However, these same local and regional portals enable the strengthening national and linguistic ties across global networks. This networked gaming becomes one way that national community is maintained and even how national identity is expressed. This suggests that the

19. Constance Steinkuehler, "The Mangle of Play," *Games and Culture* 1.3 (2006): 199-213; Dal Yong Jin and Florence Chee, "Age of New Media Empires: A Critical Interpretation of the Korean Online Game Industry," *Games and Culture* 3.1 (2008), 38-58.

capacity of network infrastructures to connect locations, across national and geographic boundaries, is enabled by knowledge that is formed and developed through shared practices of gaming.

CONCLUSION

Play across national boundaries using unevenly developed infrastructure in Venezuela, Australia and other countries was made viable by *GunBound* being a low-data game that put very little pressure on infrastructure and could thus be downloaded, installed and played on a large number of networked computers without unwanted complications. Its ubiquity at the time meant that it was a common point of experience for many people who spent time in cybercafés in distinct points throughout the globe. *GunBound* was structured to enable real-time communications, deliberately incorporating the communicative cultures of players into the game. But what made *GunBound* a useful tool relative to many other available games was its role in facilitating social relations across uneven network infrastructures. This made *GunBound* and other similar games open up the possibility of connecting locations in the global south, as well as establishing horizontally-organized constellations across the north and south, but within proximate time zones.

People at Cydus chose to play *GunBound* not just because they wouldn't experience lag, but because whomever they were playing with would also, most likely, not experience lag. However, at Cybercafé Ávila choosing to play *GunBound* was a case of "making do," from among the various free-to-play and freemium games that were available, which would also allow them and their opponents to play with consistent speed across the relatively inconsistent regional network infrastructure. The design of *GunBound* kept the possibility of an "even playing field" open. The design features that contributed to this possibility were the dual currency and the separate servers for those that had used microtransactions and wished to experience the in-game advantage they had purchased. But also crucial was the attitude of the community of gamers, who saw the "avatar off" servers as demonstrating the "true spirit" of *GunBound* competition. This meant that the mechanics of *GunBound*, and its capacity to operate smoothly over uneven networks were crucial in developing and sustaining a gaming culture that valued the ability to communicate across national borders and between cultures.

ACKNOWLEDGEMENTS

This research was funded by grants from the School of Culture and Communication, Faculty of Arts and School of Graduate Studies at the University of Melbourne.

WORKS CITED

Apperley, Thomas. *Global Rhythms: Play and Counterplay from the Situated to the Global*. Institute of Network Cultures, 2010.

—. "Understanding Digital Games as Educational Technologies." In *Popular Culture, Pedagogy and Teacher Education: International Perspectives*, edited by Phil Benson and Alice Chik, 36-52. Routledge, 2014.

—. "Venezuela." In *Videogames Around the World*, edited by Mark J. P. Wolf, 613-628. MIT Press, 2015.

—. "Digital Gaming, Social Inclusion, and the Right to Play: A Case Study of a Venezuelan Cybercafé."

In *The Routledge Companion to Digital Ethnography*, edited by Larissa Hjorth, Heather Horst, Anne Galloway and Genevieve Bell, 235-243. Routledge, 2017.

Apperley, Thomas and Catherine Beavis. "A Model for Critical Games Literacy." *e-Learning & Digital Media* 10.1 (2013): 1-12.

Bourdieu, Pierre. *Distinction: A Social Critique of the Judgement of Taste.* Routledge, 1984.

Consalvo, Mia. "Console Video Games and Global Corporations: Creating a Hybrid Culture." *New Media & Society* 8.1 (2006): 117-137.

—. *Cheating: Gaining Advantage in Videogames*. MIT Press, 2007.

Hjorth, Larissa and Dean Chan, eds. *Gaming Cultures and Place in the Asia-Pacific*. Routledge, 2009.

Hunteman, Nina and Ben Aslinger, eds. *Gaming Globally: Production, Play, and Place*. Palgrave, 2013.

Jin, Dal Yong. *Korea's Online Gaming Empire*. MIT Press, 2010.

Jin, Dal Yong and Florence Chee. "Age of New Media Empires: A Critical Interpretation of the Korean Online Game Industry." *Games and Culture* 3.1 (2008): 38-58.

Kline, Steven, Nick Dyer-Witheford and Greig de Peuter. *Digital/Play: The Interaction of Technology, Culture and Marketing*. McGill/Queen's University Press, 2003.

Liboriussen, Bjarke and Paul Martin. "Regional Game Studies." *Game Studies* 16.1 (2016).

Lugo, Jairo and Tony Sampson. "E-Informality in Venezuela: The 'Other Path' of Technology." *Bulletin of Latin American Research* 27.1 (2008): 102-118.

Mukherjee, Souvik "Videogames as 'Minor Literature': Reading Videogame Stories through Paratexts." *GRAMMA: Journal of Theory and Criticism* 23 (2016): 60-75.

Murray, Padmini Ray and Chris Hand. "Making Culture: Locating the Digital Humanities in India." *Visible Language: The Journal of Visual Communication Research* 49.3 (2015): 140-155.

Parks, Lisa and Nicole Staroseilski. "Introduction." In *Signal Traffic: Critical Studies of Media Infrastructures*, edited by Lisa Parks and Nicole Staroseilski, 1-28. University of Illinois Press, 2015.

Penix-Tadsen, Phillip. *Cultural Code: Video Games and Latin America*. MIT Press, 2016.

Steinkuehler, Constance. "The Mangle of Play." *Games and Culture* 1.3 (2006), 199-213.

Walker, Alex. "*Gunbound* Is Back As A Mobile Game." *Kotaku Australia*, 5 July 2017, https://www.kotaku.com.au/2017/07/gunbound-is-back-as-a-mobile-game/.

Walsh, Chris and Thomas Apperley. "Researching Digital Game Players: Gameplay and Gaming Capital." In *Proceedings of IADIS International Conference Gaming 2008: Design for Engaging Experience and Social Interaction*, edited by Y. Xiao and E. Ten Thij, 99-102. IADIS, 2008.

Wolf, Mark J. P., ed. *Video Games Around the World.* MIT Press, 2015.

Yoon, Tae-Jin and Hyejung Cheon. "Game Playing as Transnational Cultural Practice: A Case Study of Chinese Gamers and Korean MMORPGs." *International Journal of Cultural Studies* 17.5 (2014): 469-483.

LUDOGRAPHY

Blizzard. "Defense of the Ancients," *WarCraft III: Reign of Chaos*. Blizzard, 2003.

—. *World of Warcraft*. Blizzard, 2004.

CipSoft. *Tibia*. CipSoft, 1997.

Cryptic Studios. *City of Heroes*. NCSoft, 2004.

Dargőm Studio. *GunBoundM.* Apple/Google, 2017.

Ensemble Studios. *Age of Empires II: The Conquerors*. Microsoft, 2000.

—. *Age of Mythology: The Titans*. Microsoft, 2003.

Gala Lab. *Fly For Fun.* Webzen, 2005.

Gravity. *Ragnarok Online*. Gravity, 2003.

Maxis. *The Sims 2.* EA Games, 2004.

Rockstar North. *Grand Theft Auto: Vice City*. Rockstar Games, 2002.

Softnyx. *GunBound World Champion*. Softnyx, 2005.

—. *GunBound Revolution*. Softnyx, 2006.

Team 17. *Worms*. Team 17, 1995.

TriggerSoft. *ROSE Online*. Gravity Interactive, 2005.

Valve Corporation. *Counter-Strike: Source.* Valve Corporation, 2004.

Webzen. *MU Online*. Webzen, 2003.

THE EMERGING AFRICAN VIDEO GAME INDUSTRY

AN ANALYSIS OF THE NARRATIVES OF GAMES DEVELOPED IN CAMEROON AND NIGERIA

REBECCA YVONNE BAYECK

INTRODUCTION: THE AFRICAN VIDEO GAME LANDSCAPE

Though gaming is a global phenomenon, game development in Africa has yet to receive significant critical attention. Video games—popular interactive media played on a variety of devices such as computers, mobile devices and game consoles—are a major economic force: according to the Entertainment Software Association (ESA), the U.S. gaming industry added more than $11.7 billion to the U.S. gross domestic profit in 2016 and generated $30.4 billion in revenue.[1] Worldwide, the industry has experienced similar growth, with revenues expected to reach $108.9 billion in 2017 according to Newzoo, a research firm covering global games, eSports and mobile markets. This growth is driven in particular by the boom in mobile gaming, which, according to the same report, will account for 42% of global game industry revenues in 2017.[2] A segmentation of this revenue by regions shows that the Asian Pacific region will constitute $51.2 billion of this profit and North America $27 billion, while "Africa, Europe and the Middle East" will return $26.2 billion. Video games are therefore a worldwide phenomenon, though in Africa, the gaming industry is still in its infancy, which explains the scarcity of data on game industry revenues in this part of the world.

Nevertheless, recent reports on video games in Africa show that video games are being played more and more across the continent.[3] The increasing prominence of video game play is explained in part by the widespread use of mobile devices. A 2013 report by tech company Ericsson showed that 38% of mobile users' weekly activities in Sub-Saharan Africa (e.g., Nigeria, Ghana, South Africa, Kenya, Senegal and Cameroon) are devoted to playing games.[4] A 2018 report on entertainment and media industries in Africa by Price Waterhouse Cooper predicts that the video game market in countries such as Kenya will be worth US$118 million in 2022, growing from US$63 million in 2017.[5] This report also forecasts similar growth for countries like Ghana, Tanzania, Nigeria and South Africa, with social/casual gaming being the fastest growing segment of the market due to the growth in smartphone ownership.

Likewise, there is a growing interest among teenagers and young adults across Africa in playing video games, and although *Counter Strike* (Valve, 2000-2012), *Call of Duty* (Activision, 2003-) and *League of Legends* (Riot, 2009) are among the most-played games in the region, African game developers are increasingly trying to tap into the current generation of gamers by developing games locally.[6] Indeed, game development studios are emerging across Africa, encouraging developers to produce games on

1. Entertainment Software Association, "Annual Report 2017," *Entertainment Software Association*, 12 January 2018, https://www.esaannualreport.com/.
2. Newzoo, "Global Games Market Report," *Newzoo.com*, 12 January 2018, https://newzoo.com/solutions/standard/market-forecasts/global-games-market-report/.
3. Christopher Vourlias, "Video Game Culture Takes Hold Across Nigeria," *Aljazeera America*, 15 December 2014, http://america.aljazeera.com/.
4. Ericsson, "Bridging the Digital Divide: How Mobile Phones are Playing a Key Role in Connecting People in Sub-Saharan Africa," *All Africa*, 12 December 2013, http://www.ericsson.com/res/docs/2013/consumerlab/bridging-the-digital-divide-subsaharan-africa.pdf.
5. Price Waterhouse Cooper, "Entertainment and Media Outlook: 2018–2022, An African Perspective," *Price Waterhouse Cooper*, 2018, https://www.pwc.co.za/en/assets/pdf/entertainment-and-media-outlook-2018-2022.pdf.

the continent.[7] The emergence of locally developed games brings new voices to the medium, meaning that the narratives of games created by developers in Africa are of increasing interest, although research on this subject is sparse. Indeed, the existence of small independent gaming studios provides a new opportunity for developers to create games that reflect local cultural preferences and provide content tailored to users that would not likely be produced by "global" game developers.

With this in mind, this chapter focuses specifically on an analysis of the narratives of games developed in Cameroon and Nigeria. The chapter begins with a summary of previous research on game narratives, then applies this framework to a sample of ten games developed in these two western African nations. The chapter concludes by outlining possible paths for further research on games and game development in Africa.

APPROACHES TO GAME NARRATIVE

In literary analysis, terms like "narrative," "plot" and "story" are often used interchangeably, or subjected to a variety of divergent definitions. However, this chapter defines narrative as "the unique way in which [a] story is being presented to the audience."[8] Hence, a game's narrative "encapsulates the methods used to deliver the necessary scenes, the order of the scenes, the time taken for the events to unfold (duration) and the frequency with which these scenes occur."[9] Using this expansive definition of narrative, elements of a video game's narrative would include gameplay (i.e., player interaction with the game), cut scenes, back stories, lighting, music, promotional materials and other techniques/ elements used to present the story to the audience.[10] This broad definition of narrative is also well-captured by the concepts of interactive narrative and interactive digital narrative,[11] both of which point to the fundamentally interactive nature of video game narratives.

Rather than providing a broad and single definition of narrative in video games, some researchers go a step further to qualify narratives as emergent or embedded.[12] Emergent narrative arises from players' interactions with the game world in unpredictable and changeable manners, while embedded narrative exists prior to a player's interaction with the game and is basically the pre-generated story created by the game developer and laid out for the player to discover.[13] As previously stated, this chapter defines game narrative as the different ways in which a story is presented to the player, including the game's backstory, setting, key characters, languages, character names and objectives.[14] This open conception of game narrative is critical for understanding the local and cultural framing of African video games.

Research shows that players find video games with narratives more engaging and immersive, as narratives in games contextualize players' actions and give a greater sense of meaning.[15] The presence of stories makes a difference in players' experiences, as they generate greater identification with

6. Stephane Boyera and Aman Grewal, "Games in Africa: Opportunities and Challenges," 5 May 2014, https://www.orangepartner.com/sites/default/files/final_games_public_0.pdf.
7. Abdi L. Dahir, "African Video Game Makers are Breaking into the Global Industry with their Own Stories," *Quartz*, 7 May 2017, https://qz.com/africa/974439/african-video-game-makers-are-breaking-into-the-global-industry-with-their-own-stories/.
8. Barry Ip, "Narrative Structures in Computer and Video Games. Part 1: Context, Definitions, and Initial findings," *Games and Culture* 6.2 (2011): 107.
9. Ibid.
10. Ibid; see also Christopher Moser and Xiaowen Fang, "Narrative Structure and Player Experience in Role-Playing Games," *International Journal of Human-Computer Interaction* 31.2 (2015): 146-156.
11. Ip, "Narrative Structures in Computer and Video Games"; Hartmut Koenitz, Gabriele Ferri, Mads Haahr, Diğdem Sezen and Tonguc Ibrahim Sezen, *Interactive Digital Narrative: History, Theory and Practice* (Routledge, 2015).
12. Katie Salen and Eric Zimmerman, *Rules of Play: Game Design Fundamentals* (MIT Press, 2003).
13. Moser and Fang, "Narrative Structure and Player Experience"; Joseph Packer, "What Makes an Orc? Racial Cosmos and Emergent Narrative in World of Warcraft," *Games and Culture* 9.2 (2014): 83-101.
14. Andrew Rollings and Ernest Adams, *Andrew Rollings and Ernest Adams on Game Design* (New Riders, 2003).
15. Sean Hammond, Helen Pain and Tim J. Smith, "Player Agency in Interactive Narrative: Audience, Actor & Author," paper presented at Artificial Intelligence &

characters in the game (e.g., characters' goals and actions), create positive emotions in players and produce physiological arousal, which is known to increase learning from media.[16] Even without going into a discussion on the different types of narrative (i.e., embedded or emergent), narrative structures (linear or branching) and player roles in the construction of game narrative, the concept of narrative is a notion that has been discussed extensively in game studies.[17] Nevertheless, it is important to note that literature on video game narratives has largely focused on games produced in the major centers of global game production, and has not yet explored games designed by African developers.

AFRICAN VIDEO GAME NARRATIVES: THE CASES OF CAMEROON AND NIGERIA

In a 2014 report, Vourlias contended that video game culture was taking over Nigeria, and the same could certainly be said of Cameroon.[18] Video games have become an increasingly common part of daily life for many Africans, and game development studios are emerging across Africa, especially in Cameroon and Nigeria.[19]

Nigeria and Cameroon are neighboring countries in the sub-Saharan region of Africa. Nigeria is the most populous country in Africa, with approximately 167 million inhabitants, and is home to over 250 ethnic languages,[20] including the country's four major languages: English (the official language, due to the heritage of British colonialism), Yoruba, Ibo and Hausa. The country is bordered by Chad and the Republic of Niger to the north, Benin to the west and Cameroon to the east. In 2014, Nigeria emerged as one of Africa's largest economies, and the third-fastest growing economy in the world.[21] However, a recent dip in oil prices has slowed the country's growth, given the national economy's heavy dependence on oil revenues.[22] Nevertheless, Nigeria has a growing middle class with high purchasing power who can afford the latest electronic devices.[23]

Cameroon is located in the West-central part of Africa, and is bordered to the north by Chad, the Central African Republic to the east, Congo, Gabon and Equatorial Guinea to the south, and to the west by Nigeria, with which its shares the largest border (see Image 3.2.1).[24] Cameroon has a population of over 20 million and is often called "Africa in miniature" due to the presence of Africa's linguistic, biological and cultural diversity in this country.[25] Major languages include English and French (official languages inherited from British and French colonial rule) in addition to more than 270 other languages spoken throughout the country.[26] As with Nigeria, Cameroon has an emergent middle class with high buying power,[27] and it is a leading economic power within the central region of Africa, though the country has experienced an economic slowdown in recent years.[28] In sum,

Simulation of Behavior, University of Newcastle, 2-5 April 2007, http://homepages.cs.ncl.ac.uk/patrick.olivier/AISB07/narrative.pdf; Edward F. Schneider, "Death with a Story," *Human Communication Research* 30.3 (2004): 361-375.

16. Schneider, "Death with a Story," 2004.
17. See, for example, Gonzalo Frasca, "Simulation versus Narrative: Introduction to Ludology," in *The Video Game Theory Reader*, ed. Mark J. P. Wolf and Bernard Perron (Routledge, 2003); Simon Egenfeldt-Nielsen, Jonas H. Smith and Susana P. Tosca, *Understanding Video Games: The Essential Introduction* (Routledge, 2015); Ip, "Narrative Structures in Computer and Video Games."
18. Vourlias, "Video Game Culture Takes Hold Across Nigeria."
19. Richard Moss, "The State of Game Development in Africa," *Gamasutra*, 12 December 2016, http://www.gamasutra.com/view/news/264888/The_state_of_game_development_in_Africa.php.
20. Ibid.
21. Eleni Giokos, "Nigeria's Economy Was a 'Disaster' in 2016. Will This Year be Different?," *CNN Money*, 17 June 2017, http://money.cnn.com/2017/04/27/news/economy/nigeria-oil-growth/index.html.
22. Ibid.
23. Norimitsu Onishi, "Nigeria Goes to the Mall," *New York Times*, 5 January 2016, https://www.nytimes.com/2016/01/05/world/africa/nigeria-goes-to-the-mall.html?mcubz=1.
24. UNICEF, "West and Central Africa," *unicef.org*, 15 January 2017, https://www.unicef.org/appeals/cameroon.html.
25. Huguette G. Mbenda, Gauri Awasthi, Poonam Singh, I. Gouado and A. Das, "Does Malaria Epidemiology Project Cameroon as 'Africa in miniature'?," *Journal of Biosciences* 39.4 (2014): 727-738.
26. Ibid.
27. Danielle Resnick, "The Political Economy of Africa's Emergent Middle Class: Retrospect and Prospects," *Journal of International Development* 27.5 (2015): 573-587.

Cameroon and Nigeria have a longstanding cultural affinity that transcends nationality,[29] given that the current boundaries between both countries are remnant of the colonial era, and often serve to artificially separate otherwise unified sociocultural groups and practices found in both countries.[30] An understanding of the relationship between the two countries is helpful in understanding how local culture shapes game development in each one.

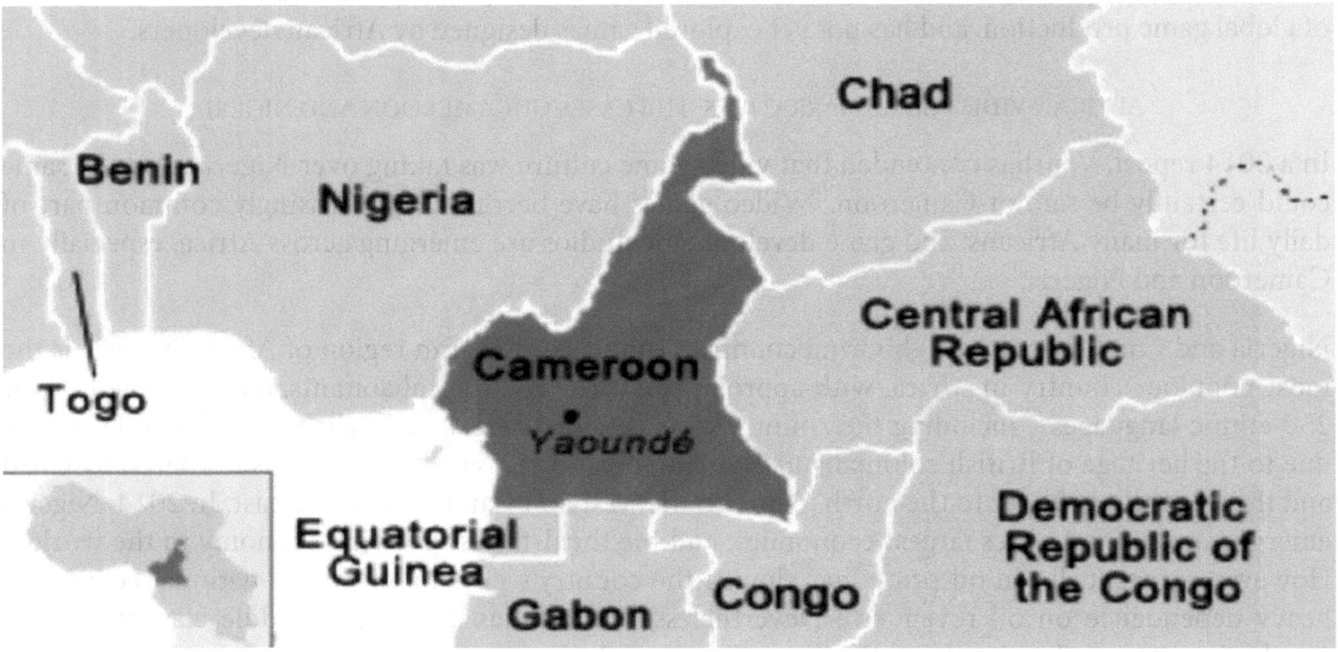

Image 3.2.1. Map of Cameroon, Nigeria and the surrounding region.

This chapter focuses on the narratives of games developed in Cameroon and Nigeria, examining the ways developers use elements such as the backstory, cut scenes, setting, key characters, character names and game objectives to enhance their games' appeal and to emphasize the Cameroonian and Nigerian characteristics of game narratives. An analysis of these games' narratives, broadly defined, reveals the many mechanisms used by game developers to evoke Cameroonian and Nigerian culture in their products.

The games selected for this chapter adhere to four criteria: 1) they were produced by one of the top three studios in their respective countries; 2) they were released in the last two years; 3) they were featured among the top ten games on the developers' site; and finally, 4) they were produced by companies aiming to reach the growing population African gamers. Based on these criteria, ten video games were selected from developers Chopup, Maliyo and Kiro'o, three of Nigeria and Cameroon's leading gaming studios.[31] While they differ greatly in genre, aesthetics and other design elements, these games share a great deal on the level of the contextualization of their narratives.

Aurion: Legacy of the Kori-Odan (Kiro'o, 2016; hereafter *ALKO*), developed by Cameroonian studio

28. Samuel Fambon, Andy McKay, Joseph P. Timnou, Olive S. Kouakep, Anaclet Dzossa and Tchakoute Romain, "Slow Progress in Growth and Poverty Reduction in Cameroon," in *Growth and Poverty in Sub-Saharan Africa*, ed. Channing Arndt, Andy McKay and Finn Tarp (Oxford University Press, 2016).
29. Olabanji O. Ewetan and Ese Ewetan U., "Insecurity and Socio-Economic Development in Nigeria," *Journal of Sustainable Development Studies* 5.1 (2014): 40-63.
30. Gabriel L. Adeola and Oluyemi O. Fayomi, "The Political and Security Implications of Cross Border Migration between Nigeria and her Francophone Neighbors," *International Journal of Social Science Tomorrow* 1.3 (2012): 1-9.
31. W. Chibelushi, "Level up!: Our Top five African Gaming Studios," *African Business Review*, 17 June 2017, http://www.africanbusinessreview.co.za/technology/2723/Level-up:-Our-top-five-African-gaming-studios; Rara Reines, "African-Themed Video Games Are a Market with Strong Potential," *Ayiba*, 13 December 2016, http://ayibamagazine.com/top-african-video-game-companies/.

Kiro'o Games, is a role-playing game that tells the story of the prince of a city called Zama, who is overthrown by his brother-in-law Ngarba Evou on the day of his wedding and coronation. Forced into exile, prince Enzo Kori-Odan and his wife Erine Evou travel the world to gain strength in the hope of returning to Zama to claim their kingdom. According to the game website, *ALKO* derives its narrative from African stories and culture.[32] Indeed, the game's backstory reveals a practice common in Cameroonian culture, as well as other cultures of West and Central Africa: the marital status of a prince often determines his ascension to the throne;[33] it is therefore not surprising that the prince's wife is mentioned in the narrative. The influence of Cameroonian culture on *ALKO* is also seen in the names used to identify characters, as well as the game setting. Names such as Evou, Ngarba Evou and Zama are reminiscent of those used by the Beti ethnic group in Cameroon. In using these names to identify characters and location, the developers situate the players in a Cameroonian fantasy world. The names add to the African-ness of the game narrative and connect the player to Africa. For instance, in the language of the Beti ethnic group in Cameroon, the name Evou means "witch," while Ngarba refers to "someone who is boastful" and Zama means "God." These names reflect the desire of developers to create narratives inspired by African culture, narratives with which Cameroonian players—and certainly many other Africans—can identify, characteristics which make *ALKO* stand out as an African-centered video game.

The localization of games can also be noted in *Ebola Strike Force* (ChopUp, 2015; hereafter *ESF*), a video game developed for mobile devices by Nigerian game studio ChopUp. *ESF* is about a team of scientists and doctors who discover that they can cure Ebola using a serum that can only be extracted from patient X with the help of a nanobot. In this description, one element that clearly stands out is the centrality of Ebola, a rare and deadly disease that caused thousands of deaths during the largest outbreak of the epidemic in West Africa between 2014-2016.[34] The use of Ebola as the game's focus situates its narrative in West Africa, and as such gives an immediate sense of the game's setting. Further enhancing the game's contextualization in the west African setting, the player is given the following background information at the beginning of the game:

> On August 19, 2014, Dr. Ameyo Stella Adadevor, a consultant physician at First consultants medical centre: a Lagos-based hospital, died of the dreaded Ebola disease, She contacted the disease while caring for an infected patient: Patrick Sawyer from Liberia. Due to the bravery and self-sacrifice of Dr. Adedevor and her team, an Ebola epidemic in the Lagos Metropolis was averted. Her heroic efforts prevented an outbreak in the most populous African country, Nigeria.
>
> This game is dedicated to her and all other medical personnel who lost their lives in the battle to keep us Ebola free. May God Almighty rest their soul in perfect peace, Amen!

In this background story, geographical references such as those to Lagos, Ameyo, Liberia and Nigeria further evidence the ways this game's narrative tackles topics and subjects related to the everyday lives of Africans. The game draws the user into this setting with references to real-life locales, situations and individuals, using names, dates and titles to enhance the realism of its west African setting.

Another recent title with a west African setting is *Aboki Run* (Maliyo, 2016), a mobile game designed by Maliyo game studio in Nigeria that tells the story of three young friends, Chinedu, Danjuma and Gbenga, who leave the city to venture into the forest, the forbidden habitat of spirits, where they are trapped by the forest gods. In order to be set free and return to the city, the three friends need

32. Kiro'o Games, Aurion, http://kiroogames.com/en/aurion.html.
33. John Mbaku, *Culture and Customs of Cameroon* (Greenwood, 2005).
34. J. Quick, et al., "Real-Time, Portable Genome Sequencing for Ebola Surveillance," *Nature* 530.7589 (2016): 228.

the player's help. In African culture, and particularly in Nigeria's Igbo culture, the forbidden forest symbolizes evil, and is the graveyard of those considered a plague to the community, individuals who have committed acts forbidden by society or those who have died of incurable diseases.[35] Hence, in the Igbo culture and worldview, the forbidden forest is symbolically the home to evil spirits and other forces of darkness.[36] In addition to the evil forest imagery that reflects Igbo culture, the three characters' names are also linked to the three major ethnic groups in Nigeria: Chinedu is an Igbo name that means "God leads"; Gbenga, a Yoruba name, is the short form of Oluwagbenga/Olugbenga, meaning "God has raised me up"; and finally, Danjuma, a Hausa name, is said to mean "son of Friday."[37] As with the previously mentioned games, *Aboki Run*, situated in Nigeria, immerses players in a variety of aspects of African culture with its narrative,.

Taking on African cultural themes in the strategy genre, ChopUp studio's *Jagun: Clash of Kingdoms* (2015) is a mobile game that narrates the story of a (fictional) prosperous medieval kingdom in the Niger region called Jagunlabi (see Image 3.2.2). The prosperity of this kingdom attracts many enemies, and in order to defend the kingdom, the *Jagun* has to use bows, fireballs and *juju*. The story sets the game in Africa—specifically Nigeria—by referring to a prosperous kingdom in the Niger area during the medieval age. As previously discussed, Nigeria is an economic power in contemporary Africa, and just like Nigeria, Jagunlabi is located in the Niger area, and the way in which its affluence attracts adversaries, could refer to the colonizers of Nigeria, or to any individual or power that might attempt to destabilize the country. To defend the kingdom, players are given bows and, interestingly, juju, a popular word in West Africa that describes an object believed to possess supernatural powers. Juju in the popular culture can be used to protect or defend the owner, and it is a concept which resonates with most West Africans, again demonstrating the relationship between the game's narrative and the African reality. In the same vein, the kingdom's name, "Jangunlabi," is a Yoruba word employed to mean "brave men or warriors," while "Jagun" is the word for "warrior" in Yoruba. The developers incorporate into the narrative African concepts reminiscent of a glorious past, and the on-screen prompts in the game (see Image 3.2.3) also evidence the inspiration developers draw from African culture and history. Historically, the Nri kingdom referenced in the game (see Image 3.2.3) was located in the east of the Nigeria, and was ruled by the descendants of King Eri from the 10th century until it was subdued by the British in 1911.[38] The prosperous kingdom of Nri is believed to be the foundation of the rich Igbo culture,[39] and thus the similarity between the historical Nri kingdom and Nri in the game points to the situatedness of the game's narrative in Nigeria.

Notably, with the exception of *ALKO*, all of the games analyzed in this chapter are designed for mobile devices. The way developers create their products and game narratives with local realities in mind is further illustrated by games designed around the theme or concept of the *okada*. "Okada" is the name used in Nigeria to refer to a motorcycle, and okadas are a popular means of transportation for many west Africans, which situates games on the okada theme of beyond the Nigerian context.[40] The following paragraphs discuss three okada-themed games, *Okada Rider* (ChopUp, 2015), *Okada vs Danfo* (Maliyo, 2016) and *Okada Ride* (Maliyo, 2013).

ChopUp's *Okada Rider* is another mobile game, this time portraying motorcycle driver Abu, waiting

35. Chinua Achebe, *Things Fall Apart* (Heinemann, 1986).
36. Ibid.
37. Name Doctor, 12 December 2013, http://www.name-doctor.com/.
38. Richard M. Juang and Noelle Morrissette, *Africa and the Americas: Culture, Politics, and History* (ABC-CLIO, 2008); all game images in this chapter are used with permission of the games' publishers.
39. Ibid.
40. Ofonime E. Johnson, "Prevalence and Pattern of Road Traffic Accidents among Commercial Motorcyclists in a City in Southern Nigeria," *Educational Research* 3.6 (2012): 537-542.

Image 3.2.2. Jagun: Clash of Kingdoms.

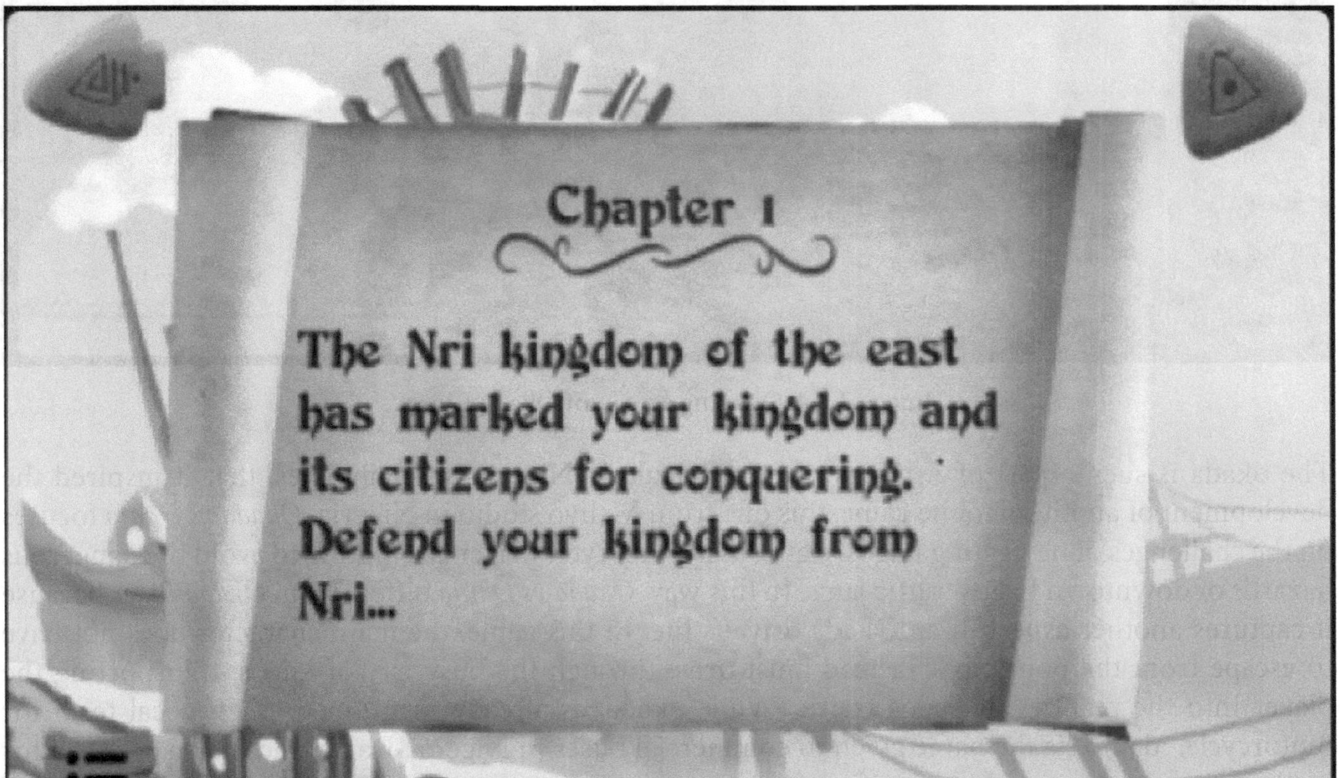

Image 3.2.3. On-screen prompt from Jagun: Clash of Kingdoms.

for customers, as usual, at a bus stop. Abu has to leave the city, when he suddenly sees police officers confiscating bicycles on the order of the governor of Lagos State. While the okada is a very popular means of transportation in Nigeria, as well as in other parts of western Africa, due to the risky behaviors drivers exhibit and their frequent accidents, okada drivers have come under strict scrutiny from authorities.[41] Consequently, it is not uncommon to see police officers seizing motorcycles, or to see drivers attempting to avoid police seizure of their motorcycles. Even still, this means of transportation is seen as fast and affordable by many residents in the region, making it preferable for avoiding the congested roads of Lagos.[42] In this way, the game relates to the realities of life in the Nigerian capital by telling the tale of an African okada driver, and thus sharing this experience with players. The protagonist's name, Abu, meaning "father of," "excellence," or "full of," while Arabic in origin, is also a popular name in west Africa, making him another example of an African-coded character (see Image 3.2.4).

Image 3.2.4. Opening screen of Okada Rider.

The okada is such a part of Africans'—and particularly Nigerians'—daily lives, that it inspired the development of another mobile game, this one from Maliyo studio in Nigeria. *Okada vs Danfo* focuses on the challenges of navigating Lagos' traffic as a motorcycle driver attempting to avoid the dangerous hazards of downtown Lagos traffic jams. In this way, *Okada vs Danfo* differs from *Okada Rider* because it captures another aspect of an Okada driver's life. In this game, the main character does not have to escape from the police, but instead must drive through the busy city of Lagos, transporting the player into the realities of Lagos traffic. While okada, as already mentioned, is the local term for motorcycle, "danfo" is the name given to commercial buses in Nigeria. Danfo and okada are used for public transportation, and competition for passengers is fierce among drivers of these two modes of

41. Adekunle Salako, Olumide Abiodun and Oluwafolahan Sholeye, "Risk Behaviors for Road Traffic Accidents and Severe Crash Injuries among Commercial Motorcyclists in Sagamu, South West, Nigeria," *Online Journal of Medicine and Medical Science Research* 2.2 (2013): 1.
42. Ibid.

transportation. As can be seen in its title, this game captures this tension by opposing okada to danfo, reflecting the ways that local reality fuels the content of the game and shapes its narrative.

With *Okada Ride* (*OKR*), players interact with Ali, a motorcycle driver who needs more money to feed his family of eight. After learning that Alhaji Shehu is looking for truck drivers, Ali has to quickly get to Alhaji Shehu in order to take advantage of this opportunity to make more money. However, on that day, roads in Lagos are blocked or busy, and Ali is forced to take a less frequented route, but one that follows a road that is filled with potholes. Helping Ali dodge these obstacles and get to Alhaji Shehu on time is the game's objective. Though similar in name to *Okada Rider*, *OKR*—developed by Maliyo studio—offers players a distinct purpose or meaning for their actions. In *OKR*, the purpose is to avoid obstacles on the road and get to Alhaji Shehu on time for a better job opportunity. The narrative highlights not only the the problems of traffic congestion in Lagos, but also the poor quality of roads in the surrounding area. Every inhabitant of Lagos, along with many citizens of other parts of Africa, can relate to this reality. Moreover, though their Arabic roots, the names Ali and Alhaji Shehu are also found among Muslims in Nigeria. The game's narrative further reflects the real hardships of this context through the fact that Ali, as an okada driver, has to look for another paying job to provide for his family of eight, since the real-life job of okada driver does not pay well enough to feed such a large family.

Games centered on the okada concept capture different aspects of everyday life and culture in Nigeria, and by extension in Africa. Thus, regional players can readily identify with the struggles of the main characters in these different okada-themed games.

In addition to *Ebola Strike Force*, *Jagun: Clash of Kingdoms* and *Okada Rider*, Nigerian developers ChopUp designed the mobile games *Ojuju Calabar* (2017; hereafter *OJC*), *Mama Put* (2015) and *Monkey Post* (2016), each inspired in different elements of local culture. This game recounts the adventure of Tunde, who finds himself in the *Ojuju* land and needs to escape to save his life, which can only be done with the help of the player. *OJC*'s Nigerian setting is primarily reflected in the reference to Ojuju Calabar: Calabar is a city in the southeastern part of Nigeria, capital of the Cross-River State; while ojuju means "masquerade." The custom of Ojuju Calabar, or Calabar Masquerade, was often used by parents in Nigeria to scare children and prevent them from doing wrong.[43] It is a fictional masquerade in Nigerian fables, and once again reflects the ways the game is shaped by Nigerian popular culture. The protagonist's name is also chosen consciously, as names in African culture are believed to not only identify an individual, but also determine character and destiny.[44] Tunde is a Yoruba name that means "return," which explains why the player has to save and return him home: as his name indicates, Tunde has to go back, and thus must escape from the Ojuju land.

Another of ChopUp's mobile titles, *Mama Put*, features protagonist Iya Basira in her kitchen, in need of ingredients as she gets ready to cook delicious Nigerian dishes. The player is invited to join Iya Basira in her kitchen, and must unlock the ingredients Iya Basira needs for each dish. "Iya" means "mother" in Yoruba, but the two-word term "Iya Basira" refers to a restaurant that specialize in local food, also known as a "Mama Put." These restaurants sell familiar food at an affordable price, making them very popular. *Mama Put* is set in Nigeria, and the dishes the player is prompted to cook with Iya Basira are popular local foods, as seen in Image 3.2.5. The on-screen prompt says the following: "Iya Basira is about to unleash her famous Jollof rice. Can you help her get the missing ingredients?" This

43. P. Sanèh, "Ojuju Calabar," *Observe Nigeria: A Sincere Look at the Nation*, 15 January 2016, https://www.observenigeria.com/cultures/ojuju-calabar/.
44. Abdulganiy Olatunji, Moshood Issah, Yusuf Noah, A. Y. Muhammed and Abdul-Rasheed Sulaiman, "Personal Name as a Reality of Everyday Life: Naming Dynamics in Select African Societies," *Journal of Pan African Studies* 8.3 (2015): 72-91.

prompt adds to the game narrative as it alludes to a dish popular in Africa and its diaspora. In these ways, game design emphasizes the African-ness of the character as well as the environment in *Mama Put.*

Image 3.2.5. On-screen prompt from Mama Put.

Based on one of Nigerians' favorite pastimes, the mobile game *Monkey Post* is a street soccer game with no penalties, red cards or corner kicks, just soccer and goals. *Monkey Post,* it should be noted, is the name given to street soccer in Nigeria because of the closeness of goal posts (Ekwealor 2006), and in addition to reminding us of street soccer gameplay, the teams listed in the league (see Image 3.2.6) reflect local reality. Players are invited to compete against friends and play the leagues choosing from teams such as Lekki Islanders, Ikeja Warriors or Agege FC. With this mobile game, ChopUp makes a virtual representation of street soccer as it is played in many African countries. For example, Lekki, Ikeja, as well as Agege are all cities in Lagos state, Nigeria. As Ekwealor (2016) has explained, *Monkey*

Post is another game from ChopUp studio that focuses on culturally-themed content aimed at a local audience.

Image 3.2.6. Monkey Post league teams.

This review of selected game narratives produced in Africa reflects the many ways in which game development is a culturally-inspired activity, that is, an undertaking framed and shaped by the context and culture of the developers. It is not surprising, then, that research on the representation of minorities such as Africans confirms that Western/colonial worldviews of Africans frequently inform the narratives of video games developed in the Western world.[45] Indie games, and mobile games in particular, certainly offer an opportunity for the diversification of game narratives, and in practical terms, for making video game development a worldwide activity in which many can participate.

CONCLUSION AND FURTHER RESEARCH

Though this study focuses on a limited number of African games designed by developers in Cameroon and Nigeria, it reflects the fact that the gaming industry is still at its infancy in both countries, as it is across the continent as a whole. But the situation remains precarious and fraught with irregularity: for example, at the time of this study, in one of the biggest independent gaming studios Cameroon had released only one video game. Reaching a level of stability for the local industry is also a challenge: more games and developers have recently emerged in Nigeria relative to Cameroon, even but even still Kuluya, one of Nigeria's leading studios in 2015, was no longer in existence by 2017. When it comes to game narratives, the games reviewed in this small-scale study all revolve around African themes, drawing from Africa's reality, folklore, environment, cultural traditions and everyday

45. Rebecca Y. Bayeck, Tutaleni I. Asino and Patricia A. Young, "Representations of Africans in Popular Video Games in the U.S," *Journal of Virtual Worlds Research* 11.2 (2018).

customs in order to tell and share African stories. The developers use African names and African characters to present unique narratives to the audience, demonstrating how bringing new voices into game development can diversify the overall landscape of games and game culture.

Though limited by its sample size and strict focus on narrative, this study was, to the author's knowledge, the first to examine the subject of African video game narratives. Further research needs to be conducted on African games in order to examine topics such as gender, language and ethnic representation. Given that video games' prominence and popularity are on the rise in Africa, exploring the content of games developed by Africans helps better understand how local developers are bringing new insights and perspectives, contributing to global trends in the gaming industry.

WORKS CITED

Adeola, Gabriel L. and Oluyemi O. Fayomi. "The Political and Security Implications of Cross Border Migration between Nigeria and her Francophone Neighbors." *International Journal of Social Science Tomorrow* 1.3 (2012): 1-9.

Achebe, Chinua. *Things Fall Apart.* Heinemann, 1986.

Bayeck, Rebecca Y., Tutaleni I. Asino and Patricia A. Young. "Representations of Africans in Popular Video Games in the U.S." *Journal of Virtual Worlds Research* 11.2 (2018).

Boyera, Stephane and Aman Grewal. "Games in Africa: Opportunities and Challenges." 5 May 2014, https://www.orangepartner.com/sites/default/files/final_games_public_0.pdf.

Brock, Andre. "'When Keeping it Real Goes Wrong': *Resident Evil 5,* Racial Representation, and Gamers." *Games and Culture* 6.5 (2011): 429-452.

Chibelushi, W. "Level up!: Our Top five African Gaming Studios." *African Business Review.* 17 June 2017, http://www.africanbusinessreview.co.za/technology/2723/Level-up:-Our-top-five-African-gaming-studios.

Dahir, Abdi L. "African Video Game Makers are Breaking into the Global Industry with their Own Stories." *Quartz.* 7 May 2017, https://qz.com/africa/974439/african-video-game-makers-are-breaking-into-the-global-industry-with-their-own-stories/.

Egenfeldt-Nielsen, Simon, Jonas H. Smith and Susana P. Tosca. *Understanding Video Games: The Essential Introduction.* Routledge, 2015.

Ekwealor, Victor. "Game Review: *Monkey Post* Will Make You Miss Your Soccer Playing Childhood." *TechPoint.* 7 December 2016, https://techpoint.ng/2016/12/07/monkey-post-game-from-chop-up/.

Entertainment Software Association. "Annual Report 2017." 12 January 2018, https://www.esaannualreport.com/.

Ericsson. "Bridging the Digital Divide: How Mobile Phones are Playing a Key Role in Connecting People in Sub-Saharan Africa." *All Africa.* 12 December 2013, http://www.ericsson.com/res/docs/2013/consumerlab/bridging-the-digital-divide-subsaharan-africa.pdf.

Ewetan, Olabanji O. and Ese Ewetan U. "Insecurity and Socio-Economic Development in Nigeria." *Journal of Sustainable Development Studies* 5.1 (2014): 40-63.

Fambon, Samuel, Andy McKay, Joseph P. Timnou, Olive S. Kouakep, Anaclet Dzossa and Tchakoute Romain. "Slow Progress in Growth and Poverty Reduction in Cameroon." In *Growth and Poverty in Sub-Saharan Africa*, edited by Channing Arndt, Andy McKay and Finn Tarp. Oxford University Press, 2016.

Frasca, Gonzalo. "Simulation versus Narrative: Introduction to Ludology." In *The Video Game Theory Reader*, edited by Mark J. P. Wolf and Bernard Perron. Routledge, 2003.

Giokos, Eleni. "Nigeria's Economy Was a 'Disaster' in 2016. Will This Year be Different?." *CNN Money*, 17 June 2017, http://money.cnn.com/2017/04/27/news/economy/nigeria-oil-growth/index.html.

Hammond, Sean, Helen Pain and Tim J. Smith. "Player Agency in Interactive Narrative: Audience, Actor & Author." Paper presented at Artificial Intelligence & Simulation of Behaviour, University of Newcastle, 2-5 April 2007, http://homepages.cs.ncl.ac.uk/patrick.olivier/AISB07/narrative.pdf.

Ip, Barry. "Narrative Structures in Computer and Video Games. Part 1: Context, Definitions, and Initial findings." *Games and Culture* 6.2 (2011): 103-134.

Johnson, Ofonime E. "Prevalence and Pattern of Road Traffic Accidents among Commercial Motorcyclists in a City in Southern Nigeria." *Educational Research* 3.6 (2012): 537-542.

Juang, Richard M. and Noelle Morrissette. *Africa and the Americas: Culture, Politics, and History*. ABC-CLIO, 2008.

Kirinya, Wesley. "Africa." In *Video Games Around the World*, edited by Mark. J. P. Wolf, 17-28. MIT Press, 2015.

Koenitz, Hartmut, Gabriele Ferri, Mads Haahr, Diğdem Sezen and Tonguc Ibrahim Sezen. *Interactive Digital Narrative: History, Theory and Practice*. Routledge, 2015.

Mbaku, John. *Culture and Customs of Cameroon*. Greenwood, 2005.

Mbenda, Huguette G., Gauri Awasthi. Poonam Singh, I. Gouado and A. Das. "Does Malaria Epidemiology Project Cameroon as 'Africa in miniature'?." *Journal of Biosciences* 39.4 (2014): 727-738.

Moser, Christopher and Xiaowen Fang. "Narrative Structure and Player Experience in Role-Playing Games." *International Journal of Human-Computer Interaction* 31.2 (2015): 146-156.

Moss, Richard. "The State of Game Development in Africa." *Gamasutra*. 12 December 2016, http://www.gamasutra.com/view/news/264888/The_state_of_game_development_in_Africa.php.

Name Doctor. 12 December 2013, http://www.name-doctor.com/.

Newzoo. "Global Games Market Report." 12 January 2018, https://newzoo.com/solutions/standard/market-forecasts/global-games-market-report/.

Olatunji, Abdulganiy, Moshood Issah, Yusuf Noah, A. Y. Muhammed and Abdul-Rasheed Sulaiman.

"Personal Name as a Reality of Everyday Life: Naming Dynamics in Select African Societies." *The Journal of Pan African Studies* 8.3 (2015): 72-91.

Onishi, Norimitsu. "Nigeria Goes to the Mall." *New York Times.* 5 January 2016, https://www.nytimes.com/2016/01/05/world/africa/nigeria-goes-to-the-mall.html?mcubz=1.

Orekan, George. "Mother Tongue Medium as an Efficient Way of Challenging Educational Disadvantages in Africa: The Case of Nigeria." *Scottish Languages Review* 23 (2011): 27-38.

Packer, Joseph. "What Makes an Orc? Racial Cosmos and Emergent Narrative in World of Warcraft." *Games and Culture* 9.2 (2014): 83-101.

Price Waterhouse Cooper. "Entertainment and Media Outlook: 2018–2022, An African Perspective," 2018, https://www.pwc.co.za/en/assets/pdf/entertainment-and-media-outlook-2018-2022.pdf.

Quick, J., et al. "Real-Time, Portable Genome Sequencing for Ebola Surveillance." *Nature* 530.7589 (2016): 228.

Reines, Rara. "African-Themed Video Games Are a Market with Strong Potential." *Ayiba.* 13 December 2016, http://ayibamagazine.com/top-african-video-game-companies/.

Resnick, Danielle. "The Political Economy of Africa's Emergent Middle Class: Retrospect and Prospects." *Journal of International Development* 27.5 (2015): 573-587.

Rollings, Andrew and Ernest Adams. *Andrew Rollings and Ernest Adams on Game Design.* New Riders, 2003.

Salako, Adekunle, Olumide Abiodun and Oluwafolahan Sholeye. "Risk Behaviors for Road Traffic Accidents and Severe Crash Injuries among Commercial Motorcyclists in Sagamu, South West, Nigeria." *Online Journal of Medicine and Medical Science Research* 2.2 (2013): 1.

Salen, Katie and Eric Zimmerman. *Rules of Play: Game Design Fundamentals.* MIT Press, 2003.

Sanèh, P. "Ojuju Calabar." *Observe Nigeria: A Sincere Look at the Nation.* 15 January 2016, https://www.observenigeria.com/cultures/ojuju-calabar/.

Schneider, Edward F. "Death with a Story." *Human Communication Research* 30.3 (2004): 361-375.

UNICEF. "West and Central Africa." 15 January 2017, https://www.unicef.org/appeals/cameroon.html.

Vourlias, Christopher. "Video Game Culture Takes Hold Across Nigeria." *Aljazeera America,* 2014 December 15, http://america.aljazeera.com/.

VIDEO GAME ENGAGEMENT ON SOCIAL MEDIA IN THE MIDDLE EAST

AHMED AL-RAWI AND MIA CONSALVO

VIDEO GAMES AND SOCIAL MEDIA IN THE MIDDLE EAST

Gaming in the Middle East is still an under-researched topic, especially if one takes into account that the region has "the fastest growing communities of online gamers in the world, and demographics mean this is likely to remain true for many years."[1] Instead of examining the portrayal of Arab characters in Western or Middle Eastern video games, conducting ethnographic research on Arab gaming communities, or treating gaming as a form of resistance—topics that are covered by Bushra Alfaraj and Pierre-Alain Clèment's essays in this anthology—this chapter is focused instead on social media engagement by players in the Middle East. As far as the researchers are aware, no previous study has explored this area of research, making this chapter unique. As indicated in the introduction to this anthology, there is a need to examine video games in culture rather than as culture alone, and this is especially so in relation to the unique consumption of video games in the Middle Eastern context. A focus on social media engagement is also relevant because social networks are important spaces to exchange gaming information and experiences as well as to create networks and connections, without which the gaming experience will be greatly lacking richness and depth.

Previous research on video gaming in the Middle East has largely focused on topics such as the pejorative representation of Arabs and Muslims,[2] while the general portrayal of race and ethnicity in video games has received significant attention from scholars.[3] Several studies have focused on the way Arab Muslims represent Westerners and themselves in video games that are produced in the Middle East, including games made by political groups like *Special Forces* (Hezbollah, 2003)[4] as well as those produced by commercial companies such as the Saudi game *Unearthed: Trail of Ibn Battuta* (Semanoor, 2013)[5] or the Syrian-developed title *Quraish* (Dar Al-Fikr, 2005). The latter game "allows the players to witness the origin of Islam and 'replay' key battles from its early history, including the defeat of the Iranian Sassanid empire and the Byzantine Empire."[6] Other examples include *The Stone Throwers*

1. Nour Merza, "Demographics, Local Tastes Fuel Arab Video Game Industry," *Reuters*, 14 March 2012. http://www.reuters.com/article/us-saudi-gaming-idUSBRE82D10N20120314.
2. Vit Šisler, "Digital Arabs: Representation in Video Games," *European Journal of Cultural Studies* 11.2 (2008): 203-220; Ahmed Al-Rawi, "Iraqi Stereotypes in American Culture: The Case of Video Games and Films," *International Journal of Contemporary Iraqi Studies* 2.2 (2008): 225-249.
3. Anna Everett, "Serious Play: Playing with Race in Contemporary Gaming Culture," in *Handbook of Computer Game Studies*, eds. J. Raessens and J. Goldstein (MIT Press, 2005): 311-326; Dean Chan, "Playing with Race: The Ethics of Racialized Representations in E-Games," *International Review of Information Ethics* 4: 24-30; Christopher L. McGahan, *Racing Cyberculture: Minoritarian Art and Cultural Politics on the Internet* (Routledge, 2013); Yasmin B. Kafai, Gabriela T. Richard and Brendesha M. Tynes, eds., *Diversifying Barbie and Mortal Kombat: Intersectional Perspectives and Inclusive Designs in Gaming* (ETC Press, 2017); Jennifer Malkowski and Andrea M. Russworm, *Gaming Representation: Race, Gender, and Sexuality in Video Games* (Indiana University Press, 2017).
4. David Machin and Usama Suleiman, "Arab and American Computer War Games: The Influence of a Global Technology on Discourse," *Critical Discourse Studies* 3.01 (2006): 1-22; Helga Tawil Souri, "The Political Battlefield of Pro-Arab Video Games on Palestinian Screens," *Comparative Studies of South Asia, Africa and the Middle East* 27.3 (2007): 536-551.
5. Merza, "Demographics, Local Tastes," 2012.
6. Vit Šisler, "From Kuma/War to Quraish: Representation of Islam in Arab and American Video Games," in *Playing with Religion in Digital Games Playing with Religion in Digital Games*, eds. H. Campbell and G. Grieve (Indiana University Press, 2014): 109.

(Hamza, 2000), which depicts the struggle of Palestinians in Israel which was produced by individual creators as well as *Quest for Bush* (Global Islamic Media Front, 2003), which was made by altering the code of the U.S.-developed game *Quest for Saddam* (Petrilla Entertainment, 2003).[7] In addition, a few other studies have focused on the use of video games by Middle Eastern terrorist organizations such as ISIS[8] and Al-Qaeda.[9] More recently, thousands of video game apps have been developed by and for Arab users, providing new horizons of gaming experience for people living in the Middle East and the Middle Eastern diaspora, including titles such as the game *Mariam* (Salman Al-Harabi, 2017), which sparked controversy by asking players for personal information.[10] Further, by examining the top 50 mobile app games in Saudi Arabia, Qatar, Oman, Egypt and Bahrain (see Image 3.3.1), we find that many of the most popular games are actually made in the Middle East and are designed for Arabic speakers, including *Drift – Hajwala* (RABABA Games, 2016), *Puzzle games* (Mesk Lab, 2014), *Words Crush* (Zytoona, 2016) and *Blue Whale* (Umayma Asfour, 2018).[11]

In general, many games produced by Arab Muslims are made to counter hegemonic Western portrayals, which are mostly negative in nature. In this way, video games provide a venue for alternative perspectives which allow some players to more readily identify with the characters and perhaps to feel empowered.

One of the benefits of using social media are its affordances, or the ways it capacitates communication and sharing of information related to other realms. In his original theory of affordances within the discipline of ecological psychology, James Gibson mentions that the environment affords people many benefits that enhance communication and interaction.[12] The term itself was coined by Gibson in the pre-Internet era to refer to the complementary nature of people and their environments—the equivalents of users and social media in the context of this chapter—, and many scholars used the theory to explain the way social media provided functional tools for their users to further communicate and interact.[13] Put another way, there is a symbiotic relationship that binds users and technologies together: "the mutuality of actor intentions and technology capabilities that provide the potential for a particular action."[14] Previous studies have shown that people who are part of a large network are more likely to talk and share ideas,[15] since networks often provide different types of support through various channels of communication.[16] In this regard, social support can be defined as "the perception or reception of coping assistance or as attributes of one's social circle."[17] And in

7. Adrienne Shaw, "Beyond Comparison: Reframing Analysis of Video Games Produced in the Middle East," *Global Media Journal* 9.16 (2010).
8. Ahmed Al-Rawi, "Video Games, Terrorism, and ISIS's Jihad 3.0," *Terrorism and Political Violence* (2016): 1-21.
9. Jarret M. Brachman, "High-Tech Terror: Al-Qaeda's Use of New Technology," *Fletcher Forum of World Affairs* 30 (2006): 149.
10. Huffpost-Arabi, "A Game that Creates Panic in the Gulf: Kuwait is Concerned and Dubai Warned Against It after its Statement on 'Punishing Qatar,'" *Huffpost-Arabi*, 9 August 2017, http://www.huffpostarabi.com/2017/08/09/story_n_17710704.html.
11. Note that Umayma Asfour's Blue Whale is a children's game that is not related to the controversial Blue Whale Challenge that has become associated with teenagers' suicide attempts in the MENA region and elsewhere; see Al Arabiya, "A Survivor of the Blue Whale Killer [Game] Reveals What Happened to Al-Arabiya.net," 14 December 2017, *alarabiya.net*, https://bit.ly/2H1p43X; CNN, "Family Finds Clues to Teen's Suicide in Blue Whale Paintings," *CNN.com*, 17 July 2017, https://www.cnn.com/2017/07/17/health/blue-whale-suicide-game/index.html.
12. James Gibson, *The Ecological Approach to Visual Perception* (Psychology Press, 1986).
13. Bernard Enjolras, Kari Steen-Johnsen and Dag Wollebæk, "Social Media and Mobilization to Offline Demonstrations: Transcending Participatory Divides?," *New Media & Society* 15.6 (2013): 890-908; Daniel Halpern and Jennifer Gibbs, "Social Media as a Catalyst for Online Deliberation? Exploring the Affordances of Facebook and YouTube for Political Expression," *Computers in Human Behavior* 29.3 (2013): 1159-1168.
14. Samer Faraj and Bijan Azad, "The Materiality of Technology: An Affordance Perspective," in *Materiality and Organizing: Social Interaction in a Technological World*, eds. P. M. Leonardi, B. Nardi and J. Kallinikos (Oxford University Press, 2012): 237-258.
15. Jack M. McLeod, Dietram A. Scheufele, Patricia Moy, Edward M. Horowitz, R. Lance Holbert, Weiwu Zhang, Stephen Zubric and Jessica Zubric, "Understanding Deliberation: The Effects of Discussion Networks on Participation in a Public Forum," *Communication Research* 26.6 (1999): 743-774; Robert Huckfeldt, Jeanette Morehouse Mendez and Tracy Osborn, "Disagreement, Ambivalence, and Engagement: The Political Consequences of Heterogeneous Networks," *Political Psychology* 25.1 (2004): 65-95.
16. Junghyun Kim and Jong-Eun Roselyn Lee, "The Facebook Paths to Happiness: Effects of the Number of Facebook Friends and Self-Presentation on Subjective Well-Being," *CyberPsychology, Behavior, and Social Networking* 14.6 (2011): 359-364; Xiaoqian Li, Wenhong Chen and Pawel Popiel, "What Happens on Facebook Stays on Facebook? The Implications of Facebook Interaction for Perceived, Receiving, and Giving Social Support," *Computers in Human Behavior* 51 (2015): 106-113.
17. Jingbo Meng, Lourdes Martinez, Amanda Holmstrom, Minwoong Chung and Jeff Cox, "Research on Social Networking Sites and Social Support from 2004 to 2015: A Narrative Review and Directions for Future Research," *Cyberpsychology, Behavior, and Social Networking* 20.1 (2017): 44-51.

Image 3.3.1. A screenshot of Jordanian game Drift in Apple's App Store.

fact, along with a strong network, social support is regarded as one of the most importance types of affordances to mental health and well-being.[18] This is also evident in research on Internet use and online communities,[19] as well as on social media use.[20] In brief, social media engagement in connection

18. Alan Hall and Barry Wellman, "Social Networks and Social Support," in *Social Support and Health* (Academic Press, 1985): 23-41; Barry Wellman and Scot Wortley, "Different Strokes from Different Folks: Community Ties and Social Support," *American Journal of Sociology* 96.3 (1990): 558-588; Brian S. Butler, "Membership Size, Communication Activity, and Sustainability: A Resource-Based Model of Online Social Structures," *Information Systems Research* 12.4 (2001): 346-362; Schaefer, Catherine, James C. Coyne and Richard S. Lazarus, "The Health-Related Functions of Social Support," *Journal of Behavioral Medicine* 4.4 (1981): 381-406.
19. Lindsay H. Shaw and Larry M. Gant, "In Defense of the Internet: The Relationship between Internet Communication and Depression, Loneliness, Self-Esteem, and Perceived Social Support," *Cyberpsychology & Behavior* 5.2 (2002): 157-171; Louis Leung, "Stressful Life Events, Motives for Internet Use, and Social Support among Digital Lids," *CyberPsychology & Behavior* 10.2 (2006): 204-214; Shereene Z. Idriss, Joseph C. Kvedar and Alice J. Watson, "The Role of Online Support Communities: Benefits of Expanded Social Networks to Patients with Psoriasis," *Archives of Dermatology* 145.1 (2009): 46-51.
20. Christy MK Cheung, Pui-Yee Chiu and Matthew KO Lee, "Online social networks: Online Social Networks: Why Do Students Use Facebook?," *Computers in Human Behavior* 27.4 (2011): 1337-1343; Kim and Lee, "The Facebook Paths to Happiness" (2011): 359-364; Robin L. Nabi, Abby Prestin and Jiyeon So, "Facebook Friends with (Health) Benefits? Exploring Social Network Site Use and Perceptions of Social Support, Stress, and Well-Being," *Cyberpsychology, Behavior, and Social Networking* 16.10 (2013): 721-727; Eline Frison and Steven Eggermont, "The Impact of Daily Stress on Adolescents' Depressed Mood: The Role of Social Support Seeking through Facebook," *Computers in Human Behavior* 44 (2015): 315-325; Meng, et al., "Research on social networking sites," 2017.

to video gaming communities is important in many ways, including its role in cementing social support among gamers who rely on each other to become more informed and efficient in their play.

In general, different types of affordances fulfill functions similar to those emphasized by gratification theory, since gaming-related engagement on social media offers certain gratifications, including sharing experiences and finding communal support.[21] Carolyn Lin, for example, mentions that Internet use has several functions, including surveillance, escape, companionship, identity and entertainment.[22] Social media provides users with the tools to understand their environment and benefit from through affordances like seeing "who else is in a chat room, who was co-sent a message, or who are the friends of my friends on a social network site."[23] Social networks also enable the establishment of connections with like-minded users in order to gain further information, spread the word about news and gaming issues or receive psychological and moral support and validation when needed. Other social media affordances include making use of status updates, which are often used to get feedback and validation from others.[24] Other types of feedback might come from offline sources, like receiving a phone call or an actual meeting that, like gaming, "provides an awareness of the attentiveness of others to one's need for support."[25] Zheng and Yu refer to this theory in their study of the Free Lunch for Children program in China, which was launched on the social media platform Weibo.[26] Their research linked the theory of collective action to the affordances-for-practice concept, while Halpern and Gibbs used the same theory to explain how social media can be a catalyst for online deliberation.[27] Likewise, Majchrzak et al. have examined how information sharing via social media can develop into "a continuous online knowledge conversation of strangers, unexpected interpretations and re-uses, and dynamic emergence," especially by providing four types of affordances: metavoicing, triggered attending, network-informed associating and generative role-taking.[28]

In sum, social media has provided gamers with affordances for personalization of their experiences by establishing a platform for online communities whose members can support one another by sharing relevant and interesting information about a variety of topics, including new video games, strategies for playing them and cheats which allow them to restructure and/or deepen their gaming experiences.[29] This chapter also takes up O'Donnell and Consalvo's 2015 challenge to more closely examine individuals' play activities as they intersect with social media.[30] Doing so both acknowledges the importance of gaming and play to activity on social networks, and also shows how activities on social media can shape game culture. With this in mind, the remainder of this chapter will offer an analysis focused on the nature of social media use by Middle East online gaming communities.

21. Robert LaRose, Dana Mastro and Matthew S. Eastin, "Understanding Internet Usage: A Social-Cognitive Approach to Uses and Gratifications," *Social Science Computer Review* 19.4 (2001): 395-413.
22. Carolyn A. Lin, "Online Service Adoption Likelihood," *Journal of Advertising Research* 39 (1999): 79-89.
23. Bernie Hogan and Anabel Quan-Haase, "Persistence and Change in Social Media," *Bulletin of Science, Technology & Society* 30.5 (2010): 309-315.
24. Keith N. Hampton, Chul-joo Lee and Eun Ja Her, "How New Media Affords Network Diversity: Direct and Mediated Access to Social Capital through Participation in Local Social Settings," *New Media & Society* 13.7 (2011): 1031-1049.
25. Weixu Lu and Keith N. Hampton, "Beyond the Power of Networks: Differentiating Network Structure from Social Media Affordances for Perceived Social Support," *New Media & Society* 19.6 (2017): 861-879.
26. Yingqin Zheng and Ai Yu, "Affordances of Social Media in Collective Action: The Case of Free Lunch for Children in China," *Information Systems Journal* 26.3 (2016): 289-313.
27. Halpern and Gibbs, "Social Media," 2013.
28. Ann Majchrzak, Samer Faraj, Gerald C. Kane and Bijan Azad, "The Contradictory Influence of Social Media Affordances on Online Communal Knowledge Sharing," *Journal of Computer-Mediated Communication* 19.1 (2013): 38-55.
29. Mia Consalvo, *Cheating: Gaining Advantage in Videogames* (MIT Press, 2009).
30. Casey O'Donnell and Mia Consalvo, "Games Are Social/Media (ted)/Technology Too...," *Social Media Society* 1.1 (2015).

ANALYZING GAMING-RELATED SOCIAL MEDIA ACTIVITY IN THE MIDDLE EAST

The study analyzes two sets of data; the first one was taken from Twitter by investigating all the Arabic tweets associated with the hashtag #PokemonGo—referencing the wildly popular augmented reality mobile game *Pokémon GO* (Niantic, 2016)—taken from a total of 11,190,283 tweets posted between 23 July 2016 and 16 August 2017 by 3,248,208 unique users (see Table 3.3.1). The data was drawn from the Boston University Twitter Collection and Analysis Toolkit (BU-TCAT).[31]

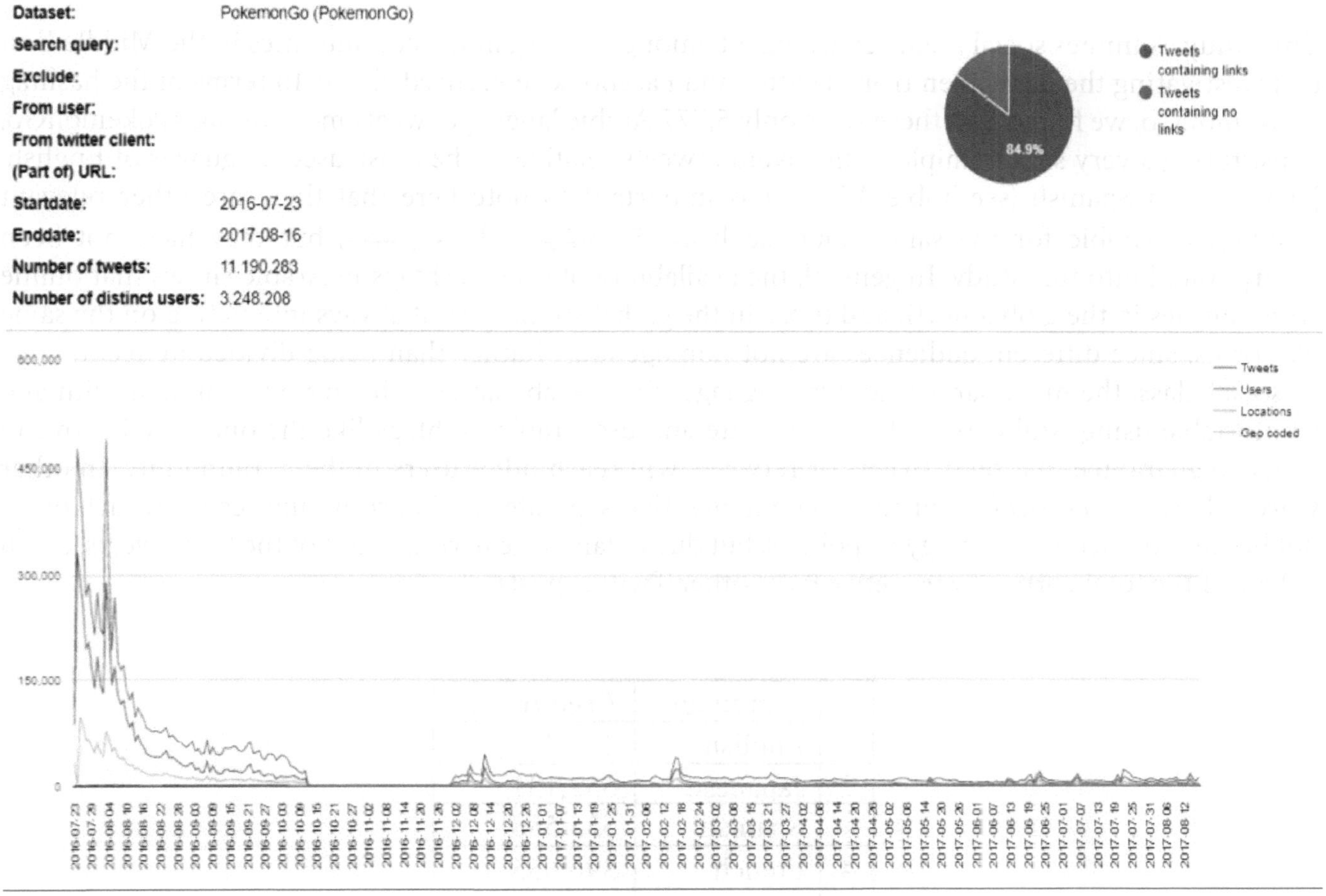

Table 3.3.1. A time series distribution of Tweets mentioning the hashtag #PokemonGo.

The second set of data was taken from Facebook. About 65,000 comments were mined on 6 December 2016 using an online tool called N-Capture for NViVO, and three Arabic Facebook pages were examined: eSports Middle East (42,673 likes, 6,447 comments, 936 images, 2,328 posts),[32] PlayStation Middle East (332,363 likes, 57,323 comments, 2,407 images, 3,515 posts)[33] and Games Middle East (77,511 likes, 1,238 comments, 112 images, 169 posts).[34] The latter Facebook page was removed from Facebook in early 2017 for unknown reasons. These three Facebook pages were selected after they were determined through Facebook searches in Arabic to be the most popular based on the number of likes.

Textual analysis of the overall comments was conducted by using a computer-based program called

31. Erik Borra and Bernhard Rieder, "Programmed Method: Developing a Toolset for Capturing and Analyzing Tweets," *Aslib Journal of Information Management* 66.3 (2014): 262-278; Jacob Groshek, "Twitter Collection and Analysis Toolkit (TCAT) at Boston University," *bu.edu*, 2014, http://www.bu.edu/com/bu-tcat/.
32. eSports Middle East, Facebook Group, https://www.facebook.com/ESME.
33. PlayStation Middle East, Facebook Group, https://www.facebook.com/PlayStationME.
34. Games Middle East, Facebook Group, https://www.facebook.com/gamesmiddleeast.

QDA Miner-Word Stat that provides indicators of audiences' online interactions. A further aspect of the study involved researching the top ten most-liked Facebook posts on each site in order to understand the issues most frequently mentioned by players in the Middle East. Finally, a social network analysis of the three Facebook pages and their connections with other pages was made using Netvizz[35] and was visually presented using Gephi, an open-source software application.[36] These tools are important in both mining the data and visualizing it, helping to offer insight into the nature of the Facebook groups and the connections they have with other online groups and communities.

This study examines social media engagement among online gaming communities in the Middle East by investigating the data taken from Twitter and Facebook referenced above. In terms of the hashtag #PokemonGo, we found that there were only 5,777 Arabic language tweets mentioning #PokemonGo, constituting a very small sample of the overall tweets relative to the most-used languages of English, Japanese and Spanish (see Table 3.3.2). It is important to note here that there are other relevant hashtags in Arabic for the same game, such as بوكيمون كو and بوكيمون جو, but they have not been incorporated into this study. In general, the availability of such hashtags in Arabic shows that online communities in the global north and those in the global south are not always interacting on the same platforms, since different audiences are not homogenous. Rather than being divided by technology or social class, the main barrier here is language, since Arab gamers who are only familiar with and comfortable using Arabic seem to disseminate and use Arabic hashtags like the ones cited above in order to guarantee that their tweets or retweets will reach other users in their community. In other words, there are *sphericules,*[37] or filtering bubbles, that separate gaming communities from each other not because of income, ideology or politics, but due to language barriers. Out of the total tweets, 3,036 (52.5% of the total corpus) were retweets of other Twitter posts.

	Language	Frequency
1	English	2,844,209
2	Japanese	553,131
3	Spanish	535,588
4	French	396,655
5	Thai	196,608

Table 3.3.2. The top five most-used languages associated with the hashtag #PokemonGo.

As for the most retweeted posts, they fell into several categories, including game cheats, technical advice, humor and social activism. We found that the most popular tweet (n=225) was related to a humorous caption for a photo showing a couple caught in a seemingly compromising position with the man pleading with another man present that: "RT @Ramy_khalifaa: Of course you won't believe me if I swear that I'm here to catch a Pikachu #PokemonGO" (see Image 3.3.2).[38] The second-most retweeted post (n=196) satirizes the devotion of football fans, featuring a photograph of two men—one perhaps chasing the other—who are in street clothes and running on a soccer pitch that states: "RT @Muhamed_samir95: When you meet your Pokemon and try to catch it???? #PokemonGO" (see Image 3.3.3).[39]

35. Bernhard Rieder, "Studying Facebook via Data Extraction: The Netvizz Application," in *Proceedings of the 5th Annual ACM Web Science Conference* (ACM, 2013), 346-355.
36. Mathieu Bastian, Sebastien Heymann and Mathieu Jacomy, "Gephi: An Open Source Software for Exploring and Manipulating Networks," *Icwsm* 8 (2009): 361-362.
37. Ted Gitlin, "Public Sphere or Public Sphericules?," in *Media, Ritual and Identity*, eds. J. Curran and T. Liebes, (Routledge, 2002)" 168.
38. @Ramyy_Rkhalifa, tweet, 11 July 2016, https://t.co/kUrRcSbaZ1.

Image 3.3.2. The most retweeted post in Arabic (n=225).

The other top retweets were related to providing practical guidelines on how to use cheats and hacks. For example, the third-most retweeted post (n=170) was for a YouTube video that explains how to supposedly catch a limitless number of Pokémon without a hack.[40] The fourth-most retweeted post (n=125) was on how to install *Pokémon GO* on the iPhone,[41] similar to the sixth-most retweeted post (n=119), which dealt with how to install the game on desktop computers or laptops.[42] The fifth-most retweeted post (n=121) stated, "Rescue Syria's children. Rescue Syria #PokemonGO" (see Image 3.3.4),[43] indicating a clear intention to spread the word about the plight of Syrian children by associating their plight with the hashtag #PokemonGo. This post is popular because it functions as a reminder to Arab Twitter users about an urgent matter that requires immediate intervention, unlike playing games like *Pokémon GO*.

39. @Ellonsh95, tweet, 11 July 2016, https://t.co/jKpaKD7KSE.
40. Kharbatsho, YouTube video, 23 July 2016, https://t.co/DZA4IbPBwv.
41. Kharbatsho, YouTube video, 15 July 2016, https://t.co/PLZl3YEMCn.
42. Kharbatsho, YouTube video, 30 July 2016, https://t.co/m9kziR3fVK.
43. @ahmednord55, tweet, 22 July 2016, https://t.co/2iz6z37wLR.

Image 3.3.3. "When you meet your Pokemon and try to catch it???? #PokemonGO."

Another connection to Syria we observed on social media came in posts linking the capture of a Russian pilot to catching Pokémon. Several Twitter users commented on a tweet that states: "RT @adilfstk: Aleppo is being liberating and is victorious while some brothers are busy catching Pokemons #PokemonGO,"[44] while another one mentions that Pokémon were found in Aleppo (see Image 3.3.5).[45] There is no doubt that there is an intended irony here, aimed at mocking those who would fervently race to take pictures of the captured Russian pilot despite his obvious suffering. Finally, it is important to note that this is a clear example of the convergence of different social media platforms, as users often create links to their Facebook pages and YouTube channels to better connect with other online communities and spread information to as many people as possible. The remaining most-popular tweets were related to game hacks, tutorials and general news on Pokémon Go. This analysis demonstrates the value of studying the intersection of games and social media—in this case Twitter. Players can use/display gaming capital to show interest in the game, offer information to other players and even relate the game to current events, in both serious and humorous ways. Gaming is not always linked to pure entertainment, as shown in the highly evident political tone of the example below, demonstrating the ways politics and gaming frequently intersect. In a country afflicted with war and terrorism such as Syria, gaming becomes another venue for

44. @adilfstk, tweet, 1 August 2016, https://t.co/iB9qYSLPtx.
45. @AboJafarMgarbel, tweet, 1 August 2016, https://t.co/WoxAenzd2S.

Image 3.3.4. Syrian children appealing for help by using Pikachu and Pokémon GO.

humorous expressions along with the ideological rejection of foreign military intervention in the region.

With regard to the Facebook data, 65,008 comments posted by members of the three Facebook groups were analyzed using a computer program called QDA Minter 4- Word Stat. Two of the Facebook groups belong to gaming companies, while the third page was a private page that was unexpectedly removed for unknown reasons. Neither the collected images (n=3,505) nor the posts sent by the Facebook page administrators (n=6,012) were included in the analysis. In order to understand the main statements shared among the social media audiences, we examined the top 50 most recurrent phrases of three-to-four words (see Table 3.3.3). The top most recurrent phrase was related to cheats, since the social media community seemed to be more focused on finding new ways to win or identifying possible cheaters. The phrase was repeatedly used in different formats (ranked 3rd, 10th, 16th and 26th). The second-most recurrent phrase references a popular YouTube channel called "Arab

Image 3.3.5. The link between capturing a Russian pilot and catching Pokémon (the tweet mentions "Discovering a PokemonGo in Aleppo").

Nerds," which posts news on game hacks and cheats.[46] Image 3.3.6 provides a visual representation of the top 100 phrases and their connections with one another. Each bubble represents a phrase, and the larger the bubble the more frequent the particular phrase was used (which is why the term "cheats, cheats, cheats" occupies the largest bubble).

An examination of the top most-liked posts shows that they are exclusively related to news about new video games and/or announcing prizes or special offers for Facebook audiences in order to encourage them to be more engaged with the companies' marketing campaigns. Here, companies are offering various rewards in order to further engage customers with their products, advertise new games, create brand loyalty and generate increased sales. Indeed, social media outlets are vital in connecting these companies with their customers, who can also be regarded as fans who often find communal spaces and connect with each other on the companies' Facebook pages (see Image 3.3.7). Only one of the top posts shared by the PlayStation Middle East Facebook page was not related to marketing. It asked the question: "Every second that passes in the gamers' lives is unique and abnormal. This is how we live our lives as PS4 players. Do you agree with us?." The post aimed to engage gamers by appealing to their emotional connection to gaming, and it received 1,026 likes, achieving the rank of the eighth-most liked post.[47]

46. DvLZGaME | دفلزقيم, YouTube video, 15 July 2018, https://www.youtube.com/user/DvLZGaME/featured.
47. The same company intends to continuously customize its print ads in order to make them more suitable to the Middle Eastern audiences. See, for example, Image 3.3.7.

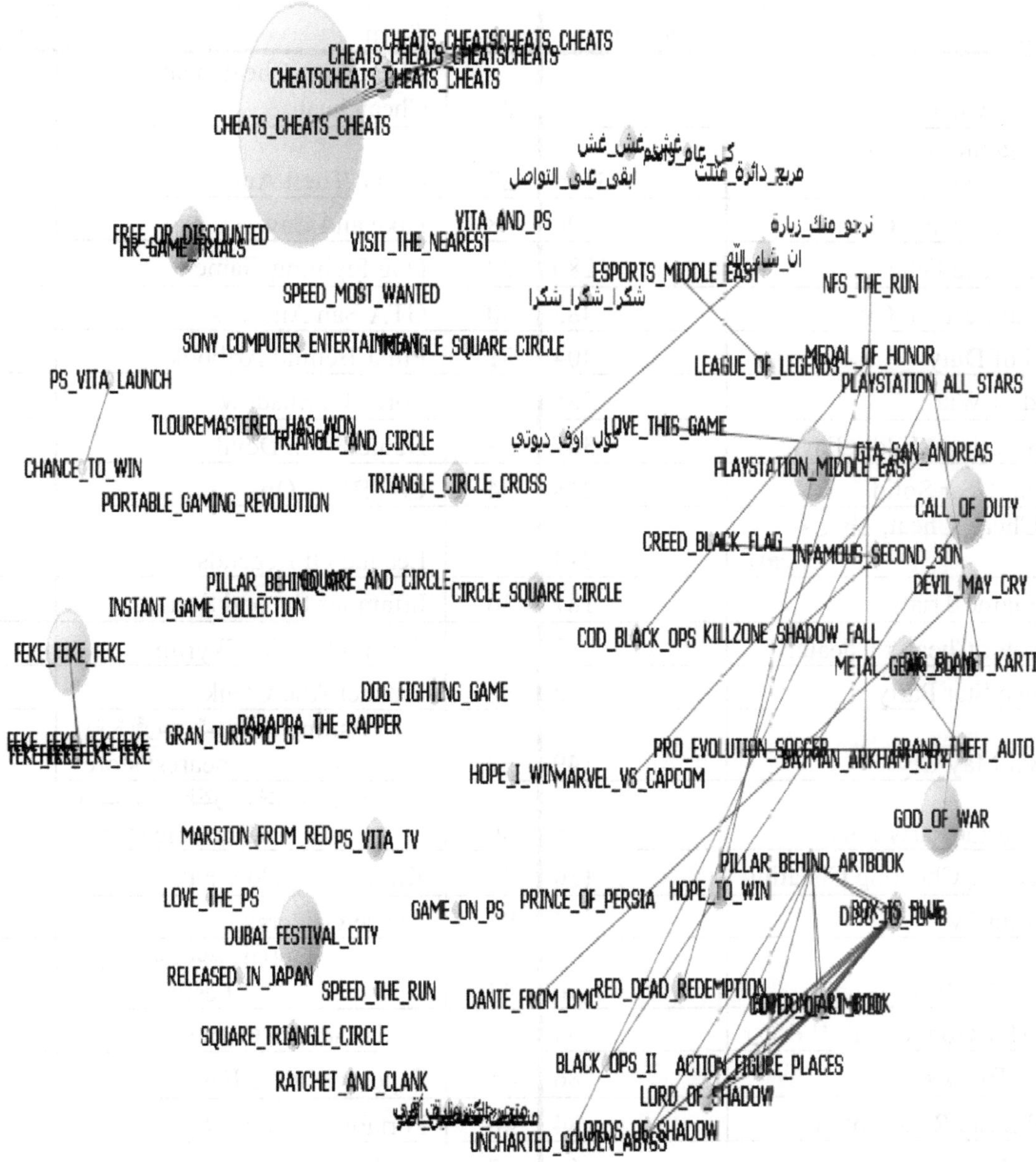

Image 3.3.6. The top 100 most frequently used phrases by Facebook audiences.

Finally, Images 3.3.8 and 3.3.9 provide a visualization of the social networking links among two Facebook pages by highlighting the connections each page has with other pages. The PlayStation Middle East page has stronger connections with other similar pages, as we can see that the majority of the connected Facebook pages are related to video gaming communities in the Middle East region, which reflects the close connections that exist among gamers.

As mentioned above, social media provides users with affordances for functional and social support. For example, many gamers from Yemen and Syria often complained on Facebook about the lack of customer support in their own countries, while other users often provided them with tips on where to purchase new games and find cheats. One user, for example, asked how to find alternative methods to update *Battlefield 4* (Electronic Arts, 2013) since his Internet connection in Syria was weak and electricity periodically got disconnected. Another user warned PlayStation about terrorism threats

	Term	Frequency		Term	Frequency
1	Cheats Cheats Cheats	10490	26	Cheatcheat Cheatcheat Cheatcheat	56
2	Dvlzgame Dvlzgame Dvlzgame	3106	27	Grand Theft Auto	47
3	Cheate Cheate Cheate	1496	28	Fake and Gay	45
4	Feke Feke Feke	1280	29	Dog Fighting Game	44
5	Dubai Festival City	482	30	GTA San Andreas	43
6	Call of Duty	404	31	Pillar Behind Artbook	42
7	God of War	385	32	Lords Of Shadow	38
8	Playstation Middle East	367	33	Dante From Devil	36
9	Metal Gear Solid	218	34	Cod Black Ops	35
10	(Cheat, Cheat, غش غش غش Cheat)	213	35	League Of Legends	35
11	Hr Game Trials	187	36	Infamous Second Son	35
12	Cheater Cheater Cheater	183	37	Skyrim Skyrim Skyrim	35
13	Dance Star Party	182	38	Ratchet And Clank	34
14	Devil May Cry	149	39	(visiting the زيارة أقرب متجر nearest store)	33
15	Dancestar Party Hits	146	40	(nearest أقرب متجر إلكترونيات electronic store)	33
16	Cheating Cheating Cheating	130	41	Killzone Shadow Fall	32
17	Ps Vita Tv	124	42	Prince Of Persia	28
18	Hope To Win	96	43	(Dubai دبي فيستفال سيتي Festival city)	28
19	(By God's will) ان شاء الله	94	44	Circle Square Circle	27
20	Duty Black Ops	86	45	Esports Middle East	25
21	Red Dead Redemption	84	46	Portable Gaming Revolution	25
22	Lord Of Shadow	66	47	Medal Of Honor	24
23	Tlouremastered Has Won	64	48	Hope I Win	24
24	Places Are Swapped	62	49	Instant Game Collection	24
25	Action Figure Places	59	50	Parappa The Rapper	23

Table 3.3.3. The top 50 most frequently used phrases by Facebook audiences.

and recommends monitoring the social media chat rooms of its games because "there are terrorist groups that use the game to brainwash the minds of children and youth." The user stresses that "we do not want to abandon PlayStation at all because we were raised since it first launched and we want to continue with it until the end." In this regard, Facebook allows this user and many others to directly interact with the video game provider (who, we should note, may or may not be taking an active role in responding to users) as well as with like-minded people who can provide extra support, guidelines and advice on different gaming-related issues.

Indeed, online space provides a venue for Middle Eastern gamers to share expressions on myriad

Image 3.3.7. An example of cultural adaptations in PlayStation marketing strategies for the Middle East.

issues, including the portrayal of Muslim Arabs in video games. For instance, one user commented on a post by eSports Middle East on *Watch Dogs* video game (Ubisoft, 2014) that depicts a criminal character having clear Muslim/Arab features.[48] One Facebook user responds by stating that "it is shameful that some Muslims support Western games that negatively portray Islam," which is followed by a variety of responses, often agreeing with the above statement. However, many other gamers stress a different view; for instance, one Facebook user speaks of how "Muslims themselves distort the image of Islam more than anyone else," while another one stresses how Da'esh (ISIS) is itself an Islamic group. Another user agrees with the above, saying: "Trust me….ur average day people…give them more juice than they cant even handle….So if the guy and the girl in this game were christians or jews…that would be alright with u?" Finally, one more user mentions the following in relation to this online debate: "The [game] developers have Raised… this idea , that muslims are terrorist , muslims do bad things , and its [sic] not too far, you can see Da'esh [and] what [it] is doing…. the world see[s] us as terrorist because what happened in syria, and the Bombing in Lebanon, and what's happening already in Iraq…." The above responses are not unusual—far more often, there are voices that blindly defend Islam and Muslims, but it seems that the nature of the gaming community's discourse is somehow different from the mainstream.[49] A few responses from conservative voices objected that some gamers spend too much time playing instead of praying, while a few others expressed concern over the impact of games on their children's beliefs, highlighting a cultural tension between Muslim audiences and Western values. Interestingly, these voices were often silenced or mocked by other gamers, making us question to what extent they were members of the group, or if they came to the space mainly to critique those active within it.

48. http://es.me/2014/06/222014 ,/واتش-دوغز-تسيء-للمسلمين.

49. Ahmed Al-Rawi, "Online Reactions to the Muhammad Cartoons: YouTube and the Virtual Ummah," *Journal for the Scientific Study of Religion* 54.2 (2015): 261-276; Ahmed Al-Rawi, "Facebook as a Virtual Mosque: The Online Protest Against Innocence of Muslims," *Culture and Religion* 17.1 (2016): 19-34.

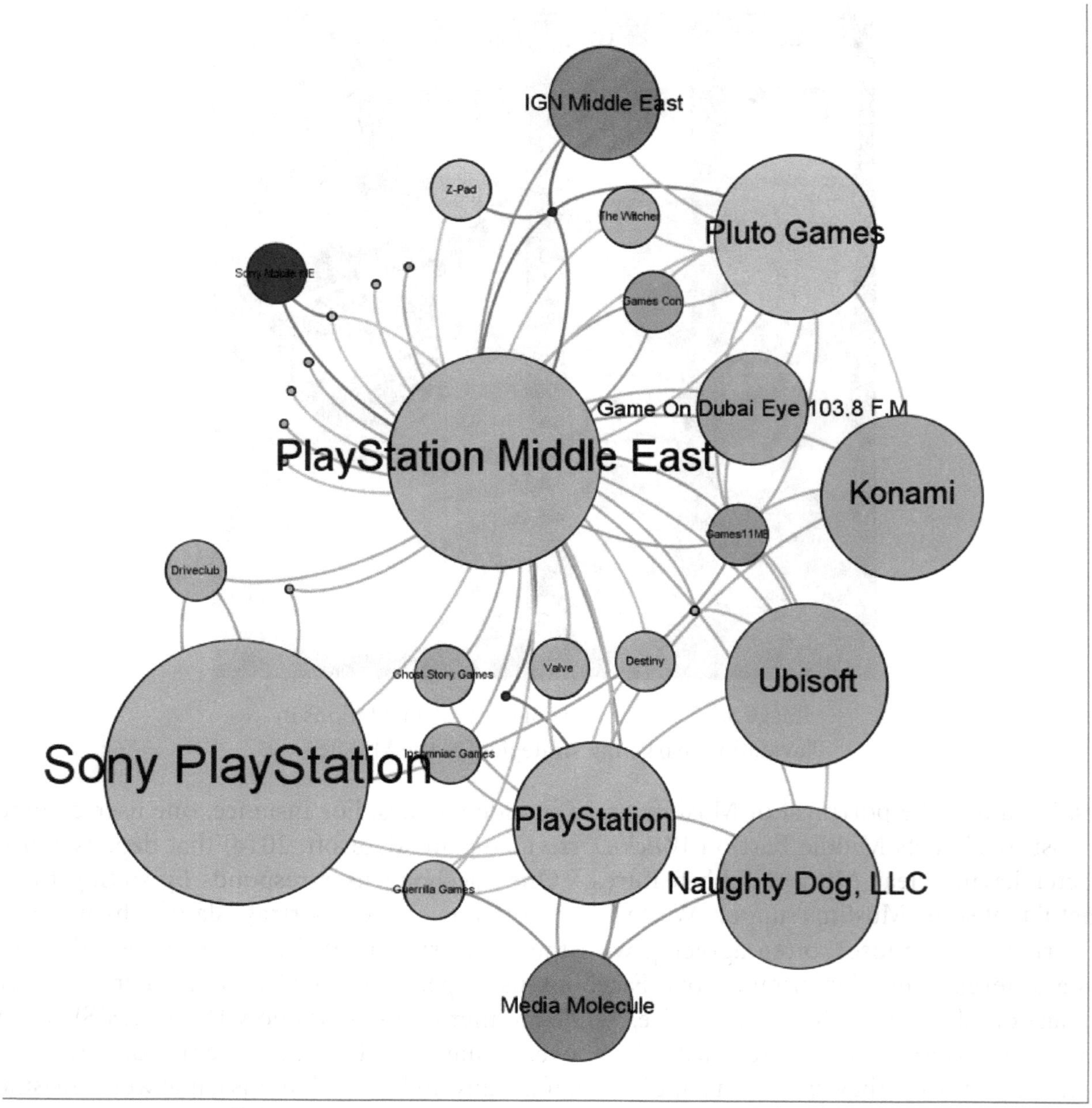

Image 3.3.8. Social networking analysis of PlayStation-Middle East Facebook page.

CONCLUSION

To sum up, different social media channels provide players in the Middle East with affordances to community-building, including various venues in which to share jokes and get practical information, tips, cheats, hacks and guidelines on how to better enhance their gaming experience; as well as opportunities to build meaningful and impactful bonds among players through the use of related but distinct media platforms—just like players in North America, Europe and Asia. More importantly, the online gaming community is publicly constructed, and therefore is not homogenous in nature and includes individuals of both liberal and conservative viewpoints. A shared identity is based on the commonalities that gamers feel due to their use of Arabic along with English, their geographical proximity and their sense of shared history and possibly religion. The war in Syria, for example, was often cited by Twitter users in order to remind gamers of the important issues taking place in the Middle East. In this way, gaming—which is frequently viewed as an activity exclusively dedicated

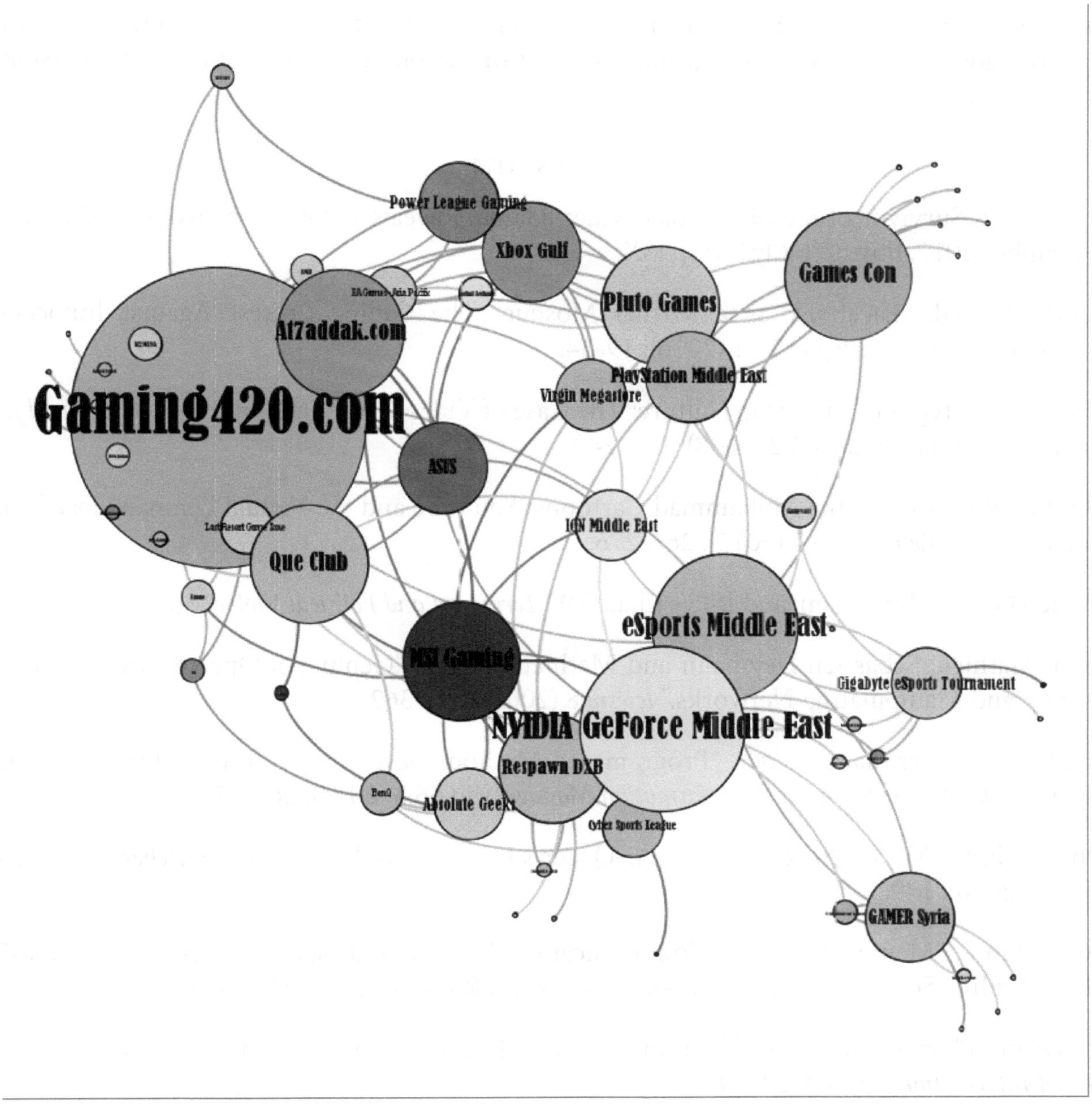

Image 3.3.9. Social networking analysis of eSports Middle East Facebook page.

to entertainment—is being utilized by Arab activists to raise awareness about the plight of Syrian refugees and civilians and to seek ways to assist the victims of war. Politics intersect frequently with the gaming experience due to the rapid and ongoing political, economic and social reforms taking place in the region. Future research might focus on other social media platforms such as YouTube, which has become increasingly popular in many Arab countries, as large online gaming communities are also being formed on this platform. In fact, YouTube can be regarded as an important alternative media outlet and entertainment hub in countries like Saudi Arabia, which has only recently legalized movie theatres. In addition, ethnographic research involving interviews with Middle Eastern game makers remains a highly under-researched area of study despite the fact that there are plenty of game companies and individual developers in countries such as Jordan. Finally, empirical research on Middle Eastern gaming audiences remains highly lacking, especially if one takes into account that young people in countries afflicted with violence, such as Iraq, are increasingly playing video games instead of leaving their homes as a safety measure. For these and so many other Middle Eastern players in different situations and contexts, gaming remains one of the most important entertainment venues available, and establishes the groundwork for the development of important relationships and social support.

WORKS CITED

Al Arabiya. "A Survivor of the Blue Whale Killer [Game] Reveals What Happened to Al-Arabiya.net." 14 December 2017, https://bit.ly/2H1p43X.

Al-Rawi, Ahmed. "Facebook as a Virtual Mosque: The Online Protest Against Innocence of Muslims." *Culture and Religion* 17.1 (2016): 19-34.

—. "Iraqi Stereotypes in American Culture: The Case of Video Games and Films." *International Journal of Contemporary Iraqi Studies* 2.2 (2008): 225-249.

—. "Online Reactions to the Muhammad Cartoons: YouTube and the Virtual Ummah." *Journal for the Scientific Study of Religion* 54.2 (2015): 261-276.

—. "Video Games, Terrorism, and ISIS's Jihad 3.0." *Terrorism and Political Violence* (2016): 1-21.

Bastian, Mathieu, Sebastien Heymann and Mathieu Jacomy. "Gephi: An Open Source Software for Exploring and Manipulating Networks." *Icwsm* 8 (2009): 361-362.

Borra, Erik and Bernhard Rieder. "Programmed Method: Developing a Toolset for Capturing and Analyzing Tweets." *Aslib Journal of Information Management* 66.3 (2014): 262-278

Brachman, Jarret M. "High-Tech Terror: Al-Qaeda's Use of New Technology." *Fletcher Forum of World Affairs* 30 (2006): 149.

Butler, Brian S. "Membership Size, Communication Activity, and Sustainability: A Resource-Based Model of Online Social Structures." *Information Systems Research* 12.4 (2001): 346-362.

Chan, Dean. "Playing with Race: The Ethics of Racialized Representations in E-Games." *International Review of Information Ethics* 4: 24-30.

Cheung, Christy MK, Pui-Yee Chiu and Matthew KO Lee. "Online Social Networks: Why Do Students Use Facebook?." *Computers in Human Behavior* 27.4 (2011): 1337-1343.

CNN. "Family Finds Clues to Teen's Suicide in Blue Whale Paintings." 17 July 2017, https://www.cnn.com/2017/07/17/health/blue-whale-suicide-game/index.html.

Consalvo, Mia. *Cheating: Gaining Advantage in Videogames*. MIT Press, 2009.

Enjolras, Bernard, Kari Steen-Johnsen and Dag Wollebæk. "Social Media and Mobilization to Offline Demonstrations: Transcending Participatory Divides?" *New Media & Society* 15.6 (2013): 890-908.

Everett, Anna. "Serious Play: Playing with Race in Contemporary Gaming Culture." In *Handbook of Computer Game Studies*, edited by J. Raessens & J. Goldstein. MIT Press, 2005: 311-326.

Faraj, Samer and Bijan Azad. "The Materiality of Technology: An Affordance Perspective." In

Materiality and Organizing: Social Interaction in a Technological World, edited by P. M. Leonardi, B. Nardi and J. Kallinikos, 237-258. Oxford University Press, 2012.

Frison, Eline and Steven Eggermont. "The Impact of Daily Stress on Adolescents' Depressed Mood: The Role of Social Support Seeking through Facebook." *Computers in Human Behavior* 44 (2015): 315-325.

Gibson, James. *The Ecological Approach to Visual Perception*. Psychology Press, 1986.

Gitlin, Ted. "Public Sphere or Public Sphericules?" In *Media, Ritual and Identity*, edited by J. Curran and T. Liebes. Routledge, 2002: 168.

Groshek, Jacob. "Twitter Collection and Analysis Toolkit (TCAT) at Boston University." 2014, http://www.bu.edu/com/bu-tcat/.

Hall, Alan and Barry Wellman. "Social Networks and Social Support." In Syme, S. Leonard (Ed). *Social Support and Health*. Academic Press, 1985: 23-41.

Halpern, Daniel and Jennifer Gibbs. "Social Media as a Catalyst for Online Deliberation? Exploring the Affordances of Facebook and YouTube for Political Expression." *Computers in Human Behavior* 29.3 (2013): 1159-1168.

Hampton, Keith N., Chul-joo Lee and Eun Ja Her. "How New Media Affords Network Diversity: Direct and Mediated Access to Social Capital through Participation in Local Social Settings." *New Media & Society* 13.7 (2011): 1031-1049.

Hogan, Bernie and Anabel Quan-Haase. "Persistence and Change in Social Media." *Bulletin of Science, Technology & Society* 30.5 (2010): 309-315.

Huckfeldt, Robert, Jeanette Morehouse Mendez and Tracy Osborn. "Disagreement, Ambivalence, and Engagement: The Political Consequences of Heterogeneous Networks." *Political Psychology* 25.1 (2004): 65-95.

Huffpost-Arabi. "A Game that Creates Panic in the Gulf: Kuwait is Concerned and Dubai Warned Against It after its Statement on 'Punishing Qatar.'" 9 August 2017, http://www.huffpostarabi.com/2017/08/09/story_n_17710704.html.

Idriss, Shereene Z., Joseph C. Kvedar and Alice J. Watson. "The Role of Online Support Communities: Benefits of Expanded Social Networks to Patients with Psoriasis." *Archives of Dermatology* 145.1 (2009): 46-51.

Kafai, Yasmin B., Gabriela T. Richard and Brendesha M. Tynes, eds. *Diversifying Barbie and Mortal Kombat: Intersectional Perspectives and Inclusive Designs in Gaming*. ETC Press, 2017.

Kim, Junghyun and Jong-Eun Roselyn Lee. "The Facebook Paths to Happiness: Effects of the Number of Facebook Friends and Self-Presentation on Subjective Well-Being." *CyberPsychology, Behavior, and Social Networking* 14.6 (2011): 359-364.

LaRose, Robert, Dana Mastro and Matthew S. Eastin. "Understanding Internet Usage: A Social-Cognitive Approach to Uses and Gratifications." *Social Science Computer Review* 19.4 (2001): 395-413.

Leung, Louis. "Stressful Life Events, Motives for Internet Use, and Social Support among Digital Lids." *CyberPsychology & Behavior* 10.2 (2006): 204-214.

Li, Xiaoqian, Wenhong Chen and Pawel Popiel. "What Happens on Facebook Stays on Facebook? The Implications of Facebook Interaction for Perceived, Receiving, and Giving Social Support." *Computers in Human Behavior* 51 (2015): 106-113.

Lin, Carolyn A. "Online Service Adoption Likelihood." *Journal of Advertising Research* 39 (1999): 79-89.

Lu, Weixu and Keith N. Hampton. "Beyond the Power of Networks: Differentiating Network Structure from Social Media Affordances for Perceived Social Support." *New Media & Society* 19.6 (2017): 861-879.

Machin, David and Usama Suleiman. "Arab and American Computer War Games: The Influence of a Global Technology on Discourse." *Critical Discourse Studies* 3.01 (2006): 1-22.

Majchrzak, Ann, Samer Faraj, Gerald C. Kane and Bijan Azad. "The Contradictory Influence of Social Media Affordances on Online Communal Knowledge Sharing." *Journal of Computer-Mediated Communication* 19.1 (2013): 38-55.

Malkowski, Jennifer and Andrea M. Russworm. *Gaming Representation: Race, Gender, and Sexuality in Video Games*. Indiana University Press, 2017.

McGahan, Christopher L. *Racing Cyberculture: Minoritarian Art and Cultural Politics on the Internet*. Routledge, 2013

McLeod, Jack M., Dietram A. Scheufele, Patricia Moy, Edward M. Horowitz, R. Lance Holbert, Weiwu Zhang, Stephen Zubric and Jessica Zubric. "Understanding Deliberation: The Effects of Discussion Networks on Participation in a Public Forum." *Communication Research* 26.6 (1999): 743-774.

Meng, Jingbo, Lourdes Martinez, Amanda Holmstrom, Minwoong Chung and Jeff Cox. "Research on Social Networking Sites and Social Support from 2004 to 2015: A Narrative Review and Directions for Future Research." *Cyberpsychology, Behavior, and Social Networking* 20.1 (2017): 44-51.

Merza, Nour. "Demographics, Local Tastes Fuel Arab Video Game Industry." Reuters. 14 March 2012. http://www.reuters.com/article/us-saudi-gaming-idUSBRE82D10N20120314.

Nabi, Robin L., Abby Prestin and Jiyeon So. "Facebook Friends with (Health) Benefits? Exploring Social Network Site Use and Perceptions of Social Support, Stress, and Well-Being." *Cyberpsychology, Behavior, and Social Networking* 16.10 (2013): 721-727.

O'Donnell, Casey and Mia Consalvo. "Games Are Social/Media(ted)/Technology Too..." *Social Media Society* 1.1 (2015).

Rieder, Bernhard. "Studying Facebook via Data Extraction: The Netvizz Application." In *Proceedings of the 5th Annual ACM Web Science Conference*. ACM, 2013: 346-355.

Schaefer, Catherine, James C. Coyne and Richard S. Lazarus. "The Health-Related Functions of Social Support." *Journal of Behavioral Medicine* 4.4 (1981): 381-406.

Shaw, Adrienne. "Beyond Comparison: Reframing Analysis of Video Games Produced in the Middle East." *Global Media Journal* 9.16 (2010).

Shaw, Lindsay H. and Larry M. Gant. "In Defense of the Internet The Relationship between Internet Communication and Depression, Loneliness, Self-Esteem, and Perceived Social Support." *Cyberpsychology & Behavior* 5.2 (2002): 157-171.

Šisler, Vit. "Digital Arabs: Representation in Video Games." *European Journal of Cultural Studies* 11.2 (2008): 203-220.

—. "From Kuma/War to Quraish: Representation of Islam in Arab and American Video Games." In *Playing with Religion in Digital Games*, edited by H. Campbell and G. Grieve. Indiana University Press, 2014.

Souri, Helga Tawil. "The Political Battlefield of Pro-Arab Video Games on Palestinian Screens." *Comparative Studies of South Asia, Africa and the Middle East* 27.3 (2007): 536-551.

Wellman, Barry and Scot Wortley. "Different Strokes from Different Folks: Community Ties and Social Support." *American Journal of Sociology* 96.3 (1990): 558-588.

Zheng, Yingqin and Ai Yu. "Affordances of Social Media in Collective Action: The Case of Free Lunch for Children in China." *Information Systems Journal* 26.3 (2016): 289-313.

THE NUANCES OF VIDEO GAME CURATION

LESSONS FROM ARGENTINA

MARÍA LUJÁN OULTON

"Add the word 'art' and you instantly create a problem."[1]

Video games have managed to permeate all levels of society and are fast on their way to becoming the dominant medium of the 21st century, like the moving image was for the 20th century and the photograph was before both of them. Eric Zimmerman's 2013 "Manifesto for the Ludic Century" summarizes in a concrete and direct manner the various reasons why we could assert we are living in the age of play.[2] Is there, then, no escape from this playful present? Characterizing games as the Copernican twist for the 21th century may be putting too much responsibility on a medium that is still fighting to shake its reputation as a form of entertainment alone, but regardless, video games are prepared for the battle.

So powerful is video games' capacity to break down boundaries that even the normally hermetic and impenetrable art world has been drawn into their technological magic circle. Perhaps it was just a matter of time, after all a flirtation between games and art has existed for centuries, as Johan Huizinga noted in *Homo Ludens*, when he declared, "All art derives from play."[3] Dadaism is one of the usual suspects when analyzing the connections between games and art, but there are traces of this intricate relationship that can be found much further back, for example in hieroglyphic depictions of the ancient Egyptian board game of Senet, dating to c. 3100 BCE. On a parallel path, art has a lengthy history of experimenting with technology, and there is a broad and deep discussion among scholars, critics and curators regarding the place and role of new media art within the art world.[4] In this context, video games represent another device with which to experiment, a logical continuation of the artistic exploration of the notions of interaction and immersion. As Arthur Danto has observed, "[n]ot everything is possible at every time,"[5] meaning that certain artworks simply could not be inserted as artworks into certain periods of art history.Since 2005, new art media curator Steve Dietz has remarked on the explosion of artistic activity aroused since the invention of the World Wide Web in the early 1990s. Dietz has long reflected on the impact that new media art has on museum collection practices, along with the importance of establishing new ground rules for this curatorship that must take into account research, presentation and conservation: "Regardless of institutional structure [...] it is important to consider how to integrate new media art into the museum's collection practices as well as to consider how its distinctive features raise certain conceptual issues and pragmatic concerns."[6] Recent scholarship exploring the historical relationship between video games and the art

1. Geert Lovink, "New Media Arts at the Crossroads," Paper presented at Conference at Argos Center for Art and New Media, Brussels, 2007.
2. Eric Zimmerman, "Manifesto for a Ludic Century," *Being Playful: Eric Zimmerman's Game Design Blog*, 9 September 2013, https://ericzimmerman.wordpress.com/2013/09/09/manifesto-for-a-ludic-century/.
3. Johan Huizinga, *Homo Ludens* (Emecé, 1968): 65
4. For deeper insight into this matter, see Domenico Quaranta, *Beyond New Media Art* (Link, 2013). Throughout the book Quaranta explores the historical, sociological and conceptual roots of New Media while suggesting new critical and curatorial strategies for its insertion in the contemporary art field.
5. Arthur Danto, *The Transfiguration of the Commonplace: A Philosophy of Art* (Harvard University Press), 44.
6. Steve Dietz, Collecting New-Media Art: Just Like Anything Else, Only Different," *NeMe.org*, 2005, http://www.neme.org/texts/collecting-new-media-art.

world, such as John Sharp's *Works of Game: On the Aesthetics of Games and Art*, shows that the time has come for video games to enter the art world and engage its debates.

Whether or not video games can be categorized as art is of no interest here—a wide range of scholars are already debating that matter and, like all discussions regarding the definition of art, it is likely to devolve into a never-ending cycle. The objective of this chapter is to deepen our discussion of how video games and the art world relate to one another. What does an *artgame* exhibition tell us? What insights can we glean regarding the society it represents? Curating video games involves merging diverse disciplines and areas of knowledge, including art history, technology and gaming. New media art is important to the art world not because of the technology it involves, but because of the uses it gives to these devices and the stories it tells. In the end, new media art it is like any other form of artistic expression—it is not about the materials, except when it expressly *is* about the materials.[7] The same goes for video games. The inclusion of video games in the art world involves examining their use for "critical play [...] built on the premise that, as with other media, games carry beliefs within their representation systems and mechanics."[8] But it also means using games to think about new forms of interactive narrative such as those envisioned by Janet Murray in her writings on cyber-narratives,[9] pushing the medium to create new aesthetic experiences based purely on play. Video game exhibitions are a great window to these important ways in which games can push us to think and create differently.

With this in mind, the remainder of this chapter will look into the way that art and video games have been interacting over the course of the last decade in Argentina, by critically examining my own experience over the past nine years curating the exhibition *Game on! El arte en juego* (*Game On! Art in Play*) in Argentina. This chapter invites readers to revisit the history of this exhibition as a way of understanding how video games have come to blur the limits of interactive art and create an aesthetic of their own. As Paul Callaghan, former director of the Australian independent game festival Freeplay, explains, "Games are an art, one of many ways of producing meaning of and about the world and our experiences."[10] Likewise, every exhibition can tell us something not only about the works exhibited but also about the society within which they were produced. Today in particular, exhibitions can speak to the transformation of the public from a passive audience into a conglomerate of curious protagonists, and about the mutations this evolution implies for art museums and galleries.

THE LATIN AMERICAN CONUNDRUM

Latin American artists and game designers have been experimenting with video games for a long time. The first approaches within the art field can be located by the early works of artists such as Venezuelan digital art pioneer Yucef Merhi, who began working with video games in the mid-1980s, and by the late 1990s games began to gain greater prominence in the Latin American art world, mostly in the form on artgame production like the game mods created by Mónica Jacobo in Argentina and the hacking activities of new media artists like Arcángel Constantini in Mexico.[11] On the other hand, the first artgame productions within the Latin American video game development community can be came at the very start of the 21st century in the works of independent Argentine developer Daniel Benmergui, who has become the leading figure for indie production in the region, in addition to being

7. For more on this matter, see Stephen C. Foster, "Clement Greenberg: Formalism in the '40s and '50s," *Art Journal* 35.1 (1975): 20-24.
8. Mary Flanagan, *Critical Play: Radical Game Design* (MIT Press, 2009).
9. For deeper insight on this matter see Janet Murray, *Hamlet on the Holodeck: The Future of Narrative in Cyberspace* (MIT Press, 1998).
10. Paul Callaghan, "Cultural Connections for Games," *British Council Film*, http://film.britishcouncil.org/comment/2017/continue (2017).
11. For more on the work of Mónica Jacobo and the beginning of the Argentine game art scene, see her interview with Mathias Jansson on *Gamescenes*, October 2011, http://www.gamescenes.org/2011/10/interview-monica-jacobo-and-the-argentinian-game-art-scene.html. Regarding the career of Arcángelo Constantini and his video game-related works, see his website: http://www.arc-data.net/. For more on Yucef Merhi's works, see his official web page: http://www.cibernetic.com/works.

internationally recognized for winning the Nuovo Award prize at the International Game Festival in 2014 with his game *Storyteller*. Since then, an increasing number of game developers have been working alongside artists, experimenting with new game mechanics and narratives.

Despite these instances of crossover between video games and the art field, there has not been a sustained tradition of exhibition and reflection on this topic. Until very recently, there had only been a few isolated exhibitions and scarce material developed by Latin American scholars regarding their cultural impact, and even less regarding the implications of video games for the art world. It is high time for local academics to join the discussion that is taking place worldwide, reflecting on the role the new media art world plays in producing, exhibiting and discussing video games. As Domenico Quaranta argues: "The importance of this should not be underestimated: even if the piece never fulfils the idea of art that other arenas have, it will have heralded a new development in knowledge that can be brought to fruition elsewhere."[12] Quaranta's writings echo the reflections of renowned art critics and curators like Christiane Paul or Sarah Cook on the new challenges that technology imposes on museums, galleries and art exhibits in general.[13] Dietz, likewise, has observed the following regarding the challenges of new media art: "Interactivity and user-friendliness are just a couple of the expectations with which we view digital art. On the museum side of the equation, there are a whole set of parallel issues to do with touch/don't touch, how much time you spend with a time-based work, and other learned gallery behaviors."[14] Academics working on digital culture are beginning to ponder the specific strategies and practices necessary for the preservation of an exhibition of video games, taking into account their incorporation into the museum as pedagogical tools and taking note of a "tendency in the future [...] to put more emphasis on permanent collections, as well as special thematic exhibitions instead of general overviews of digital game cultures."[15] We are also beginning to see academic work on the history of new media art and artgames, such as Sharp's *Works of Game*, a great introduction for a general audience to the three main fields of interaction between games and art: artgames, artists' games and game art. While this seems to be a subject of increasing interest in North America and Europe, it is difficult to find theoretical production from Latin America aside from the early writings of Mónica Jacobo or the current productions of Claudia Costa Pederson, who writes with a focus on media theory and social practice, being a strong advocate for gender issues and Latin American visibility.[16]

In 2009, the birth of the exhibition *Game on! El arte en juego* arose from this need in Argentina. As renowned Argentine curator and media critic Rodrigo Alonso asserts, "a discourse generated at the periphery is not necessarily a discourse on the periphery, nor is it a peripheral discourse," and indeed, a lengthy history of critical reflection from the southern cone has impacted global game culture. In April 2001, Gonzalo Frasca presented his Georgia Tech master's thesis "Video Games of the Oppressed," in which he argued that video games were a medium capable of fostering critical thinking and advocated for a more active presence of the global south in the gaming world. In a section of her 1994 book *Scenes of Postmodern Life*, Argentine cultural critic Beatriz Sarlo pondered the impact of video games, shopping malls and channel-surfing on postmodern society: "How can an intellectual from the southern cone respond in the face of the enormous cultural transformations of the West, which are already perceptible in her own country, and which form part of a new group of collective

12. Quaranta, *Beyond New Media Art*, 193
13. For more on this matter, see Sarah Cook, "Immateriality and its Discontents: An Overview of Main Models and Issues for Curating New Media," in *New Media in the White Cube and Beyond*, ed. Christiane Paul (University of California Press, 2008): 26-49.
14. Steve Dietz, *Interfacing the Digital, Museums and the Web*, 2003, https://www.museumsandtheweb.com/mw2003/papers/dietz/dietz.html.
15. Tiia Naskali, Jaakko Suominen and Petri Saarikoski, "The Introduction of Computer and Video Games in Museums – Experiences and Possibilities. Arthur Tatnall; Tilly Blyth; Roger Johnson," *Proceedings of the International Conference on History of Computing, June 2013, London, United Kingdom* (Springer, 2013).
16. See Claudia Costa Pederson, "Gaming Empire: Play and Change in Latin America and Latin Diaspora," *NMC: Journal of the New Media Caucus* (2016).

experiences?"[17] Since its start, *Game on! El arte en juego* has taken on Sarlo's question and has aimed to foster a space for rethinking the merger between video games and art.

The first commercial Argentine video game was created in 1982, and by the end of the 1990s the first local game development studios came about, at a similar pace to that of Mexico, Peru and other countries in Latin America.[18] Today, there are some 2,000 people involved in the Argentinean video game industry and around 100 active game development companies,[19] most of which could be classified as independent due to their financing structure.[20] That said, there is a rising community of indie developers producing creative and cutting-edge games, including some internationally renowned names like those of Benmergui, Fernando Ramallo and Agustín Cordes. These developers' productions are aimed at exploring games' inner logic and thinking about ways of constructing meaningful experiences. In so doing, they are a perfect example of the current situation of new media art, which has built upon a longstanding (if sometimes unstable) tradition of interest in the merger between technology and art, beginning in Argentina with the exhibition "Art and Cybernetics" back in 1969.[21]

Latin America has managed to develop an aesthetic of its own when it comes to new media art. Latin American new media artists have a DIY/craft tradition that translates into highly inventive low-tech art works. This is also a matter worthy of academic attention: how is technology-based art produced across Latin America? How is the art world appropriating technology and transforming it within the region? Likewise, video games need to be a part of the discussion. Developers and artists have already taken the first steps, it is now time for the local academy to acknowledge that we must look at games in culture, not only to understand them, but in order to understand ourselves as society.

GAME ON! EL ARTE EN JUEGO: AN OPEN-ENDED QUEST

The concept of culture has brought about many debates throughout history. It has been redefined over and over again, since it is a concept in constant evolution. For many, video games today seem to be the form of cultural production most fitting to the contours of the present century. For this reason, starting in 2009, subsequent editions of *Game on! El arte en juego*—each with entirely unique content—have been exploring the interactions between video games, technology and art. Thinking locally—or more properly *glocally*[22]—the exhibition has been showcasing national and foreign works in dialogue. It has been recognized as an exhibition of cultural interest by Argentina's national government, and has been hosted by several major local cultural centers and institutions, creating a constantly-evolving curatorial challenge due to both the ever-changing content of the exhibition and the material conditions of the different locations. Along the way, the exhibition itself has become an exploration of national identity vis-à-vis artgames. *Game on! El arte en juego* was the first exhibition of its kind in Argentina, and it remains one of the few events in Latin America dealing with the intricacies of artgames and experimental games in the context of the art world. This exhibition, with all its idiosyncrasies, is situated amidst myriad game festivals and exhibits across the globe, such as A MAZE. (Germany), Playful Arts Festival (Netherlands) and FILE (Brazil), among others.

17. Beatriz Sarlo, *Escenas de la vida posmoderna: Intelectuales, arte y videocultura en la Argentina* (Titivillus, 2004): 4.
18. For further information on the history of Latin American video games see Mark J. P. Wolf, ed., *Video Games Around the World* (MIT Press, 2015).
19. These numbers were reported by the Argentine Video Game Developers' Association (ADVA) in the Video Game Sector Report delivered by the Ministry of Production at its Annual Meeting. The complete report can be accessed at http://fundav.com/wp-content/uploads/2017/08/Informe-Mesa-Videojuegos-26072017.pdf.
20. For more on the "independent vs. indie" debate, see Maria B. Garda and Paweł Grabarczyk, "Is Every Indie Game Independent? Towards the Concept of Independent Game," *Game Studies* 16.1 (October 2016), http://gamestudies.org/1601/articles/gardagrabarczyk.
21. For more on the history of new media art in Argentina, see Rodrigo Alonso's chapter "Argentine Art and New Technologies," in *Elogio de la low-tech. Historia y estética de las artes electrónicas en America Latina* (Luna, 2015).
22. For an introduction to the concept of glocalization, see Victor Roudometof, *Glocalization: A Critical Introduction* (Routledge, 2016).

In 2009, the first edition of *Game on! El arte en juego* was conceived as an open question to art institutions and the video game community: Can video games be considered art, and if so, what would that mean? This initial exhibition was arranged in two separate stages on the two floors of the Buenos Aires art gallery Objeto a. When visitors entered the gallery, they were welcomed by a display of video games and interviews produced by major Argentine game developers, who explained in their own words why video games could be considered art. The interviews approached video games from the viewpoints such as narratology and film studies. Spectators were invited to reflect upon Deleuze's concept of the moving image: "It is not the same as the other arts, which aim rather at something unreal through the world, but makes de world itself something unreal or a tale [*recit*]. With the cinema, it is the world which becomes its own image, and not an image which becomes world"[23] This section invited the audience members to ponder their role as protagonists in a new immersive present to which they had been summoned in order to marvel at the virtuosity of the visual artwork incorporated into these interactive stories.

The exhibition continued on the second floor with a selection of video games that had been intentionally created as art works by game developers. Here, visitors experienced the works of Benmergui, Agustín Pérez Fernandez and the artist collective *Proyecto Untitled.* There was also a selection of international indie games from That Game Company (United States), Tale of Tales (Belgium), Amanita Design (Czech republic), Natalie Boockhin (United States) and Van Sowerwine (Australia). The exhibition brought together a variety of artgames and non-game works, encouraging reflection through the frameworks of game studies and new media theory, while helping move video games to the center of discussions on new media art and curatorial practice. As Quaranta has argued, the curator's role is ever-less-frequently that of "caretaker" of objects, and increasingly that of mediator and interpreter.[24] This initial iteration of *Game On! El arte en juego* brought to light key questions that would remain a part of the exhibition's planning and development in the years to follow: What was it that made these games suitable for an art exhibition? And what was the proper way of exhibiting them? Since video games are generally created with the intention of being played in the comfort of one's own home, resituating them within the context of an art gallery or museum implies a process of re-signification and re-contextualization that cannot be overlooked.

The first iteration of *Game On! El arte en juego* in 2009 succeeded in getting museum visitors in Buenos Aires to think about video games as something more than mere entertainment. It attained a great deal of press coverage, and over 1,500 people visited the gallery in all. Not only was 2009 the opening year for the exhibition, it also marked the initiation of the artgame genre itself and of video game curatorial practice in Argentina—there were no previous experiences related to the exhibition of video games within local art circuits, so the inspiration had to come from a merger between new media practice and the video game tradition. Here, video games were exhibited *as* video games—there was no intention of masking that. The exhibition was also accompanied by a schedule filled with activities that helped provided a 360º behind-the-scenes panorama of video game production, circulation and reception.

The second edition of *Game On! El arte en juego* took place two years later, a lapse that was due not only to curatorial decisions but also logistical choices in response to local constraints. On one hand there was the funding issue: exhibitions of this kind involve great costs and local companies are not accustomed to investing outside their pre-programmed marketing budgets. On the other hand, an exhibition of this kind would not have enough novel local production to show on an

23. Gilles Deleuze, *The Movement-Image* (University of Minnesota Press, 1997): 57.
24. Quaranta, *Beyond New Media Art.*

annual basis. Even though Buenos Aires had (and has) a thriving community of indie developers, when it comes to producing artistic or experimental projects they have to work on the side, without the time or resources needed for stable production. These kinds of works—those that step outside the mainstream arena—are the ones selected for exhibition in *Game on! El arte en juego*. A similar phenomenon has taken place in the art world—interest in video games was just getting started back in 2009, and even now, there are relatively few exhibitions that are focused specifically on games. Many recent developments in curatorial practice center around interaction, but in forms and works that are not play-related, and that therefore are not directly related to video game culture.[25]

This second edition of *Game on! El arte en juego* was presented in 2011 under the umbrella of FASE-Encuentro de arte, ciencia y tecnología (FASE – Encounter of Art, Science and Tecnhnology), the main New Media Arts festival in Argentina. The producers of FASE allotted three rooms for the exhibition at the Centro Cultural Recoleta, one of Buenos Aires' main cultural centers. Once again a program of live performances, guided tours and talks accompanied the exhibition. The previous edition had already established that video games were a cultural device and could be considered a form of art, so this edition delved into experimental works being made by indie developers and new media artists. The local artgames selected included: *Crédito ambiental/Biogame* (*Environmental Credit/ Biogame*, Joaquin Fargas, 2011), *Conflicto Local* (*Local Conflict*, Martinez-Zea,2011), *Rabbits for my closet* (Purple Studio, 2011) and *Atmosphir* (Minor Studios, 2011). The selection showed how video games can engage the audience in reflection on social issues. The main challenge faced at that time had to do with the security and functionality of the technological elements involved in the exhibition—*Game on! El arte en juego* necessarily involves a significant amount of technological equipment in plain sight, in contrast with most local new media exhibits, which tended to have more low-profile technological setups. Moreover, it was situated in a heavily-frequented cultural center near the city's downtown area. These factors had a direct impact on the content and aesthetics of the exhibition, as certain works had to be secured with padlocks, while others had to be omitted entirely because they involved wireless equipment or small devices that could be easily stolen.

That same year, the Buenos Aires Municipal Government commissioned a special edition of *Game on! El arte en juego* that was held at the city planetarium during Buenos Aires Futura, a large tech festival. This time, the curatorial challenge was directly related to the location's infrastructure and the particularities of its audience. The narrow aisles of the planetarium and never-ending lines of visitors led to a meticulously edited selection of games. The audience was taken by surprise with the exhibit—visitors would enter the building housing the exhibition as they strolled around before the planetarium screenings, so the games had to be easy to play, visually engaging and powerful enough to convey an experience or a message within a few short minutes of play. The final selection included artists' games and works by Pérez Fernández and Benmergui as representatives of Argentina's experimental and artsy indie dev scene. There was also a lineup of foreign titles that had been previously exhibited by *Game on! El arte en juego*, which were mostly puzzle games or those that allowed for brief experiences, such as *Samorost* or *Tunning*. This edition was similar in intention to the first one, as it invited the public to see video games from a new perspective, and focused on nationally-produced works but showed them within the context of current global production.

The third full edition of *Game on! El arte en juego* took place simultaneously in three locations, reinforcing the logic of working in narrative clusters. This iteration of the exhibition further developed the exploration of the artgame scene in Argentina, situating it among other countries

25. For more on the differences and similarities between interactivity and play, see Eric Zimmerman, "Narrative, Interactivity, Play, and Games: Four Naughty Concepts in Need of Discipline," in *First Person*, eds. Noad Wardrip-Fruin and Pat Harrigan (MIT Press, 2004).

of the global south by featuring Argentine production within a showcase of Latin American video games and related works. For this purpose, we teamed up with the San Martín Cultural Center as well as the Spanish Cultural Center, which has offices in different Spanish-speaking countries and a well-established cultural network, enabling us to contact a variety of game developers and artists. Each location for the exhibition dealt with a specific thematic issue: party games and workshops, indie games and artgames in Latin America, experimental games, playable media and interactive ludic installations. The public could decide to visit one or two of the locations, or all three of them. The segment of the exhibition at the Spanish Cultural Center was dedicated to the Latin American indie scene, focusing on artgames, artists' games, experimental games and serious games. The selection of games included *Consecuencias* (*Consequences*, Agustín Perez Fernandez, 2012), *Chromodigmatic* (Martin Gonzalez, 2012), *Storyteller* (Daniel Benmergui, 2012), *Intervalo lúcido del individuo inconsciente* (*The Unconscious Individual's Lucid Interval*, Alejandro Grilli, Chile) and *Laberintos Invisibles* (*Invisible Labyrinths*, Andrei Thomaz, Brasil). The second location, also belonging to the Spanish Cultural Center, was in the very center of downtown Buenos Aires and was dedicated to workshops and performances along with a selection of national party games and arcade games including *Nave* (*Ship*, Videogamo, 2012). These games were selected due to being easy to play as well as experimental and funny, with humor and togetherness connecting them all. The third and final location for this edition of *Game on! El arte en juego* was the San Martín Cultural Center. It involved a more theatrical setup displaying playable local media, interactive installations and foreign artgames and experimental indie games. This final location dealt with games that challenged the very definition of a video game, such as *Johann Sebastian Joust* (Die Gûte Fabrik, 2012), *Dear Esther* (The Chinese Room, 2012), *Passus Exilii* (Federico Joselevich Puiggros, 2011) *Anamorphoss* (Diego Alberti and Gabriel Rud, 2012) and *Profesora Clásica* (*Classic Professor*, Gabriel Rud, 2005).

The third edition of the exhibition was the first to include playable installations and new media artists producing works that challenged the standardized categorizations of video games and interactive installation. *Passus Exilii* by Federico Joselevich Puigross and *Anamorphoss 1.1* by Gabriel Rud and Diego Alberti were interactive installations that used the Xbox Kinect to produce playable experiences that actively engaged the body. *One-hit wonder* and *Ballhala*, created by Proyecto 032, were outside-the-box games created by new media artists who used standard gaming devices not only as a playful relic but also as a means of pondering the technologies used by the game industry.

One year later, the Festival Cervantino commissioned a special version of *Game on! El arte en juego* for the next edition of the festival. The Festival Cervantino, or Cervantes Festival, is a very well-known traditional event featuring all kind of art that takes place every year in a small town 600 km (375 mi) from the capital city of Buenos Aires. The director of the festival wanted to introduce the category of media art into the festival, so they asked *Game on! El arte en juego* to take care of all the details involved in setting up the exhibition. This edition took a pedagogical approach and received a very positive response from the high school teachers and other educators who organized several visits with their students, using *Game on! El arte en juego* as an example of new forms of art and new opportunities for the intersections between technology and culture.

One of the primary characteristics of *Game on! El arte en juego* has been its quest to reach different locations as a way of connecting with new audiences and trying out different combinations of works and themes in order to create novel ludic experiences. In 2015, at the invitation of Noviembre Electrónico—Buenos Aires' main technological festival, whose outreach was an acknowledgment of the impact of video games in the art field—the fourth edition returned to San Martin Cultural Center. The selection of works exhibited resulted from an open call to the media artists' community and the indie developer community. There were also a few titles that were specially invited, as well as three commissioned works: *Brain Dump* by Pérez Fernández, *The Tale of the Fox and the Crane* by visual artist Laura Palavecino and *Two Computers Playing* PONG by media artist Diego Alberti. This last work summed up the spirit of the exhibition: a media installation and homage to the movie *Wargames* (United Artists, 1983) involving two computers competing in a match of *PONG* on top of an actual ping-pong table. The installation raised several issues simultaneously, and in so doing it was able to reach different audiences at the same time: the media arts field, game developers and the general audience. This work was about the role of play in our lives and at the same time about the role of technology. It questioned what was needed for a game to occur—who set the rules and who decided the winner—and asked about the roles of both the player and the audience. This non-interactive installation, placed right in the center of a video game art exhibit, invited the audience to take a second look and to rethink what was taking place in the exhibition space.

This fourth edition of *Game on! El arte en juego* showed a marked increase in the number of proposals submitted by media artists, demonstrating increasing interest from academia and the visual arts world in exploring video games. A wide range of technological devices were involved, including interactive virtual reality experiences using Oculus Rift and alternative controls involving motion sensors or handcrafted devices. Although the technology was typical of the low-tech scenario faced by many curators across the global south, the works exhibited demonstrated ingenious creativity and were proof of the diverse ways that technology, art and games can come together.

The fifth edition of *Game on! El arte en juego*, which took place in Buenos Aires' Cultural Science Center in December 2017, was the result of an international open call that ran for a month that resulted in over 100 applications from some 25 countries. This edition incorporated a track dedicated to the state of the art in Latin America game studies, an area that would not have been possible in the first edition of the exhibition, when video games were just beginning to be taken seriously within academia. In Argentine institutions of higher education, there are currently numerous undergraduate and master's theses being written analyzing video games from an aesthetic perspective, as well as research in progress on the power of video games as communication tools and Ph.D. theses on game production focused on the relationship between video games and education. Simultaneously, an increasing number of media artists are experimenting with the language of video games, producing artworks and publications. What began as an art/video game exhibition is turning little by little into a post-media festival that explores the role of video games within the context of an emerging local ludic culture. To paraphrase Joline Blais and Jon Ippolito's iconic book,[26] *Game on! El arte en juego* is about video games at the edge of their medium.

THE NUANCES OF VIDEO GAME CURATION: LESSONS FROM THE GLOBAL SOUTH

When merging video games with the art sphere, exhibition curators have to take into consideration three main challenges: their audience's literacy, the inherent limitations of any video game experience and the criteria of selection. Curators must also be prepared for three types of audiences: the general public-at-large, who may spend only a short time interacting with a handful of the works on display; the traditional art gallery/museum audience, who may initially react with reluctance when faced with interactive technologies like video games in a gallery setting; and tech-savvy visitors, who may be prone to overlook conceptual aspects and feel drawn to the games' mechanics or to the devices themselves. Art curators have faced this divide since the dawn of new media art, and Quarante spoke

26. Joline Blais and Jon Ippolito, *Art at the Edge of Art* (Thames & Hudson, 2006).

of it repeatedly: "the audiences of the two spheres are still so different, even though the art itself is often culturally very similar; that those who write about contemporary art know nothing about New Media Art, while those who write about New Media Art hardly ever do so in a contemporary art journal."[27] Video games seem to have re-awakened this issue, and in the face of these circumstances, curators may either decide to address a particular group or try to handle the dual demands of art audiences and technological consumers. Since its inception, *Game on! El arte en juego* has been conceived as a site for shared encounters and discussions among these diverse types of visitors.

A curator's first challenge is dealing with the literacy of the audience. The exhibition brings together game developers and media artists simultaneously by focusing on current experimentations that address the audiences of both video games and art. One smart approach is to work with narrative nodes or themes, allowing curators to create parallel curatorial tracks that offer diverse paths to the audience, empowering them to choose and create their own itineraries, engaging in a ludic tour that demonstrates the variety of stories that can arise through engagement with art and experimentation with video games. Another arrangement that has proved effective is to organize a range of activities that round out the exhibition and provide a glimpse of the world of video game development. Lastly, it is important not to underestimate the significance of the human factor, especially in an exhibition focused on the use of technology. This is one reason every edition of *Game on! El arte en juego* has adhered to one tried-and-true, foolproof tactic: live, in-person exhibit guides. Of course, it is crucial to select the right profile of guides for such an exhibit, and the experience of *Game on! El arte en juego* has shown that art students are often the best fit for this kind of exhibit, since they have the historical and conceptual knowledge that allows them to make the connections between video games and the art world.

Second, a curator must consider the experience of play. German philosopher Hans-Georg once said, "In play, in every play, there is something like a 'sacred seriousness.'"[28] The role of curators is to convey this in the best possible manner, taking into consideration what is needed to convey the experience of a game, how to display video game hardware and/or software and the ways the play experience is altered when taking place in an exhibition. Any object placed within the context of an art exhibition will be instantly reframed and resignified, and this transformation is the principal task that curators must address. How should a curator proceed when faced with a game that is either too enormous to be grasped during a single visit to an exhibition, or too controversial to be included in a show for an all-ages audience? Video game exhibits raise many questions that are still being dealt with by critics and curators worldwide, and there is no magical recipe to resolve them all. Every curator has to find her own path by learning from previous experiences and keeping in mind the two traditions being brought together in this new context: commercial video game exhibitions and media art history.

The third issue curators should take into consideration when preparing a video game exhibition is the criteria of selection: why would you take a game from the living room into the museum, and what makes that particular game worthy of selection? These are questions that all curators must face, regardless their object of analysis. Curators of video game exhibitions around the world provide varied explanations for following this curatorial trajectory. The Victoria and Albert Museum proclaims that "Video games are one of the most important design fields of our time,"[29] and in a similar vein, Paola Antonelli justified the MoMA acquisition of video games in the name of a broader the

27. Domenico Quaranta, "Guest Column: When 'New Media Art' Loses Its Prefix," *Vice*, 20 May 2011, https://creators.vice.com/en_au/article/wnzmpq/guest-column-when-new-media-art-loses-its-prefix.

28. Hans George Gadamer, *La actualidad de lo bello: el arte como juego, símbolo y fiesta* (Paidós, 2008).

29. See V&A's official website: https://www.vam.ac.uk/exhibitions/video games.

understanding of design, explaining that she was drawn to video games because they place a "focus on this idea of interaction design and on behaviors."[30] Berlin's A MAZE festival is about celebrating independent and alternative games, playful media and games culture, while Babycastles is an event focused on connecting the independent game development community with the broader New York art world. *Game on! El arte en juego* was conceived as a place for experimentation and critical thinking around playful culture, where the video game and media art communities could come together in a shared creative process.

VIDEO GAMES AND ART: THE PRESENT SHAPING OUR FUTURE

Video game exhibits are now an undeniable part of our artistic present. They are being held in hybrid spaces in capital cities and at small galleries in remote towns, at internationally acclaimed avant-garde venues and traditional art institutions. The art world is courting video games like never before, taking them into account for their cultural significance rather than their commercial impact alone. Across the globe, curators are beginning to learn and work with the specific characteristics of the medium. This process of adaptation shows how video games are being reappropiated and resignified according to the idiosyncrasies of different communities, as described in the work of anthropologist Néstor García Canclini, who has proclaimed the need to understand the cultural effects of electronic media within the context of the processes of globalization that have so deeply affected our society.[31] Along those lines, Phillip Penix-Tadsen asserts that more often than not "we simply accept outdated characterization of the global south as a massive technological backwater, strictly on the downside of the 'digital divide' between hi-tech haves and have-nots when the reality of technological acquisition and usage in Latin America tells a much more nuanced tale."[32] Together with other video game exhibits in Latin America such as Anigames (Colombia), FILE (Brasil) and DevHr (Mexico), *Game on! El arte en juego* showcases the complex ways video games are merging with other forms of culture in the region today.

This chapter was conceived as an invitation to walk through the evolution of the exhibition *Game on! El arte en juego*, reviewing the history of the past decade of artgames in Argentina and the consequent birth of video game curatorial practice in the country. This journey has demonstrated the increasing interest of new media artists in the video game medium, not only as a type of work to be explored but as a device to be repurposed under the terms of new media art production. The artists' approach to video games has evolved from producing game mods and game art to developing their own ludic experiences influenced by the video game logic and game design. On a parallel path, independent video game developers have taken interest in the medium for its communicative properties and its capacity to create and explore alternative ways of storytelling. This phenomenon has been taking place worldwide and is also now occurring in Argentina, though there is not yet an Argentine identity inherent to national video game and game art production, which is still in the process of self-discovery. We will have to wait and see what the future holds for this blossoming relationship between video games and art, and when it comes the time to write that tale, Latin America will have plenty to tell.

30. Paola Antonelli, "Why I Brought Pac Man to MoMA," *TED Salon 2013*, New York, https://www.ted.com/talks/paola_antonelli_why_i_brought_pacman_to_moma
31. Nestor García Canclini, *Diferentes, desiguales y desconectados: mapas de la inerculturalidad* (Gedisa, 2004).
32. Phillip Penix-Tadsen, *Cultural Code: Video Games and Latin America* (MIT Press, 2016): 44.

WORKS CITED

Alonso, Rodrigo. *Elogio de la low-tech. Historia y estética de las artes electrónicas en América Latina*. Luna, 2015.

Antonelli, Paola. "Why I Brought Pac Man to MoMA." TED Salon 2013, New York. https://www.ted.com/talks/paola_antonelli_why_i_brought_pacman_to_moma.

Blais, Joline and Jon Ippolito. *Art at the Edge of Art*. Thames & Hudson, 2006.

Callaghan, Paul. "Cultural Connections for Games." *British Council Film*, 2017, http://film.britishcouncil.org/comment/2017/continue.

Cook, Sarah. "Immateriality and its Discontents: An Overview of Main Models and Issues for Curating New Media." In *New Media in the White Cube and Beyond*, edited by Christiane Paul, 26-49. University of California Press, 2008.

Costa Pederson, Claudia. "Gaming Empire: Play and Change in Latin America and Latin Diaspora." *NMC: Journal of the New Media Caucus*, 2016.

Danto, Arthur. *The Transfiguration of the Commonplace: A Philosophy of Art*. Harvard University Press, 1981.

Deleuze, Gilles. *The Movement-Image*. University of Minnesota Press, 1997.

Dietz, Steve. "Collecting New-Media Art: Just Like Anything Else, Only Different." *NeMe.org*, 2005, http://www.neme.org/texts/collecting-new-media-art.

—. Interfacing the Digital. *Museums and the Web*, 2003, https://www.museumsandtheweb.com/mw2003/papers/dietz/dietz.html.

Flanagan, Mary. *Critical Play: Radical Game Design*. MIT Press, 2009.

Foster, Stephen C. "Clement Greenberg: Formalism in the '40s and '50s." *Art Journal* 35.1 (1975): 20-24.

Gadamer, Hans George. *La actualidad de lo bello: el arte como juego, símbolo y fiesta*. Paidós, 2008.

García Canclini, Néstor. *Diferentes, desiguales y desconectados: mapas de la inerculturalidad*. Gedisa, 2004.

Garda, Maria B. and Paweł Grabarczyk. "Is Every Indie Game Independent? Towards the Concept of Independent Game." *Game Studies* 16.1 (October 2016), http://gamestudies.org/1601/articles/gardagrabarczyk.

Huizinga, Johan. *Homo Ludens*. Emecé, 1968.

Lovink, Geert. "New Media Arts at the Crossroads." Paper presented at the Conference at Argos Center for Art and New Media, Brussels, 2007.

Murray, Janet. *Hamlet on the Holodeck: The Future of Narrative in Cyberspace*. MIT Press, 1998.

Naskali, Tiia, Jaakko Suominen and Petri Saarikoski. "The Introduction of Computer and Video

Games in Museums – Experiences and Possibilities. Arthur Tatnall; Tilly Blyth; Roger Johnson." *Proceedings of the International Conference on History of Computing, June 2013, London, United Kingdom.* Springer, 2013.

Penix-Tadsen, Phillip. *Cultural Code: Video Games and Latin America*. MIT Press, 2016.

Quaranta, Domenico. *Beyond New Media Art*. Link, 2013.

—. "Guest Column: When 'New Media Art' Loses Its Prefix." *Vice*. 20 May 2011, https://creators.vice.com/en_au/article/wnzmpq/guest-column-when-new-media-art-loses-its-prefix.

Roudometof, Victor. *Glocalization: A Critical Introduction*. Routledge, 2016.

Sarlo, Beatriz. *Escenas de la vida posmoderna: Intelectuales, arte y videocultura en la Argentina*. Titivillus, 2004.

Wolf, Mark J. P., ed. *Video Games Around the World*. MIT Press, 2015.

Zimmerman, Eric. "Narrative, Interactivity, Play, and Games: Four Naughty Concepts in Need of Discipline." In *First Person*, edited by Noad Wardrip-Fruin and Pat Harrigan. MIT Press, 2004.

—. "Manifesto for a Ludic Century." *Being Playful: Eric Zimmerman's Game Design Blog*. 9 September 2013, https://ericzimmerman.wordpress.com/2013/09/09/manifesto-for-a-ludic-century/.

MOBILITY THROUGH GAMES

ASIAN INTERNATIONAL STUDENTS AND GAMING CULTURES IN MELBOURNE

JOSHUA WONG, WILLIAM BALMFORD, LARISSA HJORTH, AND INGRID RICHARDSON

INTRODUCTION: PLAY, CO-PRESENCE AND PLACE

> "I play with friends back home. Actually, I also play with friends here—I play with friends in general." (Sandra, female Singaporean-Chinese postgraduate, talking about Facebook games)

Contemporary media practice is dominated by the playful. For play scholar Miguel Sicart and others,[1] playfulness is a key feature of our everyday and habitual activity with media practice. However, it is important to recognize that the playful involves more than just games—it also points to an attitude and mode of engagement. As Sicart states, "Playfulness is a way of engaging with particular contexts and objects that is similar to play but respects the purposes and goals of that object or context."[2] With the rise of apps and algorithms in and around social media, the boundaries between work and leisure blur.[3] Through the lens of playful media, we can gain new insights into how "work" or "home" are negotiated, especially as we move through different places and spaces.

As reflected in Phillip Penix-Tadsen's introductory vignettes for this anthology, games can often play an important role in growing, consolidating and maintaining intimate social connections and family ties. When it comes to international students, games are a significant part of how social interaction is maintained across, and in spite of, geographical distance.

In this chapter we explore how the practices of play within new media environments—specifically, computer games—intersect with our participant international students' experience of sociality and place as they migrate between their geographical homes to the new and unfamiliar location of Melbourne, Australia. The chapter explores the ways in which games and migration interweave, both together and through lived experiences, complicating notions of locality and co-presence. Through such investigation, this chapter considers the broader concerns within the global south, particularly game and media use among migrant populations and transnational communication.

In order to address the role of games as a form of sociality among transnational students, the chapter will engage with a few key areas. Firstly, we review key literature around ideas of play, co-presence and place. We will then shift into an analysis of ethnographic fieldwork concerning Asian international students living in Melbourne—ethnography here is understood as both a set of methods and conceptual lens that seeks to document and interpret nuances and motivations informing practices.[4] The ethnography was conducted over two years and involved detailed

1. Miguel Sicart, *Play Matters* (MIT Press, 2014).
2. Ibid., 21.
3. Melissa Gregg, "Do Your Homework: New Media, Old Problems," *Feminist Media Studies* 11.01 (2011): 73-81; Larissa Hjorth, "Ambient and Soft Play: Play, Labour and the Digital in Everyday Life," *European Journal of Cultural Studies* (2017).
4. Sarah Pink, Heather Horst, John Postill, Larissa Hjorth, Tania Lewis and Jo Tacchi, *Digital Ethnography: Principles and Practice* (Sage, 2015).

discussions with 19 international students from different parts of Asia. The backgrounds of these students are summarized in Table 3.5.1 below.

In this research we consider "Asian international students" as a heterogeneous category that is in a state of constant flux, contestation and change. Just as the region is complex and disputed, what constitutes "Asian" is diverse and divergent. Throughout this chapter, particular focus will be paid to how participants' experience and enact co-presence and playfulness in social interactions through games and gameplay.

Where we play, how we play, who we play with and *who we play as* are crucial factors in how play is embedded into our everyday experiences.[5] These contexts of play inform how we navigate and understand our personal lives—from childhood through to adulthood.[6] At the same time, *what we play* has an extensive impact upon our everyday lives through informing our interpretation of social interaction and daily experiences.[7] As more and more of our playful activities have moved into digital spaces and platforms such as personal computers, game consoles and mobile devices, new scenarios and practices are emerging around personal identity; defining who we are and who we want to be through the games we play.[8]

The idea of co-presence plays a major role in weaving together notions of identity and place. Initially defined by Erving Goffman,[9] it was scholars such as Mimi Ito and Christian Licoppe that outlined the significance of co-presence in terms of mobile communication.[10] For Licoppe, when studying the use of the mobile phone for maintaining close social relationships, there are two main modes of usage—what he terms the "conversational" and the "connected."[11] The conversational mode is one where focused attention is paid to one's interlocutor. This type of exchange usually takes a relatively long period of time and the duration and place of the conversation may even follow a standardized ritual. In this conversational mode, the amount of care and intimacy is shown through how much attention and effort is devoted to the conversation, to the exclusion of other distractions.

The connected mode, however, comprises shorter but more frequent communicative messages being exchanged, where the frequency and flow of these messages are what determines the level of intimacy in the relationship. In this connected mode, the act of calling or text messaging is just as important as the actual content of the message itself, and a sense of connectedness or co-presence is established through frequent sharing of emotions or states, rather than the events or news that may be shared in the longer conversational mode. Both of these practices are crucial to international student life in Australia, and can be augmented through various media devices and social networks. Integral to this chapter are such instances of conversational and connected communication modes that occur predominantly through acts of play.

Licoppe's work was published in the mid-2000s, when social media was still in its infancy and

5. Sicart, *Play Matters*; Diane Carr, "Contexts, Gaming Pleasures, and Gendered Preferences," *Simulation & Gaming* 36.4 (2005): 464-482; Erving Goffman, *The Presentation of Self in Everyday Life* (Harmondsworth London, 1978).
6. Goffman, *The Presentation of Self in Everyday Life*; Doris Bergen, *Play from Birth to Twelve and Beyond: Contexts, Perspectives, and Meanings* (Psychology Press, 1998); Doris Pronen Fromberg and Doris Bergen, *Play from Birth to Twelve: Contexts, Perspectives, and Meanings* (Taylor Francis, 2006).
7. Isabela Granic, Adam Lobel and Rutger CME Engels, "The Benefits of Playing Video Games," *American Psychologist* 69.1 (2014): 66.
8. Nick Yee, "Maps of Digital Desires: Exploring the Topography of Gender and Play in Online Games," in *Beyond Barbie and Mortal Kombat: New Perspectives on Gender and Gaming*, eds. Yasmin B. Kafai, Carrie Heeter, Jill Denner and Jennifer Y. Sun (MIT Press, 2008), 83-96.
9. Goffman, *The Presentation of Self in Everyday Life*.
10. Mizuko Ito and Daisuke Okabe, "Intimate Visual Co-presence," *Proceedings of the 2005 Ubiquitous Computing Conference*, 2005; Christian Licoppe, "'Connected' Presence: The Emergence of a New Repertoire for Managing Social Relationships in a Changing Communication Technoscape," *Environment and Planning D: Society and Space* 22.1 (2004): 135-56.
11. Licoppe, "'Connected' Presence."

Name	Sex	Country	Ethnicity	Major
Joseph	M	Malaysia	Malaysian	Commerce
Camille	F	Malaysia	Chinese	Zoology
Steven	M	Indonesia	Chinese	Information Technology
Tamar	F	Brunei	Malay	Foundation Studies
Jane	F	Myanmar	Burmese	Construction
Samuel	M	Singapore	Malay	Physiotherapy
Rebecca	F	Singapore	Chinese	Physiotherapy
Eric	M	Singapore	Chinese	Architecture
Sandra	F	Singapore	Chinese	Speech Pathology
Nanditha	F	Sri Lanka	Sinhalese	Accounting
Peter	M	Sri Lanka	Sinhalese	Accounting
Priya	F	Sri Lanka	Sinhalese	Biomedicine
Kayla	F	India	Indian	Business Administration
Kenny	M	India	Indian	Network Systems
Amanda	F	India	Indian	Information Technology
Mark	M	Mongolia	Mongolian	Finance
Erica	F	Mongolia	Mongolian	Finance
Serene	F	China	Chinese	Arts
Pamela	F	Taiwan (R.O.C)	Chinese	Accounting & Finance
Eugene	M	Hong Kong (R.O.C)	Chinese	Finance
Sally	F	Thailand	Thai	Accounting

Table 3.5.1. Participant Details.

mobile communication was primarily centered around SMS and phone calls.[12] Fast-forward to a decade later, after the explosive proliferation of social media platforms and applications, and we see a more rich and complex picture of networked sociality emerging. In our research, for example, students frequently mentioned that one of the ways they used media for their well-being was to

12. Ibid.

chat with friends through online games or mobile media applications. Examples of these include communicative applications such as WhatsApp, Facebook–based social games like *FarmVille* (Zynga, 2009) and online multiplayer games such as *Dota 2* (Valve, 2013) and *Counter Strike: Global Offensive* (Valve, 2012). More recently, we have witnessed the convergence of social, mobile and game media, whereby sociality is often quite literally "played out" in games and playful media spaces.

Sutton-Smith argues for a rhetoric of play that has the core trait of adaptive variability, derived from human evolutionary history and the way the brain works.[13] This adaptive variability is made manifest by the sheer variety of forms of play and ways of studying it. In applying this model to our research we could argue that when international students engage in play activities, they are simultaneously employing acts of play for several ancillary uses—to feel secure (away from stressors in their lives), to gain the approval of other people in their environment (by building common interests) and in certain play worlds, feeling a sense of mastery and control over their surroundings. Examples of these forms and uses of play will be examined in the later sections of this chapter.

However, even beyond these multiple benefits to acts of play, there is more that play is capable of doing. Sicart suggests that the characteristics of play include creativity and appropriation.[14] When people play, they recognize and accept the rules and structures that govern the world, and perform within those rules to satisfy their needs or desires. Play is a way to creatively engage with the contexts we live in, and appropriate the physical, social or technological settings to enhance feelings of wellbeing. As students aspire to adjust to the new location of Melbourne, they creatively appropriate the resources around them to enable that pursuit.

In the context of this chapter, such resources include the digital technologies and games of our participants. They repurpose existing technologies such as Skype to serve more playful activities such as playing long distance board games of *Scrabble* (Brunot, 1938) or *Trivial Pursuit* (Hasbro, 1979). Similarly, their mobile phones become more than just tools for communication—they are ways to engage in gameplay in unorthodox spaces and unfamiliar locations. Examples of this include using *Pokémon GO* (Niantic, 2016) to help learn the layout of a new city, or *Candy Crush* (King, 2012) to fill in the monotony and loneliness of a long distance commute—aiming to avoid feelings of homesickness when ruminating on distant family.

Sicart also suggests that another key characteristic of play is that it exists in tension between creation and destruction—between the rational order of rules and the wild euphoria of disorder and chaos.[15] Play is deeply related to our real world experiences, rather than being separate or detached from it as previous theorists once thought.[16] Extending this idea of play as a key component of real-world experiences and everyday life, T. L. Taylor argues that the place and form of play and games can be examined to help researchers understand the "extensive range of actors, concepts, practices and relations that make up the play moment."[17] For our analysis, recognition of such an assemblage is an important step towards understanding the diverse experiences of participants across their changing environments.

Taylor argues that a focus upon these moments of playful interaction helps us to appreciate the interrelations between these various actors and worlds.[18] Examples of this include Taylor's

13. Brian Sutton-Smith, *Towards an Anthropology of Play* (Leisure Press, 1977), 222-232; Brian Sutton-Smith, *The Ambiguity of Play* (Harvard University Press, 2009).
14. Sicart, *Play Matters*.
15. Ibid.
16. Ibid.
17. T. L. Taylor, "The Assemblage of Play," *Games and Culture* 4.4 (2009): 332.

descriptions of fan "fairs" as social events blurring the boundaries between game and non-game, worlds, identities and "bodies."[19] Such understandings of play across and between worlds can be linked back to Gregory Bateson's concept of the "self between actors and worlds."[20] This concept argues that the notion of the self and human subjectivity is situated within and through the world around it. Both Bateson and Taylor alike place great emphasis upon the "networked and entangled self."[21]

Certainly there is value to such a focus on the complexity of the networked self when examining the migration of international students in Australia. By focusing on the actors, processes and their nuanced interrelations, new and previously invisible phenomena emerge around the use of play to alter and enhance the networks and quotidian life of our participants. Or, as Taylor might put it, such an approach "allows us to get into the nooks where fascinating work occurs."[22]

This idea of co-present play, or perhaps "playfulness," has been the subject of much recent research.[23] Co-presence conceives of presence as "a spectrum of presence of engagement across multiple pathways of connection."[24] Accordingly, co-present play can be understood as acts of play occurring across such pathways, going beyond rudimentary understandings of separate "online" and "offline" play.[25] Returning to Sicart, an exploration of the multiple dimensions of play helps us to frame the act within the place it occurs, and the players presence during the moment.[26] Developing this idea from myriad disciplines including architecture and politics, Sicart maps how play and playfulness migrate across all facets of contemporary life.[27] Here we see that engagement and context can become infused with playfulness, a merger between modes of presence and co-presence entangled with acts of play.

This blending of presence and co-presence in the context of play is the ethnographic focus of this chapter. Within the context of this research, the adaptive and migratory ability of play is paramount. Given the broadness of play as a category that spans cultural practice,[28] the role of play in establishing a sense of "place" and connected co-presence is a key characteristic of contemporary media. This chapter will now turn to discuss this characteristic with regard to the way co-presence and location manifest through play for Asian international students living in Melbourne.

HOME AND AWAY: IN THE ETHNOGRAPHIC FIELD

> "Basically, you try to participate in as many community activities as possible—volunteering, joining student societies, anything you can find. And hopefully there will be one spot somewhere that you can fit in." (Joseph, Malaysian-Chinese undergraduate)

Joseph, a Malaysian-Chinese undergraduate currently living and studying in Melbourne, understands that a key way to adjust to an unfamiliar living environment is to make friends via community groups. Indeed, one of the core components of international student well-being is the ability to successfully adapt to and exist in the new environment of the country they are studying in.[29] This ability to adapt

18. Taylor, "The Assemblage of Play"; Taylor, *Play between Worlds*.
19. Taylor, *Play between Worlds*.
20. Gregory Bateson, *Steps to an Ecology of Mind: Collected Essays in Anthropology, Psychiatry, Evolution, and Epistemology* (University of Chicago Press, 1972).
21. Bateson, *Steps to an Ecology of Mind*; Jos de Mul, Sybille Lammes, Valerie Frissen, Michiel de Lange and Joost Raessens, *Playful Identities: The Ludification of Digital Media Cultures* (Amsterdam University Press, 2015).
22. Taylor, "The Assemblage of Play."
23. de Mul, et al., *Playful Identities*.
24. Taylor, "The Assemblage of Play"; Taylor, *Play between Worlds*, 64
25. Ibid.
26. Sicart, *Play Matters*.
27. Larissa Hjorth, "Ambient and Soft Play"; Larissa Hjorth, William Balmford, Amani Naseem and Tom Penney, "Ethnography and Playful Interventions with Young People," in *The Routledge Companion to Digital Ethnography*, eds. Larissa Hjorth, Heather Horst, Anne Galloway and Genevieve Bell (Routledge, 2017): 288.
28. Sutton-Smith, *The Ambiguity of Play*.

has implications not just for their present living circumstances, but also can be seen as a part of a larger continuum of the student's progress towards a more cosmopolitan identity as a global citizen.

Leisure activities can often serve as a useful bridge for students to adjust to their environments in Australia. However, there are also cultural aspects to the play and leisure practices of international students, and therefore at a deeper level, the ways in which they are engaging with play and leisure also speaks to struggles of power, class, ethnicity and the clash of cultures.[30] In particular, emphasis within Australian undergraduate life, for our participants, appeared to be placed outside of study, around extra-curricular activities such as games or part-time jobs. An example of this can be seen in Joseph's story, where he recounts a feeling of "culture shock" at Australian students' categorization of daily life:

> I notice students here place a lot of emphasis—I mean, relatively to students from Malaysia and Singapore—that studies is not everything. That extra-curricular activities, part-time jobs, all these things play a very significant role in whether or not they'll have a successful career in the future, or whether or not they develop as a person in the first place. Whereas in the Malaysian and Singaporean culture, everything is just studies. You get better results than me, that's your way forward. But nobody works part-time, rarely, and leisure time is seen as a waste of time... But here if you work part-time people respect you for that, then if you are heavy on co-curricular activities but you sacrifice a bit of your results people will respect you for that as well, in the competitive academic environment and as part of a group. Whereas Asian communities—I think it applies to people from China as well—if you sacrifice results because of co-curriculum people will say that was bad time management.

Joseph's approach to his Australian migration becomes clear as he describes how he tried to get involved in community and how through these activities he built up friends. And yet, this is not uncontested. Embedded in these excerpts we can see different narratives of play clashing—the idea of play as frivolous "waste of time" alongside play as part of community identity. These interpretations of play highlight Joseph's understanding of play as a site for the contestation of power between different cultures. Joseph describes a very common perception among Asian communities according to our participants (and a key concern for them when they arrive in Australia) that the only purpose for their migration is to study. Anything else—especially leisure or extra-curricular activities, or even part-time work—is secondary, and should not interfere with one's studies. This, he contrasts openly with his perceptions of the Australian attitude towards the work-play-study balance.

The same approach to study can also be linked to aspirational mobility, i.e., what would give the best advantage in one's current and future contexts. For our participants, their previous Asian communities appear to focus on academic proficiency, whereby Australian culture takes a "wider" approach. Thus, in order to progress forward in Australian society, Joseph concluded that it was important to get involved in different aspects of community life, even at a minor cost to his academic results. Joseph's comment speaks to a larger issue of how hegemonies of power are embedded in the leisure practices of a nation or culture, and the difficulties that international students have to face when trying to navigate that cultural environment. Sutton-Smith has argued that:

> the more powerful group in power induces the subordinate group by persuasion or example to play the hegemonial group's games, under the presumption of their moral superiority... The value for the hegemonial

29. Christiane Meierkord, "International Student Migrationk," *Identities in Migration Contexts* 69 (2007): 35; Parvati Raghuram, "Theorising the Spaces of Student Migration," *Population, Space and Place* 19.2 (2013): 138-154.
30. Lorraine Brown, "An Ethnographic Study of the Friendship Patterns of International Students in England: An Attempt to Recreate Home through Conational Interaction," *International Journal of Educational Research* 48.3 (2009): 184-193; David Pyvis and Anne Chapman, "Culture Shock and the International Student 'Offshore,'" *Journal of Research in International Education* 4.1 (2005): 23-42.

> group is that playing the games can become a kind of persuasion to believe in the general ideology surrounding them.[31]

For our participants, playing games popular within Australia was not the only way such hegemonic power was experienced—ideological power was also seen in *how* these games were played.

Another participant, Sally, an undergraduate originally from Thailand, experienced a great moment of cultural foreignness when she joined a board-game group at her university on the advice of a friend. Expecting it to be a "serious" event concerned with the competition of games, she found it a largely social affair, with everyone "more concerned with talking and drinking than finishing the round (of the game)." For Sally, she had simply joined to maintain a single friendship, but found that by taking part in the (to her) unusual "Australian" form of co-present play, she found herself beginning to absorb the values and ideology of Australian students, placing social play more in line with studious focus.

Returning to our other participant Joseph, and turning back to home:

> "Unfortunately, regrettably as well, I turned back to my old gaming communities. So basically, friends who have separated, but went to UK or Singapore while I was in Australia. True, there are some delays, because internet connection and the distance... when we played games together it's like, we're back in high school again." (Joseph, Malaysian-Chinese undergraduate)

Beyond being a source of leisure and local community bonding, the games played by international students living in Melbourne can serve as a link to "home." For Joseph, as seen in the above quote, this is not always a positive link. He expands on this feeling further, sharing that:

> But if you rely on it solely to be your social support, then that's destructive. If that is your only source of social support... Then, you won't learn at all. Because... I think social life has a lot of learning involved. And, if you've already learnt a way to interact, which is through gaming, then that's it, like the next time you go into the gaming community you know how to interact again. And you never learn the outside world, how they interact. Professionals interact differently, Master's students interact differently, undergraduate students interact differently, high school students in Australia also interact differently.

For Joseph, maintaining such strong ties to home support was detrimental to his new position as an Australian undergraduate. Therefore, he began to start "cutting off" ties with his previous communities of support and patterns of play based around transnational communication. Thomas Apperley explores other examples of transnational communication within the opening chapter of Part Three of the present volume. His research focuses on a comparison of transnational communication between Melbourne, Australia and Caracas, Venezuela, highlighting how social exchange of this nature can reconnect and realign individuals from separate, and disparate, regions. While for many of Apperley's participants this transnational communication was born out of their social networks, our participant Joseph felt that transnational communication through games hindered his personal growth after his migration to Australia.

In Malaysia, it is very common to have young teenage males play networked online games together, as a form of social bonding.[32] Internet and gaming cafes dot the urban landscape, or with the advent of broadband internet, networked play now occurs more frequently at home amongst groups of

31. Sutton-Smith, *The Ambiguity of Play*, 96.
32. Sheila A. Paul, Marianne Jensen, Chui Yin Wong and Chee Weng Khong, "Socializing in Mobile Gaming," *Proceedings of the 3rd International Conference on Digital Interactive Media in Entertainment and Arts*, 2008.

friends.[33] Thus, Joseph still maintained this familiar cultural pattern of play when he came to Australia, and indulged in it as a form of psychological and social comfort, which he later regrets. However importantly, for Joseph, the reason why he harbored these doubts is not because he wanted to cut off all ties with his former life, but rather because he realized that staying in his comfortable pattern of play would lead to maladjustment with his new social context. Therefore, for the sake of his future interactions and learning, he deliberately stopped gaming with his friends from home and sought out interactions with people in his new location.

Joseph also describes changing his patterns of play to suit the Australian gaming landscape. He talks about how he had to buy an original copy of a game for the first time, instead of a pirated one, and joined Steam—an online games distribution platform and player community. This led him to play games such as *Shogun: Total War* (Electronic Arts, 2000) and *Mass Effect* (Electronic Arts, 2007) with local Australian teenagers. He then described one of the major differences between the play styles of Australia and Malaysia—the players in Australia were far more likely to use microphones and voiceover chat, compared to the typed-out text chat messages that is prevalent in Malaysian gaming circles. Joseph then started to adopt some of the local patterns of gaming as well.

These digital links to home can also be interpreted as beneficial. Such is the case for Eugene, a student from Hong Kong currently studying in Melbourne. Eugene uses the game *Dota 2* to stay in contact with his close friends from high school. By having frequent play sessions together, Eugene and his friends manage to stay in contact despite their different geographical locations. Although they have no set time to play, Eugene estimated that they probably played around once or twice every couple of weeks for several hours. Eugene described these as "gaming sessions where we all felt like we were back in high-school on a Saturday night." Contained within Eugene's practices is evidence of kinship being maintained through gameplay, enabling social mobility, in spite of distance.

We can also see how the different notions of kinship—that is, ties to friends and family—that are affected by the digital and play *in* and *through* the practices. These practices are illustrative of what Hjorth and Richardson call "ambient play."[34] That is, games have the ability to move back and forth into the foreground and background in powerful ways that reflect the participants' everyday rhythms. While Eugene plays *Dota 2*, he can be present with his Hong Kong friends. These relationships can remain comfortably in the background of his everyday life, despite his pursuit of international studies in Australia.

Elsewhere in this anthology, Jerjes Loayza also discusses *Dota 2*, exploring how the social bonds generated through the game by youths in Lima, Peru remain important beyond the acts of play the game facilitates. Eugene's example both validates and complicates these findings. While friendships built through *Dota 2* continue to be relevant despite his migration to Australia, acts of play are periodically required to refresh and strengthen these social connections. At the same time, these bonds are further mediated through Eugene's new location within Australia.

From this, we can understand how patterns of play and leisure vary significantly between cultures, and how one international student tried to negotiate the differences between the cultural values by absorbing and adapting to the local patterns of leisure and play, along with the values that are embedded in these cultural forms. For other international students, a retention of previous gaming

33. Eow Yee Leng and Roselan Baki, "An Exploratory Study on the Reasons and Preferences of Six Malaysian Students on the Video Games Played," *International Journal of Environmental and Science Education* 3.1 (2008): 19-25.
34. Larissa Hjorth and Ingrid Richardson, *Gaming in Social, Locative and Mobile Media* (Palgrave Macmillan, 2014).

practices are an important way of maintaining kinship with friends back home—a form of social mobility enabled in and through the act of game playing. For Camille, games are about relaxation, escape and recovery:

> I guess for me [online role-playing games are] like an outlet. Like, I guess in a sense you don't have to worry about, um... I guess saying "reality" is a bit weird, but it's like say if you're not happy that day, you just like take it out on whatever creature you find. (Camille, female Malaysian-Bruneian undergraduate)

Completing an undergraduate degree can be hard, even when conducted within your native country. By migrating to Australia for further study, our participants are making an already stressful and busy period of life all the more complicated, fraught with change and uncertainty. Accordingly, many of our participants stressed the need for "down time," exhibiting tendencies to engage in game playing as a form of escapism. Camille, featured above, is one such example of this consumption pattern. Originally from Brunei, she is now living in Australia studying Zoology. Another student, Steven, a mid-20s Indonesian currently completing his Information Technology degree hints at engaging games for similar reasons:

> If I have problem or something, it's like... uh, I just try to forget my problem, and then go to my games, and then... try to fight with people because sometimes we can do PvP at people... Like, in here—I don't know, people in here, if they have problem they always drunk, but for me, I always play games. Same thing.

Steven shows more classic coping strategies of playing video games to "forget [his] problem," hinting at an escapist strategy and seeking psychological detachment. This is further supported when he compares his gaming habit with people drinking to forget their problems. In addition, the types of games he plays are online games featuring intense player-versus-player combat, where there is no mercy. This interest also indicates that what attracts him to this game is the sense of mastery and achievement he gets from vanquishing other players, in an arena outside of his official studies. Likewise, it shows that he seeks out media content with high absorption potential, to change his current mood. Returning to Camille, we can see a similar sentiment in her game playing habits through her ability to psychologically detach herself from the "real world."

Both players take an emotion-focused coping strategy that relies on using gaming to cathartically vent their feelings and offload stress. However, notice that Camille takes a more nuanced approach to the coping strategy that Steven does. While Steven plays absorbing games merely to forget his real life problems, Camille views her activities in the game and in reality as two sides of her life. She is indulging in *identity play* or mimicry—one of the major forms of play identified by Roger Caillois in his book *Man, Play and Games*.[35] This is further supported by her mention of the lore, quests and people in the game. Her online persona has a full identity constructed in the world of the game. So therefore, in order to cope with stress in her real life identity, she switches identities to the other part of her life—achieving detachment through the art of role-play.

While previous studies on recovery effects have looked at video games,[36] not many have actively explored how the affordances of the medium for creative identity play interacts with the purposes of resilience and recovery. For those experiencing significant changes caused by transnational migration, online role-playing games that Camille enjoys can allow for a form of controlled detachment, as players juggle multiple roles and identities as a way of separating themselves from

35. Roger Caillois, *Man, Play, and Games* (University of Illinois Press, 1961).
36. Diana Rieger, Leonard Reinecke and Gary Bente, "Media-Induced Recovery: The Effects of Positive Versus Negative Media Stimuli on Recovery Experience, Cognitive Performance, and Energetic Arousal," *Psychology of Popular Media Culture* 6.2 (2017): 174.

stressors faced by any one identity. Although such practices are not exclusive to international students, they were consistently observed among our participants as the main reason for playing. This speaks to the ability of games to provide escape from the unknown into the familiar. Particularly for international students who are residing in a totally foreign country, this ability to find a familiar space can be incredibly useful.

CONCLUSION

This chapter has presented ways in which Asian international students in an Australian context deploy games and playful media as part of a negotiation of being home and away. The first section of this chapter provided a brief overview of the academic works crucial to ideas of play, co-presence and place. Such works are important to contextualize the experience of migrating to Australia for tertiary education. In particular, literature around the use of creative play to aid social cohesion can help to highlight the lived experiences of our international Asian participants.

Building on this review of the pertinent literature, our fieldwork explored the theoretical links between play and student aspirations. Importantly, the different interpretations of the daily focus between Australian and international Asian undergraduate students enable more nuanced understanding of the complexity surrounding migration. For our participants, the Australian focus on extra-curricular engagement led them to pursue leisure and play activities (including gaming consumption) in order to develop social communities within the locale of Australia, whilst also staying in touch with family and friends at home.

This chapter has illuminated gaming habits within international Asian student groups through its use of empirical case studies. Similar to other chapters within this anthology, our exploration has drawn attention to the different ways migrant members of the global south engage in game-based transnational communication. We see our participants repurpose video games and gaming platforms developed by the global north such as *Dota* and Steam to connect them to cultural environments—either to societies and ties back home, or as an entry point to achieve greater understanding about their host country.

With the increasing rise of mobile and casual games developed in the global south, as described elsewhere in this anthology, future research could investigate how international students can also serve as vectors through which these games become popularized in their host country. International students bring with them the games of their childhood, which may very well include video games developed within the region, and may share them with other international students from disparate nations as well as locals in their host country. These background experiences are also complicated by the identity politics of the migrant situation, as illustrated previously where the student Joseph gave up the gaming patterns of his adolescence in order to better fit into Australian society.

Future research into the area of migrant game practices within the global south could explore other migrant groups to further attend to the diversity of transnational communication and play practices currently in existence. International students do not exist as isolated individuals, but rather as nodes in a network of transnational family and kinship ties. As they are often responsible for the teaching of ICT literacy to their older family members, new forms of transnational familial interactions may arise through video games and other leisure activities, in which student and parent could play and learn together. Inter-generational play or the circulation of video games through transnational migrant family ties are another fruitful area of research to explore. Other avenues of research into migrant Asian international students would also be addressing the digital inequalities between locations (such as rural versus urban migrants). This chapter's study was informed by its urban contexts—Melbourne—a place with abundant and accessible internet broadband and digital mobile devices.

Through its exploration of how games and migration interweave together, this chapter engages with broader concerns within the global south, particularly transnational communication and the ways in which migration can alter previous play practices. By combining ethnographic analysis with several key theoretical frameworks and concepts around play, we examined how gaming consumption practices are changing the everyday lives of international Asian undergraduate students living in Melbourne.

WORKS CITED

Bateson, Gregory. *Steps to an Ecology of Mind: Collected Essays in Anthropology, Psychiatry, Evolution, and Epistemology*. University of Chicago Press, 1972.

Bergen, Doris. *Play from Birth to Twelve and Beyond: Contexts, Perspectives, and Meanings*. Psychology Press, 1998.

Brown, Lorraine. "An Ethnographic Study of the Friendship Patterns of International Students in England: An Attempt to Recreate Home through Conational Interaction." *International Journal of Educational Research* 48.3 (2009): 184-193.

Caillois, Roger. *Man, Play, and Games*. University of Illinois Press, 1961.

Carr, Diane. "Contexts, Gaming Pleasures, and Gendered Preferences." *Simulation & Gaming* 36.4 (2005): 464-482.

de Mul, Jos, Sybille Lammes, Valerie Frissen, Michiel de Lange and Joost Raessens. *Playful Identities: The Ludification of Digital Media Cultures*. Amsterdam University Press, 2015.

Fromberg, Doris Pronin and Doris Bergen. *Play from Birth to Twelve: Contexts, Perspectives, and Meanings*. Taylor Francis, 2006.

Goffman, Erving. *The Presentation of Self in Everyday Life*. Harmondsworth London, 1978.

Granic, Isabela, Adam Lobel and Rutger CME Engels. "The Benefits of Playing Video Games." *American Psychologist* 69.1 (2014): 66.

Gregg, Melissa. "Do Your Homework: New Media, Old Problems." *Feminist Media Studies* 11.01 (2011): 73-81.

Hjorth, Larissa. "Ambient and Soft Play: Play, Labour and the Digital in Everyday Life." *European Journal of Cultural Studies* (2017).

Hjorth, Larissa and Ingrid Richardson. *Gaming in Social, Locative and Mobile Media*. Palgrave Macmillan, 2014.

Hjorth, Larissa, William Balmford, Amani Naseem and Tom Penney. 'Ethnography and Playful

Interventions with Young People." In *The Routledge Companion to Digital Ethnography*, edited by Larissa Hjorth, Heather Horst, Anne Galloway and Genevieve Bell. Routledge, 2017.

Ito, Mizuko and Daisuke Okabe. "Intimate Visual Co-presence." *Proceedings of the 2005 Ubiquitous Computing Conference*, 2005

Khong, Chee Weng. "Socializing in Mobile Gaming." *Proceedings of the 3rd International Conference on Digital Interactive Media in Entertainment and Arts*, 2008.

Licoppe, Christian. "'Connected' Presence: The Emergence of a New Repertoire for Managing Social Relationships in a Changing Communication Technoscape." *Environment and Planning D: Society and Space* 22.1 (2004): 135-156.

Meierkord, Christiane. "International Student Migration." *Identities in Migration Contexts* 69 (2007): 35.

Paul, Sheila A., Marianne Jensen, Chui Yin Wong, Chee Weng Leng, Eow Yee and Roselan Baki. "An Exploratory Study on the Reasons and Preferences of Six Malaysian Students on the Video Games Played." *International Journal of Environmental and Science Education* 3.1 (2008): 19-25.

Pink, Sarah, Heather Horst, John Postill, Larissa Hjorth, Tania Lewis and Jo Tacchi. *Digital Ethnography: Principles and Practice*. Sage, 2015.

Pyvis, David and Anne Chapman. "Culture Shock and the International Student 'Offshore.'" *Journal of Research in International Education* 4.1 (2005): 23-42.

Raghuram, Parvati. "Theorising the Spaces of Student Migration." *Population, Space and Place* 19.2 (2013): 138-54.

Rieger, Diana, Leonard Reinecke and Gary Bente. "Media-Induced Recovery: The Effects of Positive Versus Negative Media Stimuli on Recovery Experience, Cognitive Performance, and Energetic Arousal." *Psychology of Popular Media Culture* 6.2 (2017): 174.

Sicart, Miguel. *Play Matters*. MIT Press, 2014.

Sutton-Smith, Brian. *The Ambiguity of Play*. Harvard University Press, 2009.

—. "The Ambiguity of Play: Rhetorics of Fate." *The Performance Studies Reader*, edited by Henry Bial. Routledge, 1997.

—. "Towards an Anthropology of Play." Leisure Press, 1977.

Taylor, T. L. *Play between Worlds*. MIT Press, 2009.

—. "The Assemblage of Play." *Games and Culture* 4.4 (2009): 331-339.

Yee, Nick. "Maps of Digital Desires: Exploring the Topography of Gender and Play in Online Games." In *Beyond Barbie and Mortal Kombat: New Perspectives on Gender and Gaming*, edited by Yasmin B. Kafai, Carrie Heeter, Jill Denner and Jennifer Y. Sun, 83-96. MIT Press, 2008.

WHOSE "GAME CULTURE" IS IT, ANYWAY?

EXPLORING CHILDREN'S GAMEPLAY ACROSS CAPE TOWN

NICOLA PALLITT, ANJA VENTER, AND MUYA KOLOKO

Gaming is a ubiquitous practice in Cape Town, South Africa, where young people across socio-economic groups partake in mobile, console, arcade, online, offline and PC gaming. In this chapter, we weave together our research about young people's gaming practices from multiple sites within the metropolis of Cape Town. In doing so, we seek commonalities, articulate differences and offer provocations about the role of place in gaming practices. We argue that gaming practices are *infrastructured* in various ways.[1]

Our cases are drawn from a range of research projects, theses and game development initiatives. We've explored gaming practices in domestic spaces in a low-income neighborhood and two public library contexts, as well as after-school settings in the wealthy suburbs of the city. These sites are characterized by differential access to gaming technologies, along with other forms of social stratification. We argue that *where* young people play and the *infrastructure* of play is as important as *who* plays, *what* they play and *how* they play.[2] Our research demonstrates that, even within the context of a single city, game cultures can be as diverse as the people and spaces of the city itself.

RESEARCHING GAMING PRACTICES IN CAPE TOWN

This chapter contributes to emerging scholarship investigating the global diversity of gaming cultures by sharing games research pertaining to young people and digital games conducted in a range of sites across Cape Town. The various projects in which we have been involved have either focused on, or included, primary school-aged children and teenagers playing games in a variety of public and private settings across South Africa's capital. The University of Washington-sponsored *Global Impact Study of Public Access to Information & Communication Technologies* (2007-2012) investigated public access to ICTs, and Walton and Donner conducted in-depth studies associated with the report's findings, focusing on the interplay between teens' public access to ICTs and private and shared access to mobile phones, which included use for gaming.[3]

The field work that has contributed to this chapter has varied by author. Following her involvement as a research assistant on this project in 2011, Anja Venter investigated communities of practice amongst PC gamers in Cape Town's Central Library, while her Master's thesis focused on children playing console and mobile games in domestic settings in Ocean View.[4] Nicola Pallitt's Ph.D. on children's

1. Susan Leigh Star, "The Ethnography of Infrastructure," *American Behavioral Scientist* 43.3 (1999): 377–391.
2. Adrienne Shaw, "What Is Video Game Culture? Cultural Studies and Game Studies," *Games and Culture* 5.4 (2010): 403-424.
3. Araba Sey, Chris Coward, François Bar, George Sciadas, Chris Rothschild and Lucas Keopke, "Connecting People for Development: Why Public Access ICTs Matter," *Technology & Social Change Group, University of Washington*, 2013, https://tascha.uw.edu/projects/global-impact-study/; see also Marion Walton and Jonathan Donner, "Public Access, Private Mobile: The Interplay of Shared Access and the Mobile Internet for Teenagers in Cape Town," Global Impact Study Research Report Series, *Technology & Social Change Group, University of Washington*, 2012, https://digital.lib.washington.edu/researchworks/bitstream/handle/1773/20956/Public access private mobile final.pdf.
4. M. Anja Venter, "Gamers in Ganglands: The Ecology of Gaming and Participation amongst a Select Group of Children in Ocean View, Cape Town," Master's Thesis, University of Cape Town, 2012.

gendered gameplay in middle-class and suburban after-school settings included a pilot study at a boys' school in Rondebosch, a children's holiday club hosted there for children from across Cape Town and an after-school gaming club at a neighboring co-ed school.[5] Muya Koloko did field work toward his Ph.D. on children's responses to violence in video games at Harare Library in Khayelitsha as well as at a co-ed school in Rondebosch.[6] While these studies share a focus—on young people and games—the papers and dissertations that were produced from this work demonstrate how radically different gaming technocultures can be, even when located within a kilometer's radius of one another.

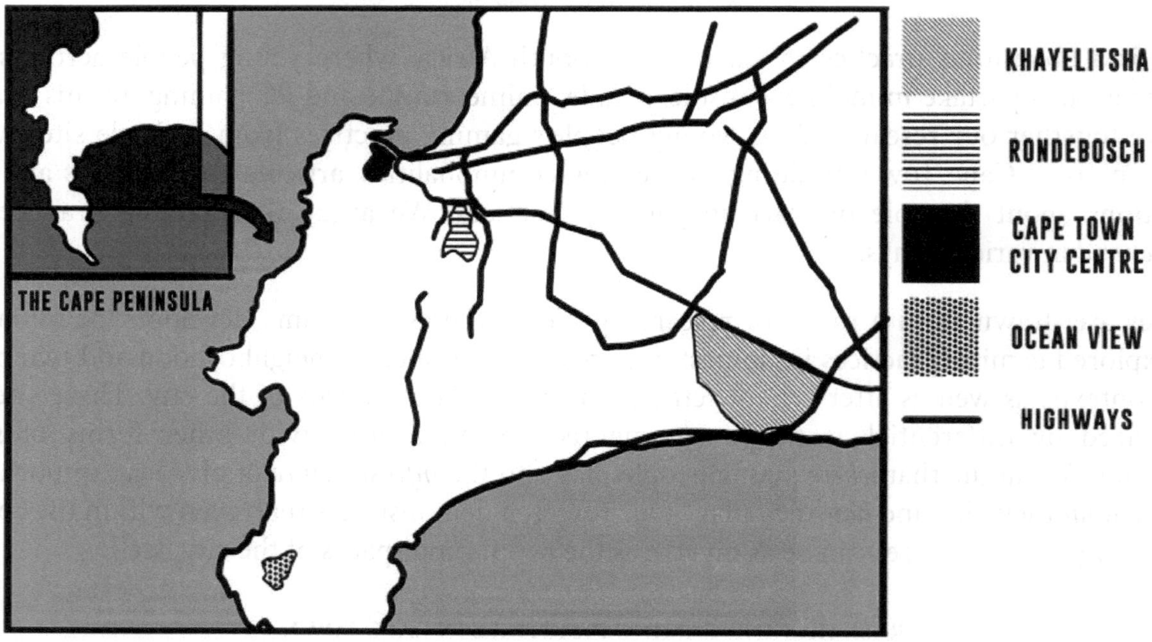

Image 3.6.1. A map of Cape Town depicting the locations of this chapter's field sites.

As each of our broader projects had a distinct theoretical perspective, analytic framework and research design, we found we needed a shared conceptual framework to discuss the infrastructure of play across sites.[7] The following section describes this framework, after which we will analyze specific cases from our research. Judging from our experiences, gaming practices in various locales are often characterized by resource constraints, necessitating a focus on infrastructure. While strides have been taken to analyze the discursive dimensions of gaming as texts that travel from the global north to the global south (such as in chapters by Souvik Mukherjee and others in this volume), in this chapter we focus on the practicalities of gaming, specifically the material and spatial conditions that support gaming practices in Cape Town.

5. Nicola Pallitt, *Gender Identities at Play: Children's Digital Gaming in Two Settings in Cape Town*, Ph.D. Dissertation, University of Cape Town, 2013.
6. Pallitt and Koloko did field work at the same co-ed school site in Rondebosch but at different times and with different children. Children played games as part of an existing extra-mural after school which became akin to an informal games club. Subsequent to our research, the school also started a multimedia room (in addition to their computer lab) where children can play games on a range of devices owned by the school.
7. See the authors' individual works for details about more specific analytical approaches, ethics, data collection, selection and analysis. For the purpose of this chapter, we acknowledge that we share broadly ethnographic approaches which included spending extended periods of time in our respective field sites, observing and recording gameplay and conducting interviews.

PARANODAL PLAY AND INFRASTRUCTURED GAMING PRACTICES

Regional "game culture" tends to emphasize consumption. Internationally, South Africa does not rank among major game consumers or developers.[8] However, figures from marketing and industry reports related to gaming in Africa and South Africa in particular demonstrate growing gaming industries.[9] Recent interest in games in South Africa has been motivated by government-supported initiatives which seek to develop an industry around serious games.[10] While local reports and proposals consider players as markets and game designers as part of a growing industry, they often fail to account for gaming practices that fall under their radar, which, from our experience, include a broad spectrum of game-related habits and behaviors. Consumption and play practices are different phenomena: researchers who "follow the money" can understand consumption, but not necessarily paranodal play practices. Ulises Mejias defines paranodal as being outside of networks and argues that the paranodal offers nuance, allows us see beyond participation and/or non-participation, enables us to question the idea of digital networks and how theorizing the outside of networks is about uncovering the paranodal contributions that nodocentrism renders invisible.[11] This concept and a critical perspective of networks more broadly provides insight into invisible players described in the introduction of this anthology. Likewise, many of the gaming experiences of South Africa's poor majority are paranodal: un-networked, offline, untrackable.

While the most common metaphor when talking about digital practices in contemporary scholarship has been that of networks and their nodocentric formulations of participatory culture,[12] few of the gamers we encountered participated in play that was networked. Rather, many of these gaming practices emerged as part of a broader phenomenon referred to as "pavement internet."[13] Walton's formulation of pavement internet builds on the work of Nyamnjoh,[14] who argues that digital social media in the context of Africa are a welcome extension of local traditions of informal word-of-mouth communication which has been dubbed *radio trottoir*—translating to "pavement radio." Radio trottoir is conceptualized as the circulation of information in the form of gossip or rumors that enhances public knowledge. For example, while some individuals might read the newspaper, or gain information from more "official" sources, news is also distributed through personal networks as a form of sociality. Walton's theorization of a pavement internet explains how information (including data such as images and digital goods such as games) downloaded from the web (making it expensive to obtain owing to young people's limited data resources) trickle down through interpersonal networks at low data costs. Owing to exorbitant data costs, these practices frequently go unregistered on the network and result in off-network workarounds, making them paranodal in nature. Gaming in public access venues such as libraries and internet cafés, as well as other localized sharing practices in which the country's poorer majority engage could thus be conceptualized as "pavement gaming"—not on the well-trodden "roads" of the networks, but just outside of their scope. As Nyamnjoh contends,

8. The authors would like to acknowledge that this depends on how consumption and development is defined (and who is doing the defining) as well as the relationship between them.
9. Recent figures are collated in Nicholas Hall, Mandy J. Watson and Adoné Kitching, *Serious About Games* (IESA, 2017). The report shares a position on the state of South Africa's local game development industry and the opportunity for serious games to create social impact. In comparison to other countries, game development in South Africa was delayed by trade sanctions and censorship which disrupted global media flows during apartheid.
10. *Serious About Games* is a Cape Town-based initiative that aims to support the growth of South Africa's serious games sector. Further information is available at http://seriousaboutgames.co.za/.
11. Ulises Mejias, *Off the Network* (University of Minnesota Press, 2013).
12. See Yochai Benkler, *The Wealth of Networks: How Social Production Transforms Markets and Freedom* (Yale University Press, 2006); see also Henry Jenkins, Mizuko Ito and dana boyd, *Participatory Culture in a Networked Era: A Conversation on Youth, Learning, Commerce, and Politics* (Polity, 2015).
13. Marion Walton, "Pavement Internet: Mobile Media Economies and Ecologies for Young People in South Africa," in *The Routledge Companion to Mobile Media*, eds. Gerald Goggin and Larissa Hjorth (Routledge, 2014), 450-461.
14. Francis B. Nyamnjoh, "Children, Media and Globalisation: A Research Agenda for Africa," in *Yearbook 2002: Children, Young People and Media Globalisation*, eds. Cecilia von Feilitzen and Ulla Carlsson (Nordicom Goteborg University, 2004): 29.

if globalization and its networked logic "is a process of accelerated flow of media content, to most African cultures and children it is also a process of accelerated exclusion."[15]

Recently, for example, the use of a game cloning application called ShareIt has become pervasive among township youth. The application uses the no-data WiFi direct protocol to quickly clone applications and games from another person's phone or device. In the case of ShareIt, the distribution of these copies cannot be measured by official distribution channels. In many of the cases presented in this chapter, players go without seeing their accomplishments recorded on official leaderboards, and without gaining visibility as legitimate, recorded consumers online like most of their counterparts in the global north.

Paranodal play is part of how we define infrastructures of play, using Star's definition,[16] which takes infrastructure as both relational and ecological, embedded in structures, social arrangements and technologies and shaped by conventions of practice.

CHILDREN'S GAMEPLAY ACROSS CAPE TOWN

Cape Town has over 600 neighborhoods, but residents tend to reduce its complexity by talking about the certain neighborhoods as being similar in economic, ethnic/racial and/or linguistic terms: "the 'Cape Flats' [former Coloured working-class townships towards the east of the city], the 'southern suburbs' [wealthy, mostly White and English-speaking], or the 'northern suburbs' [affluent, also mostly White with a large proportion of Afrikaans-speakers]."[17]

While today, people of color may legally live wherever they want, few people who find themselves in townships have the social and economic mobility to make such choices. Under the apartheid regime, Group Areas Act 41 was passed and enforced after 1950, and stipulated that the best locations were granted to White people while people classified as Black and Coloured were forcibly moved to less favorable locations.[18] These under-resourced and often overpopulated urban areas were, and are still, known as "townships." According to the City of Cape Town, 98.9% of Khayelitsha township residents earn R25,600 (US$1,969) or less per month, with 74% earning R3,200 (US$246) or less.[19] This is coupled with 38% of residents being unemployed. Conversely, Rondebosch has close to half of its residents earning a minimum of R25,601 with 6.6% earning R102,401 (US$7,877) or more per month and only 5% of residents being unemployed.

Understanding the social dynamics and implications of factors like income, infrastructure and education contributes importantly in ways that games researchers need to consider when analyzing gaming practices. The cases described in the following section are located in the following sites: domestic spaces in a low-income neighborhood (Ocean View), two public library contexts (Cape Town City Centre, Khayelitsha) and after-school settings in a wealthy suburb (Rondebosch).

15. Ibid.
16. Star, "The Ethnography of Infrastructure."
17. Ana Deumert, "Tracking the Demographics of (Urban) Language Shift: An Analysis of South African Census Data," *Journal of Multilingual and Multicultural Development* 31.1 (2010): 20.
18. "Coloured" is a highly contested—yet resilient—term, which stems from racial classification employed by the Apartheid government to refer to individuals of mixed race or Khoi heritage. The continuing legacy of Apartheid in South Africa has enforced these social and cultural divisions, and Coloured people in Cape Town continue to have unequal access to economic resources. Use of racial categories in this chapter does not indicate support for them. See also *South African History Online (SAHO)*, 2016, http://www.sahistory.org.za/.
19. "City of Cape Town – 2011 Census Suburb Khayelitsha," *capetown.gov.za*, 2011, http://resource.capetown.gov.za/documentcentre/Documents/Maps and statistics/2011_Census_CT_Suburb_Khayelitsha_Profile.pdf.

GAMING IN HOUSEHOLDS, OCEAN VIEW

Ocean View was established in 1968 under the Group Areas Act as a "Coloured area" consisting of dormitory housing, for people who were forcibly removed from re-zoned "White areas" along the South coast of Cape Town. It is situated 45 kilometers outside of the Cape Town Central Business District, between the previous demarcated "white neighbourhoods" of Fish Hoek, and the "black township" of Masiphumele. Ocean View is what Moses has described as a "geographic island" which does not share boundaries with any of the neighboring residential areas.[20] This isolation from the economic centers of the city, among many other factors, contributes to the economic stagnation of the neighborhood. Homes in Ocean View consist of small free-standing houses, semi-detached houses, and most predominantly, blocks of council flats. An informal settlement of shacks, nicknamed "little Khayelitsha" by residents, buffers the Southern margin of the neighborhood. Facilities include a multi-purpose center, a library, civic center, police station, health clinic, a soccer field and public spaces which are marked by vandalized and broken playground equipment.

Venter's study was conducted in-home among a neighborhood peer group who would often meet to game together. The participants consisted of four boys and three girls who regularly met after school to play mobile and console games. The group ranged from 9 to 13 years in age. Two older family members (ages 20 and 17) often joined them. Data was collected over a period of 9 months (August-September 2011 and February-May 2012) in the form of continual participant observation sessions, as well as formal and informal interviews with the peer group, older siblings and extended family members.

In this setting, the gamers' technologies were not connected to any digital networks. None of the digital devices (including consoles and laptops) could go online, and while most of the gaming activities took place on mobile devices, these young people did not have any substantial data usage available with which to surf the web. In fact, most of the devices were intentionally disconnected from any cellular networks, as the gamers feared their data would be "eaten up" through hidden network costs.

Despite being "off the network,"[21] members of this group would nonetheless discuss the latest technologies on offer in the mobile phone market: with better technology, they would have better gaming experiences. They often discussed asking their parents for new phones; lamented that their phones weren't compatible with certain games; and were constantly making deals with older family members who had better model phones to swap with them. Rudie had successfully swapped phones with his aunt, "upgrading" him from a Samsung E250 to a Nokia E66. Sadly, within a month this phone was stolen from him as he walked to a friend's house.

Likewise, over nine months Duke possessed three different phones: first a Samsung E250, then a Nokia music Xpress and finally a Nokia C3. Duke was an avid gamer most often glued to his phone, gaming, and therefore found it very important that his phone should be the best for gaming:

> skerm is groot, die klank is goed, die graphics is kwaai, al daai. Dis nou die beste een tussen almal.
>
> [The screen is big, the sound is good, the graphics are awesome, all of that. It is now the best out of everyone.][22]

20. Susan Moses, "The Impact of Neighbourhood-Level Factors on Children's Well-Being and Identity: A Qualitative Study of Ocean View, Cape Town," *Social Dynamics* 321.1 (2005): 117.
21. Ulises Mejias, *Off the Network*.
22. Transcription of informal conversation, 23 March 2012.

The latter phone was released with a free library of downloadable games, including titles such as *The Simpsons: Minute to Meltdown* (Electronic Arts, 2007), *Need For Speed: Undercover* (Electronic Arts, 2008) and *Need for Speed: Pro Street* (Electronic Arts, 2007). Duke downloaded these titles at great data costs, earning him bragging rights among his friends.

The boys perceived mobile gaming to be a generally solitary pastime. They were not able to play games together on their phones, so interaction was limited to talking about new games, and recommending web pages from which one could download games. At times they would take turns to play one game on someone's phone, or observe when someone had downloaded a highly anticipated game, but the small screens hindered the enjoyment of such activities.

When taking a more expansive view of gaming ecologies, one can also include the "swapping game" that these young people played with their phones. Images of celebrities or other interests were treated as commodities stored on their phones to be collected or traded via Bluetooth. This was reminiscent of playground games where children swap stickers or trade collecting cards.[23] They negotiated the relative "value" of images amongst one another (similar to sticker exchanges where furry, oily, puffy or glitter stickers would carry more currency than plain stickers). They exchanged them accordingly. Certain images were considered to be rarities; either downloaded from Google Image Search at high download costs (due to exorbitant data costs in South Africa, especially for non-contract subscribers), or purchased from "wap" sites such as Zonkewap.com. They could therefore only be exchanged for images that carried "equal monetary value."

Girls would most often swap images with girls, and boys with boys, because their preferences for content were gendered, as is found elsewhere in children's media-referenced play.[24] In this Ocean View peer group, the girls were collecting images of female pop artists such as Nicki Minaj and popular television franchises such as High School Musical or Hannah Montana, whereas the boys collected images of cars, rap artists, soccer players or the flags of their favorite sports teams.

Through the sharing game, these children created their own cultural economy which offered a low-cost alternative to collecting physical youth culture artifacts and merchandise.[25] For example, a pack of Hannah Montana stickers retailed at ±R30 (approximately US$3) for 6 stickers in 2012. To most of this peer group, R30 was a relatively large sum of money, since they reported spending that amount per month on airtime. That amount could have bought them 200 MB of data on a cheap network, which could have provided scores of images to collect, swap and barter.

While the home boasted a PlayStation 2 with scores of games, the Ocean View gamers seldom played console games over the period of observation. As the console was connected to the only television in their home, the choice of entertainment was frequently vetoed by older family members (including a grandmother and an aunt who lived in the house). These older women exerted their power to halt any gameplay, and switch the channel to their preferred daytime viewing of reality television, soap opera reruns or talk shows. Thus, while the infrastructure for console gaming exists, the ways in which these possibilities are controlled through the complex moral economy of the household strongly affects how these young people navigate the space and utilize opportunities for play.[26]

23. John Lenarcic, "Trading Card Games as a Social Learning Tool," *Australian Journal of Emerging Technologies and Society* 3.2 (2005): 58-70.
24. Pallitt, *Gender Identities at Play.*
25. Pierre Bourdieu, "The Forms of Capital Handbook of Theory and Research for the Sociology of Education," in *Handbook of Theory and Research for the Sociology of Education*, ed. J. Richardson (Greenwood, 1986), 241-258.
26. Roger Silverstone, Eric Hirsch and Roger Morley, "Information and Communication Technologies and the Moral Economy of the Household," in *Consuming Technologies: Media and Information in Domestic Spaces*, eds. Roger Silverstone and Eric Hirsch (Routledge, 1992).

GAMING IN THE LIBRARY, CAPE TOWN CITY CENTRE

Walton and Donner's work with the University of Washington's Global Impact Project explored how teenagers at Public Access Venues (PAVs) across Cape Town utilized the digital infrastructure at these spaces for various goals, in relation to their use of mobile digital devices.[27]

As part of this research project, Venter conducted interviews with a group of low-income, resource-constrained boys who played games at the "Smartcape" section of the Cape Town central library. Smartcape computers were installed at every library in the greater Cape Town district as part of a government initiative to provide free computer and internet access to the public, with the only prerequisite for use being a library card, which grants the user an allowance of 45 minutes access per day.[28] After members log in, an on-screen countdown timer shows how much time each user has left. Once the timer neared the end of the designated period, pop-up windows show a countdown timer until the session expired.

At this particular venue, a children's section of the library hosted computers for the exclusive use of young people. Here, activities mostly centered around gaming, although many students also used the computers for research purposes.

During her observation period at the library, Venter noted the gameplay activities of 18 boys, and approached four of them for in-depth interviews. The majority of these players (between the ages of 10-13) were enrolled in grade 6 or 7 from inner-city township-serving school, but her selection also included three high school learners (who ranged between the ages of 13 and 15). Computer-based play at the library included a wide repertoire of games, including online arcade games—*Snow Bros* (Capcom, 1990), *Mortal Kombat* (Midway, 1992), *Pac Man* (Namco, 1980), *Metal Slug* (SNK, 1996), *Time Crisis* (Namco, 1995), etc.—as well as flash games played on sites such as dailygames.com, freeonlinegames.com, easyretro.com, playhub.com and bodyarcade.com.

While these gaming activities were limited to a few hours a week, this constituted a large portion of available recreational time for the players involved. All of the gamers interviewed commute to school and back from their township homes for around 3 hours a day. Many reported that their time spent at the library was a strategy from their parents, who worked in the city, to keep them safe for the period of time between the end of the school day and the end of their parents' working days. Thus, similarly to the Ocean View gamers, gaming is seen as a form of childcare.

As is the case with most PAVs, there are rules and regulations in place that control how people can and cannot act in the space. In the case of these gamers, the rules that support the quiet academic practice of the library came into sharp conflict with their play practices.

The computers were arranged in two islands of four, with screens all facing away from one another, offering privacy for those who want to work or study. Yet, for gaming, where players were keen to look at each others' gameplay, cheer on progress or help out others, it was a hindrance for gamers not to be able to see the screens of the players next to them. In addition, the library's "one person per computer" rule, along with the librarians' strict enforcement of silence, limited the embodied engagement of play. Those awaiting their turn on a computer were expected to sit in a row of chairs

27. Marion Walton and Jonathan Donner, "Public Access, Private Mobile: The Interplay of Shared Access and the Mobile Internet for Teenagers in Cape Town," *University of Washington Global Impact Study Research Report Series*, 2012.
28. Ibid.

arranged on the opposite end of the room. One of the interviewees, 13-year-old Samkelo, listed this as one of the aspects that he disliked about playing games at the library:

> Like when you play in the library, you always quiet, they don't usually say [roars and punches the air] "Yeaaaaah! I win!," they just keep quiet, and the exciting part...you don't make a noise, you just say [whispers] "yes, I did it, I did kill him, yes, I win this game" I don't just jump up and [roars] "Yeaaaaah!" it is not the same thing in the library"

Samkelo's lamentations speak to the library's configuration as a space supporting only one mode of solitary, quiet and individualized learning and play, which at times is in stark contrast to the jubilant, expressive, embodied enjoyment of digital games and their culture of "backseat gaming."[29]

However, the boys were quick to transgress these embedded rules if the librarian-on-duty or security guard happened to be absent. In such cases, children flocked around the computers, attracted to the most skillful players, voiced support and concern, shared tips or assisted each other through difficult obstacles. Yet, as soon as a library-appointed authority figure stepped into the space, the children would disperse and quickly return to their seats.

Another issue that prohibited successful gameplay in the library space was the 45-minute per person allocation. In addition, gamers could not save their gameplay, and had to effectually "re-spawn" every day. In an attempt to negotiate these technical and material boundaries, one high school student, 15-year-old Wesley, set himself the objective of seeing how many levels of *Snow Bros.* he could complete within the 45 minute timeframe.

He had achieved what many of the other players perceived as mastery of the game, and was by far the most popular player to watch during Venter's time spent observing games in the library. While for many, the timer was considered a hassle, as it signaled the player's inevitable death, Wesley had incorporated the limitation into his gameplay, acceding that "in the last ten seconds [on the timer] you can't do anything though."

GAMING AT HARARE LIBRARY, KHAYELITSHA

The video games room of Harare Library forms a crucial part of the library's mission to be a community safe space and hub where patrons are able to relax through play and pursue their academic interests. The library was established using funding from the Carnegie Corporation of New York in conjunction with the Violence Prevention through Urban Upgrading, the Neighbourhood Development Partnership Grant and Provincial Grant funding. The video games room is a 5 x 3 m. room that houses three Nintendo Wiis and two PCs, which operates in a very structured way for two hours on weekday afternoons. Games included *Wii Sports* (Nintendo, 2006) and *Wii Sports Resort* (Nintendo, 2009) for the Nintendo Wii, and *FIFA 13* (EA Sports, 2012) for the PC. All games on offer are rated A (All Ages) or PG (Parental Guidance), and patrons must show their library cards to gain access to the room. Once a patron's turn is over, they must wait, and only if there is sufficient time after everyone else has had a turn may they have a second one.

The most popular games used in the room were *Wii Sports* and *Wii Sports Resort*, each of which presented players with a variety of games so players could choose what they enjoyed the most. The most popular choices were Boxing from *Wii Sports* and Cycling from *Wii Sports Resort*. Once they were cleared to play, patrons were allowed one turn and were allowed to remain and watch others play once

29. Jonas Linderoth, "Beyond the Digital Divide: An Ecological Approach to Game-Play," in *Proceedings of the 2011 DiGRA International Conference: Think Design Play* 6 (2011).

they have completed their turn (usually in the hope of getting a second turn before the room closes). Children seemed mutually supportive in that space, often encouraging or advising their peers.

Being able to watch others play appeared to encourage a communal gaming environment where cooperative gaming thrived. The cooperation took the shape of other children encouraging the player to win or achieve high scores, and giving tips on how to use the controls if the player was not so familiar with them. Playing in this way, especially in a library, functions as a way of leveling inequality, as Adams has suggested.[30] The video games room presents information to the patrons and grants them access to games that most of them would usually not have. The children of Harare library are thus exposed to video games in a more regimented way than children with more resources, but they still have their own interpretations and responses to video games.

Khayelitsha township, particularly the neighborhood of Harare, has the third-highest murder rate in the province, fourth-highest rate of sexual assault and robbery with aggravating circumstances, and the fifth-highest rate of assault.[31] Consequently, children in Khayelitsha have high exposure to violence and sometimes become its perpetrators.[32] Notably, during Koloko's research, children from the Harare Library that had witnessed violence reported playing games like *Wii Boxing* as a way of learning self-defense. They suggested that their natural inclination would be to run, but if need be they would use what they learned in the game. An example came from 13-year-old Xolani, who had mentioned being in a fight. He explained that he enjoyed playing *Wii Boxing* and watching boxing on TV because it helped him learn how to fight to protect himself. He did however also explain that this was only in self-defense, but also that this self-defense was needed against children his age:

Researcher: ucinga ngumdlalo onjani iboxing?

Xolani: Ngumdlalo ondifundisa ukuzikhusela

Researcher: Ngoku ufunda ukuzikhusela okonjani?

Xolani: ndikwazi ukuzilwela,ndingayoxela [...]

Researcher: Ngoku ucinga iboxing ikunceda uzikhusele kwabantwana abazintanga zakho okanye kwabantwana abadala kunawe?

Xolani: Kwintangazam

Researcher: Ungaiqala nawe ifight?

Xolani: Hayi,ndingaphindisa qha baumtu uyandiqala

[Researcher: What do you think of boxing as a sport?

Xolani: It teaches me how to protect myself.

Researcher: What type of protection do you learn?

Xolani: How to protect myself and not go to tell my parents [...]

Researcher: Do you think boxing is important for protection from children your age or older children?

30. Suellen S. Adams, "The Case for Video Games in Libraries," *Library Review* 58.3 (2009): 196-202.

31. "Crime Statistics South Africa," *Stats SA*, 2016, http://www.statssa.gov.za/?cat=26.

32. Debra Kaminer, Bernice du Plessis, Anneli Hardy and Arlene Benjamin, "Exposure to Violence across Multiple Sites among Young South African Adolescents," *Peace and Conflict: Journal of Peace Psychology* 19.2 (2013): 112.

Xolani: Children my age.

Researcher: Would you start a fight?

Xolani: No, I would just fight back if someone picks a fight with me.]

While having a similar discussion about video game violence with 10-year-old Lungelo, he explained having witnessed an attempted armed attack on an individual while he was walking home:

Lungelo: Izikoli zileqha ezinye izikoli

Researcher: Nyani? Wawuvela phi xaubona lonto?

Lungelo: ndandivela kwamakazi wam ndabona izikoli zileqhana. Bendikoyika kodwa ndivezke ndaqhubeka nda hamba

[Lungelo: I've seen gangsters run after other gangsters trying to stab them.]

[Researcher: Really? Where were you when you witnessed that?]

[Lungelo: I was on my way back from my aunt's place when I saw the gangsters. I was scared but I continued walking].

It is experiences like Lungelo's that led to the establishment of the library and the games room in the first place. Contrastingly, children in Rondebosch presented with less exposure to violence, but were also more competitive in their play while also sometimes behaving cooperatively as a means of demonstrating expertise.

GAMING AT SCHOOL (AFTER SCHOOL), RONDEBOSCH

This section focuses on to two sites in Rondebosch where children played digital games at schools, but not as part of their formal schooling: an after-school Arts and Crafts extra-mural program at a co-ed primary school, and a holiday club attended by children of working parents hosted at an all-male primary school. The children from both settings can be regarded as middle- to upper-class, considering the fees of the schools they attend and the holiday club fees their parents are able to afford. Cape Town's typology of neighborhoods categorizes this area as upper middle-class, predominantly English-speaking (more than 75% English, 15-20% Afrikaans), majority White (close to 90% White, around 5% Black), with low unemployment rates, medium- to high-income and high educational achievement. While linguistically and ethnically diverse, the majority of these children can all be described as "advantaged" in comparison to the country's poor majority.

The children who attended the Arts and Crafts extra-mural program were between nine and ten years old, and the group consisted of a similar number of boys and girls, although the gaming sessions were more regularly attended by girls. Many of the children were school friends who also attended other extra-mural activities together, such as choir, drama, hip-hop dancing and swimming.

The holiday club was attended by a variety of children from neighboring schools in the area, which also have high school fees relative to other South African schools. The children's ages ranged from four to 13 years old. The children attended the holiday club because both of their parents work. In some cases a domestic worker collected children from the club.[33]

33. In the South African context, "domestic worker" refers to someone who is employed to do a family's household chores, and supervise children while parents are at work.

Access to ICTs for leisure purposes can be considered an everyday domestic practice for this group. There were some exceptions, such as one case in which two children did not have access to games at all because their parents took a strong stance against games and had rules for time spent with other media, such as watching television, as well. At the time of field work Pallitt (2010-2012) and Koloko (2012-2013) found that the majority of children had access to expensive digital gaming hardware (desktop computer, laptop, standalone consoles like the PlayStation 2, PlayStation 3, Nintendo Wii and hand-held consoles such as the Nintendo DS or PlayStation Portable [PSP]) and either owned these personally or had shared access with family members and played predominantly offline. While access to gaming platforms varied, we found that the children in the school sites were generally not permitted to play games online and parents also limited their screen time and what they are allowed to play. Some children (especially the older boys) took pride in explaining how they were able to circumvent parental rules by playing games rated as inappropriate for that age at a friend's house whose parents were less enforcing, and some reported playing games using their parent's Facebook profiles. The boys in both Pallitt's and Koloko's studies were knowledgeable about age-inappropriate games such as *God of War* (Sony, 2005) and regarded violent games as a form of aspirational social capital in their (predominantly male) peer groups. Parental attempts to protect children and "moral panics" extended to children's access to mobile phones—in contrast to the children in Ocean View, mobile phone ownership was not very prevalent among the children in the middle class school sites. Expensive, offline gaming hardware and devices were parents' preferred choice.

Disney Sing It (Disney Interactive, 2008) was one of the favorite games among the children who played at the co-ed school. Once one of the children finished singing a song, the group checked where their names were positioned on the score list. Casey and Nana were both loud, competitive girls and they were surprised that Yu (who is a very quiet girl) achieved a higher score than them. Later, Casey explained to me that she achieved "full rock star" when playing the game at her cousin's house, within hearing range of her peers:

> Casey: If you get full stars, it will say your name permanently with full rock star. And if you get it three times in a row then they, like, bring you in to full rock star shows.
> Researcher: How do you know?
> Casey: My cousin has it.
> Lee: Did she make it?
> Casey: I made it. Full rock star.[34]

Casey bragged about her expertise to convince the other children that she was a better singer than Yu. Casey displayed her knowledge about *Disney Sing It* as a way to prove to her peers that she achieved the status of "full rock star," and was therefore the best singer in the group. Rather than gaming to perform their singing talents, the boys at the holiday club used *Angry Birds* (Rovio, 2009) to demonstrate their gaming knowledge and expertise.

At the holiday club, some of the children reported that they had played *Angry Birds* before. Seven-year-old Joey had played this game on his father's iPad, and eight-year-old Ray had played it on the Internet. Twelve-year-old Mark, whose father owns an iPhone that has *Angry Birds* on it, told the other boys that this game was a bestseller on the iPhone app store in 2010. In spite of the global *Angry Birds* phenomenon, fewer than half of the children at the holiday club had played it before. The game was not as ubiquitous as researchers had imagined it might be among these middle-class children. Some of the holiday club boys became frustrated waiting for their turn to play on the PlayStation

34. Interview transcript 8: "Casey the full rock star, Disney Sing It, St Mary's," 12 November 2010.

3. Their desire for quicker play turns among a larger group of boys motivated a particular take-up of *Angry Birds* on the laptop, where quick single-player turns resembled an arcade-machine style of play. When seven-year-olds Allen and Joey played the game together, they would just move on to the next level if they failed (earlier passed levels were saved on the laptop, making this possible). This was generally how the younger boys played *Angry Birds*, not taking the scoring system too seriously.

When an older boy, 12-year-old Mark, joined them, he regulated the arcade-machine style play of this game based on the boys' scores: if a boy passed a level, he played again and if he failed, it was the next boy's turn. Mark instructed the younger boys not to click on the next level if they failed "because that's cheating." Mark's expertise at the game such as telling the boys to aim higher or lower or to wait until the black bird blew itself up without being clicked (which he claimed was "more effective"), influenced the younger boys to take the game and their play turns very seriously. The game was transformed from being a casual game into a competitive one after Mark's intervention. The boys' appropriation of this game and their social rules became just as important in this setting. Although Mark did not play much himself, he managed the order of the four boys' play turns, changing players once they had used all their birds (as the levels get harder, players have fewer birds to aim at the pigs). The boys agreed that some of the levels were "way hard" (nearly impossible to complete), but at the same time, some bragged that they had finished the level before. The boys who said a particular level was easy, but failed it, were put on the spot, inviting the collective response, "If it's so easy, why can't you do it?" Therefore, the boys preferred to play up the idea of levels being "hard," which also resulted in a bigger success for those who managed to clear a "hard" level.

The boys competed against one another for status, establishing a pecking order among skilled players who could pass the "hard" levels, and who could thus earn longer turns than those who were less skilled. When Ray and Dale played the game together, they showed one another their favorite levels, also showing off their skills in particular levels where they had figured out how to kill all the pigs with a single bird.

At the co-ed school, Danny and Aaron took turns playing *Burnout Paradise* (Electronic Arts, 2008). Aaron said, "I'm not doing a race, I'm just driving 'cause it's very fun." Danny replied that "you have to actually race because you need to get money" and that "you need to work to get money, to get a new car." He explained to Aaron that "you can't customize, you need to get so much money that you can actually afford to customize" and "you have to listen to the speaker," referring to the car radio announcer in the game who announces the locations and details of races and other challenges. Danny mentioned the names of other games where players can customize their cars, such as *Grand Theft Auto: San Andreas* (Rockstar, 2004) and *Need for Speed: Underground* (Electronic Arts, 2003), which he reported playing at his cousin's house. He added that "you must modify your cars at the beginning of the game, then you can also change what you modified. Like my cousin, my cousin lets me modify any kind of car and then he—he's a nice cousin because he saves my cars for me—then when I play I have a nice car." He does not do races or challenges to win, but rather to get money so that he can play the part of the game that interests him the most: "pimping" his car or achieving a "nice car." At one of the gaming sessions, somebody forgot to save the game after playing and Danny's cars were not saved. At the next session he was frustrated that he could not select one of the cars that he found the previous time. This frustration confirmed his interest in building a collection of playable cars. Danny's display of knowledge about where the "nice cars" would be found allowed him to intrude on the other children's play turns. He would offer to find them "nicer" or "faster" cars and take up the controller. While the other children thought they were getting a more powerful or better-looking car, Danny was building up his collection.

DISCUSSION

The cases discussed highlight the importance of both infrastructure and socially-configured rules. The rules of spaces play as much a role as the rules of play that necessitate *what can be played* and how. While this has largely been understood as being prefigured by games as texts, in this chapter we argue that we need to go beyond games to understand play as a socially situated activity.

Players from Harare Library played in ways that were social and performative, but not competitive when compared to children from Rondebosch. Players at Harare Library played in a collective style as their access was such that they could only play in social settings like the Library. Further, there was less interaction with the games as possibility spaces due to the time players' had to play. By contrast, children in the after-school sites seemed more used to having direct control of their play. As such their turn taking was labored (children were hesitant to relinquish the controller when their time was up), and they appeared to try to one-up each other whenever they advised whomever was playing. Competitive play, customization and being personally identifiable and displaying expertise in the games they were playing were important features of their play compared to the children at Harare Library. The children at the co-ed school signified their role in the choir and used the game's scoring system to decide on the best singers, rather than identifying expert gamers. Despite being a racing game, Danny does not play *Burnout Paradise* to win races, collect "burnouts" and other reward points. He transformed the game into a collecting game where he could discover and play with "nice cars." This can be contrasted with the collecting games among the children living in Ocean View.

Conclusion

The cases shared demonstrate unique infrastructures of play across a range of sites in a single city. Following the work of Star, our chapter encourages games researchers to consider how play is "infrastructured." Those who study gaming practices in the global south could benefit from articulating how various material dimensions are infrastructural to play—these include spaces, configurations, bodies, hardware and software, as well as the games themselves. Scholars have largely focused on interactions between players in online games and in-game representations, but it is useful to look at the broader spaces and contexts where play is situated and subjected to available technologies, rules of the powerful, policies, moral economies, material resources such as airtime and electricity, and other constraints. Our hope is that such a focus may provide provocations and productive points of entry for game researchers who are investigating gaming in spaces where infrastructures and practices do not neatly correspond to studies hailing from or focused on the global north.

We hope to add empirical knowledge of the global diversity of gaming culture, by sharing examples of how gaming practices are situated and enabled by specific places, spaces and social arrangements. Gaming facilitates social spaces, which are given meaning over time not only by the strategies of those who yield power in these spaces, but by the tactics of those who make use of them. Infrastructure for gaming shapes possible interactions. Thus, if we are to theorize gaming in the global south, such theorizations need to encompass the gadgets of the wealthy as well as public access venues, second-hand mobile handsets and prepaid contracts of the poor.

WORKS CITED

Adams, Suellen S. "The Case for Video Games in Libraries," *Library Review* 58.3 (2009): 196-202.

Apperley, Thomas. *Gaming Rhythms: Play and Counterplay from the Situated to the Global.* Institute of Network Cultures, 2009.

Benkler, Yochai. *The Wealth of Networks: How Social Production Transforms Markets and Freedom.* Yale University Press, 2006.

Blignaut, Seugnet and Werner S. Ravyse. "Collating Researchable Issues of African Digital Games." *Proceedings of EdMedia: World Conference on Educational Media and Technology.* Association for the Advancement of Computing in Education (AACE), 2017: 313-327.

Bourdieu, Pierre. "The Forms of Capital Handbook of Theory and Research for the Sociology of Education." In *Handbook of Theory and Research for the Sociology of Education,* edited by J. Richardson, 241-258. Greenwood, 1986.

Butgereit, L. "Math on MXit: Using MXit as a Medium for Mathematics Education." *Proceedings of the Meraka INNOVATE Conference for Educators* (April 2007): 18-20.

Deumert, Ana. "Tracking the Demographics of (Urban) Language Shift: An Analysis of South African Census Data." *Journal of Multilingual and Multicultural Development* 31.1 (2010): 13-35.

Dovey, Jon and Helen W. Kennedy. *Game Cultures: Computer Games as New Media.* McGraw-Hill Education, 2006.

Elliott, Charlene, Gary Marsden, Marion Walton and Edwin Blake. "Design Notations for Creating Virtual Environments." *Proceedings of the 2009 Annual Research Conference of the South African Institute of Computer Scientists and Information Technologists* (ACM, 2009): 7-15.

Hall, Nicholas, Mandy J. Watson and Adoné Kitching. *Serious About Games.* IESA, 2017.

Hjorth, Larissa and Dean Chan, eds. *Gaming Cultures and Place in Asia-Pacific.* Routledge, 2009.

Huntemann, Nina and Ben Aslinger. *Gaming Globally: Production, Play, and Place.* Palgrave MacMillan, 2013.

Jenkins, Henry, Mizuko Ito and dana boyd. *Participatory Culture in a Networked Era: A Conversation on Youth, Learning, Commerce, and Politics.* Polity, 2015.

Kallio, Kirsi Pauliina, Frans Mäyrä and Kirsikka Kaipainen. "At Least Nine Ways to Play: Approaching Gamer Mentalities." *Games and Culture* 6.4 (2011): 327-353.

Kaminer, Debra, Bernice du Plessis, Anneli Hardy and Arlene Benjamin. "Exposure to Violence across Multiple Sites among Young South African Sdolescents." *Peace and Conflict: Journal of Peace Psychology* 19.2 (2013): 112

Kolko, Beth E. and Cynthia Putnam. "Computer Games in the Developing World: The Value of Non-Instrumental Engagement with ICTs, or Taking Play Seriously." *Proceedings of the 2009 International Conference on Information and Communication Technologies and Development (ICTD).* IEEE, 2009, 46-55.

Koloko, Muya. *Responses to Video Game Violence: Children in Middle and l\Low SES Areas of Cape Town and Represented Violence in Digital Games.* Ph.D. Dissertation, University of Cape Town, forthcoming.

Kreutzer, Tino. "Online and Digital Media Usage on Cell Phones among Low-Income Urban Youth in Cape Town." Master's Thesis, University of Cape Town, 2009.

Lenarcic, John. "Trading Card Games as a Social Learning Tool." *Australian Journal of Emerging Technologies and Society* 3.2 (2005): 58-70.

Liboriussen, Bjarke and Paul Martin. "Regional Game Studies." *Game Studies* 16.1 (2016).

Linderoth, Jonas. "Beyond the Digital Divide: An Ecological Approach to Game-Play." *Proceedings of the 2011 DiGRA International Conference: Think Design Play* 6 (2011).

Mejias, Ulises. *Off the Network*. University of Minnesota Press, 2013.

Moses, Susan. "The Impact of Neighbourhood-Level Factors on Children's Well-Being and Identity: A Qualitative Study of Ocean View, Cape Town." *Social Dynamics* 321.1 (2005): 102-134.

Newzoo. "Analysis of *Pokémon GO*: A Success Two Decades in the Making." 2016, https://newzoo.com/insights/articles/analysis-pokemon-go/.

Nyamnjoh, Francis B. "Children, Media and Globalisation: A Research Agenda for Africa." *Yearbook 2002: Children, Young People and Media Globalisation, The Unesco International Clearinghouse on Children, Youth and Media*, edited by Cecilia von Feilitzen and Ulla Carlsson, 43-52. Nordicom Goteborg University, 2004.

Pallitt, Nicola. *Gender Identities at Play: Children's Digital Gaming in Two Settings in Cape Town*. Ph.D. Dissertation, University of Cape Town, 2013.

Penix-Tadsen, Phillip. *Cultural Code: Video Games and Latin America*. MIT Press, 2016.

Sey, Araba, Chris Coward, François Bar, George Sciadas, Chris Rothschild and Lucas Keopke, "Connecting People for Development: Why Public Access ICTs Matter." Technology & Social Change Group, University of Washington, 2013, https://tascha.uw.edu/projects/global-impact-study/.

Shaw, Adrienne. "What Is Video Game Culture? Cultural Studies and Game Studies." *Games and Culture* 5.4 (2010): 403-424.

Silverstone, Roger and Leslie Haddon. "Design and the Domestication of Information and Communication Technologies: Technical Change and Everyday Life." *Communication by Design: The Politics of Information and Communication Technologies*, edited by Robin Mansell and Roger Silverstone. Oxford University Press, 1996: 44-74

Silverstone, Roger, Eric Hirsch, and Roger Morley. "Information and Communication Technologies and the Moral Economy of the Household." *Consuming Technologies: Media and Information in Domestic Spaces*, edited by Roger Silverstone and Eric Hirsch. Routledge, 1992.

Star, Susan Leigh. "The Ethnography of Infrastructure." *American Behavioral Scientist* 43.3 (1999): 377-391.

Venter, Anja and Marion Walton. "Games and Learning: A Perspective on Low-Income, Resource-

Constrained Youth and PC Gaming in Libraries in Cape Town, South Africa." *Computers in Entertainment* (2015).

Venter, M. Anja. "Gamers in Ganglands: The Ecology of Gaming and Participation amongst a Select Group of Children in Ocean View, Cape Town." Master's Thesis, University of Cape Town, 2012.

Walton, Marion. "Pavement Internet: Mobile Media Economies and Ecologies for Young People in South Africa." In *The Routledge Companion to Mobile Media*, edited by Gerald Goggin and Larissa Hjorth, 450-461. Routledge, 2014.

Walton, Marion and Jonathan Donner. "Public Access, Private Mobile: The Interplay of Shared Access and the Mobile Internet for Teenagers in Cape Town," *Global Impact Study Research Report Series*, Technology & Social Change Group, University of Washington, 2012.

Walton, Marion and Nicola Pallitt. "'Grand Theft South Africa': Games, Literacy and Inequality in Consumer Childhoods." *Language and Education* 26.4 (2012): 347-361.

Ludography

Rovio. *Angry Birds*. Rovio, 2009.

Criterion. *Burnout Paradise*. Electronic Arts, 2007.

Zoë Mode. *Disney Sing It*. Disney, 2009.

—. *Disney Sing It: Party Hits*. Disney, 2010.

Rockstar North. *Grand Theft Auto: San Andreas*. Rockstar, 2004.

SCE Santa Monica. *God of War*. Sony, 2005.

SNK. *Metal Slug*. SNK, 2006.

Midway. *Mortal Kombat*. Midway, 1992.

EA Black Box. *Need for Speed: Undercover*. Electronic Arts, 2008.
—. *Need for Speed: Pro Street*. Electronic Arts, 2007.

Namco. *Pac Man*. Namco, 1980.

—. *Time Crisis*. Namco, 1995.

Nintendo. *Wii Sports*. Nintendo 2006.

—. *Wii Sports Resort*. Nintendo, 2009.

Toaplan. *Snow Bros*. Capcom, 1990.

ABOUT THE CONTRIBUTORS

Bushra Alfaraj is a 2D artist and researcher focused on inclusivity and intersectionality in media narratives. She earned her Master of Science in Digital Media from Drexel University in Philadelphia, Pennsylvania, in 2016, where she integrated social studies to conduct research on inclusivity in video games. Prior to graduate school, she received her Bachelor of Arts in Mass Communication with a Concentration in Journalism from the American University of Sharjah in the United Arab Emirates. She aspires to continue her media research as a means to bridge identity gaps between people of different backgrounds.

Ahmed Al-Rawi is an Assistant Professor in Social Media, News and Public Communication at the School of Communication, Simon Fraser University in Canada. He holds two Ph.D. degrees, one of which is from the University of Leicester, United Kingdom (2012). His research interests are in global communication, news, social media and popular culture. He is the author of *Media Practice in Iraq* (2012) and *Islam on YouTube* (2017), and has published over 50 book chapters and papers that have appeared in a variety of journals including *Social Science Computer Review, Journalism: Theory, Practice, & Criticism, Information, Communication & Society, Public Relations Review, International Communication Gazette* and *International Journal of Communication*.

Jenna Ann Altomonte is Assistant Professor of Art History at Mississippi State University. She received a Ph.D. in Interdisciplinary Arts at Ohio University, specializing in contemporary visual culture and digital performance studies. She recently finished her dissertation project titled *Confronting Trauma in the Digital Age: Case Studies on Iraqi and American Online Performance Art Since 9/11*, which examines the works of Iraqi and American artists affected by the Persian Gulf and Iraq Wars. Her current research endeavors seek to connect representations of trauma to the virtual/digital realms, focusing on artists from diasporic communities and spaces of unrest in the post-9/11 era.

Diego Amaral is a Ph.D. candidate at the Postgraduate Communications Program of the Federal Fluminense University, Brazil and in International Literatures at the University of Tübingen, Germany. He earned his Master's degree in Communication from the Federal University of Pernambuco, and he is a member of the Media Narratives Research and Experimentation Laboratory. His main research issues are temporality, conflict, pop culture, political video games and otherness.

Thomas Apperley is an ethnographer, researcher and consultant on digital media technologies. His previous writing has covered digital games, mobile phones, social exclusion and digital literacies and pedagogies. He is a Senior Researcher at the Centre of Excellence in Game Culture Studies at Tampere University, Finland. His book *Gaming Rhythms: Play and Counterplay from the Situated to the Global* was published in 2010 by the Institute of Network Cultures. Tom's more recent work has appeared in *Games and Culture* and *ToDiGRA*.

Will Balmford is a Ph.D. candidate at RMIT University. Will's thesis examines how the Steam gaming platform is shaping everyday domestic gaming practices in Melbourne households. With a keen interest in digital play, social exchange and the relationship between device and person, he is asking questions around how Steam is being used, played and entangling with everyday media practices. He is also the Melbourne-based research assistant for *Games of Being Mobile*, an Australia-wide investigation into the modalities and contexts of mobile game practices.

Rebecca Yvonne Bayeck is a Ph.D. candidate at the Pennsylvania State University, Department of Learning Performances Systems in the College of Education, where she is pursuing a dual degree in Learning Design and Technology and Comparative International Education Programs. Her main research interests include learning and literacies in video and board games, literacy practices, representation in video games, learning and teaching in online environments, teaching and learning with technology. She also adds a cultural lens to her research as she explores the influence of culture on different environments where learning, collaboration, interaction and teaching take place.

Daniel Calleros Villareal received his Ph.D. from the University of Arizona. He is an Assistant Professor of Spanish of the Department of Modern and Classical Languages and Literatures in California State University, Fresno, where he teaches courses on Mexican culture, film and literature. His research focuses on the representation of Latino(a) identities in digital media and the study of the processes through which video games integrate cultural elements depicting specific groups.

Pierre-Alain Clement received his Ph.D. from the University of Quebec in Montreal. He is a research fellow at the National Institute for Advanced Studies in Security and Justice and editorial secretary for "Regards géopolitiques," journal of the Quebec Council for Geopolitical Studies. He published articles on popular culture, including "La signification du politique dans le rap," *Cultures et Conflits*, 2015; and, with Barthélémy Courmont, "When Geopolitics Meets the Game Industry," *Hemispheres*, 2014. He also published several works on terrorism and counterterrorism, including the monograph *G.I. contre jihad* (PUQ, 2010), articles like "Définition du terrorisme," *le Banquet*, 2010 and "Le terrorisme est une violence politique comme les autres" (*Études internationales*, 2014) and chapters including "Le contre-terrorisme à l'ère multipolaire," 2013.

Mia Consalvo is Professor and Canada Research Chair in Game Studies and Design at Concordia University in Montreal. She is the author of *Atari to Zelda: Japan's Videogames in Global Context*, about Japan's influence on the video game industry and game culture, co-author of *Players and their Pets*, co-editor of *Sports Videogames* and author of *Cheating: Gaining Advantage in Videogames*. Mia runs the mLab, a space dedicated to developing innovative methods for studying games and game players. She's a member of the Centre for Technoculture, Art & Games, she has presented her work at professional as well as academic conferences including regular presentations at the Game Developers Conference. She is the former President of the Digital Games Research Association, and has held positions at MIT, Ohio University, Chubu University in Japan and the University of Wisconsin-Milwaukee.

Gonzalo Frasca is Chief Design Officer at DragonBox and Chair of Video Games at ORT University, Uruguay. He is recognized as one of the founders of the academic discipline of game studies, and is known within this field for both his foundational theoretical writings—including "Ludology vs. Narratology" and "Video Games of the Oppressed"—and his influential online games *Madrid* and *September 12th: A Toy World*. He is currently working on "DragonBox School," a full-curriculum, game-based solution for learning math currently in use in Finnish and Norwegian schools. Frasca has developed games for Disney, Pixar, Cartoon Network, WB and Lucasfilm, and is also a columnist for CNN en Español. He received a Lifetime Achievement Award from the Knight Foundation for his pioneering work on newsgames.

Anthony Y. H. Fung is Professor in the School of Journalism and Communication at the Chinese University of Hong Kong. He is also a Professor in the School of Art and Communication under The Recruitment Program of Global Experts at Beijing Normal University in China. His research interests and teaching focus on popular culture and cultural studies, popular music, gender and youth identity, cultural industries and policy and new media studies. He has published widely in international journals, and authored and edited more than ten Chinese and English books. His recent books are *Chinese Youth Culture* (Polity Press, 2017; with de Kloet), *Global Game Industries and Cultural Policy* (Palgrave Macmillan, 2017) and *Cultural Policy and East Asian Rivalry: The Hong Kong Gaming Industry* (Rowman & Littlefield, 2018).

Larissa Hjorth is an artist and digital ethnographer in the School of Media & Communication, RMIT University. Since 2000, Professor Hjorth has been researching the gendered and socio-cultural dimensions of mobile media and play cultures in the Asia-Pacific. She is author of *Media in the Asia-Pacific, Games & Gaming* and co-author of the books *Understanding Social Media, Online@AsiaPacific, Gaming in Social, Locative and Mobile Media, Haunting Hands, Digital Ethnography* and *Screen Ecologies*. She has co-edited *The Routledge Handbook to New Media in Asia, The Routledge Companion to Mobile Media, Gaming Cultures and Place, Mobile Technologies, Art in Asia-Pacific, Mobile Media Practices, Presence and Politics: The Challenge of Being Seamlessly Mobile* and *Studying Mobile Media*.

Muya Koloko is a Ph.D. candidate in Media Studies at the Centre for Film and Media Studies at the University of Cape Town. His research focuses on how South African children between the ages of 10 and 12 respond to video game violence. Prior to pursuing the Ph.D. he attained a Master's degree in Psychological Research focusing on the effects of video game violence and the type of controller used on young adults' support for violence, also from the University of Cape Town. He teaches courses in psychology at the same institution, and is involved in education development with undergraduate students. His other research interests include sport and disability studies.

Jerjes Loayza is a doctoral candidate in sociology at the National University of San Marcos, Peru, where he also earned his Bachelor's degree in sociology and his Master of Law degree. He teaches courses in sociology at the same institution, as well as the Pontifical Catholic University of Peru. He has published work in a number of international journals on issues including education, communication technologies, gender-based violence, criminal sociology, corporeality and affect.

Rhett Loban is an Associate Lecturer at Macquarie University and a Ph.D. student at the University of New South Wales. His Ph.D. thesis focuses on how Grand Strategy games could be used to assist in higher education to teach history. He is also interested in the depiction and inclusion of Indigenous people in video games.

José Messias is a postdoctoral researcher at Federal Fluminense University under a Capes/PNPD fellowship. He earned his Ph.D. in Communication and Culture from Federal University of Rio de Janeiro under the Faperj Nota 10 fellowship. He is a former visiting researcher at University of Wisconsin-Milwaukee under the Capes/Fulbright Grant for doctoral exchange. He is affiliated with the Communication, Entertainment and Cognition (CiberCog/Uerj) and Urban Cultures and Technologies of Communication (LabCult/UFF) research groups. His research revolves around Postcolonial Science and Technology, specifically the relation between video games and modding, media/digital literacy and hacker culture.

Souvik Mukherjee is Assistant Professor of English Literature at Presidency University, Calcutta,

India. Souvik has been researching video games as an emerging storytelling medium since 2002 and completed his Ph.D. on the subject from Nottingham Trent University in 2009. He did his postdoctoral research in the humanities faculty of De Montfort University, United Kingdom and at the Indian Institute of Technology in New Delhi, India where he worked on digital media and narrative analysis. Souvik's research examines their relationship to canonical ideas of narrative and also how video games inform and challenge current conceptions of technicity, identity and culture, in general. He is the author of *Videogames and Storytelling: Reading Games and Playing Books* (Palgrave Macmillan, 2015) and *Videogames and Postcolonialism: Empire Plays Back* (Palgrave Macmillan, 2017). His current interests involve the analysis of paratexts of video games, the concept of time in video games and the treatment of diversity and the margins in video games. Besides game studies, his other interests are (the) digital humanities and early modern literature.

Thaiane Oliveira holds a Ph.D. in Social Communication from Federal Fluminense University and is professor of the department of Media Studies and of the Postgraduate Program in Communication of the same institution. She is member of Centre of Global South Studies (Tubingen University), in which she develops research about circulation of science and geopolitics of knowledge in countries of the global south. She is coordinator of Forum of Journals and Science Communication of Pro-rectory of Research, Postgraduate and Innovation of Federal Fluminense University. She is also coordinator of the Laboratory of Research in Science, Innovation, Technology and Education (Cite-Lab) and Laboratory of Experiences of Engagement and Transformation of Audience (Leeta).

María Luján Oulton is a cultural producer and curator focused in new media art and video games. She is currently working on her master's thesis on curating art games. In 2007 she co-founded the new media cultural production agency Objeto a. Since 2009 María Luján runs *Game on! El Arte en Juego*, the first and only exhibition in Argentina focused on art and video games. Luján also dedicates herself to the divulgation of video games as cultural objects and advocates for greater participation by women in games. She has given lectures at events and universities such as TEDxRiodelaplata (Buenos Aires), Universidad Jorge Tadeo Lozano (Bogotá) and DevHr (Mexico), among others.

Nicola Pallitt is a lecturer in the Centre for Innovation in Learning and Teaching at the University of Cape Town (UCT). She is also a member of the e/merge Africa team, a professional development network for educational technology practitioners and researchers in African higher education. Nicola co-teaches on a postgraduate program in educational technology, co-convenes the online course Facilitating Online and assists university staff with blended and online learning design. She received her Ph.D. in Media Studies (2013) and Postgraduate Diploma in Higher Education Studies (2014) from UCT. Nicola hopes to engage fellow researchers in research that takes critical and contextually informed approaches to educational technology. She is a networked scholar who loves Twitter.

Phillip Penix-Tadsen is a specialist in contemporary Latin American cultural studies. He earned a Ph.D. from Columbia University and is Associate Professor of Spanish and Latin American Studies at the University of Delaware, where he also teaches courses in game studies. He is the author of *Cultural Code: Video Games and Latin America* (MIT Press, 2016), which offers a synthetic theorization of the relationship between video games and culture, based on analysis of both in-game cultural representation and the real-life economic, political and societal effects of games. Professor Penix-Tadsen has published work in peer-reviewed journals including and *Letras Hispanas* and *Latin American Research Review.* His research and teaching focus on the intersections between politics, economics, new media and visual culture in Latin America today.

Boris L. F. Pun is a Ph.D. candidate in the School of Journalism and Communication at the Chinese University of Hong Kong. His research interests mainly relate to popular culture and subcultural studies, especially in Animation, Comics and Games (ACG). He is also interested in the issue of cultural identity, cultural industries and policy, and the globalization and transculturation of ACG.

Ingrid Richardson is Associate Professor in the School of Arts at Murdoch University, Western Australia. She has a broad interest in the human-technology relation and has published on the cultural and phenomenological effects of games and mobile media, digital ethnography and innovative research methods, urban screens, wearable technologies, virtual and augmented reality, remix culture and web-based content creation and distribution. She is contributing co-editor of *Studying Mobile Media* (Routledge, 2011) and co-author of *Gaming in Social, Locative and Mobile Media* (Palgrave, 2014), *Ambient Play* (MIT Press, forthcoming) and *Understanding Games and Gaming Cultures* (Sage, forthcoming).

Jules Skotnes-Brown is a Ph.D. candidate in the Department of History and Philosophy of Science at the University of Cambridge, having previously studied at University of Oxford and University of Cape Town. In the latter, he worked on video gaming, game cultures and the connection between colonialism and virtual imperialism. His more recent Ph.D. research traces the development of a settler scientific culture in southern Africa, c. 1890s-1930s, and its role in shaping a new ontology of nature. More broadly, he works on the construction of boundaries between environments, peoples, and disciplines, and the consequences of movement across those boundaries.

Claire Taylor is Gilmour Chair of Spanish and Professor of Hispanic Studies at the University of Liverpool. She is a specialist in Latin American literature and culture, and has published widely on a range of writers, artists and genres from across the region. Her particular geographical areas of interest are Colombia, Argentina and Chile, although she also worked on literature, art and culture from other regions. Within Latin American Cultural Studies, she takes a particular interest in the varied literary and cultural genres being developed online by Latin(o) Americans, especially hypertext novels, e-poetry and net art. She has published numerous articles and book chapters on these topics, and is the co-author of the volume *Latin American Identity in Online Cultural Production* (Routledge, 2012), and author of the monograph *Place and Politics in Latin America Digital Culture: Location and Latin American Net Art* (Routledge, 2014). She is currently holder of an AHRC grant which focuses on women victims, memory and representation of the Colombian conflict.

Verónica Valdivia Medina holds a degree in sociology from the Alberto Hurtado University, Santiago, Chile. In 2016, she joined the National Institute of Statistics of Chile, where she worked in the first National Time Use Survey and is currently working in Gender Studies and Statistics. She has a longstanding interest in video games and game culture, in particular the international gamer communities built around games such as *Counter Strike 1.6*, *World of Warcraft* and *Overwatch*.

Anja "Nanna" Venter is a self-proclaimed "Art-stronaut." She is fascinated by the intersection of art, culture and technology and has forged a creative career that blends these domains. She studied four years of visual communication at Stellenbosch University and has since "made pictures" for a variety of platforms and purposes, from commercial work to comics, games and apps. She has written stories, articles, opinion pieces, comics and children's books. In 2011 she completed her Master's degree in Media Studies at the University of Cape Town with a focus on video game culture in marginal settings. In 2018 she was awarded her Ph.D. which looks at how digital creative tools, particularly those on mobile devices, can assist in democratizing visual design capabilities.

Joshua Wong is a Ph.D. candidate at RMIT University. His thesis provides an ethnographic account of how Asian international students in Melbourne aspire to and pursue "the good life" using digital media technologies. His previous degrees were from the National University of Singapore, where he focused on video game design. Joshua's research interests are highly interdisciplinary in nature, revolving around the fields of mobility, well-being and everyday media practices.

Yiyi Yin is a Ph.D. candidate in communication at The Chinese University of Hong Kong. Her current research interests are mainly on fandom studies and popular culture. She focuses particularly on the shifting embodiment of fan affect and experience in relation to the evolution of digital media. As she was previously trained in cinema study and critical study at the University of Southern California, she is also interested in film theory, especially in terms of spectatorship and visual narrative.

ABOUT THE ETC PRESS

ETC Press is a Carnegie Mellon publishing imprint with a twist. We publish books, but we're also interested in the participatory future of content creation across multiple media. We are an academic, open source, multimedia, publishing imprint affiliated with the Entertainment Technology Center (ETC) at Carnegie Mellon University (CMU) and in partnership with Lulu.com. ETC Press has an affiliation with the Institute for the Future of the Book and MediaCommons, sharing in the exploration of the evolution of discourse. ETC Press also has an agreement with the Association for Computing Machinery (ACM) to place ETC Press publications in the ACM Digital Library.

ETC Press publications will focus on issues revolving around entertainment technologies as they are applied across a variety of fields. We are looking to develop a range of texts and media that are innovative and insightful. We are interested in creating projects with Sophie and with In Media Res, and we will accept submissions and publish work in a variety of media (textual, electronic, digital, etc.), and we work with The Game Crafter to produce tabletop games.

Authors publishing with ETC Press retain ownership of their intellectual property. ETC Press publishes a version of the text with author permission and ETC Press publications will be released under one of two Creative Commons licenses:

- **Attribution-NoDerivativeWorks-NonCommercial:** This license allows for published works to remain intact, but versions can be created.
- **Attribution-NonCommercial-ShareAlike:** This license allows for authors to retain editorial control of their creations while also encouraging readers to collaboratively rewrite content.

Every text is available for free download, and we price our titles as inexpensively as possible, because we want people to have access to them. We're most interested in the sharing and spreading of ideas.

This is definitely an experiment in the notion of publishing, and we invite people to participate. We are exploring what it means to "publish" across multiple media and multiple versions. We believe this is the future of publication, bridging virtual and physical media with fluid versions of publications as well as enabling the creative blurring of what constitutes reading and writing.

http://www.etc.cmu.edu/etcpress/wellplayed
Twitter: @etcwellplayed

